HARVARD HISTORICAL STUDIES, 124

Published under the auspices
of the Department of History
from the income of the
Paul Revere Frothingham Bequest
Robert Louis Stroock Fund
Henry Warren Torrey Fund

Charles Follen, late 1830s

# Charles Follen's Search for Nationality and Freedom

## GERMANY AND AMERICA

### 1796–1840

*Edmund Spevack*

HARVARD UNIVERSITY PRESS

*Cambridge, Massachusetts*

*London, England*

*1997*

Frontispiece from Eliza Lee Cabot Follen, *The Works of Charles Follen, with a Memoir of His Life,* vol. 1 (Boston : Hilliard and Gray, 1841).

*Library of Congress Cataloging-in-Publication Data*

Spevack, Edmund.
Charles Follen's search for nationality and freedom : Germany and
America, 1796–1840 / Edmund Spevack.
p.   cm.—(Harvard historical studies ; 124)
Includes bibliographical references and index.
ISBN 0-674-11011-0 (alk. paper)
1. Follen, Charles, 1796–1840.   2. Social reformers—United
States—Biography.   3. Abolitionists—United States—Biography.
4. Radicals—United States—Biography.   5. Radicals—Germany—
Biography.   6. Harvard University—Faculty—Biography.
7. Unitarian Universalist churches—Clergy—Biography.   I. Title.
II. Series : Harvard historical studies ; v. 124.
HN57.S66   1997
303.48′4′092—dc21
96-52522

# CONTENTS

# ACKNOWLEDGMENTS

For permission to quote from archival materials related to Charles Follen, I am grateful to the Harvard University Archives; the Trustees of the Boston Public Library; the Massachusetts Historical Society; the Division of Rare and Manuscript Collections, Cornell University Library; Miscellaneous Papers–Charles Follen, Rare Books and Manuscripts Division, the New York Public Library, Astor, Lenox, and Tilden Foundations; the Staatsbibliothek, Berlin; the Universitätsarchiv Giessen; and the Hessisches Hauptstaatsarchiv Wiesbaden.

For their generous help during the research for this project, I would like to thank Dr. Guiseppe Bisaccia at the Boston Public Library; Dr. Jill Erickson at the Boston Athenaeum; Dr. Eva-Maria Felschow at the Universitätsarchiv in Giessen; Dr. Herz at the Universitätsarchiv in Jena; Dr. Pult at the Hessisches Hauptstaatsarchiv in Wiesbaden; and Ernst Wilhelm Wreden at the Archiv der Deutschen Burschenschaft in Frankfurt am Main.

For their academic advice during the writing of this book, I owe thanks to Professor Otto Dann at Cologne University; Professor Heinz Dollinger at Münster University; Professor Daniel Walker Howe at St. Catherine's College, Oxford; the Reverend Walter Donald Kring; the late Professor Günter Moltmann at Hamburg University; Professor Willi Schröder at Jena University; Dr. Douglas Stange; Professors Edgar Mertner and Robert C. Walton at Münster University; and Professor Conrad Wright at Harvard University.

At Harvard University I would like to thank Professor Franklin L. Ford, and especially Professor Donald Fleming. Professor Fleming encouraged me to study history, suggested that I write about Charles Follen, and has supported my studies and research from beginning to end.

At the Johns Hopkins University I would like to thank Professor Vernon Lidtke. Thanks are also due to Professor Ronald Walters.

This book could never have been completed without the encouragement, patience, and expertise of my *Doktorvater,* Professor Mack Walker. I am grateful for his support.

At Harvard University Press, I owe thanks to Elizabeth Suttell and especially Elizabeth Gretz.

Finally, I would like to thank five individuals for their support and unfailing friendship: my parents, Marvin and Helga Spevack; Manfred Neumann; Marius Brozek; and Witold Potempa.

# INTRODUCTION

Charles Follen's life spanned the years 1796 to 1840. He began his intensely political, activist, and versatile career as a German university–trained jurist who had made a reputation for himself as a student radical and revolutionary, pressing for constitutional reform and for the achievement of German national unity. Follen's European roots were in Hesse, in a region immediately surrounding the city of Frankfurt am Main. It was here that he was born in 1796, baptized Karl Theodor Christian, and here that he attended the University of Giessen from 1813 to 1818. As a young doctor of law, Follen went in 1818 to Jena, a small town in Thuringia which contained a well-reputed, liberal university; since 1815, it had been the hotbed of German student radicalism. For the extreme views he propagated at Jena and for his secret political activities, Follen was from 1818 on persecuted by university authorities, the police of local German states, and the government agencies of the recently established German Confederation. In 1819 he chose to flee to Switzerland and found shelter there for four years, teaching at a cantonal high school and at the University of Basel.

Follen emigrated to America when it became increasingly clear that he could no longer stay in Switzerland. After landing in New York City in December of 1824, he spent a year living in Philadelphia. The Boston area eventually became Follen's new permanent home in the United States. After several years spent as an instructor in German, he was appointed professor of German literature and language at Harvard University in 1830, and began to exert a strong influence on local intellectual life. His interest in the study of religion had increased since the late 1820s, and from 1836 to 1838 he served as a Unitarian minister in New York City. At the same time, Follen also became a fervid antislavery agitator, and as a member of several antislavery societies he contributed to the theory and practice of abolitionism. The life of Charles Follen thus falls into two main parts, one European and the other American. It will have to be seen how far these two were in sharp contrast, or whether they in fact complemented each other. It would be appropriate to call this the bicultural problem of Charles Follen's life. In general, Follen is a difficult historical character to get close to: the two disparate parts of his life must be discovered by the historian in a variety of geographical places. At least partly against his own will, Follen became an international person; to get to know him means growing familiar with the characteristics and particular problems of several diverse parts of the world. It also means analyzing and comparing a variety of ways of thinking, especially about the central problems of Follen's life.

The pattern of Follen's entire public life and private personality may be explained in terms of the one goal he always pursued: freedom. This was perhaps the most important word of Follen's lifetime; it was also one of the most overused and thus one of the most unfocused and unclear. There existed an endless number of definitions of the idea of "freedom" in both the German and the American contexts. This work will try to show what "freedom" meant for Follen himself: the liberation of the individual from social oppression, moral corruption, and intellectual stagnation; the self-assertion of national states, such as Germany and the United States, against foreign domination; and finally a broad emancipation of humanity in general through the rearrangement of prevalent social, political, and theological principles and values.

Follen observed that society around him, in the age of revolutions, was in flux. Individuals whom he encountered, nation states, and in a sense humankind were in the process of throwing off an old order dominated by the political rigidities of the ancien régime, theological and scientific dogmatism, and social systems that were widely perceived as entrenching inequality. Instead, the vision of a new society was on the verge of asserting itself throughout the Western world; it was characterized by the ideals of the French and American revolutions, liberalism, and the rise of nationalism. Germany was still in the midst of a struggle to end the old order; America was perceived by Follen and many others as the land of the future. Here, the ideal of freedom was already being realized. Charles Follen wished to help steer America, and eventually also Germany, further along on this course.

Follen was a man of strong convictions, all of which developed out of his longing for the attainment of freedom. German national unity, a republican form of government, philosophical idealism, theological liberalism, and the abolition of slavery in any form, physical or spiritual, always remained his goals. When his geographical, political, and intellectual environment changed, Follen changed; but his basic beliefs, and his methods for putting these into effect, always remained fundamentally the same. Convictions, Follen thought both as a young German student and as a mature American abolitionist many years later, should never be abandoned or compromised. An individual had to stand by his political, social, philosophical or religious beliefs or else appear as a traitor to his own self and to whatever cause he was pursuing. Pressure from other persons, government authorities, or society at large could not influence and revoke the convictions a person held; only one's conscience set and controlled these standards.

Out of Follen's highly subjective understanding of convictions arose his feeling of duty to realize them in the world. If the ideal of freedom was not yet established as a reality, that reality, he thought, must be brought about at all costs. He was a man driven by the strength of his own conscience and guided by his own very subjective and independent evaluations of what was to be changed in the world. The pursuit of political and moral certainties, and rigid adherence to the guidelines he had initially set for himself, best characterize Follen's view of his successive worlds and of his own role in them. Likewise, he expected his friends always to follow their own conscience and their self-defined moral duty. Grounded in this belief in the absolute and unconditional necessity of following one's duty at all times lay the seeds of the deep conflict which eventually characterized Follen's social circumstances wherever he lived. It was impossible for him to engage even in the most favorable of compromises. When his ideals were at stake, he pursued them without any regard for the social consequences. He strongly encouraged others, whether they were German student radicals or American abolitionists, to do so as well.

Follen was a lawyer by training, and a strong legal mentality, a belief in the changeability of the world through laws, was evident in both his actions and his writings. He spent his youth in Germany at a time when, after the fall of Napoleon, the future of society and politics seemed unclear. Many intellectual leaders drafted plans for the future and made suggestions about how to organize German society; Follen's ideas were part of this wave of proposals for change. There was a feeling that whoever could map out the future first and find a working blueprint for a society to come—this person would control the future. Follen's conception of law was thus not conservative, but dynamic and progressive. It was concerned with the changing and reshaping of society as much as with giving it a secure mold. In Germany a draft for a new imperial constitution, or a political program formulated by the student movement, would contribute to social and political progress toward true freedom. When Follen came to America, he was exposed to different kinds of reform movements that were cropping up in many places. The one with which he became closely associated, the antislavery movement, always worked for legal reform during the 1830s. Those abolitionists with whom Follen wished to cooperate during this period reinterpreted documents such as the United States Constitution or the Declaration of Independence according to their own needs and goals. They did not oppose the laws of the United States on principle and did not question the fundamental assumptions of the American political or legal system; however, they wished to use existing constitutional provisions in a dynamic way in order to produce concrete social and political change.

Reform, Follen deeply believed, had to start with the individual. Along with many of his contemporaries both in Germany and in the United States, Follen ascribed to humans the potential for personal improvement. The human race as such was not static in its moral development, but could continually strive toward the elimination of vice, inequality, and injustice. In individual self-perfection lay the seed of general human progress. In the German idealistic tradition of *Bildung*, Follen thought that self-perfection was perhaps the foremost duty of every person, that it was one of the great goals of human existence.[1] This self-perfection would affect one's social and political behavior as well as one's spiritual and moral development. In Germany, Follen urged his fellow students to give up what he considered their thoughtless lifestyle of drinking and brawling, and to devote themselves instead to political awareness, national pride, and philosophical inquiry. In America, rational Unitarianism played a large role in promoting Follen's own spiritual development and moral position. When Follen's ceaseless pressure for reform was not readily successful, he demonstrated a willingness to turn to more radical means. In Germany, the political communication between youthful social reformers and the Restoration period governments had broken off by 1819. A period of harsh reaction, censorship, and political rigidity set in. Instead of retreating from the fulfillment of his goals, however, Follen subsequently came to advocate secret conspiracy and even political murder as the only way to bring about freedom in Germany and throughout Europe. To a large extent by his own choice, he eventually left the channels of socially acceptable reform agitation. In America, in contrast, when he could not achieve his goals within the institutions of civil society, such as Harvard University or the Unitarian ministry, Follen himself did not abandon these institutions; instead, unwilling to adapt himself to their principles, Follen was eventually ostracized by them, and the entire framework of society in which he lived gradually abandoned him whether he wished it or not. Once again Follen did not remain satisfied with gradual reform, but instead became convinced that a deeper transformation of American society and political attitudes was necessary. Although it cannot be decisively shown from the existing sources that Follen publicly advocated violence in America, as he had previously done in Germany, the question of violence lingered throughout his activities and between the lines of his writings.

The variety of areas in which Follen was almost constantly active in pursuit of his goals was quite remarkable. In the course of his life he acquired detailed knowledge in the fields of law, literature, theology, and politics. This largely self-taught expertise led to the writing of polemical essays, poetry, sermons, and political tracts. The diversity of his talents contributed greatly to the forceful nature of his drive for freedom. As he grew older, however, Follen came to experience more and more a paralysis and even a breakdown of his own early nineteenth-century idealistic belief in political and social progress. Evidently success in reforming human societies themselves and the various belief structures that supported them was much more complex, unpredictable, or even uncontrollable than Follen and other members of his generation had previously supposed. His own self-perfection had been strong and effective. But not many others were willing to follow him along the path to change upon which he insisted. There are several possible explanations for Follen's rigidity and the way it eventually excluded him from making greater contributions to the progress of freedom. One is the makeup of his own personality: somber, thorough, and deep. Another is the social type that he came to represent: the reformer who knows he is in the right and will not budge even though his future and perhaps even his own life may be at stake. Finally, there is the legalistic, exacting, quarrelsome, and ambitious character of the German social and cultural milieu from which Follen came. Interestingly, the qualities that Follen acquired in the environment of his home country fit perfectly into the new context and mentality of American reformers, such as William Lloyd Garrison, whom he encountered in the 1830s.

Follen was first and foremost a challenger of established authorities and truths, and he constantly had to fear persecution and the resistance of his environment to his own behavior and statements. This sort of life forced him to become a very elusive person as well. In Europe, he changed his place of residence frequently, and burned his letters and papers in Giessen, Jena, and Basel because he feared police investigations into his political engagements. Later on in the United States, his American wife wrote his "official" biography after he died in a shipping accident at forty-three years of age.[2] She only knew about those parts of his past of which he had chosen to tell her. And of that, she released to the public only what she deemed appropriate.

Again and again, Follen purposely obscured his own person from the historian of today. Any letters or diaries he possessed in Germany could have been used by the police authorities as evidence against him and the network of friends and political acquaintances he maintained; so he destroyed them.[3] In America, there was little danger of political persecution; yet the greater part of the letters and all papers and diaries of Charles Follen were protected from public view by his wife. Follen was a prolific writer, and his many essays, tracts, sermons, lectures, and poems are still available in printed form. A balanced view of the actual person and his true character, however, can largely only be reconstructed using the impressions of other witnesses: German fellow students, German police authorities, American friends, and the statements of his wife, a Boston reformer who was completely devoted to him.

This project has entailed tracing a life spent in two different worlds and in different cultural realms. Unprinted and unpublished materials are in German as well as in American archives. At the university archives at Giessen and Jena, there are files containing records of his academic career and his political activities. In the case of Giessen, student radicalism in general during Follen's stay is well documented in student disciplinary records and university administration reports. At the Hessisches Hauptstaatsarchiv in Wiesbaden, there is a complete set of the reports compiled by the Mainzer Zentraluntersuchungskommission (Mainz Central Investigation Commission), an institution of the German Confederation formed in 1819. This commission investigated the background, motivation, and aims of German radicalism from 1800 throughout the 1820s with great success and in great detail. Although the commission perhaps underestimated the potential importance of Follen, in its many reports, including the printed *Hauptbericht* of 1827, lengthy descriptions and evaluations concerning the activities of Charles Follen and his associates were included. The former Deutsches Zentralarchiv Merseburg contained files compiled by the Prussian government on Charles Follen, and particularly on his older brother August. In addition, at the Badisches Generallandes-archiv in Karlsruhe, there are legal records of the Hofgericht Mannheim dealing with the murderer Carl Sand and his possible connections with Charles Follen.

At the Harvard University Archives, records dealing with Follen's academic positions at Harvard are available. In addition, there are detailed notes of Follen's lectures on German literature and on religious topics, compiled by two of his students. About one hundred letters written by and addressed to Charles Follen, his wife Eliza Cabot Follen, and their son Charles, are preserved at the Boston Public Library. These letters cannot represent even a fraction of Follen's correspondence in America, however, and his papers and diaries, quoted extensively in the *Works,* have disappeared. The Massachusetts Historical Society holds letters and papers of several of Eliza Cabot Follen's relatives, including those of her brother Samuel Cabot.

Follen's European period forms part of the historiography dealing with the reaction in Germany to the Napoleonic wars, with the rise of German nationalism, liberalism, and the quest for German unity. Follen's career is part of the resistance to Metternich's Restoration, the discovery of nationalism urged on by Friedrich Ludwig Jahn and Ernst Moritz Arndt, and of the liberation and propagation of German unity proposed by the German Burschenschaften fraternities.[4] Follen is also a direct precursor of the political radicalism of Georg Büchner,[5] who ten years after Follen attended the same university at Giessen. The two men came from the same geographical region, pursued similar goals, and were in contact with many of the same persons of republican persuasion who dreamed of a revolution in Hesse. In America, Follen played an important role in works dealing with the spreading of German culture.[6] He has been discussed in the context of American religious history, especially that of Unitarianism,[7] and of the Transcendentalist impact on both religion and philosophy.[8] Follen also played a role in the literature on antislavery and on reform movements.[9]

Follen has remained obscure to a large degree owing to his own behavior; thus he has not been investigated closely by most established historians.[10] The two German doctoral dissertations on Follen that exist do not cover his entire life, but have instead concentrated largely on a somewhat negative analysis of his German political ideas.[11] In contrast, Follen has been seen as a positive and historically relevant figure by two of his biographers, Herman Haupt and George Washington Spindler.[12] They have shown the influence he was able to exert despite his eventual failure and early death. For them, Follen had an important role to play in the rise of the powerful and historically significant German Burschenschaft movement, and in the spreading of German learning and cultural ideas in America. Both Haupt and Spindler had a large stake in using Follen to show the importance and reality of these historical processes. This work will go beyond serving these agendas; instead, it will attempt to show how Follen's own life exemplifies the tension among the romantic aspirations of a devoted idealist, the continual setbacks of fate, and the stubborn solidity of social and political reality.

# 1

## UNITY AND FREEDOM

Karl Follen spent the first twenty-eight years of his life in Central Europe, being formed by and contributing to two major political movements of his time, nationalism and revolutionary radicalism. The first of these will be discussed in this chapter, the second in Chapter 2. The two phenomena were connected: external liberation from foreign domination and national self-realization by the German educated public were followed by an attempt at internal revolution and a transformation of German political life. When this internal revolution was blocked by the forces of reaction, however, a minority of German academics became underground fighters for radical ideals. Karl Follen did not stay with the nationalist mainstream for very long; he soon became an extreme radical and advocate of political murder and revolutionary upheaval. He was, however, born into a generation which witnessed, at first, the genesis of a new German national spirit before turning to various forms of radical activity.

### Unity, Freedom, and the German Nation

The new German nationalism of 1813 to 1818 was neither the traditional local patriotism familiar in eighteenth-century states nor identical with the aggressive nationalism of the post-1848 period. It was a movement for self-discovery and self-assertion by what in contemporary public discourse was increasingly called the German *Volk*. The nationalist mission was to define and at the same time spiritually renew a group which supposedly belonged together. Regional differences which had dominated Germany for centuries, dividing its territories and marking its people, were to lose their significance in a very short time, and a new synthesis was to be built out of the loose parts of an empire that had ceased to exist by 1806. Yet the new nationalism, though still bound together with liberalism before the middle of the century, was in its extreme forms characterized by a martial and domineering spirit similar to that of German nationalism after 1848. It was a movement for the acceptance of Germany in the world of nations, and even for its predominance over other nations. German nationalism after 1818, just as well as its "Rightist" form after 1848, has frequently been evaluated as ambiguous in its appearance and consequences.[1] The period of 1813 to 1818 was no less problematic.

The first thing to be said about the nationalist mood around 1815 is that it was dominated by an educated elite.[2] The social groups which actually endorsed and actively carried the new feeling were the academics, educated bourgeoisie, and enlightened bureaucrats. Of special significance in this context is the role of the universities, of students and professors.[3] After 1810 the university increasingly became a conscious microcosm of the new nation-to-be, and at the same time a proving ground for ideas which were to shape the future. This was the forum in which Karl Follen was first able to receive information about the political issues of his time, and it was here that he could form his own political views. Follen learned national feeling at the university, and he learned how to use it for his own purposes. At the university, he had the opportunity to study and discuss political and legal issues on a theoretical plane; he also managed to gain experience putting his ideas into practice in student politics. Follen learned that ideas were needed to change the world, to mold a character, and to manipulate others.

The nationalism which Follen lived with, like other political and social movements, had its key words. In this case the key words were "unity" and "freedom," and they were closely linked. "Unity" referred primarily to the political unification of the German nation, a higher importance to be placed on national issues, concerns of the entire *Volk*, than on problems of individual territories. But "unity" was also more: it was a term of national integration of the German people. It referred not only to the formation of an independent nation state in Central Europe but also to the relationship of the people within this state. In this sense "unity" meant the abolition of certain divisions which had previously isolated Germans from one another. This process would necessarily bring with it a larger measure of social equality and the destruction of "artificial" regimes now in power.

"Freedom" was the greatest catchword of the time. German nationalists of the time thought that when a people was truly united, it must also become free, both among the nations of the world and internally. Karl Follen was able to use the word "freedom" so much not only because he himself believed in the importance of the concept, but also because the world around him understood what he meant. "Freedom" from French influence would only be the first step for the Germans; the evolution of a domestic culture of freedom would be a much more difficult enterprise. This would involve a liberal constitution, civil rights, a free press, and the abolition of aristocratic privileges, to name some of the most important goals. The new citizen was to be free within society (that is, have certain inalienable rights), and was to be able to help shape that society (for example, by voting in elections and participating in political activities).[4]

Both terms, "unity" and "freedom," also were connected to violence. Both could only be fought for at the expense of someone else, and both were not to be achieved without the demolition of existing political and social structures. Thus one can begin to understand Karl Follen's role as that of someone who was never an affirmer of the status quo, and who in his thought and actions was not always constructive. Another strain was even more prominent in the nationalism of Follen and others in his generation: a passion to change and destroy the world into which they were born. A destruction of Napoleonic tyranny did not mean a return to the Holy Roman Empire. Particularism and noble privilege would be directly and heavily attacked and eventually were to disappear forever.

## The Spirit and the *Volk*

Karl Follen was born on September 4, 1796, in Romrod, a tiny town in Northeastern Hesse. His parents had fled their normal residence, the larger town of Giessen, because the French armies were at the time actively fighting in the area. In her extensive biography of her husband, written in 1841, Eliza Cabot Follen reports:

> It so happened, however, that General Jourdan, in a rapid retreat from the peasants of Spessart, passed through the village of Romrod, and, just as the ceremony of christening Charles had commenced, the hitherto quiet house was suddenly filled with a troop of French soldiers, with General Jourdan at their head. His mother was very weak, but fortunately the disturbance did not last long; and, owing to the judicious conduct of his grandfather, quiet was soon restored, and no evil consequences ensued.[5]

Christoph Follenius (1759–1833), Follen's father, had latinized his name. He and his wife Rosine (1766–1799) had three sons, August Adolf Ludwig (born in 1794), Karl Theodor Christian (born 1796), and Paul (born 1799), and one daughter, Luise (born 1797). Karl Follen's father was a well-known and respected judge (*Landrichter*) at the Giessen law court, and came from a family which had produced a large number of lawyers and state officials for the territories of Hesse. The Follen family may be traced back to at least the beginning of the eighteenth century in Hesse, and it has lasted into the twentieth century as well.[6]

Follen's mother died in 1799, after the birth of Paul. Karl was then only three years old, and Christoph Follenius hired a Jewish man named Süsskind to mind his household. The four children were sent to various places: August, to the maternal grandfather at Wetzlar, Luise and Paul to the paternal grandfather in Romrod, while Karl stayed with his father and the house servant in Giessen.[7] Eliza Follen, in her biography, went out of her way to show that Karl on the whole had a happy youth. However, she says of Karl's father that he "was of a very excitable temperament, and at times was even irascible." She also quotes from a letter by Luise Follen to her: "Our father was in everything excellent and worthy, excepting his temper. Charles was his favourite, yet he was sometimes impatient with him."[8] One can imagine the busy lawyer in his office at home, playing with his son. And yet the relationship between father and son in Karl's early youth seems not to have been always good. Eliza Follen thought that "Dr. Follen's recollections of his childhood were not particularly happy." Luise Follen wrote about the following incident to Eliza:

> I remember once, when his father angrily punished Charles for some fault he had committed, that the dear boy came up to him, and, extending his hand, said, "Father, I forgive you." The anger at his father, as his teacher, seemed to him of more importance than his own fault.[9]

This report may have been embellished by both Luise and Eliza. Still, perhaps one can trace in a scene like this the roots of Follen's later hatred of what he saw as tyranny and oppression, and his willingness to work for the spreading of what he considered to be freedom and independence. The earliest years of his youth must have contributed to the building of Karl's character, and their effects must have stayed with him throughout his life. He told his wife in conversation that he had "often wished himself dead, from his desire to escape this suffering," and that "there was an unnatural seriousness and earnestness in his character, when he was a child, and that it was not till he was a man, that he could learn to relish a jest." During vacation times, Follen's family problems did not change significantly: he usually went to his grandfather in Romrod who, like his father, was "occasionally very violent in his temper."[10]

Young Karl was baptized in the Lutheran Church, and his wife reports that he early showed a deep interest in religion. Many of the discussions which took place in the home of Karl Follen's father were on religious topics, and the youngster soon became convinced of a necessity for a strict Christian lifestyle. Jesus Christ was to be a model figure in Follen's life,[11] and this attraction was to be lifelong. It was to influence his character, his rhetoric as a student leader and revolutionary, and of course his turn toward an intensive study of religion among the New England Unitarians twenty-five years later.[12]

The Bible was for the young Karl Follen primarily a book concerned with morality. It was for him a guideline which would teach people to adhere to the high standards of ethical behavior which Jesus had preached. The duty of every Christian was, according to Follen's idea, self-perfection. The Scriptures were thus less a source of spirituality than a socially applicable set of rules. If followed by all Germans, they could provide a common basis of ethical conduct known to all and observed by all.

Because young Karl came from an educated family of local notables, it was expected that he would attend first the *Paedagogium* high school and then the university. Karl did both in his home town. At the Giessen *Paedagogium* he studied Greek, Latin, Hebrew, French, and Italian and passed the university entrance exam in the spring of 1813, at age sixteen. Letters written to a young friend at Darmstadt during his school years give us an idea of Karl's rather pedantic and humorless character, as well as a certain dubious reputation which was already building up. In self-defense, he wrote:

> Dear Zurbuch, I have been silent all this time not because I was too lazy to write, but because I felt insulted by you. You wrote to me that, as you had heard, I associate with bad boys [schlechte Buben] and gangsters [Ganoven]. You seem to have forgotten, that I have courage enough to keep away from bad boys. If you loved me as a friend, you would never believe such stories. . . . I wish to have an answer and an explanation in this matter from you as soon as possible.[13]

High school meant the first exposure to nationalist ideas for Karl; in one of his teachers he soon encountered a man who would indoctrinate his students with German nationalist ideas and anti-French hostility, the classical philologist and archaeologist Friedrich Gottlieb Welcker (1784–1868), brother of the famous legal scholar Karl Theodor Welcker (1790–1869), co-editor of the *Staatslexikon*.

Welcker instilled in Follen and his classmates their first consciousness of the precarious political situation of their home territory. He also outlined for them their own options for political participation in the years between 1810 and 1813. Here the students were first called upon to become politically aware and active, to think in national terms, and to plainly hate the French occupying forces. It must have been in Welcker's classes or after class that Follen first read the prose and poetry of contemporary nationalist agitators and writers such as Friedrich Ludwig Jahn (1778–1852) or Ernst Moritz Arndt (1769–1860), and that he learned to appreciate the ideals of a German ethnic identity *(Volkstum)* and national spirit, of resistance against tyrants and oppressors, and of the necessity for political and social change within Germany itself. Thus Karl Follen's mind soon became filled with overly sentimental political thoughts, and he wrote in his school essays around 1812, as a fifteen-year-old, statements that echoed the politicized and aggressive mood of the times as well as the imagination of a boy his age. In one essay he writes: "It will break my heart, when I see how the worm of tyranny daily destroys the sinews of our ancient freedom. . . . The stars of hope have passed away, and the sweet morning just will not come."[14]

At the end of the eighteenth century, Karl Follen's home state, Hesse-Darmstadt, looked nothing like the German national state, free from French influence, that Welcker, Jahn, and Arndt were imagining. The local ruler (landgrave) Ludwig reigned over a territory which seemed in many ways to be quite typical for its time: it was small, composed of a large number of districts and towns, and politically as well as militarily weak. The territory became a Grand Duchy under Napoleonic auspices in 1806, and its area was significantly enlarged. By 1824 it counted 671,789 souls within its borders. The capital, Darmstadt, including its immediate surroundings, had a population of 19,903 at that time. The Giessen area counted 28,771 inhabitants. In the entire state, there were 481,777 Protestants, 167,582 Roman Catholics, and about 20,600 Jews. Romrod, Follen's birthplace, had "three mills, 186 houses and 1032 mostly Lutheran inhabitants, who mainly lived on farming, cattle-raising, and handicrafts."[15]

The town of Giessen in the late eighteenth century has been described in the following way:

> The rise of the town at the beginning of the seventeenth century had been of short duration. The Thirty Years' War ended all that, and since then Giessen lies as if it were paralyzed behind its town fortifications, above which the houses hardly protrude. The following age has given us not a single important building; the university is alive, but it lives aside from the citizenry, and both are characterized by the plainness of their exterior life.[16]

And yet, in contrast to Romrod, Giessen must have seemed vast: by 1824 it had 740 houses, farms, mills, and public buildings. Most impressive surely were the old palace, the armory, and the university building. Not only was Giessen the seat of administrative offices and law courts, and of a garrison of soldiers, but it was also something special in the territory of Hesse-Darmstadt because it had its own university. This had first been established in 1607 and had everything from an astronomy building to medical clinics to a large library containing 18,000 volumes in 1824. The faculty consisted of twenty-eight full professors, and there were about two hundred students in the years after 1815.

The political situation of Hesse-Darmstadt at the time of Karl Follen's birth was very strained and difficult. From 1790 to 1830 the territory lived through a period of dramatic change, turbulent social problems, war, political radicalism, and severe financial crisis. The French Revolution had occurred dangerously nearby, and the landgrave was filled with fear of the new "ideas of 1789" even before his territory was invaded by French armies in 1792. Ludwig X remained loyal to the emperor of the Reich until 1796; then, however, betrayed by the emperor, who had promised protection, and snubbed by Prussia, another possible powerful ally, the landgrave was forced to sign a treaty with France in order to avoid financial ruin and the military destruction of his territory. The landgrave no longer had the funds to pay his troops by 1794. Napoleon agreed to pay and equip the troops, but only in combination with the right to use them in his own campaigns.

In an article on Hesse-Darmstadt during the years from 1790 to 1806, J. R. Dieterich has outlined what continuous warfare meant for the territory: "The constant passing through of friendly and enemy troops, the requisitions, contributions, and plundering drove the pauperized people into despair."[17] Although Hesse-Darmstadt gained territory in the reforms subsequent to the Reichsdeputationshauptschluss of 1803, and recuperated somewhat after being forced into the Confederation of the Rhine in 1806, it was once again invaded in that same year by French and by Prussian troops. It was not until the very end of Napoleon's reign over Europe that Hesse-Darmstadt joined the coalition against him. Whatever decisions the former landgrave (who became a Grand Duke in 1806) made before 1813 were thus largely dictated by financial and military emergencies.

Under such circumstances, the population was not likely to stay calm. Historians today have not finished examining all the forms of political radicalism which arose in Hesse after the first French invasion.[18] There were great famines (the worst of which was in 1816–17) and connected to these, economically motivated peasant uprisings (1819, 1830). But there were also more clearly articulated and potentially more influential forms of radicalism among students, local intellectuals, and finally professional revolutionaries. At first the protest of these groups was defensive only, focusing on the hated French military occupation, oppressive taxation, and the service of Hessian soldiers in the French army. However, it soon became apparent that the ideas of the French Revolution, brought to Hesse before and during the Confederation of the Rhine period, had a profound influence and changed the nature of the protest itself. The formulation of a new German nationalism and the cry for liberal constitutions were not only reactions to a French threat but also emulations of French historical events and political ideals.

Whether the influence of the French manifested itself in a productive, modernizing way or whether it amounted to pure oppression has been much disputed. The historian Elisabeth Fehrenbach has recently argued that it is appropriate for contemporary research to consider "the equal importance of the reforms in the Confederation of the Rhine states to those of the French Revolution itself," and to drop the old view of "unhistorical" reforms merely dictated by foreign domination. Napoleon pursued a policy of "moral conquest" just as much as military conquest, and he created "not only satellites" but also "real allies who followed him out of well-calculated raison d'état." Fehrenbach restates the accepted modern view that in the Confederation of the Rhine, "the constitutional guarantee of basic civil rights was oriented more toward the principle of equality than in Prussia," and that the Napoleonic influence decisively changed the course of German constitutional history.[19]

Among those Germans who on the one hand were stimulated by the French example of reform activity, but on the other hand were hostile to

French military oppression, there were varying degrees of commitment. For example, the conservative historian Heinrich Leo (1799–1878), whose memoirs tell us about his student years,[20] abandoned the liberal ideas he had once believed in after they were outlawed by the Carlsbad Decrees of 1819. The three Follen brothers, however, persisted, fighting illegal political battles and living at least partly underground. Finally, there were the extreme radicals who were willing to destroy their own lives in their struggle: the radical schoolteacher Friedrich Ludwig Weidig committed suicide in prison in 1837.[21] All of these persons, however, participated in one way or another in the discovery of the German nation as a new concept. This discovery was not suggested or propagated by the old order, the nobility and landgrave. There were recent proponents of a German nation, such as the philosopher Johann Gottlieb Fichte (1762–1814), who delivered his famous *Addresses to the German Nation* during the winter of 1807–1808. There had been no experience as yet, however, with a modern national state which would deemphasize the power of individual territories in the interest of further centralization. The new leading group, the educated bourgeoisie, needed to experiment and find the right path between liberalism and tolerance, aggressiveness and violence. It recognized the existence of a German *Volk,* and a spirit within it; but the idea of a political unit to contain this *Volk* was still merely utopian. To change this situation, the exponents of nationalism put to use the available means, commercialized literature and the modern press. Petitions were also circulated, and political clubs formed.

War served as a further catalyst of German national self-definition. The Wars of Liberation between 1813 and 1815 changed the nature of the new nationalism dramatically, bringing into it a sense of urgency and a militant spirit. But above all the wars were important for a mystical element which they introduced into German intellectual life. The strength of soldiers and civilians, indeed of the entire *Volk,* in the face of great adversity, soon became a focal point for the whole national movement.[22] Karl Follen and his older brother (at ages seventeen and nineteen) were among the soldiers who set out in the early spring of 1814 to pursue Napoleon's armies deep into French territory. From the University of Giessen, about 130 of their fellow students did the same.[23] Paul Follen, the youngest brother, later participated in the campaigns of 1815, after Napoleon had once again returned to power. In November of 1813, it was no easy decision for the Grand Duke of Hesse-Darmstadt to abandon Napoleon and change sides— his territory was dangerously close to France, and Napoleon himself had, through an envoy, threatened that in the case of a desertion he would destroy the territory completely.[24] Eliza Follen fully subscribed to the mythical quality of the war which came, and she embellished her report of it with rhetoric familiar from the American Civil War:

> The corps of riflemen, in which the elder Follens enlisted, consisted mainly of students. They wore no uniform, but retained their usual student's dress. They went to battle for their dearest rights, freely and from choice; they went as men, as citizens, not as hired soldiers; there was a noble, generous enthusiasm, a spirit of self-sacrifice, a religious sense of duty, among the volunteers, which gave a dignity and solemn grandeur to this national struggle for freedom.[25]

The history of the Wars of Liberation has often been told, by Friedrich Meinecke and others.[26] Likewise, the concept of a citizen army as opposed to a paid professional army has been emphasized ever since classical times. There are also detailed sources which tell how the Hessian volunteers fared who set out from their home territory in late March of 1814, participated in the occupation of France, and returned to Germany on July 3. This troop, which included the Follen brothers and their teacher Friedrich Gottlieb Welcker, had orders to march down all the way to Lyon in order to locate and destroy what was left of the Grande Armée. It was a great disappointment for these men that the outcome of the war had already been decided, and the enemy was not to be seen near or far. The entire march to Lyon took place without a single instance of combat. The only skirmish which occurred was a fistfight with French locals in a Lyon tavern.[27] Even worse, Karl Follen was seized by a severe case of typhoid fever during basic training and was thus not fit to even participate in the greater part of the marching.

There was no heroic death on the march to Lyon, as there had been for the poet and later national hero Theodor Körner (1791–1813) in August 1813 near Gadebusch in Mecklenburg during an earlier campaign. However, the aura of going to war for the newfound fatherland inspired the marching men to poetic activity and to mythologizing their own army experience. In general, the participants of this tour seem to have been better poets than soldiers. Military discipline was not held to be very important; especially August Follen distinguished himself repeatedly for being "unattentive in duty, in clothing, and equipment."[28] Many of the soldiers seem to have had interests similar to those of the twenty-year-old troop member

Georg Thudichum, who kept a very detailed diary of his adventures, was fascinated by "politics, religion, and poetry," and felt he was participating in "a crusade, a holy war."[29] Friedrich Gottlieb Welcker soon realized that he and the others were destined to "take a walk for the fatherland, not to fight for it." Although he missed his scholarly work at home, he resolved at least to enjoy the sights of the countryside while with the troops.[30]

Thus Karl Follen and his brother August did not have a genuinely military experience in France. Still, they were given a chance at least to dream of war, to quote out loud the poems of national significance which they loved, and to discuss politics with their fellow academics on a trip through France. The war gave them something they were searching for: a sense of national identity, perhaps a growing sense of who their enemy was, and an ideal of democracy and equality among the soldier-citizens participating. The war turned into an intellectual exercise and did more than that: it created expectations for the future. Returning to Germany from the army experience, these young men had experienced a change in their political mentality and were no longer satisfied with the way their territories were organized. They turned against "un-German" influences, petty particularism, absolute monarchy, and the uncontested reign of the prince in their home territory. Many of these young men upon their return home went to the university. On their way to changing the German nation, the young academics first changed these institutions of higher learning.[31]

German universities in the middle and late eighteenth century had always found it difficult to control their student bodies. At the universities of Jena and Giessen, for instance, the local government authorities had tried to curb the fist and sword fighting which was a characteristic of the existing student fraternities, known as Landsmannschaften and Orden. The former only admitted students from the specific geographical regions in Germany which they claimed to represent, and provided social activities for the students from these areas; the latter were mystical associations formed by students of varying geographical origin, derived from the model of freemasonry.[32] Both groups attempted to dominate the student body and attract as many members as possible. One of the major differences between the two student groups was that the Landsmannschaften did not require a lifelong membership; the *Orden* did. The latter had mostly disappeared by the end of the eighteenth century, leaving the Landsmannschaften in a dominant position. This group had begun to build up a body of laws from about 1770 onward; the laws were generally referred to as the *Comment*. This code was particularly important insofar as it regulated the dueling of students with each other. An example was the *Comment* still used at the University of Leipzig in 1817, which began by defining how much weight certain insults were to have and what duels were required to avenge each of them. There was also a clear statement of differences in rank and order among the students. A "senior," a "subsenior," a "new member," and so forth all had their specific places in the dueling ceremony. Infractions against the *Comment* were punishable by expulsion, either temporary or permanent.[33]

What these Landsmannschaft regulations did not include, however, was a code regulating the personal moral behavior or the political attitudes of students. They assumed that as long as relations within the fraternity were in order, and at least two or three students were familiar with the rules, there would be no problems. Similarly, the only political feature of the Landsmannschaften was the loyalty to the students' home territories; there was no moral mission to the outside world. Furthermore, the Landsmannschaften did not constitute a movement which integrated the entire student body: only students from a certain geographical area could join; others were not accepted.

The moral situation of the students has been described by many historians, especially those favorably inclined toward the later nationalist fraternities known as Burschenschaften,[34] as poor in the late eighteenth century, and this was reflected by the students' negative reputation in the university town. Those enrolled at the University of Giessen, for instance, allegedly busied themselves mainly with drinking, fencing, fistfighting, and annoying townspeople (whom they referred to as *Philister*). The Burschenschaft historian Herman Haupt wrote in 1907: "The uncouth acts of the Giessen students toward the educated girls and women of the university town seemed almost unbelievable." The following contemporary student poem is also quoted by Haupt as an indication of the student bahavior at German universities of the time:

What is a real student? One who sleeps during the day,
roams around at night, making trouble,
one who annoys the citizens, and troubles the professors,
and only associates with students of his kind,
who is frequently locked up in the student prison,
walks around like a pig,
who is very dirty, but always worried about his reputation,

and who is expelled from the university,
once he has made enough trouble.[35]

The new Burschenschaft fraternities, founded after 1811, meant to bring
about a dramatic change in German student life.[36] In that year two nationalist academics of an older generation, Friedrich Ludwig Jahn and Friedrich Friesen, had attempted to found such an organization at the University of Berlin; they too wished to reform German student life drastically.
Dueling and loose living were to stop, and the students' energy was to be
diverted to more important matters, such as the moral improvement and
national unification of the German nation. Jahn especially wished to prevent a division of the student body into many small groups according to
their geographical origin. He wanted to shape a united student body which
would serve the German national cause by reforming itself morally and
then becoming politically active. The students were to emphasize their
German rather than their regional character, and were to apply Christianity
as one of the main forces in order to hold them together.

The first Burschenschaft that was to have a major influence on students
everywhere was founded at the University of Jena, where Karl Follen
would later arrive in the fall of 1818. The motto of this new fraternity,
established in June of 1815, seemed incompatible with that of former
student organizations, being "honor, freedom, fatherland."[37] None of these
terms would have had the same meaning for students of the late eighteenth
century. "Honor" would have been related only to the dueling system, and
not to a personal moral lifestyle. "Freedom" would only have signified that
of the students in contrast to the local town surroundings and constraints.
"Fatherland" would merely have referred to the small home territory from
which the individual student came, not to the entire German nation.

With the founding of the Burschenschaft, this last term received a new
central significance at the university: the allegiance to a future German
national state would be stronger and greater than that to the home territory.
The introduction to the constitution of the new club begins: "A German
university is a common institution of the German people, for the purpose
of the entire patriotic education." After reverence for God, the "highest and
holiest" purpose was to be the progress of "freedom and autonomy of the
fatherland." The Burschenschaft and the entire university community were
projected as a microcosm of the German nation at large. The students had
a political mission. They were to fight for patriotic ideals and the unifica-

tion of Germany, first at the university, then beyond it. The Burschenschaft was to represent German academic youth, and to realize their hopes for the future.[38] The larger political goals of the Burschenschaft thus had implications for the behavior of its members at the university, and vice versa.

The Jena Burschenschaft constitution had several very democratic elements. All the student officers were elected in free, secret elections. Each student member had one vote. The terms of all offices were limited to six months. Majorities had the power of decision on difficult issues and in all elections. There was a large assembly, and small committees to deal with various areas of organization. The members were to adhere to a modern catalogue of rights and duties. Rules concerning dueling were still included, but these were to disappear from later Burschenschaft constitutions, such as the one in Giessen. The Burschenschaft would, finally, do everything in its power to prevent the spread of the Landsmannschaften and Orden.[39]

## Follen and Student Politics

In the spring of 1813, Karl Follen enrolled at the University of Giessen. At first he studied theology, but he soon turned permanently to the study of law, as was traditional in his family. He became *Dr. juris* in 1817. The title of his doctoral dissertation was "On the Abolition of Privileges Long Fallen into Disuse" *(De privilegiis non-usu longaevo omittendis)*. Follen planned to have it published in a legal journal called *Magazin für die Philosophie (und Geschichte) des Rechts und der Gesetzgebung,* edited by his teacher Karl von Grolman (1775–1829) and a colleague named Löhr at Giessen.[40] In the end the dissertation seems not to have been published, perhaps for political reasons.[41] Follen was a hard-working and successful student, but there were other matters more important to him. The ideas he had assimilated during the Wars of Liberation and at the *Paedagodium* from Friedrich Gottlieb Welcker were now to be extended into practice. While studying law with as distinguished a professor as Karl von Grolman, who was later to draft the first liberal Hesse constitution in 1820, Follen could not forget the ideas of Jahn and Arndt, the songs and poems of Körner, and the disappointment of the Congress of Vienna, as it was sensed among German liberal intellectuals.

The university town of Giessen itself lay exactly in the center of the "radical triangle," as the historian Peter Moraw has recently called it, between Mainz (a city with an important Jacobin radical tradition), Heidelberg (seat of a heavily politicized university—Follen's brother August was a student there), and Jena (the most radical German university). In Giessen, after 1813, students and professors as well were soon polarized into at least two major groups, according to Moraw: those who thought in "conservative, legalistic, dynastic, and Hessian" terms and those who considered themselves "liberal and nationalistic opponents of the absolutist state [*Obrigkeitsstaat*]."[42] Follen soon joined the new "German reading society," a political club founded at the University of Giessen in November of 1814, on a pattern suggested by Ernst Moritz Arndt. His older brother August, who had been studying philology and theology since 1811, was the leader of this group, which read Ernst Moritz Arndt's *Spirit of the Times* (*Geist der Zeit*, published in several volumes since 1806), Theodor Körner's poems on nationhood and war, such texts as the Nibelungen saga, and the political periodicals put out in a general reading room. In June of 1815 the society split, however, into two warring factions. The aggressive leadership style of August Follen seems to have caused this division.

August was soon thereafter expelled from Giessen University because of his political activism, and enrolled at Heidelberg, this time as a law student. When he was, in turn, forced to leave Heidelberg in 1817, August returned to Giessen. Alexander Pagenstecher, a fellow student at Heidelberg, remembers him there in the following way:

> Adolf [August] Follen, the Siegfried among these modern Nibelungen characters invited me to visit him and the following Sunday invited me for a walk to Neckarsteinach. . . . Our walk finally turned out to be a run from the Karlstor without interruption all the way up to Neckargmünd, an hour away. My tongue was hanging out of my mouth when we finally stopped. . . . Our selected group was still quite small back then in Heidelberg. . . . I became most attached to Follen, probably due to his poetic spirit and good looks. His outward appearance was a perfect image of a medieval knight. . . . Follen's room was our headquarters, since we did not frequent pubs. There or sometimes at another friend's house or on walks we gathered together.[43]

The Giessen "German reading society" split into the moderate "Teutonia" society, and the more radical "Germania." Karl Follen was a founding member of the latter group, in which the influence of Friedrich Ludwig Jahn was especially strong, including the emphasis on regular participation by all members in athletic exercises. This newly discovered athletic activity, known in German as *Turnen*, was good as mere physical exercise, but it also built a certain militant and militaristic spirit among the students, who would be ready to fight whomever they perceived as their enemies, be it French armies, local authorities, or princes. The motto of the "Germania" society, betraying the youth and inexperience, but also the determination, of each of its individual members, was:

> Courage in the heart
> Defiance under the hat
> Blood on the sword
> And all will be well.[44]

Karl Follen was now part of a small, narrowly defined group of politically active students, who were interested not only in university affairs but also in how they could change the political situation throughout Germany. When the Germania society was founded, more than students were present; there were also outside radicals who were seeking contacts with those at the university. Several new names now appear: Friedrich Ludwig Weidig, a clergyman and schoolteacher; Wilhelm Schulz (1797–1869), an army officer; and Wilhelm Snell (1789–1851), a local judge and intellectual, later to be a professor alongside Karl Follen in Switzerland. These individuals maintained a low profile at the University of Giessen. They met regularly in secret with the most radical students, however, and especially often with the Germania society, which was also known in a derogatory sense as the "Blacks" because of the color of "old Germanic" clothing preferred by its members.[45]

The extra-university contacts of the Blacks may be seen in the memoirs of one of their leading members, Karl Christian Sartorius (1796–1872), who, like Karl Follen, studied law at Giessen. He was able to bring various experiences to the group and, for instance, reports:

> I spent the summer of 1817 in Darmstadt, to prepare for my exams, which I had to take the following winter. . . . While I was visiting my family, I mainly associated with the young men of the liberal party, who were following the same course which I had become intrigued by in Giessen. This was to work for the unification of Germany, defend the rights of the people against dynastic interests, and inform the people about their rights. Capable men belonged to this circle, of

which I will name, among others, Heinrich Karl Hofmann, Karl Stahl, Rühl, Enslin, and Schulz.[46]

In Giessen itself, however, the continuing presence of a student leader was needed in order to direct the student group in its activities at the university. The person found for this role was without doubt Karl Follen. Alexander Pagenstecher recounts his impressions of Follen among the Giessen Blacks:

> This Karl Follen was one of the outstanding people I have met in my life. . . . He was a perfectly handsome man, of middle height, a well-proportioned body, vital and strong. . . . His speech was mild and harmonious, his expressions concise, clear . . . his posture always serene and measured, his whole appearance reassuring, dominant, but without boastfulness. . . . He had given his entire personality to the service of the fatherland, and lived, breathed, and acted only in the pure atmosphere of this idea. To realize it, and to get us and an increasing number of the people involved, those were the goals of his life. Thus he stood among us, undoubtedly our master, a savior among his disciples.[47]

About the Black members he said:

> The most loyal of these were his [Follen's] compatriots, Hessians, whom he had gathered together in Giessen; the sons of rather poor families, plain, simple youths, but loyal and full of faith, of complete moral purity and willing to sacrifice even until death.[48]

This new group of young, idealistic reformers expressed their political ideas in dicussions at their regular meetings; however, they also wrote poems and songs about their experiences and political goals. Especially talented in poetic expression of this kind were August and Karl Follen, and their fellow students Karl Christian Sartorius and Christian von Buri (1796–1850). In his poems of the time, Karl Follen dealt with such topics as the Wars of Liberation and the German nation. The sentimental poem "Körners Todtenfeier" (Körner's funeral song) combined the war experience with artistic sensibility and a passionate mystical religiosity. Referring to the heroic death in battle of the poet Theodor Körner in August of 1813, Follen wrote:

> Along with the sound of the war horns
> Angels' voices called out "Körner"!
> And the heart of the hero breaks.
> Hearts, eyes, burst into tears!
> The illumination of high faith
> Will light up your tears.
> Germany, whom you served faithfully,
> Feels, O brother, your wounds,
> bleeds along with you and—rejoices!
> You are a king, much envied,
> The purple of your blood clothes you,
> Holy thorns crown you.[49]

The politicized mood of the young students was expressed in another poem or song written by Karl Follen in 1816, entitled "Deutsches Burschenlied" (German student song):

> Storm, you sound of freedom,
> Storm, like the power of waves
> From the inside of a rocky cliff!
> Cowardly the bunch of enemies shivers,
> But our heart beats so warmly,
> Our youthful arm aches
> filled with a longing for action.[50]

These few examples illustrate the sort of discourse prevalent within this radical student group. The language of their poems was full of *Schwärmerei*, of Storm and Stress sentiments. Ideas particularly emphasized were those of the heroic character of war and of unlimited service to the German nation. But there were also other mythical components, such as a glorification of death associated with a strong religious element. In general, however, the very exuberant mood is most striking: the students are more than politically mobilized and motivated. Political involvement for them has gained a heroic quality. They understood themselves as activists longing to put their ideals into practice, not melancholy spectators of a difficult and unchangeable political situation.[51]

The new fraternity described itself as both German and Christian in character. Religious topics took up a large amount of time at the regular meetings held by the group. The students discussed Bible passages and the role of religion in the new national state which was to come in the future. The ideal of religious organization would then be a united national church, to include all Christian denominations.[52] The available sources show no antagonism against any specific Christian groups or sects, and also no statements showing opposition to Roman Catholicism. The dominant creed within the Black group, however, always remained Lutheran Protestantism. Martin Luther was seen as a national hero as well as a religious reformer, and the history of Lutheran Christianity was inextricably bound up with the time periods and the aspects of German history which the Giessen radical students admired most. The German patriot was almost by definition a Lutheran Christian, and religion was mixed with politics. The Blacks wore a black costume, which was seen as especially "German," but on the front of their black caps members had a silver cross.

The Blacks resented the influence exerted over the student body by the Landsmannschaften and soon came into sharp conflict with them. These differences became especially pronounced after December 1816, when members of the Blacks, including Karl Follen, were actively involved in the founding of the first branch of the Burschenschaft in Giessen. The goal of the Blacks was to incorporate the entire Giessen student body into this new society. Severe struggles, including sword and fist fights, ensued between the adherents of the old Landsmannschaften and the new Burschenschaft, and both found themselves in conflict with the very conservative university rector, Franz Josef Arens (1779–1855). He immediately became particularly suspicious of the new Burschenschaft, and at a social evening at the home of a Giessen professor he interrogated one of the known members of the new fraternity regarding its goals. To whom would this student be loyal if forced to decide, Arens asked: to the local territory and its prince, or to some kind of general German fatherland? The student hedged on his answer, but Arens became more and more convinced that the new group was national and liberal in its opinions and should therefore be suppressed by the university authorities, who after all were officers of the principality.[53]

The new Burschenschaft had been planned and formed by Karl Follen and a few fellow students. It had also been given a constitution radically different from the *Comment* observed by the Landsmannschaft groups. The *Ehrenspiegel*, or "register of honor," adopted by Follen and his friends had two main themes: reforming the notorious student lifestyle and giving the students a sense both of local and particularly of national mission. But its most radical departure from previous student fraternities lay in the idea of total equality among members. There was to be no more ranking among the students: all enjoyed equal rights, privileges, and duties. The officers, as was the case with the Jena Burschenschaft, were all freely and secretly elected for a limited term.

The *Ehrenspiegel* document was composed in 1816, largely by Karl Follen himself. It had three parts, beginning with the "General Part," followed by an "order of punishment" for those who broke the rules, and then an "order of fighting" to handle differences which developed among the members. The "order of punishment" was meant to enforce a strict moral code among the students. The unruly student life common before 1816 was to be abandoned, and what was conceived of as honor, loyalty, chastity, and honesty were to be upheld by students at all times. The "order of fighting" strictly limited the resort to duels which had traditionally been used to solve conflicts among students. The many useless duels fought by the Landsmannschaften were to be avoided. Duels would be used only if all other attempts to solve the problem had failed. The winner of the duel was then believed to have been preferred by an "act of God."[54]

A major theme in the new constitution was that of honor. There existed a distinction between "exterior" and "interior" honor. The honor of the student was not only shown and restored in an exterior way, by dueling. Now every student also had to possess "inner" honor by living a personally moral life, which meant sexual abstinence, Christian uprightness, and personal integrity. There was to be no more wasting of energy on drinking and fights with local townspeople. Rather, the students would focus on the reform of the German universities and the nation as such, in spiritual and political terms. A ideal Burschenschaft member was to become more than an organized, moral student; he also had to be transformed into a responsible citizen with a moral and political mission, inspired by mystical religious values and German national feeling. He lived above all not for his alma mater or his home territory, but for his people and the dream of a united Germany.[55]

As an intellectual leader at the local university level, Karl Follen needed national role models to look up to. The influence of major figures such as the philosopher Fichte was already felt around 1808. But two contemporary personalities were the most influential on Follen and his generation: the prophet of *Volkstum* and gymnastics, Friedrich Ludwig Jahn (1778–1852), and the poet and historian Ernst Moritz Arndt (1769–1860). Jahn is probably the less profound thinker of the two. He was a practical man, emphasizing action and active behavior on the part of the German people on a very broad level. Today he is remembered more for his contribution to modern gymnastics than for his nationalistic tone; however, in Follen's time, both were equally important.

Jahn opened his first athletics training ground in Berlin's Hasenheide park in 1811. The exercises performed there by his devoted students can be examined in the instruction book which Jahn published.[56] Jahn's gymnastics improved the physical fitness of German youth, its cooperative spirit, and its willingness to engage, if necessary, in physical battles. At the universities, Jahn's movement was not one of withdrawal from the world; rather, it was meant as a preparation for young men to go out and change the world. Gymnastics also provided, along with the Burschenschaft, the German reading societies, and the constitutional movement (to be considered in Chapter 2), a way for German youth to meet, form a coherent group, and to develop a distinctive national consciousness. The gymnasts tried to show in many different ways how German they were: by singing patriotic songs, wearing special clothes, and engaging in semireligious rituals. Some of the most common songs were published by August Follen in an anthology in 1819.[57] The gymnastics movement soon spread from Berlin to many other places in Germany. In Giessen, the Blacks built their own athletics exercise ground. Karl Follen spent much of his time as a student on the sports field, and excelled at fencing, swimming, and other forms of physical exercise. Many members of the Giessen student clubs and the new Burschenschaft joined him there, and friendships developed within the relatively small student body which would carry over into future political activities. The gymnastics ground thus provided another forum for Follen and a few others to influence the rest of the Giessen students.[58]

Gymnastics, as Jahn saw it, was to have a strong political component. During the Wars of Liberation, he had published his main work, entitled *German Ethnic Identity (Deutsches Volkstum)*.[59] This programmatic work called for a renewed attention to things German in general, but particularly in the cultural and spiritual realms. The German language was to be preferred over others, especially over the French, and specifically foreign patterns of behavior, clothing, and taste were to be avoided. Xenophobic attitudes thus played a large role here, as in Jahn's other writings. The worst enemy for the Germans was France. French political and intellectual influence was not to be accepted under any circumstance. Germany had to find its own identity, and did not need foreign suggestions in the process. Jahn clearly supported an end to particularism and a future united Germany. One can even argue that he was a proponent of a national *Machtstaat*, a unified Germany able to wield its economic and military power against other nations and thereby improve its own position. Jahn also introduced into Germany a popularized version of thought in terms of the *Volk*. His ideas could certainly not be considered as profound and forceful as those of Herder and Fichte; however, they were easier to understand, aimed at a wider audience, and more aggressive. Not only was the German *Volk* bound together by its common past and destiny, but it was proclaimed by Jahn to be heroic, having been maltreated and exploited by Napoleon and subsequently having fought for its own liberation. A common culture and political consciousness were now needed.

Karl Follen to a large degree eventually rejected the culturally xenophobic and especially the unrefined political views of Jahn, although in his own intellectual development he had to pass through the stage of considering what Jahn had to say. The published works of Jahn had a dreamy quality, however, a component of unrealistic *Schwärmerei* which Follen soon could no longer accept. The works of Jahn became for Follen a means to an end: they would get students involved in the cause which interested both Jahn and Follen, the struggle for a united Germany. The gymnastics meetings inspired by Jahn provided an occasion for Follen to discuss politics with those around him as Jahn had suggested. In the end, however, Follen adopted certain political ideas which Jahn could not have shared since they were informed by the principles of the French Revolution: the problems of individual civil rights, freedom of the press, and a participatory democracy. In this sense, Follen realized which sort of political arrangements would be influential in the future, while Jahn did not. Although the development of Follen's thought is unthinkable without the reference to Jahn, Follen soon developed in a different way, becoming more realistic and calculating.

The character of Ernst Moritz Arndt was quite different from that of Jahn. Arndt was a poet, a mystic, and an author who liked to view himself as a prophet. He claimed that he had a special capacity to save his country and fellow Germans because only he was capable of clearly discerning the truth, and of recognizing the most pressing political and social issues of his time. Knowledge of such things would be propagated by the printed word; and from Arndt, Follen and his friends received the idea of a German reading society which would further the nationalism among academic youth throughout the German territories.[60] Arndt's writings were extraordinary not only for their nationalistic and radical contents, but also for their highly polemical tone and finger-shaking rhetoric. A prime example was his work entitled *Über den Deutschen Studentenstaat* (1815), in which he described the students' role in the creation of a German national state. Follen's defense of the Giessen Burschenschaft,[61] to be discussed below, was written in rhetoric and style very similar to that of the *Studentenstaat*: there appeared the mythical, the heroic, and the religious elements. Arndt's text was meant to convince the reader less in intellectual than in emotional terms. Arndt appeared as more of a poet than a political theoretician, preferring poetic imagery to rational analysis. Yet he wished to analyze the German political situation, and often adopted a highly belligerent tone.

Arndt's most important text, and one which was certainly read, studied, and quoted by Karl Follen and his Giessen friends, was the work *Geist der Zeit*.[62] The book consisted of four parts, and rambled widely. It related dense historical tales and investigations into specific historical periods and problems, probed into the character of Germany and the Germans in the past and the present, and made many programmatic suggestions for the future. In Arndt's work there was a discomfort with the present, and disgust with moral and political laxity of the time. But there was also a hope for the future, a sense of the necessity of a better life, and an idea of what history could and could not do to instruct the modern reader. Arndt was strictly against political arrangements which seemed to him "un-German" and contrived; he claimed to be in strict opposition to the conventional wisdom of the time, and believed it necessary to change the spiritual values of the Germans before one could start changing the political situation. For him, the essentials were not only external matters such as those discussed by Jahn—language, dress, manners, activities, and so on. Arndt went deeper and was so more of a genuine Storm and Stress intellectual: art and spirit were essential to the building of a new Germany. Not only would its civil community, national unity, and moral citizens distinguish the new Germany, but also its grand spirit, once this was set free.

Arndt wrote during the Wars of Liberation, and he strongly emphasized liberation by violent struggle. Many songs and poems composed by Arndt thus dealt directly with military themes and subjects. There are calls for destroying the enemy of the fatherland, and for breaking the chains of slavery and tyranny. Arndt believed that violent struggle was going to be necessary in order to liberate and consolidate Germany. In 1813 Arndt had begun to emphasize this point in his pamphlet entitled "Aufruf an die Deutschen zum gemeinsamen Kampf gegen die Franzosen." In 1812, he had published his "Kurzer Katechismus für deutsche Soldaten." In these works Arndt did not suggest negotiations with the French; instead he called for the willingness of every individual German to sacrifice his life in battle. Arndt has been called a "crusader and militant German patriot."[63] It appears clear that after 1815 he more and more turned his hopes toward Prussia, which had shown such strength and perseverance even in times of great crisis, as the necessary agent for the unification of Germany. For Alfred G. Pundt, an American historian, it was in his militaristic preaching that Arndt made perhaps the greatest departure from the pacific and humanitarian nationalism of Herder.[64] Arndt was thus also an example for Karl Follen because he was a multifaceted character, in favor of a liberal constitution and individual rights including freedom of the press, but nevertheless at the same time a militarist, a proponent of violent solutions to political problems: a revolutionary intellectual. The modern civil society ruled by law (Rechtsstaat), Arndt said, would not evolve by itself. It would have to be fought for. Karl Follen took much from this attitude as his student days were drawing to a close and as he was probing the nonuniversity political world.

## From the Wartburg Festival to the Unconditionals: The Radicalization Process

In October of 1817 the Burschenschaft movement won nationwide attention for the first time when it organized a national meeting at the Wartburg castle near Eisenach. The most liberal prince in Germany, Carl August of Saxony-Weimar, provided for the students the same site in which Luther had hidden from his enemies three hundred years before. The Jena Burschenschaft initiated the idea for the festival, and sent letters of invitation to students at all Protestant German universities. Students from the University of Jena, which was nearby, were the most important and numerous participants.[65] There were also nonstudents involved, including professors and persons not at all associated with a university. Whether the list of participants was representative of German academic youth at the time or not, here was the first national youth forum to hold discussions and attempt to formulate resolutions with a national significance. Karl Follen was taking his doctoral exams in Giessen that October and thus could not attend the festival, but other members of the Giessen Blacks did travel to Eisenach to represent their university. The students gathered at the Wartburg to discuss the current political situation of Germany, to listen to speeches by fellow students and professors, and to come to understand their own roles as agents of nationalism. There was also a religious component in the celebration, and a commemoration of the three hundredth anniversary of the Lutheran Reformation. Religious motifs occur throughout the speeches held at the festival.

Lutz Winckler has argued in a study of the religious aspects and political implications of the Wartburg festival that "the history of Luther and of the Reformation is in a sense the history of their interpretation."[66] In the contemporary descriptions of the festival, the songs, and the speeches, there was a strong identification among the participating liberal students with Martin Luther as a figure who combined a religious mission with a patriotic one. The religious issues of the Reformation and its leader were incorporated into a secular religiosity which was to provide the strength for the new national movement in Germany. The commitment to a united Germany was thus reinforced by a national religion. Luther became the key symbol of freedom and progress.[67]

The opening speech held at the festival was by the student Heinrich Riemann. He welcomed the other students and emphasized the fact that he was speaking in the place where Martin Luther had once stayed. Luther had been sent by God "out of the dark walls of an Augustine monastery . . . to proclaim a better teaching, to destroy the Roman money-changing tables, and free the world from the worst of all bondages, that of the spirit." From the spirit of the Reformation, and of Luther as a national symbol, Riemann went on to observe that, during the Napoleonic wars, "slowly the longing returned for the lost freedom, for the restitution of the destroyed fatherland; soon the longing became loud and called out for a savior." Riemann ended his speech with a statement phrased as a prayer to God: "Look down with benevolence on our German fatherland, let it blossom in freedom and justice."[68] In this speech, political demands of the present were legitimized with the traditions of the past: if God was on Luther's side, He also had to be on the side of the Burschenschaft and its ideals. Who among the critics of the festival could dare to argue against Luther?

A speech delivered by a Jena professor of natural science, Lorenz Oken, called above all for unity among the festival participants. A way had to be found to unite all German students, be they organized and politically active in the new Burschenschaft or still members of the old Landsmannschaften. Oken called for the establishment of a set of laws applicable to all German students, which would make it possible for them to live together in harmony and thus be able to donate their energy to nationally important goals. The speaker urged the students to be a vital group in the ultimate creation of a German national spirit and a national state. Students could be especially effective fighters for nationalism because of their great personal mobility: the student might find a job not only in his home territory but anywhere in Germany, and "he no longer speaks the language of his village, of his home town . . . he is a universal man!" Oken believed that it was "a shame to be satisfied" as a student if one has "not become more than a provincial yokel" as a young academic. The new national young academic should always remember: "It is a rule in human history just as in nature: always link up with the mass: the individual always goes under against the whole: and the individuals always perish if they choose to fight each other."[69]

Perhaps the most important speech was given by the student leader Ludwig Rödiger, a philosophy student. His rhetoric was purely nationalistic, with no effort to give it any other framework, religious or secular. Rödiger chose not to speak carefully; rather, he said directly what he thought, and clearly expressed the mentality of the politically motivated youth movement. There was a "clear distinction between the shame of past years and the wonder of the recent ones." Rödiger recalled the Napoleonic time, when Germany was "under the iron yoke of the destroyer," when "princes shamelessly destroyed" Germany and its people. Finally, there was the great disappointment of the Congress of Vienna, upon which Rödiger commented: "In great danger we were promised a fatherland, a united, just fatherland, but the much-prayed-for *Bundestag* has not yet begun."[70] Moreover, the liberal constitutions which had been anticipated still had not been introduced in the individual German states. The only exception was Saxony-Weimar; Rödiger praised its ruler Carl August and called him an example to other German princes. Rödiger continued with a famous phrase: "Who bleeds for the fatherland, he may also talk about it, how it may best be shaped in peacetime." Here he spoke as a representative of his generation of War of Liberation soldiers. These men argued that they had risked their lives for the external liberation of Germany, but were after 1815 denied a word of comment on the German domestic scene. To such veterans, the denial of freedom of speech practiced in Germany seemed more than an insult: it was a betrayal of those who had fought bravely and had received the promise of a better life upon their return home.

Immediately after the oratorical part of the festival had ended, there occurred the event that caused perhaps the greatest stir among the German Restoration governments, and deeply offended many moderate as well as conservative intellectuals of the time. After most of the students had left, a small number stayed behind and publicly burned books and symbols which they saw as hostile to their cause. A number of items symbolizing French military aggression and domination, the German Restoration after 1815, and the contemporary German governments were burned. So were certain "un-German" books, such as the attack of the Jewish publicist Saul Ascher on "nationalistic fanaticism" and the Burschenschaft movement.[71] Another book burned was the conservative legal work *Restauration der Staatswissenschaften,* written by the Swiss author Karl Ludwig von Haller (1768–1854); it had given its name to the entire period of German history. This book burning was a deliberate imitation of Luther's public burning of the papal bull "Exsurge Domine" in late 1520, and was used to legitimize the cause celebrated at the festival.

Soon Metternich and the Prussian authorities demanded decisive steps to reduce the influence and liberty of students at German universities. The Restoration governments became uneasy when faced with the main program formulated at the end of the Wartburg festival, the "Principles and Resolutions of October 18." This document was obviously national, rather than particularistic, in its focus, but was phrased in a deliberately moderate and objective way in order to be firm in its demands but at the same time as inoffensive as possible. The tone and language of the document were clear, lacking the confused and overly romantic elements of other contemporary student writings. Thus it seemed to the state authorities that perhaps not only students but also professors or other advanced academics had participated in the formulation of these ideas. It is fairly certain that not only the students Heinrich Riemann (who had spoken at the festival itself) and Karl Müller had been involved, but also the professor Heinrich Luden and the Kiel medical doctor Franz Hegewisch.[72]

The "Principles and Resolutions" were intended for wide public distribution; they were to show citizens and governments exactly what the student movement, or at least its leadership group, demanded. The most important point stressed was German unity: there had to be one national state, since wars between individual German territories, and of members of the German people against one another, would be unthinkable. There was to be a citizens' army, not a standing army of mercenaries. Toll barriers between the individual German states were to be abolished. The document also, however, made more aggressive proposals: the "longing for emperor and *Reich* should not be forgotten"; it had to be "nurtured" by each individual German youth. The German Confederation was considered too weak and splintered to replace a centralized and powerful empire. The "Principles" continued: "All German states have the right and the duty to take revenge on other peoples for what they have done to the German people. In the relationship of the peoples the main rule must be: 'measure for measure' in war and peacetime." The document even went on to welcome "national hatred" as a legitimate force as long as it "jealously guarded the nation's rights" and rejected all foreign insults.[73]

The constitutional ideas which followed were strikingly modern, and influenced by the ideals of the French Revolution, when placed alongside traditional German political beliefs. There was an insistence that the will of the people, not that of the prince, should steer the policies of the government. For all power proceeded from the people; the prince could only be an executing agent, and had to adhere very strictly to the law when doing his duty. Furthermore, the most important principles of government should no longer be the *Ständestaat* or absolute monarchy, but "freedom and equality" for all. There was to be "no freedom but that dictated by the law, and no equality but that regulated by the law." The representative constitutions promised in Article 13 of the *Bundesakte* in 1815 should be introduced as soon as possible. All governments would in the future be composed of "freely elected representatives," chosen by the people alone and not by a prince or king.

Private property held by any individual was to be protected. There was also a guarantee of inalienable personal freedom—serfdom, for instance, being described as "a matter of disgust before God and every good human being."[74] Those released from serfdom were to be assisted so they could enter independent, productive, and prosperous lives. Freedom of personal opinion and freedom of the press received special attention. Legal reform would bring the equality of all citizens before the law and the introduction of public trials and the jury system. The police should be controlled by local authorities only, and any secret political police were to be abolished. Finally, every citizen was called upon to uphold the German language and indigenous culture. These program points were voiced in a clear and objective way—very different in style from writings by Jahn or Arndt. The style alone was an indication that this document, produced as a cooperative effort of political professors and engaged students, was meant as a mature expression of contemporary political dissent and proposals for the future. Perhaps one can argue that it was more moderate than aggressive. Karl Follen until 1817 shared many of its assumptions; yet his political ideas were quickly becoming more radical than those expressed by the student leaders involved with the Wartburg festival.

Follen's own history and description of the Giessen Burschenschaft, which he entitled *Beiträge zur Geschichte der teutschen Samtschulen seit dem Freiheitskriege 1813*[75] and published in 1818, was quite different in tone from the "Principles." Follen articulated an outspoken and contentious defense of the student movement in which he had been engaged, and although he tried to discourage those who thought of the Burschenschaft as illegal, illegitimate, or criminal, his language was more radical than most of that produced at the Wartburg festival. This aggressive text cannot have appeared soothing to the university and state authorities: rather, it irritated them greatly.[76]

Follen compiled more than a description of the goings-on in Giessen; he created a powerful counter-manifesto on behalf of the academic youth movement of his time. In the prefatory section, he urged the students to "pray, think, and act" only for their "fatherland." What the radical students had been doing was to organize a "Christian-German free state" and to "realize, in the people, the original image of all humanity." The beginnings of the "spirit of freedom" were seen in the external struggle of the German nation against the French during the Wars of Liberation; this spirit was then carried into the universities and further developed there.[77] Follen told the story of the Burschenschaft's struggle against what he saw as the particularistic, narrow-minded Landsmannschaften, and quoted the proposed motto of the Burschenschaft, voiced at a student assembly meeting, calling for "freedom, equality, and unity" among all students.

Follen denounced the disciplinary measures of university officials against the new student fraternity at Giessen as being exaggerated and even absurd. Follen always claimed to be representing the *Gesamtwillen*, the common will of all students, as he spoke—a term immediately reminiscent of Rousseau. He also used the dichotomy of "slavery" versus "freedom" to describe two different views of society, that of his opponents (the Landsmannschaften and university officials) being that of "slavery." His next statements were as radical as they were illiberal: among the student groups as among all Germans, as there was to be "one fatherland," so also "one religious creed" and "one freedom" to unite all. The entire population was to be made up of "German Christians." Those who did not fulfill these qualifications, coming from a different people or religious tradition, were to be excluded first from Burschenschaft activities and then eventually from the "German free-state." Only Christian Germans, then, would be united by a powerful "bond of conviction."[78]

The personal rights of the individual, however, were not as much emphasized by Follen as they had been in the Wartburg festival "Principles."

Follen used the term "freedom" primarily as defined by the common good of the German nation as a whole, and not the happiness of each individual. The unambiguous identification, and rejection of, ethnic and religious outsiders in Follen's scheme did not fit in well with his insistence on the more cosmopolitan principles associated with the French Revolution. The text was thus a mixture of various political ideas modified by Follen's own attitudes. The ideal of an "original image of humanity" re-created in Germany did not seem in harmony with the restrictive character of the future Germany which Follen tried to outline. He mixed elements of "Germanomaniac" *Schwärmerei* with French Jacobin ideals.

This contradiction between the French ideals of humanity and cosmopolitanism on the one hand, and a rigorous proposal for the specific rights of the German nation and people on the other hand, did not seem as ambiguous to Follen as it may to today's observer. When he spoke of the "horrors of the French Revolution," he seemed indeed to decry some of his own basic beliefs in republicanism. On closer reading, however, it becomes more apparent how carefully and skillfully phrased Follen's essay was. It constituted propaganda rather than a critical analysis of the contemporary situation, and a cover-up of Follen's true intentions, according to which "freedom, equality, and unity" would play at least as much of a role as "faith" and "fatherland." The accusations made by the university authorities that the Giessen Blacks were a secret group plotting to "destroy everything that exists" and that Follen and his friends were "treasonous" and "guilty of lèse-majesté" were denied. However, these accusations were actually well founded; the nationalist and liberal movement had become more widespread, articulate, and influential than was publically known.

A program for national change could never have been, and was never, formulated by the students of Karl Follen's generation alone. Rather, much in the Burschenschaft movement was due to the support of nationalistic "political professors" who had witnessed the period of French domination in Europe as mature men, and who before and after 1815 did everything in their power to awaken students to political issues.[79] Not all professors, to be sure, were part of this national and liberal group. The Giessen rector Franz Josef Arens, for instance, was strictly opposed to any student movement which dared to question the status quo in Germany. All were state appointees, and many had direct ties to the government; they would thus never have supported the Burschenschaft. Into this category falls Follen's teacher in law at Giessen, Karl von Grolman, later to become minister of Hesse-Darmstadt. The university professors who did join the national and liberal course, however, came from a wide variety of disciplines; here we will discuss a classical philologist, a philosopher, and a historian. The first was a professor at Giessen, the latter two at the University of Jena, the nationwide center of student radicalism.

The classical philologist at the University of Giessen was Friedrich Gottlieb Welcker, who had taught Karl Follen at high school in Giessen; he then spent time with him in the army during the Wars of Liberation; finally, he maintained very close contact with Follen at the university, where he lectured on classics. By 1815 Welcker was not only influencing his students but at the same time publishing a great variety of political tracts on contemporary issues. These included "Von ständischer Verfassung" (1815) and "Über die Zukunft Deutschlands" (1816).[80] The first pamphlet called for the establishment, in a literal and concrete sense, of the representative constitutions for all thirty-five German states, as previously promised in vague terms in Article 13 of the German *Bundesakte.* Not only external liberation from the French but also domestic reorganization was called for here. The second pamphlet was even more interesting, since it attempted to predict the future of Germany. Contemporary conservatives must have been seriously upset by Welcker's declaration that "if the *Bundesakte* will be and remain our basic law, internal wars or violent upheavals will be impossible to avoid."[81]

Welcker wrote another document significant in this context: the introduction to his lectures on German history delivered at Giessen University in 1815. Here there was a clear distinction made between the "German and the French characters." Welcker based his assumptions on a strong feeling of "Germanness," defined by national sensibility and historical tradition. While on the one hand he did read and discuss French thinkers such as Montesquieu, on the other hand Welcker tried to define a specific, indigenous "Germanness" which he wished would develop more thoroughly among the people he knew. There was a synthesis of natural law and what he referred to as "historic sense" in Welcker's thought, which might be seen as quite contradictory. He also stressed the need for "inner freedom" in the mind of a people; only in this way could there be a free and democratic national state.[82] As the teacher of the young Follen, he realized that both components must go together; the political order could not be modernized and improved without a preliminary change in the consciousness of the people, particularly the intellectuals.

In a portion on religion which followed, Welcker warned against a conception of religion which was too "ethereal" and took the attention of the people away from the affairs and necessities of the world. The "tendency to be complacent and introspective" could be dangerous to the individual and the nation. Religion too must become a "source of freedom" and a support for the demands of the people, instead of a tranquilizer. The lack of true religious faith in Germany was a proof, Welcker argued, for the soullessness of German society, and its pessimism about the future in general. He claimed that in England, which he considered to be an enlightened country with a free constitution, unbelief never became as widespread as in Germany. The French, in contrast, were the most atheistic people of all, a fact which was well suited to their "evil role" in the world of politics and intellectual thought.[83]

The role of history was central for Welcker; but history had to be employed in an appropriate way. The Germans were to be proud of their historical achievements, but to carry their pride in silence rather than in boastfulness. History was to be "like a look back into a youth filled with activity and strength," and it would be helpful in the "elevation of the *Volksgeist*" and in the "political rebirth" all Germans were looking forward to. The most important images to keep in mind would be the "freedom, rights, and greatness of our forefathers."[84] Welcker did not present these thoughts only in published form; during the winter of 1815–16 and the summer of 1816 he lectured regularly to groups of Giessen students brought together at the initiative of the Blacks. His topics were "religion, ethics, *Volksgeist*, public opinion, education, and teaching." The lectures were evidently closely related to the contents of Fichte's *Addresses to the German Nation*.[85] They dealt with the current weak and disturbed situation in Germany, and tried to set an agenda of national moral, ethical, and political reform for the future.

Perhaps the most influential political professor to affect Karl Follen was the Jena philosopher Jacob Friedrich Fries (1773–1843). He incited his students to think about nationalism, constitutional reform, and moral improvement in Germany, participated in the Wartburg festival, and was a radical theorist. He was not, however, a radical in practice, and far from a Jacobin or revolutionary. When Karl Follen arrived at the University of Jena in the fall of 1818, he quickly broke the influence of Fries over his student followers, and Follen himself became the leader of the Jena "Unconditionals," a group much more radical than Fries would ever have accepted, as we shall see in Chapter 2. Fries would never himself have committed a violent act in order to achieve political goals; however, he conveyed much to the radicalizing student movement through his philosophical teachings.

Fries introduced to the student radicals and revolutionaries the concept of personal "conviction" *(Überzeugung)*, which was needed to legitimize the actions a person might undertake in order to achieve an important goal.[86] Thus, for the students who felt it crucial to improve their nation, their convictions served to outweigh any illegal acts they might have to perform to achieve a change for the better. Fries did not preach the legality of crimes as grave as political murder by any means; however, he gave to his students a set of philosophical terms which they could use and interpret for themselves as they wished. Fries had derived his concept of "conviction" from the philosophy of Immanuel Kant, and then popularized it for a broad student audience. He differentiated between knowing *(Wissen)* as the "natural conviction," and believing *(Glauben)* as the "ideal conviction"; the latter had the highest status in his metaphysical ranking system.[87]

But Fries went still further in his teaching. The decided "conviction" at which a person arrived must lead him or her to an "act of conviction" *(Überzeugungstat)*. Fries believed that there were certain transcendent, super-individual truths which must lead a person to act in specific ways. The "good spirit" of a whole people had to "realize itself" in this way. Fries's principle of "conviction" might, on the one hand, legitimize moral relativism and give license to an infinite number of valid ways of living, acting, and thinking. On the other hand, it could also give legitimacy to the destruction of the wide range of permissible opinions in a free society, and make possible the total dominance of only one kind of thought, branding all its opponents as "enemies of morality."[88] This fidelity to a certain conviction led necessarily to ethical rigidity and intolerance. Without perhaps explicitly wanting this, Fries thus provided the glue which would hold secret groups of radicals together. He also supplied the excuse, if not the incentive, for political murder.

A third major influence on the student generation of 1813–1815, and a major voice of Karl Follen's time, was the Jena historian Heinrich Luden (1780–1847). During the terms of 1806–1807 he hardly had an audience for the course of lectures he was offering; some students were absent from the university during the war, others were not seriously interested in historical studies. This situation changed dramatically when Luden announced a series of lectures on contemporary German history and politics in the winter of 1808, and attracted over seventy listeners.[89] From that point on, his lectures on the most recent German history were a meeting place for all students with radical tendencies. One historian has commented, "Luden had firmly decided to live and die in his role for the rebuilding of the shattered fatherland."[90] In his lectures, Luden demanded that his listeners give up their noncommittal passivity and actively engage in thinking about the Germany of recent times. He glorified what he called the "German character," noting that a great part of this consisted of a natural "resistance to slavery and oppression." Luden also used expressions very similar to those employed by Friedrich Ludwig Jahn, including *Volk* and *Volkstum*. A *Völkerrecht*, making national self-determination a prerogative for Germans, would help to build out of several Central European states a German national state to house the entire *Volk* within it.[91] Before a *Rechtsstaat* was introduced in Germany, first of all the nation had to be liberated from outside aggression and oppression; autonomy was "the first thing every people should strive for" in order to "remain free and independent."[92] In order for the *Volk* to achieve true autonomy, however, it must first rediscover its own indigenous traditions, habits, culture, and language.

Luden was also able to influence a large circle of educated readers outside the university community in Jena by means of a periodical he founded in 1813. It appeared under the aggressive title *Nemesis: A Journal of Politics and History* (*Nemesis: Zeitschrift für Politik und Geschichte*). Through this magazine he sought for as many Germans as possible to "forget all old conflicts, and, with a great faith in freedom and rights, filled with a childlike love for the common fatherland, [to] bind themselves closely together." As editor of this periodical, Luden engaged in unrelenting competition with the playwright August von Kotzebue (1761–1819), who had been editor of the *Literarisches Wochenblatt* since 1817 and was widely perceived as an enemy of German nationalism and liberalism. After Luden found himself in the middle of a lawsuit which Kotzebue had initiated against him for his opinions expressed in the *Nemesis*, he had to be increasingly careful. The local government became even more suspicious of his activities despite the fact that he was cleared of all charges brought against him in court. Eventually publication of the *Nemesis* had to be discontinued.[93]

Luden had a considerable guiding role in the founding of the first Burschenschaft in Jena in 1815, and an influence on the formulation of its constitutional document. Although he did not get directly involved with the Burschenschaft and was careful to protect his public image, he did help behind the scenes, notably with the "Principles and Resolutions" drafted after the Wartburg festival. In this instance too he urged the students to be careful about what they published and to formulate their political demands in as clear and as inoffensive a way as possible.[94] The influence of Luden had become decidedly moderate by the time August Follen spent the spring of 1818 in Jena and Karl Follen arrived for a term the following winter.[95] Luden had once been a strong voice in formulating the new nationalism, but he was not willing to take a position of complete opposition to the state in which he lived. Karl Follen had also arrived at a point of decision when he arrived in Jena, fleeing a disciplinary charge at Giessen. Was he to quiet down, or to fight in the underground against the prevailing situation in Germany? Unlike Heinrich Luden, Karl Follen would choose the latter option.

While Follen was making crucial decisions about his future personal life and political goals, leading to increased political radicalization, the more moderate Burschenschaft movement achieved the creation of a national organization with the founding of the Allgemeine Deutsche Burschenschaft in October of 1818. This league of all the Burschenschaften at all individual Protestant German universities provided both the student movement and the entire nationalist movement with a broader base and a better organization. The national movement was now on its way to becoming much more formidable, controlling not only small groups of local students but, at least in theory, the entire German Protestant student body. The philosopher Fries even spoke of a *Jugend-Bundesstaat,* a confederation of German youth which was to bring about the unification of all Germans into one state.[96]

The constitution of the new general Burschenschaft was based on two main principles:

a. Unity, freedom, and equality for all members; equality of all rights and duties.
b. Christian-German formation of all spiritual and physical strength in order to serve the fatherland.[97]

The structure of the new organization was to be that of a confederation. All individual Burschenschaften would remain intact. But they would pool their strength and resources, and it was agreed that "the common will stands above that of each individual Burschenschaft." This new national student organization would try to monopolize German student life as much as possible: the old Landsmannschaften or other fraternities would not be tolerated if they appeared on the scene. The general Burschenschaft would hold regular meetings and festivals in order to demonstrate unity and strength.[98]

This new organization was both an asset and a weak point for the national movement in Germany. The conservative governments around Central Europe were growing uneasy about a student body which was becoming too well organized and putting too much emphasis on a national community. Nobody was sure how effective this new organization could be. Either it might develop enough strength to influence politics on a national basis and force local governments into gradual concessions, or it would become a target for a decisive and formidable attack by the German Confederation and eventually be shot down. Perhaps by 1818 the way to influence the course of political events in Germany was through secret, behind-the-scenes agitation, and not by taking a public stand.

We have seen the rising wave of nationalism in which Karl Follen was swept up at the time he was initiated into political consciousness. He actively participated, on a local level, in the sort of projects which figures of national prominence such as Jahn and Arndt had outlined. He was active in the Burschenschaft movement and was willing to give his time and attention not only to the political issues of his home territory but also to those of the entire German nation. It is significant that he did not participate in the Wartburg festival, where he could have tried to gain national attention. The fact that Follen had to take his university exams exactly at the time the festival occurred may not be a full explanation for his absence. From early on, Follen was just as determined as the student leaders Riemann and Rödiger, who spoke at the festival. By 1817, however, he may have preferred to be comparatively quiet about his true goals, so as to guard them and not endanger their positive outcome.

Follen's group, the Giessen Blacks, was determined to be distinct from the local Burschenschaft: it was more elite, more radical, and less publicly visible. In his pamphlet "German Universities" (the archaic German title read "Teutsche Samtschulen") Follen had made every attempt to portray the local Burschenschaft as inoffensive, harmless, and essentially conservative in outlook and goals. The ideas and goals of the Blacks, however, were in fact extremely radical, and were actively fed by contacts with agitators outside the university. His leadership position within the Blacks forced Follen to lead an unstable personal life as early as 1818: he had to change universities, fleeing to Jena in order to avoid extensive investigations into his political background at Giessen, and he had to be increasingly secretive and careful.

Follen's thought by 1818 indeed emphasized a national framework of ideas; however, his conception of "national" was changing. He was quickly drifting away from the mainstream of liberal academic sentimental feelings for a united fatherland, and toward intense radicalism and advocacy of violent revolutionary change. His new group in Jena, the "close-knit club" of the Unconditionals, was secret, very radical, and generally suspect to the local authorities, insofar as they could grasp what was going on at this time. Follen was by then no longer an impressionable young student. He had become a determined and single-minded revolutionary interested in planning concrete violent actions which would destroy the German Confederation, radicalize German nationalism, and lead to a social and political revolution.

# 2

# FREEDOM AND VIOLENCE

While leading members of the German Burschenschaft movement were formulating plans for national reform as well as for the renewal of university life, Karl Follen was engaging in activities not at all related to the university and prefiguring the role of revolutionary he was to assume in the near future. Follen's political career began at the local level, in his home territory. In 1818 the effects of the Napoleonic wars were still felt very strongly in Hesse-Darmstadt: Hessian soldiers had died in battles fought for and against the French armies, and the countryside had been plundered and destroyed. Moreover, the wars which Napoleon fought cost Hesse-Darmstadt tremendous sums of money as well. The Grand Duchy still remained in deep financial crisis even after 1815. These war debts had to be paid back, and the government decided to set up an agency which would help raise money from the individual peasant communities.[1] This demand for the rural population to bear the responsibility for the war debt was extremely unpopular throughout the state. The anger and unrest among the peasants which resulted was immediately of interest to Karl Follen. He was at once willing to help peasants who protested government decisions and who urgently sought leadership and legal advice.

## Publicity and Conspiracy

Follen was now in a position to apply what he had learned in his legal studies at Giessen, to analyze and understand a situation, to give directives on how to modify it, and to fight back against intrusion by the state. While Follen lent his skills to the peasant communities, they also gave him something: his first opportunity to deal directly with a large group of common people and their relationship to the state. Follen wished to probe the potential for protest and the inclination to armed revolt against the government, which he would have to learn from personal experience. The new law calling for the raising of a war tax, in addition to an already very heavy taxation load, was issued at the beginnng of July 1818. The peasant communities were exhausted. Attempts to gather a group of deputies and discuss the matter were immediately criticized by the government. Finally, a committee representing a group of communities sent a letter to Karl Follen, asking for his help. The peasants needed a petition drawn up by a legal expert, to be signed by members of the common folk or their representatives, and handed over to the government. This sort of document was to become very important and frequent in Hesse-Darmstadt and other German territories in this period, especially in the petition movement for the establishment of liberal constitutions in the individual territories.[2]

The drawing up of a petition was not a revolutionary undertaking as yet: Follen worked within the system of legal complaints (Gravamina) established by tradition and observed for many centuries. He made a case, following these existing laws, that the new governmental measure was in fact not legitimate. Thus he composed "A humble petition of several hundred communities of the province of Hesse, beseeching the Grand Duke of Hesse-Darmstadt to repeal the establishment of the commission for paying off the debts of the communities, and to continue to them [sic] the administration of their own affairs."[3]

It is doubtful that as many as a hundred communities were actually involved. Yet Follen's petition was presented to the Grand Duke Ludwig I and was also printed, distributed, and commented upon in the newspapers. Public opinion soon became even stronger against the new law. Follen's statement had evidently been powerful enough, for the law was repealed on November 28, 1818. At age twenty-two, Follen had succeeded in helping to defeat the government. From then on, he was well known to the officials in Darmstadt, who feared him and in the next few years would try to make his life as uncomfortable as possible. The good standing that a young lawyer might have enjoyed in this small territory was thus destroyed. Follen had now established himself as an undesirable person not only with the university administration in Giessen but also with the state government in Darmstadt.

Follen's subsequent political work was to be done in secret, since he had reached the limits of government tolerance with his antitaxation petition. He now significantly expanded the scope of his political activism.

During 1818 he had not abandoned his contacts with the Giessen Blacks at his home university; rather, he had intensified his activities with this secret student group and also, at the same time, with a similar group in Darmstadt.[4] The Giessen members had all been students together with Follen; most of them had since finished their studies and had entered positions in the lower levels of the state bureaucracy. The Darmstadt members, however, on the whole belonged to an older group.[5] Even though the Blacks at Giessen and Heidelberg lost members who graduated from the university and took up jobs in their home states, a hard core of followers still managed to stay together and keep in touch even over considerable distances. The Darmstadt group had been founded, for instance, by Karl Christian Sartorius, a leading member of the Giessen Blacks, and by Heinrich Karl Hofmann (1795–1845), a former law student at the University of Heidelberg (where he had met August Follen), and now a lawyer working for the Hessian state government at Darmstadt.[6] The other founding member of this group in the capital was the civil servant and lawyer Georg Rühl (1793–1861), from Rüsselsheim near Frankfurt. In Darmstadt by 1816 there was thus a club of about fourteen radicals, who included six lawyers, among them Hofmann and Rühl, military officers, artisans, and various local bureaucrats.[7]

The topics discussed at regular meetings of the Darmstadt group were mostly related to questions of local and national politics and religion. Of special significance to the radicals, however, were the concepts of German unity and freedom. All members shared the as yet rather unfocused goal of revolutionizing German society in order to put unity and freedom into political practice, and in a letter of March 5, 1816, Hofmann declared how they were to be realized: "If something good is to happen, then it must come up from below, and not down from above." Hofmann elaborated his tactical suggestions a year later, in a letter of April 1817:

What seems most important to me now is the encouragement and enlightenment of the less-educated part of the people; heaven has already prepared the way, it incited the hope for a better future by letting things get very bad, by letting life get wretched. Now let us act, before new prosperity shall wipe out these impressions. . . . Even if we lose a head or a few worn-out bones, they can't do more than kill us! But we must inform the people, so when a revolution comes we can lead it to the victory of freedom and not through horrors to a new form of slavery.[8]

The first thing the Darmstadt Blacks did was to obtain a printing press and inform the people of its rights and duties—not an easy undertaking, considering the harsh censorship laws. They soon began to turn most of their attention to the establishment of liberal democratic constitutions (*Landständische Verfassungen*) in Hesse-Darmstadt and throughout Germany. The establishment of these constitutions, the Blacks argued, had been promised by article 13 of the German Confederation's *Bundesakte* of July 8, 1815, although it had not been specified exactly what the "representative constitutions" were to consist of.[9] In 1816 the nature of such a modern, liberal constitution was already being considered and plans for a series of petitions to the government were being drawn up.[10] The first such popular petition had been introduced in Baden by a Heidelberg university professor named Christian Reinhard Dietrich Martin (1772–1857) and his local associate, the bookdealer Heinrich Winter (1773–1853). Soon thereafter the Darmstadt Blacks became more heavily involved in a movement which pressed for the introduction of a liberal constitution specifically in the Grand Duchy of Hesse, to fulfill the promise of a constitution made at the Congress of Vienna. Since 1816, there had been public pressure for this in a campaign by members of the Blacks, organized by the lawyer Karl Beck (1789–1862), with propaganda and signed petitions. In 1817 Beck and his friend Ludwig von Mühlenfels appeared at the Wartburg festival and attempted to win support there for the constitutional movement in Hesse.[11]

The Darmstadt group also followed Christian Martin's and Heinrich Winter's example and drew up a much grander project: a national petition to be signed by prominent liberals throughout all of Germany and then sent to the German Confederation in Frankfurt. In his work *Geist der Zeit*, Arndt had proposed a national German parliament, which would consist not only of princes but of representatives designated by all social groups in the population. An army officer named Christian Massenbach (1758–1827) had then brought up the idea again in 1817, and this time it was discussed by the Blacks as well. A meeting on this subject in May 1817 was attended by Heinrich Karl Hofmann, the lawyer Karl Beck, and the Giessen Black Karl Christian Sartorius. A national club of liberals was planned; it was to rally support for the idea of a national parliament.[12] An invitation to join this club of liberals was sent to concerned individuals all over Germany: to Martin in Heidelberg, Christian von Massenbach in Stuttgart, Arndt in Bonn, Joseph Görres (the still liberal Catholic publicist) in Koblenz, Jahn in Berlin, and Karl Follen in Giessen. The government authorities who examined this case in the 1820s thus had grounds for belief that a national conspiracy was being founded which had revolutionary goals, socially as well as politically. Perhaps its members would not hesitate to grasp political power in Germany if the time was right and the support of the masses was evident. What Karl Follen suggested in 1817, for instance, was that the national club, a risky and easy-to-detect group, would have to wait until the Blacks and their allies could manage to gain more support among the common people. Follen thus was convinced by 1817 that real political change in Germany would not be possible without support from the lower social strata.[13]

The idea of forming a national club of liberal personalities failed for the moment in 1817, but the signatures for a national petition of leading liberals were indeed collected between October 1817 and May 1818 by radicals traveling from Darmstadt and students from Giessen. This procedure was agreed upon and organized at a meeting at Frankfurt in which the following radicals participated: Hofmann, Beck, Sartorius, Karl Follen, and a young local pharmacist named Löning. Joseph Görres promised to collect signatures in the Koblenz area; a large territory was meanwhile being covered by the lawyer Beck and the student von Mühlenfels, the latter a personal friend of Karl and August Follen. Beck also met with the Jena professsors Fries and Oken, both of whom he had first seen at the Wartburg festival, and won their support for the plan initiated in Hesse.[14]

The petition idea was less successful than had been hoped. Some leading liberals did sign, but others refused, and some even handed over the document they had been asked to sign to the local authorities. Still others later demanded that their signatures be taken off the list, because they no longer were willing to support the cause sponsored by a group as radical as the Blacks had by then already proved to be. Karl Follen and his associates had to realize that not only was the public at large not prepared to lend its support to a radical program of national reform, but neither were a great number of the leading liberal intellectuals. Evidently a semi-legal method of political change at the national level, such as the collecting of signatures for a petition, was destined to fail for two reasons: the governments and the German Confederation were prepared to suppress the petition movement, and the liberal party was unorganized and disinclined to forceful action.

The first incentive for constitutional rights in Hesse actually had come from the group of nobles known as Standesherren, who wished to secure the protection of the countryside against the centralistic government in Darmstadt. In 1816 a group of them had sent a petition to the Grand Duke describing their own difficult situation, but also the desperate economic state of the Hessian peasantry. Taxes to the government could no longer be paid, these nobles argued, because the peasants did not even have enough to live on before taxation occurred, let alone to pay dues to the *Standesherren*. The warning of the nobles was, however, disregarded in Darmstadt.[15] With this fact, the initiative in the constitutional movement passed into more radical hands, using other means. The historian Adolf Müller has described in detail how the Darmstadt Blacks worked in the Hessian constitutional movement. They again drafted petitions to the government, and then let younger associates, preferably students, distribute them throughout the territory. These students otherwise had very little influence within the group. The leaders were all older men who had entered professional life much earlier.[16] Rector Arens, who had previously had enough trouble with Karl Follen, supposed that Giessen students were the leaders of the constitutional movement, but actually the students were mere instruments of their elders. With the help of students, the older radicals collected signatures in their place of residence and then dropped them off at the group headquarters.

In August of 1818, the first illegal regional assemblies, organized by the Blacks, met in several Hessian localities; these were to elect representatives from the local communities to act on behalf of their specific concerns. The first such assembly met in the towns of Grünberg and Zwingenberg in the northern part of the territory. Its purpose was to emphasize the plight of the countryside, call attention to the poverty and hunger crisis which the peasants were going through, and to convince the government to radically change its policies. Karl Wegert has remarked:

> Resistance to the state's meddling in local affairs might not have been so adamant had the communities not been able to provide specific evidence of purported state mismanagement. . . . On top of the financial burden came, in 1816/17, a series of disastrous crop failures, intensifying the already widespread feelings of despair at the community level.[17]

The theory assumed by the Blacks was that, shaken by economic crisis, Hesse-Darmstadt would be compelled to move toward a modern democratic form of government based on free general elections and a legislative process shaped by the representatives of the people in a statewide governing body. The more desperate the economic situation of the population in the countryside grew, the greater the success of the Blacks was in pressing for a liberal form of government which, they claimed, would be more capable of handling such severe problems. The strongest factor aiding the cause of these illegal regional assemblies was that they might gather enough power and popular support not to topple the state government, but at least to prevent the prompt payment of taxes by various regions.[18]

Aided by the Blacks, the peasant communities indeed soon became more militant in their resistance to the government. The peasants complained that the terms of duty in the army units were too long and too tedious, that the local forests were never properly administered, and that they would no longer respect the power of rude and self-seeking officials sent to them from Darmstadt.[19] The Hesse-Darmstadt government now had to face not only a bad economic situation, but also political efforts to exploit popular discontent for radical political purposes. On July 31, 1819, the Grand Duke appointed a new chief minister: the candidate preferred by the Prussians, the former rector of the University of Giessen (and Karl Follen's law teacher) Karl von Grolman. His first goal was to regain firm control over the political life of the territory: "Every subject who resists the military and is armed when arrested shall be shot dead immediately."[20] Von Grolman also began to draft a more liberal constitution for Hesse-Darmstadt. But as soon as his proposals were made public, he was attacked severely from various quarters. The conservatives in the government thought his position was too extreme; for the liberals he did not go far enough. Many nobles rejected the changes Grolman proposed; the Blacks also were completely dissatisfied, and stepped up their demands. Ultimately Grolman and his government could curb the unrest only by issuing a genuinely liberal constitution, which took effect in late December of 1820.

The historian Siegfried Büttner has written that no one can claim that a truly powerful contribution to politics was made in this period by Follen and the other Hessian radicals.[21] It is also possible to argue, however, that the Darmstadt and Giessen Blacks served as catalysts for the real political change which did occur. In any event, Follen was part of a group which forced the Hessian government into concessions by 1820: a liberal constitution was indeed introduced against the resistance of a stubborn, very conservative high bureaucracy. The extremely conservative character of the Restoration period territorial leadership appears in the example of Baron du Bos du Thil (1777–1859), one of the key Hesse administrators of the time, and a firm advocate of political centralization, particularistic patriotism, and omnipotent princely rule.[22]

Du Thil had a complete lack of faith in popular discussion and democratic decision making on public issues. His opinions were not much different in constitutional matters. The edict which Grolman issued on March 18, 1820, calling for elections and the establishment of a legal assembly of representatives in Hesse-Darmstadt, was applauded by du Thil only because it was "written to support princely authority, and thus monarchy." Du Thil also felt that Grolman issued this edict because he felt under pressure to do so, not because he thought it the best solution to allow a discussion of a new constitution with the estates. In fact, he thus "had an excuse, to which he was pressured, and by which he could save his face." Du Thil was firmly convinced that "Von Grolman wanted a mainly monarchical constitution; that is evident not only by the edict of March 18, but also by his whole behavior all along."[23] However, Grolman had indeed set his mind on introducing a new constitution, and du Thil was forced to accept this by 1820, if grudgingly. On December 12, 1820, after seven months of discussion within the assembly of estates, Grand Duke Ludwig I proclaimed the new constitution which provided the political guidelines for Hesse-Darmstadt until 1848, and which guaranteed the responsibility of the state ministers to the representative assembly, and called for the right to autonomous administration by the individual communities.

As will be seen in detail below, by the time the new Hesse-Darmstadt constitution was in fact proclaimed, Karl Follen had first left Giessen for Jena, and then fled from Germany to Switzerland. Still, the Darmstadt Blacks had continued to agitate without him. The character and agenda of the liberal movement, which was faced with attempting to influence men like Baron du Thil, may become clearer if one examplary and relatively systematic work is examined here. In a closely argued pamphlet of 1819, the lawyer and bureaucrat Georg Rühl explained what he and his associates meant by a representative constitution (landständische Verfassung). This interpretation in many ways ran counter to whatever the Congress of Vienna had intended to create. Rühl had been a member of the Giessen Blacks during his student days, and was now a member of the Black group in Darmstadt. For several years he had been in direct personal contact with Karl Follen. Although his piece was written as late as 1819, in a turbulent year full of violence, his tone was moderate and respectful. His pamphlet was addressed to "the friends of the German fatherland," for their enlightenment and guidance.[24]

Rühl began by asking "what the expression 'a free people' actually means," and concluded that the "freedom" of a society was defined by the rights of all of its members. These included inalienable personal rights, such as personal security from violence, and inviolable property rights. If the individual was not "free," Rühl argued, neither could the state and its government be. Individuals, like nations, were entitled to self-determination. Only a people could decide what form of government it preferred, and every citizen had to be engaged in this decision. The well-being of the state depended on the happiness and wealth of its individual citizens. Thus the citizens must be able to determine how they wished to establish this happiness and wealth. The first step in this direction was the abolition of all aristocratic privileges, so that all citizens might have an equal chance to achieve happiness and wealth, and so that those persons who were the most skilled could fully develop their potential in a free environment.

The key to the participation of all citizens was modern representative constitutions, to be introduced as soon as possible. Rühl named several conditions for this system to work; these typify, at the same time, the demands of the constitutional movement. The new constitution was to be a contract between people and government; it had to truly represent all citizens, whatever their social background; all representatives would be eventually united in one great governing body; the people themselves would elect their representatives freely; the representative body must be allowed to decide on its own agenda; all of its discussions would be publicly accessible; and the representative assembly should meet and stay together continuously without interruption.

In a moderate and reasonable, if at the time strictly illegal way, Rühl had so articulated the political goals of the Darmstadt Blacks and much of the Hesse constitutional movement. Karl Follen agreed with him, at least until 1818, that increased freedom would come through legal and constitutional reform. German national unity and regeneration seemed utterly impossible without the previous establishment of modern representative governments in the individual states of the German Confederation. The Hesse government had thus, by 1818, already been forced to make concessions to the popular movement and to at least take notice of men like Georg Rühl and their suggestions. At the same time, however, in 1819 it had begun a crackdown on the illegal assemblies which had met in various towns, and ordered an investigation of Giessen student radicals by April of that year. The struggle between friends and enemies of the Congress of Vienna, the Restoration, and of particularism continued.

Karl Follen meanwhile had decided to keep up his contacts with local radicals by working with the Darmstadt Blacks, but he had also begun to turn in another direction, gathering a core group of extremists around him in Giessen who would follow him where many prominent liberals would not. This radical group, as we have seen, was known as the Unconditionals. A police report of 1827 defined an Unconditional as one "who pursues what he has recognized as good and true unconditionally, without any allegiance except to his own conviction." The report also stated that "Karl Follen is often quoted as saying that there are cases in which common morality must be ignored at the advantage of higher purposes."[25] The Mainz Central Investigation Commission for political crimes (Zentraluntersuchungskommission), in this report of 1827, estimated that in 1818 about forty Hessians belonged to the Giessen Unconditional club. These probably included August and Karl Follen, the brothers Wilhelm and Ludwig Snell, Heinrich Karl Hofmann, von Mühlenfels, Friedrich Ludwig Weidig from Butzbach, and Karl Christian Sartorius. Their activities and contacts were illegal and therefore secret. If legal reform and political efforts failed to bring about rapid change throughout Hesse and the entire German Confederation, then, the Unconditionals held, it was time for violent measures.

## Imagining the Future Germany

Because of the secrecy the Unconditionals maintained it is difficult to find out more about their activities and purposes. However, one major document was seized from them which indicates that their goals and political views were as radical as they were utopian. This document, a "Draft of the Constitution for a Future German Empire" ("Grundzüge für eine künftige teutsche Reichsverfassung"), was written by August Follen early in 1818 and revised by Karl soon thereafter.[26] The historian Hardtwig Brandt has called the document the most extreme of the many constitutional drafts made during the period 1815–1819. Brandt argues that "the external features hide the fact that [Karl] Follen was an unconditional Jacobin" whose thought was dominated by "moral rigor and a glorification of the ends of politics over the means," and that Follen would shy from no political terror in order to achieve his goals. His "Draft of the Constitution" showed this by its "leveling rationality, puritanical illiberality, and a spartan attitude toward education."[27] A tendency toward radical democracy and social equality was certainly evident; and a rigidly authoritarian tone pervaded the entire document.

Most remarkable about Follen's "Draft" was the ambiguity of its derivation: the mixture, current among Follen and his circle, of French democratic and republican ideals (derived largely from Rousseau) with native German traditions and nationalistic ideas concerning the role of the individual within society (derived from Friedrich Ludwig Jahn and others). Here we gain a true sense both of Follen's idealism, oppressed by those who currently governed his society, and of his own personal hardness. None of his writings expressed more directly his actual personality and his political thought as a mature revolutionary, because the "Draft" was never published, and fell into the hands of police investigators entirely without Follen's consent. It was intended as a memorandum for the Unconditionals only.

The "Draft of the Constitution" began by declaring the Germans a *Volk*. Membership in this entity was defined by a common biological and "spiritual" background, common language, history, and religious faith. Politically, the *Volk* required a united empire *(Reich)* to encompass it. Germans were thus to be defined by their ancestry as much as by the political organism to which they belonged. Follen declared his opposition to the inequality of the legal estates when he explicitly argued "that all Germans are completely equal in their rights." In the next set of phrases, on the legitimization of authority, he declared that "the Germans' rights and laws are made by ways of a majority vote of all Germans" and insisted on "the legal omnipotence and exclusive power of the people"; this was strictly Jacobin language. Similarly, there was a demand for tight control over the salary and term in office of public officials, the wording of which could almost be taken from a modern constitution. There was even a provision for public access to all judicial trials, and for a judicious and controlled use of public funds. All these demands were certainly formulated in response to the problems of the time; however, it is uncertain how significantly they catered to the real needs of the German masses, or even how much to the very specialized needs of the radical movement.

The utopian and intolerant quality of Follen's thought became clearly apparent in section 10, which dealt with the role of religion in a future German empire. This required a single Christian state church which would include within it all German denominations. How this undoing of the last three hundred years of German religious history was to be accomplished was not specified in any detail. Follen declared nevertheless that he did not believe in "religious coercion" and approved of free worship at home by any Christian sect. His raw illiberalism, and his reliance on the prejudices of his home territory, appeared, however, in his attitude toward Judaism, which he described as "opposed to the ends of humanity." It therefore "will not be tolerated in the Empire." Here Follen was not following the cosmopolitan French models which appeared in other parts of the text; instead he was turning toward the parochial "Germanomania" of the nationalist movement during the Wars of Liberation, as best expressed by Jahn and Arndt.

Sections 12 through 14 were devoted entirely to schooling and education. All students in Germany were to receive the same education, whatever social stratum of society they might have come from, in a well-rounded program of religious education, history, and natural sciences. Perhaps more unusual was the importance given to physical exercise, and the familiarity all students were to have with manual activities such as farming or making their own clothes. The schooling a German child was to receive was oriented very strongly toward national integration and unity. The sections on military matters were again an affirmation of German nationalism and the building of a united German state. The soldier of the future, following classical models, but especially the mythologized student ideals of the Wars of Liberation, was supposed to be a free citizen defending his home country, not a mercenary paid by a specific prince. Through a prolonged army service in the reserves that would last well into middle age, every German male would be made to feel part of the *Volk*. The Germans would be part of a military culture; bearing arms would be an everyday experience for everyone. The individual was to be well prepared by physical exercise during his school years, and was then to become part of a military system which would last practically his whole life. Follen wanted to guarantee the constant readiness of the German *Volk* to defend itself against both potential outside aggressors and opponents of German unity. Moreover, he wanted to achieve a national integration of the German people, and also wished to enable this people to define itself by being militarily strong.

The rest of Follen's "Draft" again constituted a mixture of radical ideas for innovation, which seemed quite utopian for their time, and rather conservative and traditional measures. Freedom of the press and freedom of speech were concrete demands shared by all mainstream liberals of the day. Censorship, also explicitly mentioned, had to be abolished if Follen and the nationalist movement were to have any chance to influence the future. The idea of leaving society divided into what Follen referred to as estates, however, persisted within the Constitution. But perhaps this was done in order to veil how radical Follen's other demands really were. In fact, the estates were assigned a much-reduced significance because any German might join and belong to any one of them. Estates had thus become a sociological category, not a system of rights. They merely denoted the professional occupation of any given citizen.

Follen constructed a modern system of administrative levels, which reached from the common man *(Der Mann)*, to the local community *(Gemeine) (sic)*, to the region *(Gau)*, the state *(Land)*, and finally the empire *(Reich)*. There were to be two state assemblies (the Landtag and the Landtagsausschuss), and two imperial assemblies (the Reichstag and the Reichsausschuss). The members of all administrative and legislative bodies would be elected directly from the populace and would enjoy no special rights. The princes would lose all their personal, formerly God-given power, and would become mere executing agents of the will of the people in their territories. The king was, in Follen's scheme, reduced to service as a mere administrator to the empire; he too was to be an elected official.

Because it was Jacobin and national at the same time, Follen's "Draft" denied many of the central principles of Restoration statesmen. The whole document was strongly oriented both toward Jacobin ideas of equality and toward a powerful nation state which defined itself by training its members and excluding outsiders.[28] National integration required an equality of rights for all legal members of the *Volk,* and also the elimination of as many potential divisions and conflicts in society as possible. The "Draft" did not attempt to forecast, however, just how long it would take to produce a society in Germany which was as homogeneous and as equal in its educational abilities as Follen suggests. It was very unlikely that such a plan could have been made comprehensible and profitable to the peasants of Hesse in 1818. It was a product of doctrine and intellectual speculation rather than a prospectus based on actual experience with the needs of the people, a utopian document stating aspirations rather than a proposal of an organized program.

Other characteristics of the "Draft" were its inflexible and dogmatic tone, and the illiberal strands which ran through it. The principles expressed in each case seemed very final, with little room for discussion and change. Follen was not a compromiser, and not willing to accept certain restrictions of his time. German liberalism during the period from 1813 to 1818 has been described by a modern constitutional historian as a development from "radical individualism" to "radical nationalism" to, finally, a sort of "radical statism" ("radikaler Etatismus"). The main characteristic of the last phenomenon was, instead of a stress mainly on the freedom of the individual, a marked intolerance against those who might hold contrary opinions.[29] Citizens would receive their identities and rights directly and exclusively from the state, instead of being able to establish these themselves. Follen's "Draft" demonstrated the split within German liberalism by 1818 between moderates (see Riemann's "Principles" of the Wartburg festival, discussed in Chapter 1) and its most radical and rigid leftist element. Follen's constitutional thought thus was not so integrating and not so unifying as one might think. Rather, it was a symptom of the deep rift developing within the German liberal movement. Follen was power-centered rather than generous in his approach; he did not include very many guarantees of individual freedom, but rather pressed all Germans into his own very specific framework. The individual citizen would only be significant as a small part of the collective.

As we have seen, Karl Follen intended to admit only Christian Germans, and not Jews, to his utopian "German Empire." This plan, and the personal sentiments it betrays, is surprising in that his father's attitude toward Jews was evidently known to be decidedly favorable.[30] Still, hatred of Jews was present in the culture of even educated Germans of the time, and the increasingly aggressive character of certain radical parts of the German liberal movement appears in their anti-Semitism (Jahn is a prime example here) and in their attempts made specifically in Hesse in 1819 to use the anti-Jewish tendencies of the peasant population in order to bring about social revolt in a time of severe economic crisis.

The original Jena Burschenschaft did not mention Jews in its constitution of 1815; for its members, the "Jewish question" did not exist. There were Jewish students at the University of Jena from 1790 onward, and some of them had taken part in the Wars of Liberation. While there is no definite record of a Jewish student having wished to join or having been a member of the Jena Burschenschaft, Jews were not explicitly denied the right to membership.[31] From the beginning, however, there was a tendency in the more radical Burschenschaft movement in Giessen to avoid contact with Jews. The Giessen "Christian-German Burschenschaft," founded with Karl Follen's help in 1816, stipulated that "only Germans and Christians" could join their fraternity. The Jews at universities were seen as outsiders who could not possibly share in the ideals followed by Christian students.[32] The discovery of the German *Volk,* in its most radical and overdrawn form, thus demanded the separation of "Germans" from "foreign" peoples such as the French, and also from the Jews. Nationalism carried with it a tragic determination of whom to include in and whom to exclude from the new nation.

Many of the arguments used by the early student movement were provided by Professor Fries, who polemicized against the Jews in a 1816 pamphlet entitled "Über die Gefährdung des Wohlstandes und Charakters der Deutschen durch die Juden." Fries believed in a much harsher form of dealing with the Jews, who for him were "despoilers and exploiters of the German people" contributing to the "urbanization and commercialization of the German."[33] The attempt of Saul Ascher, in pamphlets such as "Die Germanomanie" (1816), to counter Fries's opinions on the Jews and warn against an overly raw tone of nationalism, did not exert much influence.[34] In fact, as already noted, Ascher's pamphlet was burned in the fire at the conclusion of the Wartburg festival along with other hated works, while the following comment, attributed to the influence of Fries, was read aloud: "Woe to the Jews who hold on to their Jewishness and make fun of our *Volkstum* and Germanness."[35] In his play *Almansor*, written in 1820, the poet Heinrich Heine observed on this scene: "This was only a prelude; where one burns books, one will eventually burn people."[36]

By 1819 anti-Jewish incidents were occurring more and more frequently in the universities. At Würzburg, for instance, during the inauguration ceremony of a new professor, one of the older faculty members who had written on behalf of the Jews was jeered by the student crowd. Ultimately this older professor was physically attacked by members of the Burschenschaft and had to flee the scene. By 1820 the constitution of the General German Burschenschaft, founded in 1818, was changed to provide that Jews, "who have no fatherland and thus cannot be interested in ours," could no longer be accepted as members.[37] A long tradition of virulent anti-Semitism in the Burschenschaft, which ran deep into the twentieth century, was thus launched. At the same time, counterparts to the anti-Jewish feelings introduced into the Burschenschaft movement by Follen's Giessen Blacks were also to be found among other parts of the population. In 1819 there were widespread riots against Jews throughout southern Germany, beginning in Würzburg. There, a mixed crowd of students and local townspeople attacked Jewish stores and homes during the summer months. The riots soon spread to other areas, including the cities of Frankfurt am Main and Darmstadt. Everywhere the riots carried out by peasants and townspeople were related to the general economic crisis of the time: Jews were accused of overcharging for certain products they sold, especially grain. In Darmstadt, soldiers had to patrol the streets for many days in order to restore peace.[38]

Karl Follen and the Black radicals at Giessen and Darmstadt meanwhile were pleased with the political unrest of the population. It showed that it was evidently possible to incite the peasants and townspeople to violent revolt against an oppressor, whether this was to be a specific group of the population or the German princes themselves. A government report of August 1819 unequivocally expressed the opinion that, most likely, the Blacks were actively involved in the disturbances which were going on. This must, they argued, be another instance of the excellent ability of the Blacks to carry their ideas into the masses.[39] By 1818 Karl Follen had thus split off from the moderate mainstream of the German liberal movement, and had turned his direction toward more radical paths to political change. Not many of his student friends in Giessen, or those participating in the Wartburg festival, were willing to follow him on this new course. There were, however, a few radicals who shared his ideas, as formulated in the meetings of the Giessen and Darmstadt Blacks, and also voiced them independently. Two radicals willing, like Follen, to go underground and to live in the realm of secrecy and illegality were Friedrich Ludwig Weidig and Wilhelm Schulz.

Friedrich Ludwig Weidig (1791–1837) was a Hessian revolutionary who never became a figure of national significance or prominence in Germany; but he was able to exert a powerful influence primarily on a local level. He is best known for having composed the famous and radical *Hessischer Landbote* journal together with the poet Georg Büchner in 1834, and for his suicide in prison in 1837, which shocked the liberal sensibilities in Germany deeply, and which was much discussed in pamphlets by various prominent intellectuals.[40] Weidig studied theology at Giessen, and in 1813 he was hired as a schoolteacher in the town of Butzbach (thirty miles north of Frankfurt). When the Wars of Liberation began in the fall of that year, Weidig joined the same Hessian free corps in which Karl Follen and his older brother had enlisted. After the war he again followed the same path as did Follen, became highly politicized, and organized a German reading society in Butzbach by November 1814. This new society managed to gather over forty members in a short time, and the nationalistic lectures and meetings which Weidig organized were popular.

Weidig also succeeded in introducing the gymnastics movement into Hesse. After meeting Jahn on a trip to Frankfurt in 1813, he opened the first gymnastics training ground in Hesse in 1814, and began to inculcate in his athletes what he had learned about history, politics, and nationalism from reading the works of Jahn and Arndt. Weidig's example of using athletic exercises as a means of political influence was soon followed by members of the Giessen Blacks, whose first attempts at gymnastics in 1816 were supervised by Charles Follen and his fellow Giessen Black Karl Christian Sartorius. On Sartorius's trip home to Darmstadt in the summer of 1817, he came into contact with the Darmstadt Blacks, and also engaged in athletic exercises on a new gymnastics ground in Darmstadt. Next to Heinrich Karl Hofmann, another participant in the exercises inspired by Weidig was the young Darmstadt military officer Friedrich Wilhelm Schulz.[41]

Weiding had first met the Giessen liberal students Sartorius, Wilhelm and Ludwig Snell, and Karl Theodor Welcker during his studies at Giessen and had stayed in close contact with the Giessen student groups that formed after 1814. Here he met Karl Follen, and played a key role in establishing contacts between young enrolled Giessen students, and older, more radical alumni who had become strong advocates of liberal and national ideas.[42] His recent biographer, the historian Harald Braun, doubts whether Weidig ever fully subscribed to the teachings of the Giessen Unconditionals.[43] It seems more than likely, however, that Weidig was radical enough to participate fully in their activities, and thought of the university students he was dealing with as instruments for formulating a truly revolutionary program, much as Karl Follen did. He was a central figure in the opposition movement forming in Hesse-Darmstadt from 1814 to 1818.

Most remarkable is Weidig's ability to dodge the provisions of the Carlsbad Decrees of 1819, which will be discussed shortly). Unlike Follen, he was able to hide his political sympathies from the authorities and able to exert a continual influence on those around him.[44] His friend August Becker introduced him to the young Giessen medical student Georg Büchner at the beginning of 1834. During his literary and political cooperation with Büchner, Weidig's whole political work and existence were at stake. If the investigation committee had managed to unravel the net of past intrigues, all of the future work of the opposition party would have been threatened, Weidig himself exposed, and his whole movement stripped of its leader.[45]

The *Hessischer Landbote*, written and distributed in Hesse by Weidig and Büchner in 1834, proclaimed the motto "peace to the cottages, war to the palaces," and openly attacked noble privileges and the rule of the German princes. It even incited the Hesse peasantry to armed revolt, and is considered to be the most significant revolutionary pamphlet in Germany before the Communist Manifesto of 1848.[46] By the year 1834, Weidig and Büchner had thus arrived at the stage which Karl Follen had already reached in

1818: they advocated violence as the only means which would effectively bring swift political change in Germany. Both believed that a revolution would only be possible if the simple peasants were reached by propaganda which was short, easy to read, and uncompromising in its radicalism. Karl Follen can be seen as a direct precursor of Georg Büchner: both men were Hessians, both had studied at Giessen (one decade apart), and had come to hold political opinions that had matured in the same environment.

Weidig's radical career ended soon thereafter—he had become a dangerous threat to the government, and the authorities were therefore prepared to deal with him in the harshest of ways. By 1833 he was being observed by the police in an ever more careful way, and was finally arrested that same year after a close associate betrayed him and leaked information to the government. Weidig was imprisoned, and questioned continuously for months on his radical activities and contacts. On the morning of February 23, 1837, Weidig was found dead in his prison cell. He had cut his veins with pieces of broken glass, and marked, in his own blood, on the wall: "Since the enemy will not grant me a proper defense, I choose suicide."[47] Several pamphlets were subsequently written vindicating Weidig, and telling of the brutality and illegality of the police investigations.[48] The Weidig case suggests how radical revolutionaries could be treated in Germany if their plans should be discovered. Karl Follen was able to escape this fate early on only through emigration to Switzerland.

Friedrich Wilhelm Schulz (1797–1860)[49] is another leading figure associated closely with Karl Follen, willing to sacrifice a "normal" bourgeois life for radical goals extremely difficult to realize under the conditions of the time. Wilhelm Schulz was born in 1797 in Darmstadt, the son of a civil servant and archivist. In 1811 he began his army career in Hesse-Darmstadt, and was made a lieutenant in 1813. After he took part in the campaign against Napoleon in 1814, that same year he received permission to take leave from the army for several months in order to study law at Giessen University. In Giessen he soon met Karl Follen and joined the Blacks.[50] Schulz became very involved with student radicalism at Giessen, and also established contacts with the revolutionaries of Darmstadt. In 1819, after leaving the university, he had arrived at a high degree of radicalization. That year he wrote, printed, and distributed a pamphlet which would cause a great stir in the peasant population and greatly disturbed the government, entitled "Frag- und Antwortbüchlein über allerlei, was im deutschen Vaterlande besonders Not tut. Für den deutschen Bürgers- und Bauersmann."[51] This work has been called "one of the most important revolutionary pamphlets in the German language."[52] It was prepared by Schulz under the influence of the revolutionaries with whom he was then associated: Karl Follen, Karl Christian Sartorius, and Heinrich Karl Hofmann at Darmstadt. Like Weidig, Follen, and the others, Schulz was convinced of the importance of winning influence over the common people. The local peasants and townsmen had to be informed about their own situation and the range of their possibilities before one could count on their support in the case of a revolutionary situation.

Perhaps Schulz' pamphlet is somewhat more moderate than Karl Follen's "Draft of the Constitution," which the historian Karl-Ludwig Ay has analyzed and shown to contain a mixture of both "intelligent insight into the necessities of a democratic society" and "misguided fanaticism." Yet Follen's work is a secret memorandum, and thus was necessarily different in substance and presentation from the widely distributed "Frag- und Antwortbüchlein." Schulz' wording was such that he never directly urged the common people to overthrow their government; rather, his ostensible purpose was merely to educate the peasants and townsmen, to make them realize their situation and then draw their own conclusions from it. However, Ay has shown an astounding number of parallels to Follen's constitution.

Unlike Follen's constitution, the "Frag- und Antwortbüchlein" had a definite influence on the life of the Hesse region. Schulz' strong criticism of taxation as "public theft" spoke directly to the hostility of the peasantry against the government. In the summer of 1819, the peasantry in the Odenwald area, south of Darmstadt, did begin to show signs of unrest and resistance to state legislation and local state officials. In his pamphlet, Schulz emphasized above all that the "German townsman and peasant" had to start thinking for himself: "He shouldn't put his hands in his lap and wait until God lets the pigeons fly ready-cooked directly into his mouth." The most important starting point was to rely on one's "own reason" rather than on the omnipotent government: reason will tell the common man himself what is "right" and "wrong." Freedom, again, was an important word, and was defined in two ways: one, that "nobody else can take away one's life or property through murder or robbery of unnecessary taxation," and two, that the common man "must have a clear conscience." Thus freedom consisted of individual civil rights and of noble conduct within society. Freedom could not conflict with public morality and conscience; if it was not realizable within the current political system, Schulz advocated a right of resistance for the common man against his superiors.

The Hesse-Darmstadt government could not, or at least it did not, imprison Schulz when he first went on trial as a suspected revolutionary in 1820. He was temporarily cleared of all charges, and was able to finish his doctorate in law at the University of Giessen and settle down as a lawyer in Darmstadt soon thereafter. When he made a renewed attempt to influence public opinion with two revolutionary pamphlets in the 1830s, he was officially charged and sentenced to three years' imprisonment in the fortress of Babenhausen. He was luckier than Friedrich Ludwig Weidig, however, and was able to escape from the fortress with the help of his wife on New Year's Day 1834, and to flee to France.[53] The careers of Friedrich Ludwig Weidig and Wilhelm Schulz differ from that of Karl Follen only in the years after 1819. Follen might have shared either fate: death in prison or a lucky escape. But he could not succeed in either changing the German political system or even living in safety in Germany as a radical critic. By 1819 Follen had decided, perhaps more firmly than Weidig and Schulz, what Georg Büchner was to express in a letter of April 1833: "My opinion is this: if anything at all is going to help us in our time, it is violence. We know exactly what to expect from our princes. Everything they have ever granted us was conquered by force."[54]

## Follen at Jena: The Turn to Violence

By 1818 Follen, influenced by the thought of Weidig and Schulz, was independently composing propaganda which was especially violent and harsh in tone. The most well-known and notorious example was his long poem entitled "The Great Song," which was sung by members of the Blacks and Unconditionals and even printed and distributed in a shortened version in the countryside, during the Hesse peasant unrest of 1819. The title of this shorter and more popular version, sung by peasants rather than intellectuals, was "German Youth Addressing the German Masses."[55]

Follen's lyrics were not phrased as discreetly as the prose of Wilhelm Schulz would be in 1819. Follen was less interested in the education and rationality of the common folk than in stirring them up, making them hate rather than reflect. The three main themes of this poem were raw appeals to violence and popular self-liberation from tyranny; a mystical celebration of secret revolutionary groups (such as the Blacks themselves); and prominent religious imagery replete with emotionality and *Schwärmerei*. "The Great Song" was an emotional rather than an enlightening poem, a piece of powerful propaganda rather than information to be evaluated in the light of common sense. It was blunt and unveiled in its call for an armed uprising of the common folk against those who were their oppressors, the German princes and their executing agents:

> Take out the knife of freedom!
> Hurray! Pierce the dagger through the throat![56]

Freedom, the old key concept, could now no longer be taken for granted or peaceably awaited; rather, it would have to be fought for in a violent and bloody revolution. The new key words that pervaded Follen's lyrics were "revenge," "blood," and the "anger" of the people.

At the beginning of this long poem, Follen called upon both the princes and the common people to "wake up" so they "would not be found sleeping in the hour of the world conflagration." A violent revolutionary upheaval that might cover greater parts of Europe or even the entire globe was, according to "The Great Song," to be expected very soon. What would happen next, Follen predicted, was:

> Then lightning must flash,
> Storms full of rage must crash,
> To make men out of shadows,
> To make day out of night!

The poem conveyed the impression that these cataclysmic occurrences would completely destroy the existing social and political world order, created by reactionary princes, and instead fully empower the masses. The apocalyptic revolutionary event, furthermore, would be initiated under the leadership of a chosen few, but when fully set into motion would certainly involve the active participation of common people everywhere as well:

> Crowd of men, great mass of humanity,
> Touched in vain so far by the spiritual spring,
> Rip, break finally, old ice!
> Attack in strong proud waves
> The lackey and tyrant who insult you,
> Be a people, a free state, become hot!

The people, according to Follen, had to arm themselves and destroy the established system in order to actively change their own fates for the better:

Brothers, it can't go on like this,
Let us stand together,
Don't endure any longer!
Freedom, your tree is rotting,
Everyone is desperately hungry
And will soon die of starvation;
People, arm yourselves!

The final section of the poem was devoted entirely to religious motifs: the political and social salvation of the Hessian subjects and eventually of all humanity was here compared with the Christian incarnation:

Man, you have fled from yourself,
You shall become a Christ,
Just like you, a child of the earth
Was the Son of Man.

These lyrics signified more than what one historian has called a mixture of "fervent piety" and "blood-curdling brutality."[57] They provided a framework for Follen's revolutionary demands, made accessible to the common man in the Hessian village through the Christian concept of Incarnation and brought into political discourse. The biblical motif also added special legitimacy and urgency to the political demands of Follen and his fellow radicals. At the Wartburg festival, religion had also played a role as a legitimizing force; however, it was used only to back up German nationalism with the explicitly nationalistic tendencies of Luther. The religious components of the "Great Song" did more: they justified the role of violence in Follen's political agenda, and explained how a pious person could very well use violence to achieve his goals. Follen wished to clarify the role of martyrdom and of divine wrath in his view of human history. Salvation had to have a price, and had to be fought for in order to punish or even eliminate those who oppressed others. Violence thus became a justified and necessary component of the radical crusade.

By early October of 1818, when "The Great Song" had been introduced to university students as well as to peasants in the Hesse countryside, the situation in Giessen had become too uncomfortable for Karl Follen. He had long been notorious for his student activities at the University of Giessen, and the administration, under the leadership of Rector Arens, was trying to persecute the troublemaker as best it could. Although there was no way

Arens could be sure about what Follen was planning, he always remained suspicious and did not discard the idea that a secret club of radical students was in existence in Giessen.[58] After Follen had received his doctorate at Giessen in 1817, he had stayed on as a *Privatdozent*, and had begun to teach and lecture as a member of the law faculty. But since his work defending the interests of the Hessian communities in the taxation dispute, Follen was now also known to the government in Darmstadt, which was beginning to investigate his role with the help of the Giessen disciplinary board. Although the investigation was dropped after his departure, with the provision that he was never again to be allowed to teach at Giessen, Follen thought it better to move away at least for a while, and to seek employment elsewhere.[59] Upon his arrival in the Thuringian town of Jena in October of 1818, Follen wrote to the university senate, asking for permission to teach in the law faculty. He stated that he had been a faculty member at Giessen, and that his parents would see to it that all the necessary steps would be taken for his transfer to Jena. "Only the delay in the delivery of his suitcases" made it impossible for him to present the neccessary documents and credentials immediately. Follen had "asked Professor Fries to guarantee his speedy recognition" as a lecturer in law, while he was waiting for his papers to be sent.[60]

There was no place which could have been more adequate for Follen than Jena. The town was located in a comparatively liberal state, ruled by an enlightened prince, Carl August of Saxony-Weimar, who acted as the sponsor of Goethe and many other great literary personalities of the time, and who also favored the student movement: in providing the Wartburg for the 1817 student festival, he had greatly annoyed his fellow princes of the Restoration. Jena, which was close to Weimar, had been able to maintain an intellectual life of international importance during the late eighteenth century, and in the early nineteenth developed into the most radical center of the student nationalist movement, even surpassing Giessen. In the late eighteenth century, the University of Jena had attracted a truly incomparable faculty, especially in philosophy, history, and arts and letters. Johann Gottlieb Fichte arrived in 1794 to teach philosophy, staying for five years, Friedrich Wilhelm Joseph Schelling joined the factulty in 1798, and Georg Wilhelm Friedrich Hegel in 1801. In 1789 Friedrich Schiller began his professorship in history by lecturing on "What does universal history mean, and why should one study it?" Other important personages living in Jena around the turn of the century were August Wilhelm Schlegel and Friedrich Schlegel, and both Humboldt brothers. Anselm Feuerbach received his professorship in philosophy at Jena in 1799. Goethe, who lived a few miles away in Weimar, received as one of his tasks as a state official the order of organizing and administering the university library. In the late eighteenth century, he had already explicitly complained about the unruly students at the local university and their "false idea of freedom," academic and otherwise.[61] Despite Goethe's criticism, Jena retained its attraction to radicals. In 1817 Friedrich Ludwig Jahn received an honorary doctorate, and so did Friedrich List in 1840. Karl Marx completed the requirements for his doctorate in philosophy at Jena in 1841.[62]

The town of Jena was, however, not only blessed in the early beginning of the nineteenth century. It suffered wartime experiences similar to those of Giessen. By 1805 the French and Prussian military presence greatly increased. On October 13, 1806, a day before the battle of Jena, which ended in total defeat for the Prussian forces and a decisive victory for the French, French soldiers finally entered the town and plundered it. Even the philosopher Hegel was forced to flee from his house, carrying the manuscript of his new work, the *Phenomenology of the Spirit*, with him in his coat pocket.[63] Heinrich Luden, who had recently assumed his professorship in history at Jena, in his memoirs recalls the great battle and its aftermath.[64]

Considering the direct experiences with Napoleonic troops and the liberal attitude of the territorial government, it is not hard to see why Jena could become one of the hotbeds of the new student radicalism. The first influential Burschenschaft had been founded there in 1815, and Jena students and professors had organized the Wartburg festival in 1817. In addition, there existed by 1818 a smaller, more radical club of students gathered around the philosopher Jakob Fries, who had been in Jena since 1816, after teaching at Heidelberg for ten years. Fries participated in the Wartburg festival and provided leadership for the most active and committed students, but his opinions by 1818 were by no means as extreme as those of Karl Follen. In a short document aimed at his students, his so-called "Confession of Faith" of October 1818, for instance, he rejected the idea that his students should join a secret society of radicals; instead, they were to found an open "religious group with republican tendencies" which could attempt to influence public opinion.[65]

When Follen arrived in Jena in October of 1818, however, the influence of local role models on the most radical students soon faded. Follen at once came into sharp conflict with the law student Robert Wesselhöft (1797–1853), who had played a major role in the Wartburg festival and the founding of the General German Burschenschaft in that same year. Weselhöft was a moderate who wished for as little friction with the government as possible, but who also wanted to unite the Burschenschaft movement of all German universities even though concessions toward a hard radical line might have to be made. Follen soon denounced Wesselhöft's mediating attitude as a cowardly denial of radical student convictions and thus broke almost at once with the ideas and tactics advocated by the mainstream of the Jena academic liberal movement.[66]

The philosopher Fries did not fare better than Wesselhöft. He was soon replaced in the leadership position by the young and charismatic Follen, who sought to retain only those members in the student club who would unambiguously accept his doctrines of political terrorism.[67] Follen had thus taken the principle of "conviction" from Fries, but had reinterpreted it according to his own purposes while shoving its actual author aside. It was clear that by the fall of 1818, Follen was no longer interested in the broader, more moderate Burschenschaft scene, and no longer attempted to win the support of a large number of students for his ideas. He now preferred to gather a small number of fanatical personalities around him, such as his Jena roommate Johann Ferdinand Wit von Dörring (1800–1863), whom he had first met en route from Giessen, and the theology student Carl Sand (1795–1820). Most of Follen's former friends now rejected the new path he was following.[68]

Follen was officially lecturing on law (specifically on the Pandects, the fifty books of Roman civil law compiled under the emperor Justinian in the sixth century) at the University of Jena, but at the same time he was secretly involved in activities with his small group of followers, including the discussion of how to change the political situation in Germany in a concrete and especially in a speedy way. In this context, Follen was work-ing on his new doctrine which his recently acquired friend Ferdinand Wit referred to as "la guerre des individus."[69] It called for strong-minded and radical individuals to sacrifice their own lives for the cause of freedom and revolution by assassinating particular personalities of high significance within the German Confederation, such as politicians, diplomats, and intellectual leaders.

Ferdinand Johannes Wit von Dörring had been born in Hamburg in 1800. Three years after his birth, his mother had been divorced and had married the Danish officer von Dörring. As a child Ferdinand lived an unstable and changeable life, attending various schools. In 1817 he enrolled at the Uni-versity of Kiel in order to study law, but soon thereafter transferred to Jena, where he befriended Karl Follen. His involvement in student radicalism was strengthened by a trip to Paris in October of 1818, during which he attempted to associate with French revolutionaries.[70] Wit publicly denounced Follen as a criminal only a few years after they had first become close political associates at Jena and violently dissented from his opinions, but his description of Follen's intentions at that time still seems quite accurate:

> The main goal of Follen was to root out all prejudices (as he called them), especially the quality of shying away from murder. Thus he always referred to murder as "la guerre des individus," the war of individuals against other individuals, and this idea was legitimized by his whole system of thought.[71]

Follen had now turned not only to a glorification of political murder but also to a fanatical attachment to martyrdom. As in the mythologized Wars of Liberation, when patriots gave their lives for the resurgence of the German nation, the post-1815 radical was to die willingly in preparation of the future revolutionary transformation of Germany. Follen had especially admired the poet Theodor Körner from early on, and had praised him in the poem "Elegy on Körner" ("Körners Totenfeier"). He was most impressed by the fact that Körner did not remain only a poet and artist; rather, he knew how to achieve "the great connection between poetry and action" when he died in the wars.[72] Follen was now intent on instilling a similar radical state of mind in his followers.

The positive image of violence and bloodshed that Follen had thus accepted had been introduced into German political culture long ago and was already familiar during the early nineteenth century in the case of Ernst Moritz Arndt, who had called for strong reprisals by the Germans against their French aggressors. There was one playwright, however, whose militant views particularly influenced Karl Follen: this was the Prussian playwright Heinrich von Kleist (1777–1811). In 1808 Kleist finished his radical and highly emotional drama *Die Hermannsschlacht*, a rendering of the Germanic tribes' legendary struggle against Roman aggression.[73] The leadership figure of Hermann (or Arminius) stood at the center of the play. His struggle to overcome the divisions and the self-interest among the Germanic tribes and the battles he led against the Romans constituted much of the plot in the drama. However, the essential significance of the historical episodes presented lay in their relevance for the early nineteenth century. In fact, historical facts were changed by Kleist in order to fit the current political situation; the mythological aspect of the Arminius story was the most important to the playwright. Since the drama was too politically provocative, it was not allowed a premiere in Vienna in 1809, and could not be legally printed until 1821.

The list of violent acts in the *Hermannsschlacht* was long: the play is "not adequately described by the term 'furor teutonicus,'" but rather goes beyond such a category. Kleist believed that there was only one cause worth fighting for, the fatherland, and all means were allowed in order to liberate and strengthen it. All voices dissenting from this opinion within the German people were to be ignored. Kleist the nationalist, the artist struggling to be heard above all the dissenting voices of his time, was thus introducing a jingoistic and intolerant strain into his work.[74] The solution to contemporary problems, in his personal opinion, lay not in clever crisis management or in diplomacy, but in violence and martyrdom for the almighty fatherland.[75]

Following the rhetoric of Kleist, a small group of students in Jena became particularly fascinated by the strong, militant personality of Karl Follen, and turned into ardent disciples willing to put their master's plans into practice. Thus Follen was able to gather at least some true believers around him. One was the originally Bavarian (but Protestant) student Carl Ludwig Sand, born in 1795, who had studied in Tübingen and Erlangen before arriving in Jena in the fall of 1817. Sand had taken part in the Wars of Liberation as part of a South German unit, but like Follen had experienced no combat. He attended the Wartburg festival but did not play any significant role; after the festival he proceeded to Jena, and eventually became close to Follen, as a devoted member of the Unconditional club.

By the early months of 1819, the overly serious and isolated student was systematically preparing for a deed which he thought would be a first great step forward on the way to a liberated Germany. Sand took part in regular meetings with Follen, and recorded his entire spiritual development of the time in a detailed, tragically honest diary.[76] On March 9, 1819, he set out for Mannheim, and after making stops in Erfurt, Frankfurt, and Darmstadt, arrived there on the morning of the 23rd. At 11 o'clock he went to the house of the playwright and journalist August von Kotzebue (1761–1819), whom he thought of as a cynical mocker of student patriots, and expressed the wish to see him. Kotzebue, however, was busy and asked Sand to come back in the afternoon. At five P.M. Sand returned, was admitted to Kotzebue's study, and after a few words revealed a dagger and stabbed the writer to death immediately, exclaiming "Here, you traitor of the fatherland!"

Unable to flee the scene as he had originally planned, Sand then attempted to commit suicide by stabbing himself several times. He failed to end his life and was ultimately seized by Kotzebue's servants.

This bloody scene, described in many contemporary and later accounts, completed the turn to outright violence which the tiny minority of absolute radicals around Follen had been preparing for several months.[77] The moderate Burschenschaft adherents everywhere were deeply shocked, as were the territorial governments all over Germany. The radical fringe of the revolutionary movement found in Carl Sand its first martyr, but the profit it would reap from this acomplishment would be very meager indeed. August von Kotzebue had long been an eyesore to the radicals, because he ridiculed their behavior and goals in his writings, refused to join the nationalist movement, received subsidies from the Russian government which was seen as the mainstay of reaction in Europe. But it proved ineffectual to assassinate an individual who was not even a political decision maker when one sought to change the entire structure of society. In fact, such actions instead supported the viewpoint of those conservatives who wanted a tighter, more rigorous control over the Burschenschaft movement.

Doubts such as these, however, seem never to have occurred to Sand. For several months before he committed the murder, he was convinced that his deed would help to quicken the pace of political change. Furthermore, Sand felt that in August von Kotzebue he had found a victim who combined in one person all the evils which he saw, or at least imagined, in contemporary German society. The very detailed personal diaries kept by Sand until the beginning of 1819 are quite clear about this.[78] The historian Günther Heydemann believes that Sand saw in Kotzebue a sort of "antipode" to his own being, an incarnation of all that he opposed and wished to fight against.[79] What the playwright stood for in the eyes of Sand may be seen in a letter which the assassin carried on his way to Mannheim. The document, written by Sand, bears the heading "Death to August von Kotzebue! Only in virtue is there unity!"[80] In this letter the outsider, the isolated, intellectually limited student did something characteristic of many German intellectuals of recent history. He showed his disgust at the cultural and political situation which currently characterized Germany. Public opinion was controlled and perverted, wrote Sand, by "half-educated idiots and crippled smart-alecks." The German elite saw its main values in loyalty to particularistic courts and to moneyed interests, instead of turning to genuine virtue. It was hindered by "slavish laziness" and had thus become unable to fulfill its role in society with any sort of "enthusiasm." Sand wrote that he "hated nothing more than the cowardice and laziness of the day." He called upon the German people to "lift itself up," and admonished it to realize the duties and role which God had originally intended for it. All Germans were finally to have a "free conscience" and "free will," and should realize themselves.

Into his derivative text, Sand interjected several distinctive and significant phrases, some of them in language identical to Karl Follen's "Great Song." Calling upon the German people to rise up from humiliation and death and assume a mighty and virtuous position, he uses Follen's image, saying "You shall become a Christ." It seems likely then that many of the other expressions used by Sand, and the combination of political criticism with religious, mythical elements, were first employed by Karl Follen. Sand was not a young man who set his own agenda, who could himself identify enemies and friends in more than a simplified, stereotypical way. Rather, he had two main sources for his ideas, and for his expression of these ideas in writing: his participation in the Wartburg festival, and his friend and adviser Karl Follen. Sand was a follower, not an independent agent, and the police authorities at Jena promptly concluded that he could not have acted alone. Very soon, therefore, Karl Follen knew that he was again bound for a confrontation with government inquiries.

The question as to whether Karl Follen was indeed actively involved in driving Sand to his deed, or if he had only been an indirect influence through his Jena circle of Unconditionals, has been frequently disputed.[81] The direct accusations voiced against Karl Follen by several of his closest associates are not shared by most commentators who have subsequently dealt in a critical way with the case. Eighty years after the murder, the German scholars Wilhelm Hausenstein and J. Hermann both examined the testimony involving Sand and Follen given by various sources, and both came to the conclusion that Karl Follen was not directly responsible for Sand's deed. Both in fact thought that Follen had no knowledge of Sand's plans before they were carried out, and that he therefore did not help with the preparation for the murder.[82]

It was impossible in 1819 for the investigating law courts in Weimar and Mannheim to prove Follen's guilt, both because of the strength of his personality and because of the detailed training in law which he had received. In 1827, however, the Mainz Central Investigation Commission eventually did come to the conclusion that Karl Follen had been directly involved in the murder. Follen had apparently accepted a packet of Sand's letters and papers when the latter set out on his journey, he had probably had an early knowledge of his friend's plans, and had even lent him money for his trip.[83] The main report of the Mainz Commission, compiled in 1827, which anticipated the statements subsequently made by several of Follen's former friends, claimed:

> According to a later interrogation, Karl Follen mentioned to one of his friends not only that he had pertinent personal papers belonging to Sand, but also that the latter told him about his plan when leaving on his journey to attempt Kotzebue's murder; and that even though Follen did not think of the plan as useful, he still gave Sand the necessary money for the trip.[84]

Friedrich Münch, another one of Follen's friends and confidants, emigrated to America in 1836 with Paul Follen and a group of Hessian settlers. Many years later, in 1873, and far outside the reach of German law courts, Münch published his memoirs.[85] On the basis of what he remembered, and what he had heard in conversations with Paul Follen, Münch said that Karl Follen was directly responsible for the murder of August von Kotzebue. Follen, Münch argued, had had full knowledge of what Sand was going to do long before the murder was carried out. In a calculating way, he had influenced Sand intellectually, and had even provided him with money in order to travel to Mannheim. Indeed, the only reason why Follen did not carry out the act himself was because he wished to save his own life, so as to become the leader of a future revolution in Germany.

The most powerful accusations against Follen, however, came from his former friend Ferdinand Johannes Wit von Dörring. After 1819 Wit became more of an adventurer than a student, little interested in finishing his studies and making a career, and disinclined to keep his attention on one cause for long. He filled his time with restless traveling throughout various parts of Europe, including England, France, Switzerland, and Italy, and in many forms of employment, especially in journalism. It is clear that after 1819 Wit had turned away from the position of radical republicanism which Follen supported. For some time after the murder of Kotzebue, Wit had been in doubt as to what his own political persuasion was to be, and he had wavered between support for Follen, the moderate Burschenschaft, and the Restoration governments. Eventually, by the early 1820s, he could no longer believe in the possibility or even in the desirability of a revolutionary upheaval in Germany. In his three-volume memoirs, published between 1827 and 1830, Wit set out to clarify the role which Karl Follen had played in the murder of the playwright Kotzebue.[86] He wrote:

> Hatred of Kotzebue affected Sand without special influences . . . [but] a powerful outside incentive was needed to turn this hatred into murder. This was the business of Follen; he was then a *Privatdozent* at Jena and entranced the excited youths there. . . . But not only in this way was Follen *socius,* or even *coauctor delicti,* he was this also in another much more specific way. Sand had told him about his plan in order to get the necessary travel money. Follen not only told this to me, but also to others who have testified to this. . . . Follen did not care much about Kotzebue; he just wanted . . . to attain satisfaction for the German people by means of a murder, and to scare the governments. For this plan (which turned out to be false) he sacrificed not only Kotzebue but also Sand.[87]

Whatever Follen's role in the Kotzebue murder case actually was, the event had an immediate, strong effect on Follen and his relations to other radicals. Soon after the news of Sand's deed spread around the universities in Giessen and Jena, the great majority of even the most radical students very quickly began to dissociate themselves from Follen and his beliefs. The regular Burschenschaft movement had for a long while abandoned its cooperation with Follen; now, however, he was being rejected by his own most devoted followers. The conservative historian Heinrich Leo, initially a radical Jena University student in 1819 and a follower of Follen's, described in his memoirs many years later the reception of the news among the students. He stated that the initial sympathy eventually changed into sullenness and fear:

> On the afternoon when the news of Sand's deed arrived in Jena, since Sand was beloved and Kotzebue hated, in the excitement which was caused by the deed, one could have gathered whole droves of new murderers for supposedly great deeds, and this mood continued for several days. . . . For three days after the news arrived the mood was still such that Dr. jur. Kassenberger, who a short time before had still been a student leader, felt obliged to exclaim that instead of a student dormitory one should build a madhouse for the students. . . . Some days later, however, this mood evaporated, and what followed was a great depression of all spirits. . . . Through Sand's deed the Jena Bur-

schenschaft received the mortal blow, after the arrival of Karl Follen there had already fatally wounded it.[88]

There were, however, voices which were in principle not so critical as the later conservative Heinrich Leo. The most well known was the liberal Berlin professor of theology Wilhelm Leberecht De Wette. Shortly after Sand had been thrown into prison to await his trial, De Wette wrote a public letter addressed to the assassin's mother. The theologian conceded that Sand had committed a moral infraction by breaking the law and killing another person. However, the young man had been true to his own heart; he had followed his own conviction and thus could not and should not be found guilty. De Wette further argued: "The error is to be excused and even canceled out by the strength and honesty of conviction. . . . He [Sand] was firmly committed to carrying out his deed, he thought it just to do what he did, and thus he acted in the right way."[89] This letter immediately caused a great stir, and De Wette soon lost his chair at the University of Berlin—he would end up at the University of Basel together with Karl Follen two years later. De Wette's isolated statement of solidarity with Carl Sand did not, however, produce the desired effect. Very few academics were willing to support it, antagonize the government, and risk their teaching posts. The general public was overwhelmingly shocked by Sand's deed and under no circumstances would they openly agree with any aspect of it. Understanding for men like Sand and Follen was wearing thin, in general, and not only among government officials.

## Revolution and Reaction

The Kotzebue murder, however, did not remain for long the only politically motivated crime to send shock waves through the German states in 1819. On July 1 of that same year, a young pharmacist from Idstein in Hesse, Karl Löning (1791–1819), attempted to assassinate the leading minister (*Regierungspräsident*) of Nassau, Karl von Ibell (1780–1834). Löning had traveled to Schwalbach, a resort town where the minister was vacationing, in order to carry out the murder. He was unable to kill Ibell, however, only injuring him, was apprehended, and immediately imprisoned. On July 11, Löning killed himself in prison by swallowing pieces of broken glass. The historian Hans Schneider, who has dealt extensively with the Ibell assassination attempt, has remarked on Löning's unhappy childhood, his own and his brother's drinking problems, and his girl friend's abortion.[90] More significant, however, were Löning's connections with the Giessen Blacks, especially Karl Follen's younger brother Paul, then a leader among Giessen radicals, since Karl had left for Jena. Other Hesse revolutionaries, such as Heinrich Karl Hofmann, were also implicated. Inspired by these people in the Giessen area, the young student Löning became obsessed with revolutionary ideas much as had Carl Sand at Jena. He became convinced that his deed was "something absolutely good, which pleased God and humanity." Löning's friends and the eye witnesses of the murder attempt were struck by his "fanaticism" and "insane face" while attacking Ibell.[91]

As in the Sand case, the police authorities immediately tried to ascertain whether Löning had shared his plans with others around him or if his attempt had in fact been planned by a secret conspiratory group of murderers.[92] Again, one can turn to the memoirs of Friedrich Münch, a close friend of both Karl and Paul Follen. Münch includes the opinions of Paul Follen on this case: the latter insisted that Löning discussed his plans with local Hesse radicals, and that he was sent out specifically by them to execute Ibell.[93] Münch in fact argued that it was "obvious" the second political murder attempt of the year would come this time not from Jena, but from Giessen, the other town where Karl Follen had connections. He firmly believed that Karl Follen wished to intimidate government authorities in as many parts of Germany as possible, and make these authorities think that his secret conspiracy of political murderers could strike anytime and anywhere they chose to.

Hans Schneider, in contrast, came to the conclusion in 1920 that the radicals in Hesse talked more about violence than about being actually willing to endorse it: "Not only radicals and revolutionaries would make such statements, but also people who would never have thought of realizing their threats."[94] However, it seems likely that the Giessen Blacks and Paul Follen had a greater influence on Löning than one can ever possibly prove. They imbued him with the most radical of ideas, similar to those which Karl Follen was preaching in Jena, and the Sand murder must have been received very differently in their circle than it was among the larger Burschenschaft scene. Rather than being shocked by Sand's act, the Giessen Blacks immediately looked for other key figures whose murder could damage the Restoration governments and their supporters. They thus also searched for other martyrs among the Giessen student population who would be willing to commit such a deed. In July of 1819 August Follen wrote in a personal memorandum, later confiscated by the police:

The German youth movement has sworn to bring virtue and a Christian spirit back into the feeble German fatherland. If this oath is declared a crime and treason, then the time of the apostles has come, in which only martyrs and blood witnesses can any longer attest to the truth. This is what German youth longs for.[95]

On the background of the Löning case, Wit von Dörring contributed his own view:

Who knew of Löning's deed I cannot say; but Löning belonged, at an earlier time (if I am not wrong, during his stay at Heidelberg), and also later, to the most fervent revolutionaries, and was close friends with Follen and the Darmstadt and Nassau Unconditionals. . . . But it becomes even more certain that the deed was known to others if one considers the following circumstances.[96]

Wit then wrote that Ibell had received several letters threatening assassination in the previous months. These letters, Wit argued, point to an organized effort on the part of local revolutionaries not only to scare Ibell personally, but also to increasingly intimidate the local government. The authors of these letters intended to rush the government authorities into faster political reforms, and also led them to believe that a large conspiracy existed which had the power to plan and execute strikes against the state and its most prominent personalities at any time.

In his testimony in prison before his suicide, Löning said that "while executing his deed he believed that, if his motive was good, the will was pure, and the deed was likely to be successful, he was allowed to use any means available" to carry it out. The government authorities concluded that "in this we can only find a repetition of the 'principle' by which Sand was guided in his murder, and his friends in their justification of it."[97] Thus there may be a connection, if indirect, to the doctrine which Karl Follen had endorsed in Giessen, and which he was now passing on to his followers in Jena. The "principle of conviction," popularized by Jakob Friedrich Fries and used by Karl Follen, had thus contributed to two murders, by Sand and by Löning. Behind both criminal figures stood an intellectual leader with high tactical skills, Karl Follen. Follen may not have directly ordered Sand and Löning to murder specific individuals; he did, however, explicitly recommend murder to them as a political tool as often as he could.[98]

In the summer of 1819 an important political guest arrived in the state capital, Weimar: the Empress Dowager of Russia. She had come to visit her daughter, who was the wife of Duke Carl August of Saxony-Weimar.[99] All enrolled Jena students were invited to the celebration, but the Burschenschaft members as a whole refused to come. Russia was seen by them as the most reactionary power in Europe. It was for the Russian court that the subsidized August von Kotzebue had written reports on the political situation in Germany. It was Russia that urged for the implementation of the decisions of the Congress of Vienna, and that was the mainstay of the Holy Alliance. Several sources, however, agree that the Jena Unconditionals not only were hostile to the Empress, but also tried to formulate concrete plans to assassinate her. This plan, if there was one, was never put into practice, though probably it was heatedly discussed. In her biography of her husband, Eliza Follen commented upon the visit of the Empress':

> The public authorities caused triumphal arches, decorated with evergreens and complimentary inscriptions, to be erected in the streets through which she would pass. . . . But Mr. Ferdinand John Wit, who seemed anxious to make himself famous, set himself to work to destroy the arches, which he succeeded in doing.[100]

In his memoirs, Heinrich Leo reports another plan debated by the Jena Unconditionals: when Czar Alexander I of Russia (1777–1825), the founder of the Holy Alliance, himself visited Weimar in the fall of the same year, Karl Follen once again proposed an assassination by one of the Unconditionals. Leo claims than when the radicals were actually considering this proposition, the Czar had already left, so there was no chance of actually carrying out this deed. However, while Follen knew the Czar was in fact no longer in the city, the rest of the group did not; according to Leo, Follen thus wished to strengthen the willingness of his associates to commit themselves to his principles. The event was a test: if there were members of the group who opposed murdering the Czar, they would be seen as unreliable in future undertakings. While there was no chance of actually committing the murder, it is clear that Follen aimed at accustoming his followers to complete devotion to the most radical of ideas, as well as at breaking their capacity to think critically about their own behavior and to resist the orders he gave.[101]

During the winter of 1818–19, Follen remained in Jena and strengthened his ties with the small circle of radicals he had gathered around him. He was no longer interested in increasing his influence on Jena students, but rather in producing a widespread revolutionary movement in Germany. The first step was to conceive a theoretical framework for any uprising that was going to take place in the future. In the summer of 1819, Karl Follen wrote an essay on the potential for revolutionary change throughout the German Confederation. It was entitled "Report of Carl Follenius on the Revolutionary Mood in Germany" ("Bericht des Carl Follenius über die Revolutionäre Stimmung Deutschlands"), and was later published by Wit von Dörring in his memoirs.[102] The document should be read with care, keeping in mind Wit's bias against Follen. Nevertheless, it doubtless represents Follen's thinking in 1819. Follen wrote that Germany had now arrived at a time "when one can no longer recognize the history of a people in its government." He argued that "only for the people themselves does there remain an independent political role." This utopian proposition for direct popular democracy set the tone of the entire document. The cleavage between constitutional reality and demands for radical political change affected only a small number of largely academic people. The consciousness of the population at large was in general not yet set on a radical transformation of society, but it should be.

Still, Follen firmly asserted that the spirit of the *Volk* seeks "unity and free constitution":

> The same spirit that struggled for liberation from foreign oppression in the years 1813 and 1814 is still alive. . . . Whoever is familiar with the enduring, broadly supported struggles of that time, knows that not a battle of despair, and still less a blind following of the government's will, drove the Germans to fight, but they fought for their conviction that once exterior liberation would be achieved, the inner freedom, which had been promised so often, would come about on its own.

Follen went on to describe how, at the Congress of Vienna, the German people had subsequently been betrayed, and how it now had to fight for the rights it had long ago been promised, the rights it truly deserved. Instead, what had followed the great Wars of Liberation were "suppression of free speech, erection of domestic trade barriers and tolls, oppressive taxes, standing armies, false justice and all kinds of arbitrary legal measures."

One of the first signs of hope, Follen wrote, was the martyrdom of Carl Ludwig Sand. He was not an individual maniac, but rather a "representative of the people" whose deed had "originated without the influence of others" and who wished to destroy the "representative of all that was bad about these times," August von Kotzebue. The police investigations into the Sand murder, which were soon to affect Follen as much as anyone, he described as evil, arbitrary, and "terrible." Follen was here attempting to clear his personal record as much as possible. At the same time, regarding contemporary Germany, he was convinced that, despite the criminal investigations which ensued, "such a state, even if it manages to oppress the popular masses, can easily be destroyed by the struggle of annihilation by individuals against other individuals."

About the general political situation, Follen predicted that "all this points for Germany toward a bloody future." He ended his essay with a call to arms aimed at all those who could possibly have been willing to follow him on the path to revolution: "The governments have supported the monarchical principle, and so have prompted all those who until now wished a moderate constitution, not to stop halfway down the road, but rather to place principle against principle (the republican against the monarchical)." Follen here affirmed his readiness to violent struggle and his support for those who were willing to sacrifice their own lives in this process. In this he did not, however, show much political realism. His tactic for destabilizing the German governments through individual acts of terror could not succeed, and instead of solidifying his tactical plans he was becoming increasingly isolated among German radicals. Soon, in the fall of 1819, the Carlsbad Decrees would follow, ending any chance for Follen's political future in Germany. The only options which would remain were his own self-sacrifice in a violent act, long-term imprisonment, or involuntary exile.

The role of Karl Follen within the German political tradition as a whole, and specifically in the Restoration and Vormärz periods, must be considered here. Follen's career has not been seen in a positive light by most historians, for a variety of reasons. The Prussian national conservative Heinrich von Treitschke was perhaps the most brash in his attack on Follen and his ideas. He saw him as a "bloody German Robespierre" and a "hard fanatic, but basically unproductive thinker" who was led by egotism and irrationality while more or less ignorant of the actual laws of political change and development. Follen's energies had, according to Treitschke, been exerted in vain; they had discredited the work of other, more realistic and capable reformers of the day, and obstructed the path to an improvement of the German political condition.[103]

For a contemporary view of these issues, consider the judgement of Robert Wesselhöft, originally a Jena radical of 1818–19 and later a moderate who was deeply shocked by Follen's opinions when they began to be propagated on campus. Wesselhöft and the great majority of Jena Burschenschaft members not only avoided Follen and his program. In fact, they did everything to oppose it and deprive the newcomer of the audience he had hoped for in Jena.[104] On Follen's time in Jena, Wesselhöft claimed in an 1828 pamphlet that "Lucky for the rest of the world, among about thirty friends who formed the intimate club of Karl Follen, there were only three who became absolute unconditionals, and about five who were undecided."

However, Wesselhöft went on to say about Follen and his influence at Jena University: "He was a German devil. . . . Dr. Follen was a bloody revolutionary. Not only did he carry the death of the enemies in his heart, and the heart was not only on his tongue—he clenched his strong fists when he heard the sound of shackles and chains." Wesselhöft confirmed Follen's readiness for armed struggle, but he also contended that "Follen's fate was already decided. He himself recognized that he would lose—but he still wanted to engage in the fight."[105] Follen was not able to convince those around him morally; instead, his ethical standards were sharply rejected by most of those surrounding him by 1819. Follen frightened the Jena radicals too much. He was mistrusted and considered dangerous and irrational, not only by his enemies in the government and police, but also by his own potential allies, whether professors, students, or nonuniversity radicals. The Sand murder had its sympathizers, but their number was bound to be very small, even within the Burschenschaft environment. Follen's tactic of "la guerre des individus" was destined to failure from the start. Julia Wüst, writing on Follen in 1936 during the National Socialist era, thought of him as full of "self-deceit" and "falseness," lacking true moral stature, as opposed to fanatical moralizing, and above all, as unrealistic: "Follen's cause broke apart over the resistance of the political and social reality. He underestimated the . . . strength of tradition, of the historically grown, and overestimated the power of ideas."[106] According to Wüst, "as democratic as Follen's teachings were supposed to be, they still worked against democracy," and "the doctrines of the convinced democrat in reality led back to enlightened absolutism."[107] The East German historian Günter Steiger wrote in 1967 that Follen did not possess "the most important virtue of revolutionaries: patience." His goals were therefore "dangerous" and his means of achieving them useless for social progress.[108]

And yet several historians have warned against considering Follen and his closest friends as members of a "lunatic fringe," as marginal figures in German history with no competence to promote political and social change. Burschenschaft historiography has often been accused of an attempt to save the honor of the Burschenschaft against the suspicion of Jacobinism. The 1819 governments were, according to Ernst Rudolf Huber in 1961, "not wasting their time struggling against a phantom when they turned against the revolutionary spirit of contemporary youth." In fact, had the governments, under the leadership of Metternich, not decided in the aftermath of the Sand murder to crack down on the revolutionary movement, "a powerful oppositional party, libertarian and national in character, would have established itself in Germany." Huber argues that Follen is to blame for not stopping Sand from committing the crime at a critical time in political development. By turning to violent tactics too early, Follen ruined the chance for a revolutionary group to gather sufficient strength and membership before attempting to deliver a serious blow against the German governments.[109]

How Follen alienated his own close political allies and personal followers appears in the case of Wolfgang Menzel, a radical member of the Jena Burschenschaft in 1818–19 and later an influential literary critic. Menzel surely did not think of himself as a political moderate; and yet, after Follen's appearance in Jena, Menzel sensed a strong polarization within the radical scene. Follen's conception of freedom was much more radical, more daring and unusual than that of the Burschenschaft majority ever could have been. The students mostly were reformers but loyal to monarchical authority; Follen, in contrast, was by this time a radical Jacobin willing to engage in violence without the slightest reservations. Menzel wrote to Follen and suggested that he "control himself a bit more." Follen soon responded to this criticism in a harsh way by calling Menzel and his type "practically useless and the first whose heads he would have chopped off."[110]

The student radical Ernst Münch, a friend of Menzel's, was also included in this threat. He wrote of Follen and his role in his memoirs of 1836:

K. Follenius presented himself as a true Proteus. He could be cold or warm, he could rave or be philosophic, be a Christian or a nationalist, a poet and a politician at the same time. His pious mystical poems were meant to directly impress young people, and he used these young people for his purposes, while he could talk to adults, if he had to, either in a Fries-Arndtian manner, or in a French-liberal one, à la Benjamin Constant. Robespierre was his idol, and he would have acted just like him if he had had the chance to do so. . . . He was one of the greatest egotists, but only for his own political system; on the other hand, he was also a very morally pure person, whom one would do an injustice if one would deny this even partially.[111]

Richard Pregizer argued in 1912 that Follen was firmly convinced by 1819 of the need to "justify the right to revolution," which was for him "a legal principle, an ethical law, and a religious dogma." He also believed in an "extreme subjectivism to govern his actions."[112] Personal conviction and the necessity of political violence were thus no longer disputed. Follen's inspiration by 1819 were no longer Arndt and Jahn, but Rousseau and especially Robespierre. Follen wished to be dangerous, not conciliatory. There is no reason to doubt his eagerness to become a key figure in a German revolution, had one taken place during the years of 1819 or 1820. It is important to realize as well, however, that Follen lacked support for whatever he was going to do. The Blacks tried to emotionally manipulate the peasants of Hesse, and to mobilize them politically. However, they did not even have the aid of the liberal academic mainstream on their side. Figures like Arndt and Jahn, on the one hand, were certainly not overly hostile to violent solutions to the German question, but they were also not republicans who could have accepted the plans Follen had for political and social upheaval in German society after a bloody revolution. The professors Fries, Welcker, and Luden, on the other hand, were not very given to the use of violence, and neither were they willing to consider "French" solutions to German political problems. Follen was thus increasingly isolated; it had become impossible to convince others of his opinions. Those who were by 1819 still willing to fight along with him, such as Weidig and Schulz, would soon be eliminated from active political engagement by the severe measures of the Carlsbad Decrees.

# 3

# STAGES OF EXILE

By the fall of 1819, Karl Follen's days in Germany were numbered. He returned to Giessen so as to escape possible investigations at the University of Jena, and stayed for a while at his father's house. The Giessen University authorities were well aware that Follen had arrived and might attempt to win a renewed influence among the local student body. He had not applied to the university for a teaching job, yet his presence was at once regarded with suspicion. The academic senate specifically stressed in a written statement that he should not be allowed to take up teaching at the University of Giessen any time in the near future.[1] Follen realized that he would not have a chance of escaping a prolonged prison term if he remained within reach of German authorities. He was well aware of the new legislation which had been introduced in the fall of 1819 by the German Confederation, at the suggestion of Metternich. The Carlsbad Decrees of September and their rapid implementation in the German states mandated the investigation and punishment of all those involved in the national or radical movements. Criminal sanctions were thereby placed on anyone who engaged in activities which were even slightly suspicious to the government, at a university or in the press.

Follen thus had no choice but to flee to Switzerland via France in the winter of 1819–20, and Switzerland too eventually failed to provide sanctuary. His time in Switzerland, spent as a teacher at the cantonal school in Chur and as a lecturer at the University of Basel, was productive and happy, since he was temporarily free from persecution and other revolutionaries from Germany joined him there. To the German police authorities, Basel soon became a notorious place for assorted exiles to gather and formulate political plans. From Switzerland, Follen eventually tried to influence the German political situation one last time, by founding the

League of Young Men (Jugendbund). This secret revolutionary group spread to several places in Germany. A League of Elders (Männerbund) which was to work in conjunction with it was never actually established. Eventually, however, Follen's German past caught up with him in Switzerland as well. In 1823 and 1824, the Prussian government made several attempts to convince the Swiss to extradite him and several other German exiles. While the authorities in Switzerland were still deciding on this matter, Follen fled from Basel to France with a false passport and eventually, with the help of Swiss and French sympathizers, managed to board a ship from Le Havre to New York in November 1824. His five years in Switzerland were to be the last Follen was to spend in Europe.

## The Carlsbad Decrees and Dismissal from German Academic Life

At least since 1817, after the Wartburg festival, the governments in Germany had been increasingly concerned about the political activities of academic youth around the entire German Confederation.[2] The senior Prussian police official Karl Albert von Kamptz (1769–1849), in particular, believed that the nationalist movement was getting dangerously large, organized, and visible, and that it was was time to curb its influence and investigate the backgrounds of its members. He and several members of the Prussian government by late 1817 began to speak of a "Wartburg conspiracy" which would grow and become a serious political threat unless it was suppressed. Kamptz tried to convince the King of Prussia, Frederick William III, that the Prussian state must take action against this threat or suffer serious attacks.

Kamptz was angered by the news of the book burning which had taken place in Eisenach after the conclusion of the Wartburg festival; one of his own works, a police law code entitled *Allgemeiner Codex der Gendarmerie* (1815), had been thrown into the fire. Kamptz became convinced that the true purpose of the festival had been "political and demagogical," and that the main goal of its participants was the notorious struggle for what he called "inner freedom."[3] By this expression Kamptz did not mean the "external" liberation which the wars ending in 1815 had brought, but rather the revolutionary upheaval and domestic liberalization for which the Burschenschaft movement was prepared to fight. He dramatized the student movement as "illegal" and "subversive" in a report dealing with the Wartburg festival which he submitted to the Prussian government authorities.[4]

The question of what to do with the student nationalist movement and possible radical factions within it was introduced into the Austrian-Prussian political dialogue and placed among the topics of the Congress of Aachen in 1818. Günter Steiger has noted that an effect was soon felt in various areas: the gymnastics movement was condemned and the training grounds shut down, the Prussian constitutional question was handled in a more rigid, cautious way, measures against the Burschenschaft were announced, and a governmental decision to arrest and question suspected "demagogues" (as the police authorities called the student radicals and their adult leadership) was announced.[5] The Berlin police thus began collecting material on the student movement at Prussian universities.[6] The governments of other states soon followed the Prussian example, placing more restrictions on the activities of students and liberal professors and providing information about local radicals to the police at Berlin.

The factor that contributed most to a concentrated governmental effort throughout the German Confederation to attack and destroy the liberal movement systematically was Metternich's own growing interest in pursuing such a course. The event which led Metternich to focus more of his attention on the Burschenschaft situation was the news of the Kotzebue murder. Metternich's close political associate Friedrich von Gentz emphasized the possibility of a widespread conspiracy in a letter to Metternich of April 1, 1819:

> This issue is bad enough as it is, however its origin and its probable, almost certain connection with the greater ills and dangers of the time causes everyone who is able to see the large framework of things to experience an even higher degree of terror and disgust. Look what the "innocent, virtuous aims of German youth" and its "teachers full of merit"—this is what we were told when we tried to warn against the dangers of the Wartburg festival—have accomplished! . . . The necessity of dealing with the situation at the universities is now more evident and important than ever before.[7]

Metternich answered Gentz on April 9:

> I have received the message of Kotzebue's murder with all available details. . . . I have no doubt that the murderer did not act entirely by himself, but rather in connection with a secret society. . . . I want to react in a harsh way to this issue, and will try to exploit it as much as I can.[8]

Metternich thus had been alerted to the possible dangers involved, but he had also understood that it would be possible to use the Sand case in order to further his own political goals. The fact that several violent acts had been committed by members of the Burschenschaft scene made it possible to justify a tight control on the universities and on liberal professors, limitations on freedom of the press, and severe restrictions on any other way in which the liberal movement might articulate its opinions. All liberals in Germany, whatever their true political stance, could now be classified as potentially dangerous and subversive. Metternich now had a pretext for formulating and implementing a grand strategy for the prevention of social and political change throughout Germany, under his own and Austria's leadership.

The principal instrument which Metternich used to cripple the liberal and national movement, and thus to secure his own dominant position until 1848, was the Carlsbad Decrees of September 1819. Metternich met with the Prussian head of state, Hardenberg, at Teplitz on August 1, 1819, in order to prepare for a larger conference at Carlsbad which was to begin a week later, and to establish Prussia and Austria's common position on the issues to be raised. At Carlsbad, the ministers of the ten largest German states were present, and they agreed on four new laws to be introduced throughout the German Confederation. These were a University Law, a Press Law, a law providing for the investigation of political activities hostile to the Confederation, and an executive order governing the execution of these laws.[9] These new decrees were not accepted everywhere in Germany without criticism and dispute. Because a unanimous decision of all members of the German Confederation was necessary, Austria and Prussia between them simply forced the smaller states to comply. In this the decrees exemplified the unbalanced constitutional situation within the Confederation. By October 1819, the individual states had been forced to accept the new rulings and began to implement them within their individual territories. Decisions reached mainly by Austria and Prussia were thus to have a strong impact on university towns such as Giessen in Hesse-Darmstadt and Jena in Saxony-Weimar.

On September 20, 1819, the first law, known as the University Law, was introduced. At every German university, a special state officer was installed who watched over disciplinary matters and compiled reports on the activities of the Burschenschaft and the entire student body. The autonomy of the universities from the state goverments was henceforth severely damaged. The law also stipulated that the universities must dismiss immediately any professor who had in the past been publicly known to sympathize with the Burschenschaft or the national movement, or who had tried to influence students' opinions in a decidedly liberal or even radical direction. Among those who lost their professorships for long periods of time were Jakob Friedrich Fries and Lorenz Oken at Jena, and Ernst Moritz Arndt at Bonn. The Berlin theologian Wilhelm Leberecht De Wette, author of the famous letter expressing his sympathy to Carl Sand's mother, lost his chair at Berlin and had to emigrate to Switzerland and accept a new teaching post at Basel. Another stipulation of the University Law was a complete prohibition of the Burschenschaften or any other form of student organization which would be conducive to a national or liberal spirit and would encourage students to formulate political plans. Every student was obliged, at the end of his studies, to apply for a political evaluation signed by the special state officer supervising the local university. Without this document, the student could neither take his final exams nor enter into the service of the state in any capacity whatsoever. Those who were known to have a radical past or a membership in the Burschenschaft were effectively excluded from finding employment for which they were otherwise well qualified, and which for many was the main purpose of their university training.

The new Press Law was aimed at the many oppositional pamphlets and periodicals which had served the liberal movement and its propaganda effort. Short pamphlets had been very effective in several liberal states which had previously abandoned censorship, especially in Saxony-Weimar. Under the new Press Law, all printed items of less than twenty pages could no longer be distributed without express prior permission from the state authorities. Censorship was now reintroduced throughout the German Confederation. Printed items under twenty pages were usually read by more people than long tracts, and they were also much easier and cheaper to distribute. Radical propaganda intended for wide popular distribution was now made nearly impossible. If the individual states should allow the publication of materials which the Confederation at large did not approve of, the Confederation was authorized to interfere in the affairs of the individual territories.

The most powerful and most notorious of these new laws, however, was the Investigation Law, which established a Central Investigation Commission, to be set up by representatives of the largest individual territories. The seat of this special commission, which reported directly to the German Confederation, was to be in Mainz. The Central Commission was to probe into the character, scope, and goals of the national and liberal movements at large, and the student movement in particular. It would attempt to find out whether there were in fact "seditious, treasonous" groups which were plotting to overthrow the German Confederation and its individual governments, and especially, whether and how these secret groups were connected to one another. Was there even a national secret revolutionary group which had to be actively suppressed?

Seven representatives, sent by the largest German states, headed the commission, which met from 1819 until 1827 and investigated thousands of liberals and suspected political deviants throughout the German states.[10] Every major liberal who had ever become known to the governments, from Jahn to Arndt and from the Snell brothers to Wit von Dörring, was given an individual file, and even the most inconsequential persons were investigated as well. Furthermore, every political association which came to light, whether it was the Polish Friendship Club in Berlin (a group of German and Polish revolutionaries) or the Giessen Blacks, was considered individually by the investigators. The main report of the Mainz commission *(Hauptbericht)* was presented to the Confederation in 1827. It consisted of a summary of all the investigation results, and it showed that the commission had been able to find out a considerable amount about the contemporary liberal and radical scene. The report was a result of many years of careful evaluation of a formidable mixture of suspicious persons and facts. There was a four-volume extensive version (handwritten) and a condensed one-volume version (typeset).[11] An outline of the report was also printed in the official records of the German federal diet *(Bundestagsprotokolle)* of 1827.[12]

It now became clear that out of the secret nationalistic groups founded in resistance to Napoleon as early as 1808, such as the League of Virtue *(Tugendbund)* or the German League *(Deutscher Bund)* founded by Friedrich Ludwig Jahn, there had developed other, much more radical conspiratory groups which had attempted to create nationwide networks and prepare for a violent revolutionary upheaval. These concrete radical activities had been greatly influenced by specific intellectuals and prominent individuals such as Jahn, Arndt, and Luden. Documents such as Wilhelm Schulz' "Frag- und Antwortbüchlein" and the poem "Teutsche Jugend an die teutsche Menge" ("German Youth Addressing the German Masses"; a section of Karl Follen's "Great Song") had done their part to bring Germany closer to a revolutionary situation. It is surprising how much this commission, with the help of local police authorities, was actually able to find out. For evidence, the commission used transcribed interrogations of the leading liberals who had been arrested and imprisoned, and letters and personal papers owned by these persons. The officers of the commission also became familiar with all the pamphlets, newspapers, or leaflets ever printed and distributed by radicals all over Germany, and they compiled substantial reports on all of these. Attempts by the radicals to burn all their papers, almost entirely successful in the case of Karl Follen (only his Draft of the Constitution was discovered), very often came too late for the great majority. At the same time, the police worked with great efficiency and speed throughout the German Confederation.[13]

Because of the Carlsbad Decrees, both Karl and August Follen faced a very similar situation in the early fall of 1819. The brothers were each arrested and thoroughly interrogated. Directly after the Sand murder, Karl was taken to the criminal court in Weimar for investigation, but then the authorities let him return to Jena to continue his teaching there. The case against him had only just started, however, and would now be pursued with greater intensity. His wife reported in her biography:

> In the following October, he was suddenly waked, one night, by a noise in his room, and found himself surrounded by gens d'armes. Upon asking what they wanted, he was told, that they came to take him to Manheim [sic]. As this was the place where Sand was imprisoned, he understood well the object of taking him there; it was to confront him with Sand. The officers busied themselves with seizing all his papers.[14]

During the arrest, Follen managed to burn some politically very sensitive letters that were lying around his bedroom. Still, the next few months were a very difficult time. He was again taken to Weimar, and interrogated a second time there, and then driven directly to Mannheim in order to be confronted with Carl Sand in the latter's prison cell. Nothing, however, could be discovered about a connection of Follen and Sand other than that they had maintained friendly relations when both were present in Jena, and that Follen had lent Sand money in order to finance his trip to Mannheim. The authorities could not find grounds to suspect Follen of being a possible accomplice to the Kotzebue murder at this time; they had not yet gathered enough information about his secret activities at Jena.[15] Even the Mainz commission, which was by then at work piecing together bits of evidence at a fast pace, was evidently not yet clear in the fall of 1819 about the dangerous role of Karl Follen; the leader of the Unconditionals remained free and in early 1820 he managed to escape arrest by flight.[16]

Before this, however, Follen's teaching career in Jena was over. From the fall of 1819, he was no longer allowed to lecture there, and was advised to return to Giessen pending further proceedings against him. The Hessian authorities had by then also been alerted to his case, and were prepared for his appearance in their territory. They knew, according to a Giessen University report to the state government in late 1819, that

> Dr. Carl Follenius from Giessen has for some time been present here in a quiet manner and has so far not tried to deliver any lectures. According to a member of the academic senate, Follen has remained here since his return from Mannheim, at the express wish of his father and with the specific permission of the investigation commission at Weimar. He does not wish to lecture, and has not left Jena forever, but only for an unspecified length of time, and is convinced that he wants to return there, although he has been forbidden to lecture in the coming winter term. In addition, he is not finished with the Weimar law courts but is still to be dealt with in the future.[17]

Follen's academic past in Giessen and his role in past radical activities throughout Hesse-Darmstadt were now coming back into view. Franz Joseph Arens, special state officer at the University of Giessen according to the terms of the Carlsbad Decrees, reported to the state government on Karl Follen's Burschenschaft membership, while the government reported to the university on his participation in the petition movement, which it was beginning to uncover.[18] Connections between the Giessen Blacks, led by Karl Follen, on the one side, and the Darmstadt Blacks, including individuals such as Friedrich Ludwig Weidig and Heinrich Karl Hofmann, on the other, were now beginning to be investigated.[19] Arens had already begun in the spring of 1819, several months before the Carlsbad Decrees, to order that the rooms of many suspect students at Giessen be searched. Whatever papers or letters could be found had been seized, and later evaluated for their possible political contents. The Follen brothers at this time believed that they were still safe. Full of self-confidence, in a letter of May 1819, August Follen stated about the intensive Giessen investigations, and their relative failure up to that point, that "this time Arens had put his dog's nose into shit [*Scheissdreck*] instead of into pot roast."[20]

This initial feeling of security was not to last for very long. Authorities at the University of Giessen reached a firm resolution even before Karl Follen had made any attempt to contact them and explain his situation. In Karl Follen's file at the university, reads: "Should he come to Giessen, this university will under no circumstances allow him to lecture without permission, and it will write an evaluation of what sort of measures shall perhaps be directed against the person under immediate consideration."[21] Follen therefore could remain in Giessen only under the most difficult of circumstances. His father kept him in his house and was urged to accept the legal responsibility for his son while he was under investigation. Follen was not permitted to leave Hesse-Darmstadt, nor was he allowed to move anywhere within his home state. Finally, there was no way in which he could exercise his profession as a *Privatdozent* in law and earn a living. Any kind of political engagement was totally out of the question, since every step he took was under constant supervision by the police, while the universities with which he had been connected, the state governments, and the Mainz commission were all hastening to put together and evaluate the evidence against him and prepare the trial which was to take place in the near future.

On May 20, 1820, the murderer Carl Sand, a symbol of courage and patriotism to the radicals in Germany, and of fanaticism and evil intentions to the governments, was executed by the authorities at Mannheim. He had survived the wounds which he had inflicted upon himself after his deed, and had been thoroughly interrogated. The police had not been able to learn as much as they would have liked from interviewing him. However, they were convinced that he was part of a whole network of radicals waiting to kill key figures of the Restoration governments and of German cultural life. To political radicals everywhere in Germany, Sand became a martyr not only because he claimed he had committed his deed for the good of the fatherland, but also especially because of his harsh trial, followed by his execution by the sword. The death of Sand was supposedly deplored even by the executioner, who asked his forgiveness before he fulfilled his duty.[22] Pieces of the wooden block on which Sand's bloody head fell were collected by radical friends present during the execution. The wood was later used in the building of a garden house where conspiratory meetings of revolutionaries took place throughout the 1820s and 1830s.[23]

For Follen and his closest associates, the Sand murder had a different, more powerful message. In it they saw very clearly what would happen to them if they resorted to violent action against the established governmental regime and its leadership. Execution or another harsh form of punishment threatened everyone who was convicted of plotting to overthrow the existing political arrangements. The Sand execution provided a signal for a number of radicals who were still in the country to leave Germany as soon as possible, and to try to influence German politics only from outside the country.[24]

## The Basel Sanctuary and the League of Young Men

Karl Follen had already responded in the only way still open to him: he had fled Germany, and spent the early months of 1820 first in France (January 1–February 13) and then in Switzerland. His brother August chose the same destination after his initial prison term, a year later. Eliza Follen reports Karl's flight by quoting from a letter which she received several years later from Follen's stepmother:

> He was satisfied that his only safety was in flight, and he resolved to leave Germany. He told his family that he was going to Coblenz (he did not mention to them that he should never return), and bade them farewell forever. . . . It was in the winter of 1819 and 1820 that Dr. Follen left his home. . . . Hearing from a good friend that he was to be imprisoned, to prevent this, he left us . . . sparing us the anguish of such a leave-taking, and went to Strasburg [sic].[25]

After passing through the city of Koblenz, Follen spent several weeks in Strasbourg in the beginning of 1820; unfortunately all his clothes and his papers which his family sent to him were lost when the riverboat which was supposed to bring them along the Rhine accidentally burned. In February of 1820, he traveled on to Paris for two weeks in order to learn about French radicalism. He was introduced to a number of leading French liberals and radicals, and made the personal acquaintance of one of the central figures of French political life, the Marquis de Lafayette (1757–1834). Follen also met the liberal constitutional theoretician Benjamin Constant (1767–1830); Victor Cousin (1792–1867), the Germanophile philosopher and political radical; the Marquis Marc-René d'Argenson (1771–1842), a political associate of Lafayette and Constant to whom he ascribed a radical political orientation; and a Paris lawyer named Joseph Rey, who had been suspended from professional life for writing several radical pamphlets.[26] He thus began to establish international connections with persons who had goals very similar to his own. In Paris, Follen was escorted around once again by Johannes Wit von Dörring, his former roommate at Jena, who had also chosen to leave Germany. At this time, Follen did not yet know that Wit would later bitterly oppose him and relate his secret political plans to the German governments.

The Mainz Central Investigation Commission was able to find out that Rey, a lawyer who was politically radical, took Follen and Wit on a trip to a forest outside of Paris and there mentioned to him that there was a secret revolutionary society with contacts throughout France which was well organized and waiting to start a revolutionary upheaval once the time was ripe. Follen evidently replied that a similar organization with decidedly republican goals was to be established in Germany and Switzerland with his help, and that both the French and the German revolutionary groups were to work together in the future.[27] The contacts with Victor Cousin were just as intensive. Follen saw him in Paris at least six times, and wished through him to be introduced to other French radicals. Follen also asked Cousin, among others, for money in order to support revolutionary efforts in Germany and Switzerland. Finally, Cousin and Follen discussed the Italian situation, and Cousin's forthcoming academic trip to Turin, Milan, and Bologna, which could be used in order to establish further radical contacts. Follen was especially eager to stay in contact with Cousin in order to be informed about the potential for revolution in northern Italy and the Piedmont.[28] Follen and Wit established a connection to French radicals and hoped that a revolution in France would help bring about a similar upheaval in Germany.

After the murder of the Duc de Berry on February 13, 1820, however, all foreigners were immediately asked by the French government to leave the country. Follen thus had to find an alternative to France. He was lucky enough to find a noblewoman, the Countess Benzel-Sternau, wife of the German liberal politician Karl Christian Ernst von Benzel-Sternau (1767–1849), who invited him to stay at her country seat at Mariahalden near Erlenbach on the Zürichsee.[29] This relationship grew more personal as time went by; the countess finally invited Follen to stay as long as he wished at her residence. Follen explained that he had to move on. He had not yet given up hope for a political upheaval in Germany and preferred to go to a place where he could be with like-minded intellectuals and from which he could perhaps influence the events in his home country in a more effective way.

After this stay near Zurich throughout the summer of 1820, Karl Follen decided to move permanently to a different part of Switzerland. In mid-

September of 1820, he received an invitation to teach at the cantonal school of the Grisons at Chur. His radical friend from Nassau, Wilhelm Snell (the younger of the two Snell brothers who had worked in the constitutional movement with the Darmstadt Blacks), joined him there. Follen gladly accepted his new post as schoolteacher. However, by the spring of the following year, 1821, he was again hampered by serious problems. While most of his students and fellow teachers were deeply impressed by the intellectual abilities he demonstrated in his history and religion classes and by his commanding personality, the more conservative and traditional members of the Calvinist community at Chur were disturbed by the religious opinions which Follen voiced in the presence of his pupils. Several Calvinist clergymen claimed that Follen had actually denied the existence of God in what he said to his students.

According to Eliza Follen, Follen had argued that there were two great principles, one that there was "but one spiritual God," and another, that "all men ought to love one another as brothers, and strive after godlike perfection." He stressed that the adoption of these principles would lead to "the destruction of the basis of all heathenish institutions, idolatry, and unnatural distinctions among men."[30] Follen argued that man had not been born in a sinful state, and that he had the freedom to decide himself between a good and an evil life. These assertions ran directly counter to Calvinist doctrine.[31] Eliza Follen reports the reaction of Follen's audience:

> The warmth, with which this simple doctrine was received by the young men, who had been brought up in gloomy and perplexed religious ideas, roused the fanatic zeal of some highly Calvinistic ministers, who spread an alarm through the canton, that Dr. Follen had denied the Godhead of Christ Jesus, the doctrines of original sin and the absolute moral depravity of man.[32]

Follen was forced to defend himself publicly and ask for an audience before the evangelical synod of the canton of the Grisons in order to clarify his religious views and his fitness to serve as a schoolteacher in the canton. The constant troublemaker had once again drawn upon himself the anger of his neighbors. The president of the cantonal council of education, a man named Bernegg, praised Follen's commitment to teaching and his intellectual skills in a letter of July 1821,[33] but Follen, recognizing that the resistance of the rest of the council was formidable, had already asked for his own dismissal from his Chur teaching post that same May.[34]

By the same time, evidently, the Austrian and Prussian governments had begun to find out where Karl Follen was hiding.[35] At the Congress of Troppau in 1820, there were decisions made which extended the Metternich system to all of Europe. According to the new "principle of intervention," all European countries were required to deliver political radicals up to the states in which they were to be prosecuted. The groundwork was thus laid for capturing Follen and the other German emigrés in Switzerland, by asking the Swiss government to extradite the supposed criminals and to allow Prussian officers to bring them to Köpenick near Berlin, where the political police was waiting for them. The Swiss government did not, however, yield as yet to the pressure which was being exerted from outside, and Follen was, for the time being at least, safe from German prosecution.

The problem for Karl Follen was to find a new intellectual and political environment in Switzerland, since he had lost his school teaching post. Once again, he managed to come upon just the right place: the University of Basel. It had been an important intellectual center in the sixteenth century, and then had fallen into decay. In 1817, however, the university was refounded and reorganized. Professors' chairs were being filled with German exile intellectuals, many of whom the Swiss authorities could find throughout the country. What was being set up at Basel was an international center of liberal and even radical ideas, a place from which the Swiss students would profit because of the excellence of the new German scholars, and from which the liberal scholars would gain because there they would be allowed to freely discuss their political and religious ideas, and make plans for the future of Germany.

Follen was appointed as a lecturer on natural, civil, and ecclesiastical law, and found many of his former friends already installed at Basel. The exact title of his designated academic field *(venia legendi)*, awarded to him in November of 1821, was "psychology and logic." Follen taught as a member of the philosophical faculty. His lectures were on the Pandects, philosophy of law, public law, and canon law. In January of 1824, it was suggested by the university administration that he should be made a full professor because of the "thoroughness of his knowledge and his constant work for the best of the university." He remained at the university until the summer semester of 1824, during which he was on sabbatical from his teaching responsibilities.[36] The social surroundings at Basel were as agreeable as the university scene. Follen became engaged to marry Anna de Lassaulx, the daughter of a local professor (she later refused to follow him to America). While the city council was quite conservative and dominated by a group of older local notables, there was also a set of younger, more liberal, and modern-minded intellectuals around the city with whom Follen and others like him could come into contact, for instance through a new "literary society" founded in the fall of 1821. Most important for Follen, however, was the opportunity to once again gather with many of his longtime political associates from Germany, many of them now refugees at Basel University.

The most prominent of the German exiles, to be sure, was the new professor of theology. Wilhelm Leberecht de Wette, author of the open letter of sympathy to Carl Sand's mother, had now found a new home in Basel, and began editing a university scholarly journal together with Karl Follen. De Wette had been a student and *Privatdozent* in Jena from 1799 to 1807, and then professor of theology at Heidelberg. In 1810 he accepted a chair at Berlin, from which he was removed by the government in 1819. After a stay in Weimar he arrived in Basel in 1822, staying there until his death in 1849. He was known throughout the scholarly world not only for his important research in Protestant theology but also for his unambiguously liberal opinions. He was an open sympathizer of the Burschenschaft and one of the closest friends of the Jena philosopher Jakob Friedrich Fries.[37]

Another German scholar at Basel was De Wette's stepson Karl Beck, who would eventually accompany Follen on his journey to America three years later. In addition, there was the legal scholar Wilhelm Snell from Hesse, who had worked with Follen in the Hesse German reading society and the Blacks, and another radical, a medical doctor named Carl Gustav Jung. The Burschenschaft leader Wilhelm Wesselhöft, whose brother Robert had been a key speaker at the Wartburg festival, was also present on the university faculty. De Wette tried in 1822 to pursuade his friend Jakob Friedrich Fries, who was being investigated at Jena and would soon lose his professorship there, to move to Basel. Fries would not himself come, but he suggested someone else to be hired in his place.[38] This was Karl Seebold, one of Follen's closest friends and a very early member of the Giessen Blacks. Only a few years later Wilhelm Snell's brother Ludwig was also able to join the philosophical faculty. He was given the *venia legendi* for philosophy.[39] It is astounding how these radicals, who had been working together for over ten years, were able to gather once more in the same town; many of the original Giessen Blacks were together again at Basel.

An attempt by De Wette to gain a professorship in Basel for the now unemployed Jena natural scientist Lorenz Oken (1779–1851) failed because of a veto on the part of the Swiss board of education. Perhaps even more interesting to Follen at this point, however, were the emigrés from France and Italy who now came to Basel. These were the Italian legal scholar Pellegrino Rossi of Carrara, a later member of the French upper house *(Pair de France)* and minister of Pope Pius IX, and a French economist named Charles Comte, who had previously been sentenced to imprisonment in France as the editor of the anti-Bonapartist journal *Le Censeur.* Basel thus became a center of radical intellectuals with a greater European significance.[40]

During his time as a teacher at Basel, Karl Follen published two articles in the local scholarly journal he edited with De Wette, called the *Wissenschaftliche Zeitschrift der Universität Basel.* The titles of the two essays were "On the Destiny of Man" and "On the Legal Teachings of Spinoza." These short contributions were mere splinters of a much larger work that Follen was planning to publish. Follen was in the process of conceiving a major book on law to be entitled *Das Naturrecht,* and to be published with the Gessner bookdealers of Zurich. Most of the work was to be based on the lectures Karl Follen was at the time holding at Basel University. In the summer semester of 1824, for instance, he taught a university seminar devoted to the historical development of natural law. Basel University was known as the only academic institution in the German-speaking world where natural law and its practical applications were still primarily taught. It had not as yet been rejected, and replaced by the historical school of law *(Historische Rechtsschule)* founded by the Berlin jurist Friedrich Karl von Savigny (1779–1861), and influenced by the ideas of Hegel. The faculty at Basel believed in immutable and omnipresent natural law; they disagreed with seeing law as historically ever-changing and shaped by a specific local *Volksgeist.* This fact was praised especially by Follen and his radical friends, who adhered to the legal and philosophical conceptions proposed during the French Revolution; because of its political atmosphere, Basel now became very attractive for German emigrés interested in law.[41]

While his larger work was never published, the essays he did complete tell us what sort of legal theories Follen was interested in at this time in his life. "On the Destiny of Man" was perhaps the most concrete and forceful statement of his own moral stance that Follen ever made. It revolved around the concept of man's decidedly moral nature, the role of conscience, self-control and self-perception, the relationship of duty to an individual's deeds, and liberation. It proposed a moral agenda which could be applied to many different realms of human existence, including the political and the religious, and prefigured Follen's later engagement with the antislavery movement in America. Follen began by conventionally pointing out basic differences between the animal and the human being. Human existence manifested itself in three chief ways: man was physically present, he lived his biological life, and he was also spiritually alive. The human was at the top of a hierarchy of creatures because, as opposed to the animal, he was a spiritual being intrinsically equipped with a conscience to guide his behavior. Thus the human being was destined to live and experience life on a much higher plane than was the animal. Conscience was not an attribute which was conveyed by education; rather, it was present at birth and could never be completely extinguished.

A further fundamental characteristic of humans, according to Follen, was that they all had an innate drive to be religious. Even the most primitive people had their myths to believe in. At birth, there was already what Follen called *Gottgefühl*, a feeling that life was guided by a divine being and that man must establish spiritual contact with this being. Children were particularly apt to feel in touch with the divine, and Follen strongly argued that their feelings were genuine and that childhood did not represent, as some rationalist philosophers supposed, a "dark or benighted state of being" *(Nachtzustand)*. In addition, all humans had the very important capacity to become free. There would always be obstacles to be overcome on the way to true human freedom, but man could use self-perfection and self-control in order to strive for the goal of freedom. Even slaves in the ancient world had felt an urge, Follen argued, to liberate themselves from their state of misery. Modern man had to muster that same strength, had to follow the call of his own conscience, and strive for his own liberation. He argued

> that it was good for the human being who wished to grow into a state of freedom, to run into obstacles at the beginning of his course. These should not suppress his powers to achieve freedom, but rather should foster them and bring them into his own conscience. In blissful laziness only despots and those with servile mentalities can blossom.[42]

Man should not attempt to flee from the world, or to avoid its problems. Neither should he become addicted to the pursuit of physical delights. Instead, Follen demanded of the individual a willingness to sacrifice his personal well-being and focus on the progress of self-perfection, and on the liberation of humanity. If man was to make a contribution to the world, he had to first bring his own passions, wishes, and emotions under strict control. The best guide in the struggle for freedom, Follen argued, was a careful study of the history of mankind. History had consisted of "a great variety of states, and a continuing change" between freedom and slavery. There had existed, on the one hand, heroes of freedom and self-liberation, such as Aristides, Cato, Hutten, and Winkelried, and, at the other extreme, also "shadowy outcasts which were halfway between humans and animals." Follen continued to describe how freedom and slavery had alternated during human history:

> Slaves harvested from the earth that free men had fought for with their own blood, and had left to them. On the other hand, black slaves destroyed the legitimacy of whites, who had enslaved them because they happened to have been born in a higher social place. These blacks founded free states and allowed their former oppressors equal rights.[43]

Man's struggle for freedom would go on; and to succeed in finally eradicating slavery from the face of the earth, it must follow a series of steps of development, from the conscience of the individual to the liberation of all mankind. First, conscience *(Gewissen)* would tell man that his current state was deficient and needed to be changed. Man would then recognize that it was his duty, and therefore virtuous, to strive for change. Thus man would arrive at the conviction *(Überzeugung)* that he must act. This conviction in turn would force him to do what was necessary to change his own situation first, and then eventually that of all humanity.[44] Piety and freedom were, according to Follen's argument, the two concepts on which human self-perfection, and the improvement and fulfillment of all human life ultimately hinged. Those who had combined a firm belief in God with the courage to fight for freedom had always been successful in history. Thus Christianity had a prime role in human progress toward self-liberation. It endowed man with a moral code as guide, and it gave him a mission to sacrifice himself for the good of mankind.[45]

In the second article, "On the Legal Teachings of Spinoza," Follen used the writings of the philosopher Baruch Spinoza in order to demonstrate the validity and usefulness of natural law for the establishment of modern republican nation states: "Among the most important things which have ever been achieved by our science is the philosophy of right [*Rechtslehre*] of Spinoza, which I will discuss here as a contribution to the history of natural law."[46] Spinoza was not to be called an atheist, but in fact someone who had dedicated his life's work to the search for truth. Follen argued that Spinoza saw God as "the substance, the origin, and the law of the world," from which everything in existence proceeded. Only God could be completely free, and He spoke to people through natural law. God had made the world not arbitrarily, but according to his own plan. This plan was dictated by freedom and necessity, both of which could be seen in an examination of natural law.

Again Follen was concerned with the question of liberation. Spinoza had recognized that humans were not quite strong enough to achieve complete freedom independently. Indeed, some patterns which human life had to follow were dictated by the provisions of nature. Still, humans had to pursue freedom as best they could in their own individual positions in life. The prime tool for this pursuit was law. Humans could achieve freedom by "collectivizing" law in a social contract, and then obeying this contract as closely as possible. The ideal form this contract should take was that of popular sovereignty *(Volksherrschaft)*. The rules of natural law had to become as nearly identical as possible with the laws postulated in civil society. Follen went on:

> Even if the state may use its force to all ends, the actual point of its existence is reason, that means freedom, peace, and unity. The more reasonable the laws of the state are, that is, the stronger they guarantee the equal freedom of the individual against all intervention and hindrance, the firmer the state will stand. Rules which anger the majority will lead to the downfall of the state.[47]

The discussion on Spinoza was to be continued in the major work on natural law that Karl Follen was writing and that he planned to publish with the Gessner company.[48] Follen and his brother August (who had also arrived in Switzerland in 1821) also made contributions to the periodical *Schweizer Volksblatt* which the Gessner brothers published, but which was censored by the Swiss government in late November of 1821. The brothers tried to reestablish the magazine under a new name, but were finally kept from doing so by the end of the year.[49] Most of their energy from then on went into support of both Karl Follen's renewed efforts to influence German politics and the radical group that became known as the League of Young Men, or Youth League.

From the beginning of his stay, Karl Follen had not devoted his entire time in Basel to teaching and intellectual speculation. He still wished to actively change the German political situation. Several German revolutionaries, including Heinrich Karl Hofmann of the Darmstadt Blacks, and the enthusiastic supporter of Friedrich Ludwig Jahn's gymnastics movement, Franz Lieber (who would, like Follen, shortly emigrate to America and become known as Francis Lieber), visited Follen and his friends in Switzerland in the summer of 1821. Georg Rühl, who had worked with Follen in the Hesse constitutional movement, came to visit in the summer of 1822.[50] The most significant visit, however, was that of the former Burschenschaft leader and Berlin philosophy student Karl von Sprewitz (born at Rostock in 1800), who came to see Karl Follen in Chur in the spring of 1821. Follen gave this young radical a mission to carry out in Germany: he was to found a secret group of young academics at as many German universities as possible. The Youth League (Jugendbund) was to be known to nobody except the members, who were to be in close communication with one another and to gradually expand their number as much as they safely could. Once a potentially revolutionary situation was evident in Germany, this group of young intellectuals would attempt to topple the existing governments and seize power.[51]

Having received these instructions from Follen, Sprewitz continued his travels through Switzerland, visiting Wilhelm Snell in Basel and the Gessner brothers in Zurich. The first new member whom Sprewitz was able to gain for the new radical youth league was the student Heinrich Gessner (born in 1798), who came from a prominent Swiss family of writers and poets. Together with his brother, the book dealer Eduard Gessner (born in 1799), he maintained close contacts with the German refugees in Switzerland. Soon, however, Gessner went off to continue his studies in Jena, Göttingen, and Heidelberg, and sought to win new radical members at these universities. Among those who joined were the brothers Wilhelm and Robert Wesselhöft, both medical students, the church historian Karl Hase, and the important radical publicist Arnold Ruge.[52]

Christoph Heinrich Gessner and his brother Eduard were the grandsons of the Swiss poet and bookdealer Salomon Gessner (1730–1788), and they had inherited a Zurich bookstore and printing shop called the Swan Publishing Company from their father. By 1820 Heinrich Gessner had begun studies in theology at the University of Zurich, while Eduard was running the book business. It was about this time that the Gessners began to regularly take in German political refugees and offer them their hospitality for lengthy periods of time.[53] Their most important acquaintance had been made in the spring of 1820, when Karl Follen himself arrived in Zurich. Follen had impressed the Gessner brothers a great deal, and they were almost immediately ready to support whatever political cause he might suggest. Both brothers began to share in Karl and August Follen's revolutionary goals and their hatred for the enemies of German radicalism. Thus the two Follens had quickly found politically committed and financially potent supporters in Switzerland.

In the summer of 1820 Wit von Dörring had likewise arrived in Zurich. The Gessner brothers did not like him personally, and, in addition, they noticed an increasing antipathy between Follen and Wit while both were in Zurich that summer. Eventually the Gessners were forced to write letters to several radicals in Germany, warning them against political contacts with Wit. Karl Follen did not want to write these letters himself, ostensibly because it would have been very dangerous for anyone in Germany to be receiving mail from him.[54]

The Gessner bookstore was meanwhile being used as a front. It was a meeting place and point of reference for political radicals coming across the border from Germany. Wilhelm Snell, among others, was able to receive mail addressed to the bookstore from associates in Germany. When Sprewitz visited in the summer of 1821, Heinrich Gessner was made a member of the Youth League. From now on, visits from German radicals became even more frequent. Members of the Youth League's Jena branch visited Zurich, and so did Franz Lieber, one of the closest associates of Jahn. When August Follen arrived after his release from prison in the summer of 1821, he was invited to live in a room at the Gessners' house from October to December of 1821. He went on to publish a songbook entitled *Harfengrüsse aus Deutschland und der Schweiz* with the Gessners' publishing company. In order to explain and coordinate the goals and tactics he advocated, Karl Follen had initially jotted down the main principles of the new League of Young Men and conveyed them to Sprewitz, on a small piece of paper. This short document was later seized and publicized by the police authorities:

a. The purpose of the League is to be the destruction of the contemporary constitutions, in order to produce a situation in which the people may give itself a constitution through elected representatives.
b. The League should have two groups, one composed of somewhat older men who are already in the professions, the other composed of youths who are still in the process of educating themselves. The latter should not have so prominent a role.
c. The youths shall follow the orders of the elders of the League as long as these orders correspond to their convictions.

d. This League must be organized in such a way that each member personally knows only very few other members.

e. Each member shall acquire weapons and practice with them.

f. Nothing about the League may be written down.

g. Each member must pay a contribution.

h. Each member must swear an oath that he will betray nothing.

i. Any traitor will be punished with death.[55]

The Youth League, consequently, was to serve several concrete purposes. First, it would be a partner group for a League of Elders which Follen wanted to found among the most prominent liberals throughout Germany. This league would include intellectuals, professors, and even government or military officials. Second, the Youth League could try to help Follen and his closest friends seize power in case a revolutionary situation arose in Germany. If the German Confederation collapsed owing to an outside revolutionary event (for instance in France), Follen would thus already have at his disposal an organizational structure which would be valuable in times of turmoil. Third, the Youth League was supposed to influence university students continually and preserve their nationalist consciousness even though all Burschenschaften had been officially banned. The old support group in which Follen had previously placed his confidence, academic youth, thus was not to be given up under any circumstances.

From 1821 on the Youth League gradually expanded its scope. Sprewitz traveled around Germany to several universities, including Freiburg, Tübingen, Erlangen, and Jena, and secretly recruited new members. He also sent out friends to those places which he could not himself reach.[56] It is unlikely that concrete political actions were planned at this meeting: the league, according to Karl Follen's orders, was to be prepared in case the League of Elders (which supposedly existed) needed it in a revolutionary situation; it was not to attempt to start upheavals in Germany by itself. Once a circle of supporters and members had been won for the Youth League in various places, Sprewitz proceeded to call meetings in order to organize the league and familiarize the members with one another. The first Youth League meeting was to take place in Dresden in early June of 1821; however, only one of the invited radicals appeared at this organizational meeting. Sprewitz was thus faced with the fact that organizing a radical conspiratory group was not going to be as easy as he thought at first. The next meeting, held in Erlangen the following August, was more of a success: representatives from at least four universities appeared and actively took part in the discussion. In late October, there was another meeting which took place on Kyffhäuser Mountain, the symbolic site where, according to legend, Emperor Barbarossa was waiting to return and save Germany. There were also successful meetings in May and in September of 1822, both held in the Würzburg area.[57]

During the last two meetings, the participants actually hoped that the Swiss initiators of the league, perhaps including Karl and August Follen, would arrive and talk to them in person. This did not happen, however. Evidently Follen and the other important radicals now in Switzerland were too afraid of the security risk involved if they ventured so deep into German territory. Lack of contact with the actual leadership group, be it in fact organized in a League of Elders or only in theory, and lack of clarity about what the format and the goals of the league were in fact to be began in late 1822 to destabilize the Youth League. The members were increasingly puzzled about where funding was to come from, how extensive the membership was to be, and how far there was to be a cooperation with the Burschenschaften, which were still unofficially and secretly active. It was not surprising that in October of 1822 the Jena student leader Robert Wesselhöft suggested that the Youth League be dissolved and refounded, if at all, with a completely new orientation. He favored a loose association that would be more concerned with shielding those radicals who were being persecuted by the German authorities than with violent interventions into the interior affairs of the states of the German Confederation. Wesselhöft's suggestions were voted down among the key members of the league; nevertheless it was clear that full support from all members was on the wane.[58]

The League of Elders, which Follen had hoped would be established throughout Germany, never actually came into existence. Prussian statesmen and generals, including reformist figures like August von Gneisenau (1760–1831) and Heinrich von Bülow (1792–1846), could never actually be won as members of such an organization, nor could more openly radical figures such as Jahn or Arndt. Yet Follen attempted to convey the impression to members of the Youth League that there was indeed a complementary organization of high officials and intellectuals who would, in the case of a sudden development toward political change, come into contact with the young men and provide the national leadership which was necessary. The League of Elders thus served mainly as a contrived means of keeping the Youth League together and of raising the morale among the mostly very young radicals.[59]

It is evident, throughout the existence of the Youth League, that Karl Follen and the other German radicals at Basel were mostly concerned with the question of how they could most effectively start a revolution in Germany.[60] But they also hoped to bring about change in their home country with the support of radicals in other European countries. Eventually, as well, they were concerned with building up a European-wide network of radicals and producing uprisings and political change in as many countries as possible. Perhaps tapping the strength of foreign radical movements such as the French and Italian was a distinct possibility. By 1822 Karl Follen and Wilhelm Snell had realized the importance of international radicalism as a base for their own operations aimed at the German situation. They established further connections with Italian radicals and their secret leagues. While teaching school in Chur, Karl Follen had met the north Italian lawyer Joachim de Prati, whose association with the Carbonari had been discovered and who had thus fled to Switzerland. The Italian secret Sublimi Maestri Perfetti group, which advocated a free and united Italian nation but also strove for the revolutionary transformation of the world at large, wished to establish contacts to German radicals through de Prati.[61]

The Darmstadt revolutionary Heinrich Karl Hofmann had meanwhile continued his activities within Germany, in order to consolidate German radicalism. Even the Burschenschaften which had been forbidden after 1819 were soon thereafter reestablished unofficially, and in secret, at many universities throughout Germany and potentially could have helped in future revolutions. The politically engaged among the Jena University students, by 1821, were in fact expecting a European revolution to occur very soon. They continued to meet in secret and to observe as closely as they could the developments in radicalism outside Germany. The possible international contacts which German student groups would make at the same time always remained highly important to Follen. He had by this time clearly realized how important outside influences such as revolutionary stirrings in France or Italy could be for the German situation. In 1823, in addition, there was great distress among the Swiss emigrés. They strongly reacted to the news that the Spanish liberal government, installed after the revolutionary upheaval of 1820, had been abolished and that the liberal military leader, Rafael del Riego y Nunez (1785–1823), had been executed by the Restoration government. Every promising event within a possible Europe-wide revolutionary process was, from 1820 to 1823, of prime interest to Follen and his fellow radicals.[62]

## Prussian Pursuit

Even before the Mainz Central Investigation Commission had taken up its work, in September 1819 a state police agency was already collecting and evaluating large amounts of data in Prussia. This Immediate Investigation Commission at Berlin was headed by the Prussian minister of police, Wilhelm Ludwig Georg Fürst Wittgenstein (1770–1851), and its work was under the immediate direction of the senior police official *(Geheimer Regierungsrat)* at the ministry, Karl Albert von Kamptz.[63] While Wittgenstein took his duties as police minister seriously, wishing only to preserve tradition and suppress all new ideas, Kamptz became almost obsessed with actively fighting German radicalism, and with punishing those who had burned his military law code book after the Wartburg festival.

The Berlin commission itself became a center for the persecution and interrogation of German radicals from all over the German Confederation. It had its prison facilities in Köpenick, near Berlin; August Follen, Jahn, Wit von Dörring, and many others were held there and questioned extensively. Each interrogation was conducted very carefully, and personal papers, letters, and other evidence was carefully evaluated. One of the senior officials working for this commission and compiling its reports was the well-known poet and musician E. T. A. Hoffmann (1776–1822). Hoffmann's worldly profession was that of a lawyer in the service of the Prussian state, at the Ministry of Justice. This professional attachment provided for him a good salary, and even material for several of his books. His legal works were also quite extensive; it was he who compiled the reports on a number of radicals including Jahn, Rödiger (the Jena Burschenschaft leader and Wartburg speaker), Karl Follen's friend and confidant Ludwig von Mühlenfels, and also August Follen.[64]

Hoffmann had ridiculed the student groups and their romantic attachment to "Germanness" in the second volume of his satirical work *Lebensansichten des Katers Murr* (1821–1822). In his legal work, however, Hoffmann did not let these private sentiments influence him and recommended mild treatment for the prominent radicals being held in Berlin. In the case of August Follen, Hoffmann had to insist that Follen be kept in prison, but in many other cases he pleaded for a quick release, as with Rödiger. Hoffmann's liberal attitudes soon led to serious disagreements with Kamptz. The latter began to criticize Hoffmann's reports whenever he could, and challenged most of his decisions. Kamptz had Rödiger returned to prison, for example, after he had just been released by Hoffmann. In general, Kamptz often encouraged the police officers and the many secret agents sent out to catch fleeing radicals to be tougher in their approach. His goal was to get as many radicals imprisoned for long terms as he could. The Prussian police soon was burdened by a very bad reputation owing to Kamptz' unfair methods of interrogation, and the illegal, sometimes violent treatment which he tried to give prisoners at Köpenick. Eventually the only protection which remained for important radicals such as Jahn, imprisoned at Köpenick since the summer 1819, was to write directly to the king of Prussia and to take Kamptz to court himself.[65]

All of these radicals, captured and imprisoned for long periods in Köpenick without a clear idea of what they were being accused of, were interrogated at great length. What was also of particular concern to the prisoners was that the Berlin commission working on them had to first clarify for itself what the punishment for various suspicious acts was to be, and which courts were to be responsible for which crimes, since the commission could only hold prisoners for interrogation, but could not actually judge them itself. From 1819 to 1821 the life of August Follen intersected with the decisions of the Berlin commission in an unfavorable and consequential way. While Karl Follen had escaped imprisonment and interrogation in Germany by fleeing to Switzerland, the case of his brother August provides a marked contrast. For two years, the latter remained in prison and was not able to follow Karl to Switzerland until late 1821. There he lived a life dominated by his interest in German cultural romanticism and characterized by a withdrawal from politics, never able to return permanently to Germany until his death in 1855.[66]

## The End of the Youth League

By the summer of 1822 significant rifts had developed within the Youth League which Karl Follen had founded through Karl von Sprewitz. Many of the members were not as much in agreement on tactics as they had previously thought, and the hope for a revolutionary uprising, which had kept the league alive for over a year, was fading more and more into the background. Key members such as Robert Wesselhöft began to withdraw, at least temporarily, from the league and from the student scene in general.[67] Even at the University of Jena, at which the idea of revolution had been welcomed most ardently, the students were by the spring of 1822 losing confidence in the league. Sprewitz later told the police about the mood in the league during the year 1822: "I have to confess that I never opposed the League because the law forbids political associations, but only because I had come to the conviction that our [German] people neither wanted a revolution, nor could it possibly have wanted one, because of the level of its education."[68]

The actual activities of the Youth League had been minimal since it had been founded, and by the time of a secret general meeting at Nuremberg in October of 1822, Robert Wesselhöft was speaking for most members when he suggested that the league disband. He noted that the chances of actually influencing political events were minute, that the league posed great personal dangers for each member, and that the mysterious League of Elders, which was supposed to be cooperating in secret, had so far never been in evidence.[69] The Youth League did struggle on with little success until August 1823. Subsequently, before it had had a chance to formally disband, the entire organization was discovered and destroyed by the Prussian government. A Bavarian student named Johann Andreas Dietz, worried about his ability to take the upcoming university exams, and accepting money for the information he could provide, betrayed the league to the Prussian government. He was interrogated very carefully on August 31 and September 1 of 1823, and provided a list of thirty-five names of Youth League members.[70] On December 3 the territorial governments were informed by the Central Investigation Committee in Mainz, and many of the members were arrested and pressed to make disclosures about the group's activities. Sprewitz was arrested on January 24, 1824. Everything about the league had already been betrayed to the authorities by then. Sprewitz stabbed himself in the chest three times with a knife while in prison, but then recuperated sufficiently to tell the police whatever they were still unclear about.

The total number of Youth League members was subsequently estimated at no more than two hundred. The great majority of these, though not all part of the leadership group, had been Burschenschaft members in the past and had been willing to extend their political commitment beyond 1819. Most of Sprewitz' closest associates soon were imprisoned at Köpenick near Berlin. By 1825 twenty-six former Youth League members were temporarily released, eleven were cleared of all charges, four were no longer alive, and many others were sentenced to long prison terms in jails all over the German Confederation. The administration of punishment was particularly harsh for the 120 to 150 members arrested in Prussia. Most of these had previously been members of the Burschenschaft. The leadership group of the league had looked upon these students as willing instruments for their cause. The governments were very harsh in their response to suspected conspiracies, whether they were persecuting young students or older revolutionary leaders.

Karl Follen's revolutionary message had carried the Youth League only that far; his hope that revolution would break out again in France, and that this upheaval would spill over into other European countries including Germany, did not materialize. Rather, Follen was now forced to watch as each one of his young associates in Germany was picked up by the Prussian authorities and questioned. A note by the Prussian police chief Kamptz was sent around to various territorial governments and universities in Germany; it urgently requested information on the whereabouts of Heinrich Gessner, whom the police supposed to have been one of the main actors in the Youth League in Germany. Gessner was finally arrested and brought to Berlin, where he was extensively questioned and thereafter imprisoned.[71] The role of the Prussian police authorities, meanwhile, was attacked frequently as unfair and unjust. The radical Arnold Ruge, one of those investigated at Köpenick, for instance reported in his memoirs that the official questioning him only dictated to the stenographer what he found worth noting, but suppressed the rest of the proceedings. Many of the detained radicals thus thought of themselves as martyrs for the cause of a united Germany when they were given an unfair trial and then handed a harsh prison term.[72] This conception of martyrdom, rather than any form of concrete political influence, had been the league's main achievement.

The harsh persecution of the Youth League also ruined such political activities of the Burschenschaften as still existed, if only in secret, at the individual German universities. Since the Burschenschaften were now known to be still active, they were drawn into the Youth League investigations and their structure was increasingly discovered by the authorities. Thus they suffered the loss of many members, as the governments were alerted and watched the student scene even more closely and carefully. The governments now decided to legally categorize the Burschenschaften in a different way: they were now classified not only as illegal but also as subversive, and their members faced prison terms of six to ten years if discovered.[73] With the arrest of most of the members and sympathizers of the Youth League throughout Germany, the Swiss leadership group which had attempted to exert total control over the league, and thus over much of the radical potential in Germany, suddenly became again the focus of German police interest and antagonism. Once the significance of the Swiss actors for the German scene had been recognized in Prussia, Austria, and the other German states, the demands for extradition which had already posed a great danger to Karl Follen during his stay at Chur were immediately renewed.

The Swiss and the German governments had both been suspicious about the German refugees in Switzerland ever since 1820. Even before Karl and August Follen's arrival, there had been rumors that the persecuted Burschenschafter of Germany were planning to meet at a second edition of the Wartburg festival, this time on the Swiss mountain Rütli. Leadership was to be provided by the former German professor Lorenz Oken, who had himself been viewed with reservations by the Mainz commission because of his outspoken liberal opinions. Karl Follen's position in Switzerland was, in addition, made especially difficult from the start by a series of newspaper articles which Wit von Dörring had written about German radicalism for the English newspaper *Morning Chronicle* from November 1819 to January 1820. Revealing many previously well kept secrets, Wit wrote about the political situation in German universities and the character of the German nationalist movement. He was also frank and outspoken about the aggressive revolutionary goals of the Giessen Blacks. Wit's article of November 16, 1819, for example, entitled "German conspiracies," never specifically mentioned Karl Follen's name, but it did reveal intimate details about the "Giessen friends" of whom Follen was known to have been the leader. The subtitle of the article, revolutionary and inflammatory in tone, consisted of the motto of the Giessen Blacks: "Si medicina non sanat, ferrum sanat, si ferrum non sanat, ignis tunavid [sic]."[74] Although the main aim of Wit's articles may indeed have been self-aggrandizement and an attack on the Prussian legal system rather than betrayal of his former radical friends throughout Germany, the latter effect certainly occurred. Even the radical statements which Wit made on the nature of and necessity for revolution were assumed in Germany to have had their origin in Karl Follen's radical thought.

In a letter of late October 1820, Karl Follen sent a warning to Wit von Dörring, whose loyalty he no longer fully trusted:

Remember the importance of this point, . . . that every unreflected step, which draws attention to this country and thus to us all, is in fact an act of treason. Remember that you belong to us, whether this is good for you or bad. You may understand the meaning of this sentence in terms of what I wrote to you before, and know that every false move will threaten not only our physical existence, but also all that for which we are striving.[75]

After he had returned to the Continent, Wit was imprisoned in Milan toward the end of 1822, because the local government did not trust his political activities in northern Italy. He was soon able to escape, however, and thereafter returned to Zurich. The Gessner brothers were by then not willing to meet with him. Eventually Wit claimed that Eduard Gessner and the former German Burschenschaft member Graf Theodor von Bocholz, now living in Swiss exile, were planning to take him outside the city of Zurich, shoot him, and abandon the body where it would be hard to find. Bocholz later denied this, but Heinrich Gessner confessed during his interrogations in Berlin that Bocholz had in fact threatened to shoot Wit in his own presence. Wit thus had been forced to leave town as soon as possible.[76]

The situation became critical when both Sprewitz and Wit von Dörring were arrested and brought to Köpenick near Berlin for interrogation in early 1824. Faced with the Prussian investigation committee, and risking life imprisonment if they did not tell all they knew, both radicals had no other choice but to describe in a detailed way Karl Follen's role in their activities. Follen had indeed been the actual founder of the Unconditionals, in his room in Jena plans for the assassination of Czar Alexander of Russia had been discussed, he had established connections with French radicals in Paris in 1820, and he was, finally, responsible for the formation of the Youth League. Even Victor Cousin, the French subject Follen had met earlier and remained in close contact with, was arrested in Dresden in December of 1824 and intensively interrogated about his recent travels, which included visits to Switzerland. Although the Prussian police could find out very little about the supposed League of Elders, they were able to completely break the resistance of Sprewitz, who was still recuperating from his suicide attempt, and to establish clearly and in detail the organization and membership of the Youth League. Those members who were not able to leave Germany immediately were arrested a few days later and eventually sentenced to long terms in prison.[77]

Karl Follen's role meanwhile was increasingly given bad press not only by the Berlin and Mainz investigation results but also within radical circles themselves. Arnold Ruge, formerly a devoted member of the Youth League, purposely revealed in his 1862 memoirs that Karl Follen had been the "originator of the myth of a League of Elders," and had thus tried to secure the loyalty of young and inexperienced students to his own true purposes, which he kept secret. Ruge went further than this in his accusations. When he heard that the league was disintegrating and in great danger of being discovered, Karl Follen evidently panicked. The Youth League member Hildebrandt visited Karl Follen in Basel just before the league was discovered by the authorities, and brought back to Germany the message that "we must all take up the dagger and immediately kill all German princes. Only in this way can the people be awakened out of its death sleep. Something incredible has to happen, or nothing at all will change." The league members were all united in their immediate rejection of this order, which called for an immediate practical application of Follen's tactic of "la guerre des individus." The trust they had once been willing to place in Karl Follen, whom most had never personally met, was gone once and for all. Arnold Ruge himself was one of the most outspoken opponents of taking up arms and turning to assassinations which would not necessarily produce a revolutionary situation, but rather waste the lives of many young students.[78]

Karl Follen and his brother August did not fare much better in the opinion of Friedrich List, the German economist, liberal, and emigré in Switzerland. A dispute over finances and political tactics ended List's relationship with August Follen, to whom List wrote in June of 1824: "That we will in the future have nothing to do with each other anymore is obvious; you don't even have to tell me this."[79] Only because of the danger to his own safety, should August Follen choose to betray him to the government, List said, "am I holding back what I should really tell [the authorities about] you, your brother, and all those who have played a role in this game." List now realized why August Follen had earlier told him about Karl Follen's radicalism, including the assertion that for the latter, "everything was just calculation."[80] So Karl Follen's enterprises were being successfully prosecuted and dispersed by the German authorities, and were increasingly falling into disfavor with his own political associates as well. But even toward the end of his stay in Switzerland, Follen still hoped for a return to Germany, and expressed the wish to do so in a letter to his sister Luise (who was still living in Giessen) dated March 8, 1820:

A while ago I asked father about a visa for him [August Follen] and myself, issued by the Hessian government, but I have not yet heard from him. Was the letter perhaps lost in the mail? In any case I would like to ask you . . . again to write a note to father, that he should go to the Grand Duke with this request! I have been cleared of all charges in the Sand case by the Weimar courts. August's case is being dealt with by the Prussian courts. Should there have been any legal decisions in Hesse against us, those have lost their validity because of our long exile.[81]

## Karl Follen's Flight to America

As stubbornly determined as the Swiss government was in resisting foreign interference in its own affairs, the pressure from Prussia and Austria to extradite both Follen brothers now increased to an almost intolerable level. The question of bringing German emigrés in Switzerland like the Follen brothers, the Snell brothers, and their acquaintance Karl Völker to trial in Prussian courts now became an international diplomatic issue.[82] Not only the Prussians and Austrians but also the French and other governments soon sent numbers of agents to Switzerland in order to find out more about the whereabouts and activities of the refugees hiding throughout the country. Although the radical emigrés had the sympathy of a large part of the educated Swiss population, they still could not completely escape the surveillance of agents sent out by their home governments. Furthermore, the foreign secret police agents were paid more when they produced interesting results: this was a strong incentive to exaggerate the frequent reports they sent home, claiming that the Germans, the French, and others hiding in Switzerland were still politically dangerous to their home countries.[83]

The person nominated by the Prussian foreign minister Count Bernstorff to travel to Switzerland and seek the extradition of the Follen brothers, certain other Germans, and even to interrogate the Gessners, who were Swiss citizens, was the diplomat Sixt von Armin. He was not necessarily a reactionary enemy of Switzerland, but still a Prussian government official who was required to fulfill his duty.[84] Von Arnim's first interest had to be to return August Follen, against whom an official court sentence had been pronounced, to Prussia. When informed that his brother now faced a renewed threat of extradition, Karl Follen wrote a calming letter to Süsette Ritzmann, August's Swiss bride, as late as February 16, 1824:

The court sentence against my brother would probably never have been made public, had not his enemies contacted the Prussian ambassador in order to raise up . . . suspicions. For the Prussian government itself cannot be interested in forcing my brother, through new acts of violence, to publicize all the injustice which he has had to endure from it. Thus I don't believe that the Prussian government will insist on its demands.[85]

August Follen was indeed able to resist extradition and finally to escape it altogether. When he was to be taken from Switzerland to Berlin in 1824, he became very ill, and was much too sick to travel.[86] Von Arnim, who visited Follen with the intention of forcing him to return to Berlin immediately, decided that Follen could not have survived the long trip to Berlin. When he had recovered again, the fact that he had been made a Swiss citizen added to the difficulties of the Prussian cause. Finally, in December 1824, the Prussians gave up on their claim to August Follen, even though the Swiss cantonal government of Aargau seemed almost willing to let him be taken off.[87] Evidently the Prussians had now decided to concentrate their efforts on securing Karl Follen and his friend Wilhelm Snell, who were both active in Basel, along with several other German emigrés.

While August was thus able to remain in Switzerland, the events of Karl's life developed in a much more dramatic way. In a letter to Karl Christian Sartorius in Mexico, written in early 1825, Follen described the last several months of 1824:

> For almost three years I had been a law instructor at the University of Basel, and taught there with great enthusiasm. On November 27 of last year three diplomatic messages suddenly arrived from Prussia, Austria, and Russia, which demanded that Switzerland and Basel in particular extradite Wilhelm Snell and myself, as the leaders of a great conspiracy, to Prussia as the general inquisitor of the Holy Alliance. This request was supported by two messages from Giessen and Nassau, who wanted us, as their born citizens, to be extradited to Prussia.[88]

At first the Basel government was not willing to cooperate with the Prussian authorities and extradite Karl Follen, Wilhelm Snell, Wilhelm Wesselhöft, and Karl Völker, all of whom were to face charges in Berlin of taking part in a revolutionary conspiracy against the German Confederation. The Basel authorities wrote that they "wished to protect the professors Snell and Follenius, and reserved the right to conduct their own investigations of participants in revolutionary activities."[89] Follen and his friends soon had to swear an official oath stating that they had never acted subversively in Switzerland or elsewhere, and were thus eligible for Swiss governmental protection. The Swiss government decided to initiate its own investigations of Follen and others before ruling on the extradition issue.

The oath Karl Follen had been required to take was part of a new Swiss legal measure known as the *Press- und Fremdenkonklusum* (Provision Concerning the Press and the Treatment of Foreigners) of July 14, 1823, which called for severe systematic control over all foreign subjects in Switzerland. Its concrete measures included press censorship and investigation of those persons who seemed suspicious on account of their political past or their supposed subversive activities while in Switzerland. Actually, this new set of regulations was intended more to pacify hostile international opinion held by the Restoration governments against Switzerland than to institute domestic suppression. The Holy Alliance, in any case, was not satisfied, and the Swiss increasingly had to come to the conclusion that they were heavily vulnerable to the other European governments. The danger of armed intervention could no longer be completely ruled out.[90]

As the efforts of his persecutors were thus continually being stepped up, Karl Follen's ideals of freedom, equality, and unity did not seem achievable in Germany by 1824. Follen had to realize that life in Europe free from difficulties with police and legal authorities and free from employment restrictions was going to be impossible, at least in the near future. Therefore he was forced to look around for new horizons, for an environment which would allow him to be safe from persecution on the one hand, and on the other hand would give him time to think and plan for the future of Germany and Europe. There had already been speculation in Follen's circle about a possible refuge for German radicals in North America by 1819 or 1820. America was the last hope for these men who understood that their situation would get progressively worse and more restricted in Germany. A poem, probably written by one of the Follen brothers, was found among the papers of one of their closest friends. Two stanzas show Follen's current state of mind and his expectations for life in the United States:

> Freedom is dying! The old Greek heroes,
> Who died for their country's rights,
> They are buried! Broken-down halls,
> are all that remind us of the better worlds.
> Cross-bearers, who carry the sins of the world,
> have now become sons of their grandchildren.

No daring will, no strength!
No! Men kneel here before the despotic hordes.

I will go out to look for a new fatherland,
Which father Franklin's love built up,
The worthy world, trusting its own strength,
the young rights of freedom want to glow.
Over there she is growing up like a young oak tree.
We bring strength to the young flames,
to the new crusade, the promised land.
Rome is where free Romans stand together![91]

There is also an early statement by Karl Follen himself, drawn up in Germany, on the possibility of emigration to America. The Prussian police authorities captured his "Memorandum on the Founding of a German-American University"[92] (written in 1819) when they arrested Ludwig Snell in January of 1820. The "Memorandum" made three points clear. One was Follen's realization that his political mobility was becoming extremely limited in Germany. The next was his trust that America possessed a republican form of government and a free society which would grant protection for any European refugee. The third point was that Follen hoped he could emigrate to America, but retain a primary concern with the German political situation while in the United States. He was not interested in working at an American university, but rather in founding a German one in America. He wanted to avoid assimilation into the American way of life, and keep the German ideals of his followers intact. It seems evident from this third point that Follen hoped to return to Germany one day with a whole group of like-minded men who had physically survived, and had also reconstructed their political views and theories, in the free society represented by America.[93]

Follen began his "Memorandum" by describing how the hopes of 1813 had been shattered in Germany, and how, instead of freedom and democracy, a stubborn system of oppression had been established. He made clear how wrong all those had been who hoped for improvement to come only from God, or only from outside Germany, or only from the highest government officials. But even those who placed their hope in political change to be brought about at the hands of the popular masses or through an organized bloody revolution did not see their dreams fulfilled. Plans for reform through the influence of education or the press could never be strong enough to force the powerful governments into submission. The "friends of freedom," as Follen called the organized political radicals in Germany around 1819, thus faced the dilemma of how to preserve any chance of influencing German politics and of returning to their home country in the future. He recognized the need for shelter as well as for intellectual discussion:

> We are lacking an independent meeting point, and this can only be based in a German educational institution which includes all areas of human knowledge. This institution must become the refuge of spiritual freedom, which is suppressed so harshly in Germany, and the refuge of all those who have fought for spiritual freedom and have lost their employment in the process.[94]

Follen thought that the new institution could "work for the German cause in America," that country which was the "archetype of a free state constructed according to the laws of reason." The new institution had three main areas of importance: as a refuge and source of income for political emigrés; as a center for the association of all Germans in America in a free state; and as a means to teach the North American people their duty to bring freedom to the whole world. It is evident that emigration to America was attractive to German radicals even as early as 1820. By the 1830s, this idea would attract an ever-increasing number of people. Paul Follen, the youngest of the three Follen brothers, founded the "Giessen Emigration Society" in the middle of the decade and eventually organized a voyage for a large group of Hessians, farmers, workmen, and intellectuals who wished to begin a new life in Missouri.[95]

Having considered emigration to America at least in some detail, late in the fall of 1824 Follen hastily left Basel, claiming that he wished to visit his brother August, who was still extremely ill in Aargau. But Follen never returned to Basel. He had been tipped off by local friends that he should have himself smuggled out of the country within the next few days, or he would inevitably be extradited to Prussia and face a long and strenuous trial and possible execution for high treason.[96] Leaving Switzerland with a false passport and travel money collected by his Basel friends, Follen hid in a horse-drawn wagon which left Basel at night. He was able by early November to proceed through France to Le Havre and to board a ship, the

*Cadmus*, for New York. He traveled with Karl Beck (1798–1866), a south German radical who had also been a political refugee in Switzerland. Beck was the stepson of the theologian Wilhelm Leberecht De Wette. Himself also a doctor of theology, Beck was not allowed to take an academic job in Germany after his stepfather had been removed from the University of Berlin. Beck had managed, however, like De Wette, to find a teaching post at Basel. Follen had been invited to join one of his closest Giessen friends, Karl Christian Sartorius, who had recently emigrated from Darmstadt to Mexico, and who wished to gather a colony of German radicals there in order to build up a German free state. However, Follen decided to go to the United States instead, since he had been able to acquire several recommendations from the Marquis de Lafayette which would help secure him a place to stay and rather quick academic employment.

The journal which Karl Follen kept on the sea voyage to New York City shows a mixture of relief that he was able to escape persecution and hope for a better and freer life in America.[97] The ship sailed via the Bermudas to Virginia, and finally entered New York harbor on December 19, 1824. Once on land, Follen and Beck exchanged their money and spent a few days in New York before traveling south to Philadelphia, in order to be nearer to the German community and look for possible employment. One of the first letters Follen wrote upon his arrival in New York was to his family in Hesse:

> From Basel, where I just sent my first letter from New York, you must have already received the news of our voyage and our happy arrival in the homeland of freedom. Considering the season we had a good trip; the storm of November 19 was not dangerous for an American ship on the high seas. In New York we were received very cordially by the men to whom we had been recommended. We got a room in a French boarding house, because our English is not adequate as yet. . . . From New York, I wrote to Lafayette to tell him about the reasons for our emigration and our current situation.[98]

Follen maintained his battle for the abstract ideals of freedom, social justice, and political commitment in the New World, but the concrete issues he became interested in changed greatly owing to his completely new surroundings. Follen eventually abandoned any activism that had to do with German politics, and began to concentrate on conveying German cultural values to his new American friends. The idea of a German university or free state in America gradually waned. Follen did not follow the invitation of Karl Christian Sartorius to Mexico. He cut himself off from the German community in Philadelphia by moving to Boston. More central in his life became American religious issues of the time, and the specifically American problem of slavery.

# 4

# GERMAN CULTURE AND AMERICAN REFORM

With his arrival in the United States, and in the sixteen remaining years of his life thereafter, Karl Follen (who now began to call himself Charles) discovered completely new social and political crusades to engage in, but at the same time saw no significant change in his own personality or fundamental ethical outlook. Follen made contributions to several areas of American life which, during the 1820s and 1830s, were characterized mainly by rapid change and heated controversy. The Unitarian Church, in which Follen became first a lay preacher and eventually a minister, separated itself from orthodox Calvinism and, in a difficult process, defined itself as an independent denomination. Follen also joined the antislavery crusade, at this time perhaps the most spirited but also least popular and least socially accepted of reform movements. He began his energetic activities, however, by bringing German cultural ideas and assumptions with him across the Atlantic.[1]

The first half of this chapter will focus on characterizing the cultural setting into which Follen entered upon his arrival in New England; the second half will be concerned primarily with the representations of German culture that Follen conveyed to Americans as instructor in German, and later as Professor of German, at Harvard. These views, expressed in conversations, lectures, and essays, were not what other Germans might have brought; in fact, they were dominated by his very own personal biases and preferences. On the one hand, Follen certainly contributed in a significant way to the spreading of conventional knowledge about German literature, theology, and philosophy in the United States. On the other hand, the personal agenda which lay behind his message of what the German nation was, and what it should be, dominated the influence he was able to exert.[2] Follen meant to tell Americans about those aspects of Germany which he considered important for the furthering of national consciousness, human freedom, and moral perfection; he did not concur with those currently espoused by the Restoration governments. Eventually, Follen's idealist and libertarian vision of German culture and thought was amalgamated with the world view and current intellectual needs of his new American environment.

When he came to the United States in December of 1824, Follen was twenty-eight years old. Almost five years of exile in Switzerland lay behind him; now he was once again uprooted and about to begin a new life. An American witness, writing in 1853, recalled his first impression of the European newcomer:

> Dr. Follen had the features and stature of the Suabian race. He was rather short, with a round and large head, set very closely on square shoulders, a large mouth which easily relaxed into a broad smile, eyes set very far apart, large and somewhat projecting, a great width at the temples, and a broad and retreating forehead, on which a little thin brown silken hair lay softly.[3]

Follen was now a mature man, trained and ready to work in a profession and contribute actively to the intellectual and political life of his surroundings. He had acquired his education in Germany, but had had little chance so far to put it to use in civil society.

The first thesis of this chapter is that Follen gradually became fully assimilated in America. After a few years, he was forced to abandon the plan which he and other German radicals had speculated about from early on, and which he had discussed in his "Memorandum on a German-American University" (1819),[4] that of an autonomous German free state on the North American continent. Instead, like many other German exiles in the first half of the nineteenth century, Follen perfected his English, acquired American citizenship, and married an American woman. He gradually turned from unfulfillable German dreams to an active engagement in American reform. The second thesis is that while adapting to specific American conditions and American issues, Follen did not significantly alter his own radical and activist personality in the United States. He always remained a man who found it extremely difficult to form compromises with the society in which he lived, and he retained a fanatical commitment to political and social reform. The attainment of his own ideals was always more important to him than the dire consequences for his own life in society. In America Follen once again pursued the course which he believed to be the only "moral" one, without flinching. He was still driven by his never-failing sense of social and political "duty." Once again he needed outlets, this time specifically American ones, for the energy which he had previously put into political radicalism in Germany and Switzerland. And again he made more enemies than friends, and could not remain in one job for more than a few years, whether as Harvard professor of German language and literature (from 1830 to 1835) or as Unitarian minister in New York City (from 1836 to 1838). Time was to show that even in a free country with a republican form of government, Follen could find flaws to recognize and attack; his career in America was thus to be as turbulent and changeable as that in Europe had been.

## America as Image and Reality

Disembarking from the ship *Cadmus* in New York in December of 1824, Follen was faced with a new world in many different respects. He had to learn a new language and find employment in order to ensure his personal survival. He also had to come to terms with a new political system and a different organization of society. However, the recent political development of American society toward liberty and democracy was in many important ways congruent with the vision presented in the plans which Follen had made for Germany during his youth. Jacksonian America had embarked on the course of industrialization and popular democracy in the modern sense,[5] and was engaged in a quest for a national identity that had begun in the last quarter of the eighteenth century and was now more vital than ever before.[6] The republican political system, a daring experiment in modern times and previously unparalleled throughout the world except in France, had to prove its own stability and be consolidated. Complementary to issues of practical politics, there was also the question of national symbols and of an independent national literature, particularly one free from the domination of Great Britain.[7] In certain ways, the American experience was similar to that of the German nationalist movement that had arisen during the Napoleonic period. Although Germans had only been able to dream of a democratic future, many Americans became absorbed by a strong sense of mission, by a desire to reform and improve their communities and their country. They believed that progress was definitely possible in such areas as political and economic development, social justice, and moral behavior.[8]

Russel B. Nye has argued that the War of 1812 had hastened the completion of a national feeling in America. It had made Americans "feel and act more like a nation."[9] There is a distinctive parallel here to the German Wars of Liberation of 1813, which had at the same time functioned as a catalyst of nationalism in Central Europe. The Union, according to Nye, was essential to American political thought and national feeling after 1812; the German liberal movement of the same period also pressed for the creation of a unified German nation state. The idea that America was destined to national greatness and that Americans had a moral and political mission to fulfill in the world, which gathered momentum during the Jacksonian period, was similarly to be found in Germany in the writings of Jahn and Arndt and their followers after the defeat of Napoleonic France.

As a recent arrival in America, Charles Follen in 1825 had a fixed image of his new home in his mind, dominated by the concepts of freedom, equality, and the rights of the individual. This decidedly European view of America had been fostered repeatedly by travel reports about the United States that had become available in Germany after 1800. The reports had been received enthusiastically by most European liberals, who recognized the realization of their own dreams in what they heard about America. Follen's reactions to this new world may for instance be compared with those of Duke Bernhard of Saxony-Weimar, detailed in the latter's travel description.[10] Bernhard of Saxony-Weimar arrived in America in 1825, at the same time as Charles Follen, and traveled extensively for more than a year. Duke Bernhard's report, although written in an objective style, conveyed the image of a new society full of vitality and hope in the United States.

Another German contemporary who arrived a few years after Follen was the German radical student, gymnast, and revolutionary Francis Lieber (1800–1872).[11] Lieber had visited Karl Follen in Switzerland in 1821, and may have been a member of, or at least associated with, the Youth League. By the early 1830s, his political career in Germany was over. This emigré wrote to his family just before setting out for America:

From all the letters I should judge you have taken a wrong view of my hopes and anticipations with regard to America. Believe me I do not expect a paradise, but I look forward eagerly to the prospect of a more settled and active life, and an honorable and useful position in a young republic, which, however imperfect it may still be, yet gives a field for the practice and application of talent and ability. I shall of course miss much that I have been accustomed to in Europe, especially the intellectual life; but it will be more congenial to me than Europe with her effete institutions, for I shall feel that I am in a land of progress, where civilization is building her home, while in Europe we can scarcely tell whether there is progression or retrogression.[12]

Another example of travel reports as sources of a specific image of America is the extensive panorama of American society, politics, and geography provided some years later by Ludwig De Wette, son of the theologian, who traveled widely throughout the United States for sixteen months in the 1830s, and spent much of his time in New England.[13] De Wette was in general extremely impressed with the progress of American society and politics, with American reform efforts, educational opportunities, and the great interest in the discussion of religious topics among most people, even those who were less well educated. At the same time De Wette did not fail to mention some of the problems of his host country, especially the fate of Native Americans, who lived in what he considered miserable poverty, and the blacks, who were being mistreated by what he termed the "awful slave-trade." He was convinced that slavery was "highly unnatural and unjust," and that society was going to have to be changed in order to destroy this social and economic institution.[14] Despite these negative aspects, however, the concept which seemed central to De Wette and which fascinated him most about the country he was visiting was that of social equality.[15]

It is in the context of these descriptions that Charles Follen's own expectations and first impressions of America must be envisioned. His thoughts in late 1824 and in 1825 are recorded in a diary which he kept while crossing the Atlantic and during his first few days in New York; and in several letters written to his family in Germany. On November 19, 1824, Follen wrote the following poem into his diary:

> If you love me, take my hand,
> Let us wander, let us roam,
> Westward with the sun;
> There on the other side of the ocean,
> There is the home of freedom, the home of humanity.[16]

Similarly, Follen's first elated letters to his family in Hesse restate the widely held image of America as a place of democracy, freedom, and hope for oppressed German refugees.[17] In a letter written shortly after Follen had landed in New York, he said about American politics, which were so different from those he had known in central Europe:

> Politics concerns everyone here; it is really true that every kitchen maid takes part in it and reads the public papers which are published in a great number here. There are no secrets kept from the people, but instead the rule applies that the care for the entire polity is up to everyone, including the common people. Whoever comes here citing conceptions of noble privilege is taken to be a fool. This world of political reason has so greatly affected some noble fools that they had to be brought to the local insane asylum, which is established in a very wise and humanitarian fashion.[18]

In the same letter, Follen added to his first impressions of American freedom:

> The government interferes scarcely at all, but acts merely as a defense against breaches of the law; and there is certainly no country where one lives more securely without passports, police officers, and soldiers, than here. Almshouses and penitentiaries are more perfect here than elsewhere. In education they make rapid progress. For the rest, they let men alone; and thus every thing is much better done than when it is accomplished by direction of the authorities.[19]

Follen at first saw America as a haven of safety and a liberal republic worth preserving and improving, and referred to it in a letter, as previously in his poem, as the "native land of freedom." The image in his mind contained many of his radical European ideals: popular sovereignty, civil rights, freedom of the press, and social equality of all citizens. However, Follen was also bound to notice how significantly different specific American political issues and social conditions were from those in Europe. Although many of his most basic German assumptions about politics, religion, and social issues remained applicable, they had to be transposed to a new society.

In addition, during his life in the United States, Follen's largely positive view of American society and politics had to be amended in many ways. While he was strongly convinced that the new form of government and politics being tested in America should be defended and upheld, after several years of residence in the United States Follen saw much room for improvement. As had been the case with De Wette, Follen began to look critically at those aspects of American society which he considered negative, such as slavery. Again he recognized that the United States, so recently founded, could not remain politically and socially static, but instead was in need of carefully orchestrated change. Follen's active involvement in several reform movements once again characterized his way of life.

Many reform movements sprang up in America beginning in the 1820s, including the temperance movement, many forms of social benevolence motivated by religious and humanitarian ideals, and the communitarian movement; the 1830s saw the sudden and dramatic rise of the immediatist antislavery movement.[20] According to Russel B. Nye, American reformers were driven by the following principles: faith in progress; faith in the individual's ability to control himself and his society and to direct both toward higher ends; what Nye calls the Enlightenment tradition of benevolence; and a sense of national mission. Citing the strong connections which American reformers had with their counterparts in England, he claims that "reform was in the air on both sides of the Atlantic, and the winds of change blew equally strong in London, Paris, Frankfurt, and Boston."[21] Charles Follen, of course, was no stranger to the problems, as well as the possibilities, of such movements.

The reformers themselves constituted a group which is not easy to interpret today. They exhibited pragmatism, social awareness, faith in the perfectability of man, and a strong commitment to their goals. But they have also been criticized by historians for their "extremism, fanaticism, eccentricity, and contentiousness," and even for "working to extinguish basic liberties" in society.[22] Charles Follen's career in Germany had shown a similar tension between high ideals and ruthless ways of achieving them. Eventually he would again move back and forth between these two extremes in the United States. Writing home to his father and stepmother in Giessen in 1826, Charles Follen promised that "there is in this country, where law alone governs, no more quiet citizen than I."[23] He soon realized, however, that he could not remain as silent and satisfied as he had thought upon his arrival.

## Follen Arrives at Harvard

The first order of the day for Follen, in the winter of 1824–25, was to secure the support of some influential Americans who sympathized with his problems and would write him letters of recommendation. The Philadelphia businessman Peter DuPonceau, for instance, wrote to a certain John Davis in 1825, introducing Charles Follen:

> I do myself the pleasure of introducing to your acquaintance Dr. Charles Follen, late Professor of the Civil Law in the University of Basel in Switzerland. The Holy Alliance have thought him dangerous, because he was a Republican in a Republic, and the government of Basel, much against his [Follen's] will, have been compelled to expel him. He is come to this, the only country where he can be safe. He is studying the Common Law and intends to practice it in our German Counties, for which he will soon be qualified. I doubt not his succeeding well in this state—General Lafayette thinks highly of him and recommended him to me.[24]

Follen's first year in the United States was spent in New York and Philadelphia. He arrived in New York City on December 19, 1824, together with Karl (Charles) Beck, the stepson of the theologian De Wette. Both emigrés were aided by the merchant De Rham, who exchanged their money and found them lodgings. This reception had previously been arranged by General Lafayette, who had written in advance to several American friends in order to ensure the aid Follen would need to begin a new life. Once in America, Follen again wrote to Lafayette asking for advice on how to proceed in this new environment. He received an answer, dated January 2, 1825, containing references and names of prominent Americans to whom he could turn for help:

> Although Upper Pennsylvania is peopled mostly by old Germans, their occupations, more agricultural than literary, if they offer good opportunities for husbandmen, are yet not so favorable for your companion and you as a residence in Cambridge, near Boston, which is the part of the country where German literature is held in the highest honor. You will find, in that university, the Professors Everett and Ticknor and some others, and the President himself, Dr. Kirkland, all much disposed to aid you. Appointments to office, and other literary advantages, are things which do not depend upon their favor; but they will render the time agreeable to you which is necessary for learning English, an indispensible condition in the United States.[25]

In January of 1825 Follen moved to a boarding house in Philadelphia and tried to establish contacts with the German community there while he looked for a means of employment. It was from here that he wrote his first long letters home to his father and stepmother, describing his impressions of America and his own situation at the beginning of a new phase of life:

> I, with my jurisprudence and philosophy, can only find a sphere of action, suited to my former life, in some one of the higher seminaries in this country. From Lafayette I received a very friendly answer on the subject. He advised me to go to Philadelphia first, and then to Cambridge, near Boston, the seat of the most celebrated university in the United States, and promised to give me, at this place, letters of introduction there.[26]

Follen soon realized that a career in law would be almost impossible to pursue in America. He would have to learn the legal system of the United States from the very beginning, and it would take him years before he could become a practicing lawyer. Thus Follen eventually decided on a career in teaching. Beck had already turned in this direction, and had found employment as a teacher at the newly established, educationally progressive Round Hill School in Northampton, Massachusetts.[27] In Philadelphia, at the end of January, Follen met George Ticknor, a young professor of modern languages at Harvard University. Ticknor had recently returned from Göttingen University, where he had studied philology, and had been among the first Americans to receive German academic training. General Lafayette had now asked Ticknor to find employment for Follen, if possible at Harvard University. Follen had already begun to learn English while on the *Cadmus*. In Philadelphia, however, he strove to perfect it enough to qualify him for an academic career in the United States. The first American novel he read in order to improve his English was *Redwood*, by Catherine Sedgwick. Little did he know at the time that this author, a prominent New York Unitarian, was a friend of his future wife, and would introduce the two to each other in Boston during the fall of 1826.[28]

With the support of George Ticknor, Follen was appointed as instructor of the German language at Harvard on November 19, 1825. The oldest institution of higher learning in America was rapidly expanding.[29] John Thornton Kirkland, a Unitarian and a Federalist who was president of Harvard from 1810 until 1828, was a well loved, tolerant, and respected man. However, he lacked the authority and perhaps the vision to transform Harvard into a full university which was truly in touch with the academic changes taking place in Europe. Plans for ambitious academic reforms, mainly propagated by George Ticknor along with Edward Everett and

Joseph Cogswell, two other Americans who had studied in Germany with Ticknor, challenged tradition. The curriculum and student requirements were to be changed, and the teaching of modern languages was to be intensified.[30] The reforms included stricter discipline among the students in order to counter the rebelliousness of the student body during the 1820s. The entire college academic landscape was to be divided into individual departments, so that related scholarly subjects could be grouped together. Ticknor's plans for curriculum reform were, however, largely obstructed by the Harvard faculty members, and the students rebelled against his disciplinary measures.[31]

The intellectual composition of the university faculty was also in transition, as the religious orthodoxy guaranteed for many decades by the unchallenged reign of Calvinism was fading and a more secular variety of philosophical teaching was being introduced. The appointment of the theologian Henry Ware to the Hollis Professorship of Divinity in 1805 had introduced into the college a new liberal Unitarian spirit, which soon became dominant. In the era that followed, Ware firmly defended Unitarianism against its critics on the right, while his colleague Professor Andrews Norton defended the new creed against "atheistic" strains of thought on the left.[32] When the lawyer and former Boston mayor Josiah Quincy became the new president in June of 1829 (he remained in office until 1845), a conservative and authoritarian man took charge of an intellectually fractious faculty and a rebellious student body, both very liberal in their religious and social views.

Into this academic setting, in December of 1825, arrived Charles Follen. He was immediately able to take up his new teaching position.[33] Eyewitness accounts of Follen's teaching activities were recorded in memoirs by several of his American students,[34] and notes taken by students from Follen's lectures on German literature have been preserved. They show the competence and efficiency with which Follen lectured in the English language. His topics were the general history of German literature and language and a full discussion of selected works such as *Die Nibelungen*.[35] There had never been an official instructor in the German language at an American college before 1825; Follen's teaching was thus genuine pioneer work.

One other important aspect of Follen's early work at Harvard was the fact that he taught the French language as well as German. There is extensive proof of this in the Department of Modern Languages reports which Follen wrote and submitted to President Kirkland.[36] In these reports, Follen commented in excellent, surprisingly fluent English on the size of his classes during the years from 1826 to 1828, as well as on the academic progress of individual students. On June 1, 1828, for instance, Follen noted down that he had twenty-eight students to teach in German, and forty-nine students in French. The students were assigned to "divisions" according to their class and level of proficiency (juniors, seniors, theology students, beginners, advanced). The texts Follen read in his advanced German classes included Friedrich Schiller's *Kabale und Liebe* and *Die Räuber*, as well as Goethe's *Faust*. In French, Follen had his students read classic plays by Molière.

Knowledge of the German language had been almost nonexistent in New England before the 1820s, and at that time almost no German books could be bought in Boston bookstores.[37] Elsewhere, resources were just as limited; there were, for instance, hardly any German books available in the Harvard College library until 1825. Charles Follen thus had no texts available to teach his classes. He was forced, during his first term, to compile an unsystematic anthology of German primary sources himself. Follen eventually responded to the lack of a German textbook or anthology for the classroom with his first contributions to American intellectual life, the compilation of a *German Reader* (Boston, 1826) and a *German Grammar* (Boston, 1828). Both went through many editions as college textbooks. The twenty-first edition of the *Grammar* appeared in Boston in 1859.

Follen's selections for the *Reader* are primarily interesting in that they show which authors Follen promoted, and which ones he chose to slight or even ignore. The majority of the German writers Follen considered appropriate for America had a strong interest in political and social reform, and were part of the Enlightenment or Romantic movements of literature. The place in German literature of Gotthold Ephraim Lessing (1729–1781), Johann Gottfried von Herder (1744–1803), Friedrich von Schiller (1759–1805), Christoph Martin Wieland (1733–1813), and Novalis (1777–1801) was discussed in a brief introduction, and Follen edited selections from their works for his American readership.[38] Follen was presenting a view of the canon of German literature upon which only a fraction of German academics would have agreed. He even included in some of the editions selections from Theodor Körner and poems by his brother August Follen. Follen conveyed an image of German literature that had as its mainstays the Middle Ages, the Reformation, and the Enlightenment (which he referred to as the period of "new German literature"). Even within these periods, he only selected very specific authors, those who had contributed, in his own view, to German unity and human liberation.

The authors favored by Follen, from Martin Luther to Friedrich Schiller, had worked to define German nationhood and supported modern ideas of individual and social freedom of the kind which Follen himself had tried to implement in his short political career in Germany. Writers such as Schiller, Lessing, and Körner were now being used to create a specific image of Germany for the American reading public. Follen hoped that Americans would be best able to understand and relate to the ideas and purposes of these specific works. The concepts of nationality, social reform, and human freedom, as expounded by the writers Follen suggested, would fit into the American intellectual context just as much as they did into that of the German liberals. Americans would be able to comprehend their beliefs and sympathize with them.

Follen was also a founding member of a Harvard German Society in 1828. This academic group included Francis Lieber and George Ticknor, along with several others. The society engaged in the exchange of knowledge of German literature, theology, and philosophy. Its existence reflected the increased interest in things German among Harvard faculty members, and their wish to make the study of Germany more systematic. German ideas were also increasingly influential regarding Harvard faculty members' opinions about the organization of education in their own university. Göttingen and other German centers of academic excellence had by now become models for American higher education. The Harvard German Society played a role in the realization of this idea.[39]

## Harvard Academic Reform and Boston Intellectual Culture

Charles Follen's influence on American scholarship and thought manifested itself particularly in two spheres. On the one hand, the academic life of Harvard University was increasingly receptive to German scientific ideas and teaching methods. Leading academics such as George Ticknor were highly interested in reforming Harvard according to German models, particularly that of the University of Göttingen. On the other hand, the cultural pursuits of Boston's social and intellectual elite began to center on German philosophy, theology, and science. Thus prominent figures in Boston such as William Ellery Channing and Ralph Waldo Emerson began to shown an active interest in things German.

Several American students (later to become professors and college officers) from 1815 onward for the first time experienced direct contact with German conceptions of how a university was to be fashioned, how science and scholarship were to be conceived, and what subjects in general were to be taught.[40] The young American scholars George Ticknor (1791–1871; Dartmouth B.A. 1807), Edward Everett (1791–1871; Harvard A.B. 1811, M.A. 1814; Göttingen Ph.D. 1817), Joseph Cogswell (1786–1871; Harvard A.B. 1806), and George Bancroft (1800–1891; Harvard A.B. 1817), among others, had by the early 1820s all returned from extended study trips to Germany, and one of them held a German academic degree.[41] All of these students had studied at the University of Göttingen, but had also traveled throughout Europe. They were most impressed with the German teaching methods and scientific training.[42]

The newly forged contacts between American and German institutions of higher education were made even more fruitful by the importation of German academics to America. Hence a tradition of migration began which lasted until well after World War II. German scholars such as Charles Follen (German), Francis Lieber (Gymnastics, Political Science), and Charles Beck (Latin) were by the late 1820s the first generation of Germans to make their presence felt in American universities.[43] Lieber, a Prussian Burschenschaft member and revolutionary, had been imprisoned for four months after the murder of August von Kotzebue. He then traveled to Greece to fight in the Greek war for independence from the Turks. After a short stay in Rome under the protection of the German historian Barthold Georg Niebuhr and a temporary return to Berlin, Lieber again fled, this time to London, in 1826. In June of 1827, Lieber landed in New York, and then found a job as gymnastics teacher in Boston. Two lengthy personal letters from Charles Follen to Francis Lieber, written that same year, document the important advisory role Follen played in bringing Lieber to the United States.[44] Eventually Lieber went on to become a pioneering political scientist and encyclopedist in the United States, teaching first in South Carolina and then at Columbia University in New York.[45]

Before Lieber was hired in Boston, there had even been plans to bring Friedrich Ludwig Jahn to Harvard as an instructor in gymnastics and the German language.[46] Jahn was seen as the ideal combination of language teacher and gymnastics instructor: he would work for the development of the body as much as for that of the mind. Furthermore, he had always instilled in his German students, such as Francis Lieber, a feeling of intense patriotism; perhaps he could do the same in America. Jahn's position in Germany stabilized somewhat during the 1830s, however, and he chose not to emigrate. Had the offer from America come at an earlier time, during the 1820s, when Jahn had suffered persecution and imprisonment, his decision might have been different. His presence in America probably would have brought many more German emigrés to New England, and the German influence there might have been even stronger.

Even without well-known, established figures such as Jahn, the German university now came to be used as a model for the shaping of its American counterpart. Follen and his colleagues particularly wished to implant in American minds the German concept which they described as freedom of thought and inquiry. Reginald Phelps, discussing the influence of German academic thought on America during the period, has referred to freedom of thought as "the center from which other freedoms radiate."[47] Göttingen, among all other German universities, became a symbol of academic progress to Americans, and exerted a strong attraction on students wishing to travel to Germany. In the eyes of Americans, it offered, writes Phelps, "universality, freedom, devotion to the truth, ceaseless diligence in seeking it; the surroundings and the materials necessary for the welfare of a republic of scholars."[48]

Charles Follen was expected by his American hosts to be an active exponent of the academic environment that they had witnessed at Göttingen. He was to bring the best qualities of the German university to the American campus, and become a living symbol of freedom of thought and modern conceptions of scholarship (*Wissenschaft*). Follen did take on this academic role; in addition, however, he brought more to Harvard than some faculty members had bargained for. His conception of freedom was stronger, less conducive to compromise on political issues, and extended well outside the classroom and the realm of pure ideas.

Within one year after he had landed in the United States, Charles Follen had chosen Boston as his new home, and began to make as powerful an impact outside the Harvard academic community as he made within it. He felt that Boston would be the place where he could best build a new career using his European background to his own advantage.[49] Although the city of Boston was controlled primarily by financially powerful and socially conservative merchants, there was also a receptive atmosphere for controversial intellectual activities and for thought which aimed at social and religious reform, in and around Boston. The rise of the Brook Farm experimental community, abolitionism, the Unitarian controversy, and the Transcendentalist controversy demonstrate this point.[50]

The close links of the Boston social elite to Harvard University have been described by Ronald Story, who has shown in detail the funding patterns of Harvard and other institutions such as the Boston Athenaeum. Story has described how Harvard could play such a large role as "the centerpiece of the elite institutional constellation" of Boston and as the foundation of the "Brahmin Aristocracy" in that city. This "aristocracy" was achieved through the pursuit of a "class ideal" among Harvard students and through a strong "process of exclusion" directed against provincials and poor potential students.[51] Interested primarily in the history of the anti-slavery movement, Lawrence Friedman has spoken of a "Boston Clique" of devoted political, social, and religious reformers which was crystallizing and forming in the early 1830s. This "Boston Clique," to which Follen eventually managed to become attached, was formed of men and women with various professions. There were ministers such as William Ellery Channing (1780–1842) and Samuel Joseph May (1797–1871), lawyers such as Samuel Sewall (1799–1888) and Ellis Gray Loring (1802–1852), journalists such as William Lloyd Garrison (1805–1879), and writers such as Maria Weston Chapman (1806–1885).[52]

Martin Green has in turn characterized the Boston of the early nineteenth century as "The City of Culture" and "The City of Literature" which was the most prolific in America. The intellectual class was interwoven with the business community and the political elite. The leading thinkers came from Boston's socially prominent families and had a sense of responsibility for the community at large. They each were, as was George Ticknor (whom Green uses as one of his examples), an "Aristocrat in Democracy." Several periodical journals were published in the city, and countless lecture series were offered in many areas of knowledge.[53] The educated elite, from which Charles Follen's wife Eliza came, wished to move beyond a merely English-dominated literature and develop a tradition of letters unique to the United States. For this purpose, studies in European writings could be a valuable guide; they were to show the way to the formation of a unique American national literature and scholarly tradition. The Boston intellectuals and reformers active around Follen, who during the 1820s became fascinated with European literature and philosophical thought, turned to the new arrival as a living representative of German scholarship.[54] Follen was able to gain access to the most elite social circles in Boston, at least until he became an antislavery activist. His especially close friendship with William Ellery Channing and his marriage to Eliza Lee Cabot are indicative of this.[55]

In the winter of 1826–27, Follen was first invited to attend one of the many evenings of discussion which frequently took place in the home of the great Unitarian leader William Ellery Channing and his wife. The topics of interest usually included literature, religion, philosophy, and education.

In the realm of education, Follen was able to report on the pedagogical work of Pestalozzi and Fröbel, then being developed in Europe. In philosophy he was able to provide information about the thought of Immanuel Kant, who was not yet well known in America, and about whom Follen's hosts wished to learn more.[56] In religion Follen was able to discuss the ideas of Schleiermacher and De Wette. Finally, he introduced his new social circle to those works of contemporary German literature which he found most appealing.[57] The time of Follen's arrival in Boston coincided with what has been referred to as the "German craze" in New England. German science, literature, theology, and philosophy in particular were soon profoundly influential among Unitarians, Transcendentalists, and the authors and literary critics of the New England Renaissance.[58] The work of Madame de Staël, whose famous study *On Germany* was first published in an American edition in 1814, was especially influential in persuading Americans of the attractions offered by continental European culture.[59] Thomas Carlyle and Samuel Taylor Coleridge also conveyed their interest in German Romanticism to many educated New Englanders. They produced English translations and editions of current German texts, thereby making them accessible to an English-speaking and highly interested American readership.

The central tendencies of German culture and philosophy only really began to be incorporated into serious American intellectual endeavors when New England saw the rise of Transcendentalism in the 1830s. Charles Follen's influence on its main proponents, such as George Ripley (1802–1880),[60] Margaret Fuller (1810–1850),[61] Bronson Alcott (1799–1888), Theodore Parker (1810–1860),[62] and Ralph Waldo Emerson (1803–1882),[63] was clearly substantial. All of these thinkers and reformers knew Follen in person and wrote about him in their articles (especially Ripley), memoirs, journals, or letters. Although he rarely mentioned Follen in his letters and diaries, Ralph Waldo Emerson was at least aware of Follen's activities, and his interest in German philosophy and culture steadily increased from 1829–1830 onward.[64] From that time on, Emerson's appetite for German literature and philosophy was tremendous. He began by reading the relevant works of Samuel Taylor Coleridge and Thomas Carlyle, and then developed the desire to read Goethe in the original. His next step was to acquire a reading knowledge of the German language, as did many other educated Americans.[65]

The Transcendentalist who contributed most to the reception of German culture in America, and the only contemporary who was perhaps even more important in this respect than Follen, was Frederic Henry Hedge (1805–1890).[66] In 1818, at the age of twelve, Hedge had been taken to Germany by George Bancroft and enrolled at the famous boarding school of Schulpforta near Naumburg, and also at two other schools, for four years. In the 1820s, Hedge went through Harvard College and the Harvard Divinity School and was ordained in the Congregational Church in 1829. The Transcendental Club, which began to meet regularly in 1836, was founded by Hedge and sometimes also referred to as the "Hedge Club." As editor of the *Christian Examiner* and contributor to the *Dial*, Hedge shaped the American opinion of Germany at least as much as did Follen. When Follen lectured on Schiller (1831–32) and edited Carlyle's *Life of Schiller* (1833), Hedge published articles on the same topics.[67] In the late 1840s, finally, Hedge provided Americans with a substantial German reader including what he considered the "classics" when he published his *Prose Writers of Germany*.[68]

With Follen present at Harvard, those Americans interested in German thought, such as Hedge and other Transcendentalists, actually had an living exponent of it to turn to for intellectual exchange. Follen's acquaintance with Jakob Friedrich Fries at Jena, and his own work on philosophical topics at Basel under the tutelage of the theologian Wilhelm Leberecht De Wette, had prepared him adequately for the task of instructing American thinkers in the academic culture and idealist thought of his home country. The "Inaugural Discourse" delivered by Follen at Harvard in 1831 and his *Lectures on Moral Philosophy* of the same year did much to popularize current German ideas in New England by defending them against frequent American accusations of moral laxity and atheism, and showing their place in the new continental European cultural orientation which was so strongly affecting the Boston reading public. Several periodicals published in New England at the time were also highly significant in the dissemination of German culture. The increasing proliferation of articles on German topics is striking after 1830 in the *Christian Examiner,* the organ of Unitarian scholarship.[69]

*The Dial,* which appeared from 1840 to 1844, played perhaps the greatest role in promulgating German literature and thought in New England.[70] The many articles on German topics show how widely accepted German thinkers and writers had become by this time. Theodore Parker published a piece entitled "German Literature" in January of 1841. It enthusiastically acclaimed German intellectual achievements which, according to Parker, had absolutely no equal in the Anglo-Saxon world. Kant, Schleiermacher, and Goethe, Parker argued, were the best scholars and thinkers to be found, and those still skeptical in New England had to rethink their views. Continuing his interest in Germany, Parker was to write an article in 1843, entitled "The Life and Character of Dr. Follen," which also appeared in *The Dial*.[71] It contained what was perhaps the most positive and engaging account of Charles Follen's personality ever published. Parker discussed Follen as a man who embodied what Boston reforming intellectuals believed to be the message of modern German idealism and cultural liberalism.

Eliza Lee Cabot (1787–1860), the American woman whom Follen married on September 15, 1828, was a daughter of the Boston "Brahmin" class which combined business skills with a strong interest in education and culture and a vital sense of civic responsibility.[72] Eliza was nine years older than her husband, having been born in Boston on August 15, 1787. Her late father, Samuel Cabot (1758–1819), had been engaged in foreign commerce. His three older brothers had made great fortunes in privateering during the American Revolution.[73] Eliza's mother was Sally Barrett Cabot (1763–1809). There were thirteen children born into the family. After her parents' early deaths in 1809 and 1819, Eliza and two of her unmarried sisters had established an independent household,[74] living in comfortable, if not wealthy, circumstances. Eliza was well educated and maintained a keen interest in intellectual, theological, and social issues and problems. She was a well-known author of children's books (many of them related to the antislavery cause), a founder of the Sunday school connected to William Ellery Channing's Federal Street Church in Boston, and in her later years a fervent antislavery agitator. From 1828 to 1830 she edited the *Christian Teacher's Manual*.[75] Follen had first met Eliza in the fall of 1826. Their first encounter is described by Eliza in the "Life of Charles Follen" (Volume I of Follen's *Works*):

> It was in the autumn of this year, 1826, that I first saw Dr. Follen. He was introduced to me by our mutual friend, Catherine Sedgwick, who was in Boston on a visit. He accompanied us and some other ladies to his gymnasium, to see his class of boys go through their exercises. . . . All of us noticed the simple, good-humored dignity of his manner, and his unaffected enjoyment of a jest at his own expense. The childlike earnestness, the sublime simplicity, of his character made an indelible impression on me, as I saw him then for the first time. He did not seem a stranger to me. I believe he never seemed like a stranger to a human soul.[76]

Attending a series of meetings on Sunday school issues together at the home of William Ellery Channing, they soon became intimate intellectual friends. They took part together in reform discussions, and Follen began to acquaint Eliza Cabot with German literature and his own cultural background. Charles Follen soon began to deeply influence his wife's views. In the spring of 1828, they became engaged, and they were married only a few months later. Follen joined the household of Eliza and her two unmarried sisters in Boston in 1828.[77] The couple's first and only child, Charles Christopher, was born on April 11, 1830. He would later attend Harvard University and graduate with the class of 1849.[78] Eliza was one of the many Boston women of the time who took as active a part in reform activity as did men. On the one hand, her views were often not compatible with those of the socially rather conservative Boston business community. On the other hand, Eliza wisely avoided a complete break in relations with her powerful and socially established family. Her brother Samuel Cabot, a businessman, joined by several other wealthy friends, sponsored a professorship in German language and literature at Harvard for Follen in 1830.[79]

Thus, by the end of the 1820s, Charles Follen enjoyed the support of the Cabot family and was firmly established in Cambridge. Some of the correspondence which Follen had in the summer of 1830 is preserved, and shows his personal and professional circumstances at that time. He was vacationing with his wife in Artichoke Mills, near Newburyport, in northeastern Massachusetts, and finalizing plans to buy a large new house in Cambridge. To Charles Folsom, the head of the university press at Harvard, Follen wrote several letters at the time which expressed the optimism he had about his newly found prosperity in America:

> We are safely and very pleasantly lodged here, four miles from Newburyport. Mrs Follen and my sisters who arrived here the day before yesterday after a voyage that had nothing but safety to recommend it, are very well. . . . I would further request you to have the goodness to make such enquiries for a house for us, as would not take up too much of your time. I wish that my name should not be mentioned until I can decide whether the one offered answers our purposes better than that which we now inhabit. A higher rent, unless it be very exorbitant, would not be an objection.[80]

Charles Folsom was soon sucessful in finding several appropriate houses from which Follen and his new family could choose. On August 9 Follen again wrote to him about the subject of housing:

Mr Curron's intention to set out for Boston this morning leaves me but just time to thank you for your kindness, and request you to engage, if not possible [sic], this referral of Mrs. Beal's house till commencement when I shall go and see it. If she should wait upon an answer until that time, have the goodness to write to me a few lines by mail. If you should see Mr Coit, you would oblige me by addressing him about the house, and the cause why he left it.[81]

When he was inaugurated as professor of German language and litera-ture in 1830, Follen and his wife were able to move to their new home, located at 11 Waterhouse Street on the northern boundary of the Cambridge Common. It soon became a social center where prominent Unitarians and reformers as well as Harvard faculty and students met.[82] Eliza Follen later described her optimistic mood when the couple moved in during the year 1831, still untroubled by the difficulties she and her husband were fated to have and the unstable life they would be forced to lead because of their social commitment and her own poor health:

When we took possession of our new house, in the autumn of 1831, Dr. Follen's pleasure was very great. "At last," he said, "I have a study to my mind. It is, indeed, a blessing to me to have a place for my books and papers; now I shall be able to do something.". . .We had already moved twice since our mariage, and his hopeful spirit relied almost with certainty upon the thought, that now he was established. . . . And his generous heart rejoiced at the prospect of long and liberally exer-cising that simple but true hospitality, which, with him, was so un-questioned a duty, that he never asked whether it was a pleasure, and so high a pleasure that he never thought of it as a duty. As we had some rooms to spare, we took four young men to board with us, who made a part of our family. . . .[83]

There is, in the same source, an indication of the Follens' conception of marriage, which was modern and liberal, but pedantic at the same time. The passages which Eliza wrote about marriage demonstrate the ideal of marital equality to which Charles and Eliza aspired. Eliza Follen used a statement her husband made, in his notes to a sermon he later wrote, as a justification of her own relationship with him:

His views of the duties, of the high purposes of the married state, will be best represented, by his own words, in the following notes for a sermon on the subject. . . . "Object. To preserve and promote their physical, moral, and religious perfection. . . . Love an eternal principle. Hence, all false, all merely temporal motives are wrong. Suicide, from disappointed love, better than marriage from mercenary motives. Parents are apt to have low motives upon the subject. They educate their daughters to be married, setting love aside. . . . "Female mind" and "female heart" about as proper as "female conscience." The marriage state cannot change the principal ground of equal, mutual respect; otherwise it would be a degrading, immoral connexion. Equality of the sexes. Equal moral obligations."[84]

In the early 1830s, it thus looked as if Charles Follen, who was by then married, held a good job, and lived in a new comfortable house, had found himself and his destiny in America.

## Follen on History

When Charles Follen had established himself in Cambridge, he immediately began to produce academic work at a high rate. While still a German instructor at Harvard in 1829, Follen published a review of two works by the German historian Arnold Heeren (1760–1842) that had recently appeared in English translation. He briefly treated the *History of the States of Antiquity* and the *History of the Political System of Europe and Its Colonies* in one review, and then used the opportunity to add his own views of history.[85] Follen was on the one hand providing insights into German scholarship and intellectual debates for his American audience; on the other hand, he was continuing a crusade for the acceptance of natural law and human self-determination which he had begun previously in his two articles published at the University of Basel.

Follen began his critical treatment of Heeren's scientific methods with a discourse on what he considered the essentials of historical scholarship. He criticized the "propensity to exaggerate the merits or the faults of individuals," of religious and political parties, or of noble families. The worst of all examples for Follen was the historian in Europe who attempted to "pass over the faults of his prince and his august family." He called this kind of historiography a "conscientious servility," and "the greatest triumph of falsehood over truth." Many historians, including Heeren, had attempted to "trace the designs of Providence" in their works. While many "hidden links" between events had been discovered, this enterprise should not be carried too far, especially in the writing of ecclesiastical history.

Follen thought that "most of these speculative historians suppose the object of divine Providence, in the direction of human events, to be the gradual improvement of mankind." Agreeing with this proposition, Follen once again stated his own view:

> The constitution of nature and the course of events are sufficient to convince us, that it was the plan of Providence to make mankind the free and responsible authors of their happiness or unhappiness. . . . The time will come for the slave to break his chain; and the savage will see the light breaking through the wilderness of his mind. Our faith in an overruling Providence leads us to believe, that every nation and every individual, however degraded, will, at some time, obtain the means of the highest happiness of which human nature is capable.

Humans should therefore become aware of their own position, and should not be tempted to fall into "dangerous self-satisfaction, and a regardlessness for their own responsibility."

Follen also contributed a decidedly negative treatment of the philosopher Hegel and his followers. While Follen held fast to his concept of human freedom and responsibility, he severely criticised Hegel's idea that historical events developed according to preconceived, uncontrollable rules:

> Some philosophers, especially, in our times, those of the school of Hegel (now Professor at Berlin), pretend to a still higher intelligence, than the anticipation of future events from the knowledge of the past. They think themselves possessed of the universal theory, according to which, all things that have been, are, and will be, are preconceived and produced. They maintain, that all that exists and comes to pass, must be and ought to be; subverting, in this manner, the proper ground of history as well as of morality.

Instead of making the historiography of individual nations merely an examination of the great deeds of high-ranking individuals, and turning international history into only a description of "wars, conquests, treaties of peace and alliances," Follen called for an "internal" and "external" social history of nations. In both his ancient and his modern histories, Heeren had succeeded admirably in paying attention to the domestic life, culture, and religion, and also to political arrangements and commercial relations of the nations he described. At the end of his review article, Follen turned to his proposals for an American national historiography. He warned against a general "overrating of the past," an "idolatry of history, which in Asia and Europe keeps down, in millions of human beings, every spontaneous effort of the free-born mind." However, he did advocate the study of history among Americans, so they could "watch the progress of the human race, and its improvement." Follen hoped that this "spirit of improvement" had "found at last a permanent home" in America, where individual liberty, popular sovereignty, and religious freedom had been accepted and transformed into law.

## Follen as the First American Germanist, 1830–1835

Charles Follen played an increasingly important role in the rapid spread of interest in German culture in America after he was appointed professor of German language and literature in September of 1830.[86] The endowment for his new chair was at first to run for five years, as a document formerly in the possession of Follen's brother-in-law, Samuel Cabot, indicates:

> Whereas the subscribers, together with Samuel Cabot Esquire, have heretofore agreed to contribute the sums set against their respective names, to be paid annually for the term of five years towards the salary of Dr. Charles Follen as Professor of the German language and litera-ture in Harvard University; and the said S. Cabot has bound himself personally for the payment of the whole sum to the Corporation of the University, being five hundred dollars a year for five years. . . .
> Boston, Sept. 14, 1830
> T H Perkins, One Hundred Dollars
> Jonathan Phillips, One hundred Dollars[87]

Follen laid the groundwork of his activities as professor of German in his "Inaugural Discourse," which he delivered on September 3, 1831.[88] He began by stating his pleasure at being allowed to offer instruction at Harvard, which through expansion was becoming a true university meas-uring up to the European standard. Follen proceeded to briefly examine the contributions of several of the German writers, thinkers, and scholars in various fields which he held to be the most valuable for American intellectual discourse: the jurists Gustav Hugo (1764–1844) and Friedrich Karl von Savigny (1779–1861); the philosophers Samuel Pufendorf (1632–

1694), Christian Thomasius (1655–1728), Immanuel Kant (1724–1804), and Johann Gottlieb Fichte (1762–1814); and the historian Barthold Georg Niebuhr (1776–1831). Follen mentioned many fields in which Germans were at the time beginning to excel, such as philosophy, literature, medicine, and history. He went on to describe how German literary writers had recently been able to emancipate themselves from the "slavish imitation of French taste and manners" which "had crept into all departments of social literary life" and had led the German nation "to the brink of a disgraceful intellectual bankruptcy."

The recent revival of German literature and thought had been dramatic. Follen above all credited Madame de Staël with renewing the cultural and literary eminence of the Germans. He mentioned her in the same breath along with the French heroine Charlotte Corday, who had stabbed Marat, and with Joan of Arc, as a supporter of freedom and true art. Madame de Staël had elevated the tastes of her own home country by winning many admirers for German literature among the French. Thinkers such as Victor Cousin and Benjamin Constant (whom Follen had met in Paris in 1820) were drawing their ideas from Germans such as Kant and Jacobi. German literature had become of great interest to the English as well, through the translations of Romantics such as Coleridge and Shelley. German literature, thought, and conceptions of history were also arriving in America through other English writers, particularly Thomas Carlyle.

Follen suggested to his audience that German literature, theology, philosophy, and culture had much to offer if Americans would explore them in greater depth. German metaphysics were to him "the best gymnastics of the mind," and "everyone who had enjoyed a German education had been nurtured in religion." There were many points of convergence between American and German culture, beyond the basic affinity of the English and the German languages. The means for a turn to the culture of Germany were all available for the interested New Englander:

> There are German books and teachers in every place of importance in this country. In Boston, particularly, where, I am assured, about fifty years ago, not a German grammar or dictionary was to be found, there are now a number of persons who speak, and a large number who read, and enter into the sense of the German spirit. Many German authors have already found a place in private libraries.[89]

In addition, Follen attempted to liberate German philosophy and theology from the stigma of immorality, of skepticism and atheism which had been placed upon it by conservative American theologians and scholars. There was indeed a tradition of free inquiry in German scholarship, a great freedom of thought and plurality of opinions. Nevertheless, the great majority of German philosophers and theologians, unlike the French and English, were far removed from atheism, materialism, or even skepticism. There was such a great variety in German scholarship, Follen argued, that the previous American negative judgments about it were much too partial and too narrow and could never truly assess the situation of the early nineteenth-century German mind.[90] A frivolous author such as Kotzebue (very popular at the time as entertainment on the American stage), in whose murder Charles Follen himself had been implicated, was indeed "bad," and fostered "immoral excitement" and "impure pleasure." By contrast, Schiller, Kant, and De Wette presented examples of the noble contributions which German scholarship and the German arts could offer to Americans.

At the end of his "Discourse," Follen reviewed the tradition of German literature for his American audience. There are strong parallels to the introduction to his *German Reader,* published a few years before. First, he mentioned the medieval "Love-Singers" *(Minnesänger)* of the twelfth and thirteenth centuries, with their message of "courage, truth, honor, trust, and love." The Reformation was for Follen the next highlight of German literary tradition. It represented "the first powerful manifestation of the principle of freedom awaking in man, and striving to liberate his highest interests from the tyranny of presumptious self-constituted authority."[91]

More recently, there had followed "the independent genius of Lessing," which helped the young national literature in Germany to rise above "the self-imposed bondage of foreign taste and manners." The great poets to which Germany's "new republic of letters" owed its existence and its glory were Lessing, Klopstock, Wieland, Herder, Goethe, Schiller, Richter, and Tieck. The last passage of the "Discourse" was devoted to philology. Follen had already discussed concepts which linguists such as the Grimm brothers were beginning to research in Germany. He argued that "the ancient German language is the mother of the English," in somewhat broken English; recent German scholars and poets had made the German language of prime interest to English speakers once again. In discussing literature, Follen thus combined a prominent anti-French bias with a strong tendency toward establishing links between Germany and the English-speaking world.

The "Inaugural Discourse" was reviewed very favorably by George Ripley for the *Christian Examiner* in January of 1832. There were also enthusiastic reactions by former President John Quincy Adams (1767–1848) and by the well-known politician and diplomat Edward Livingston (1764–1836), both of whom were interested in the promulgation of German learning in New England. President Adams corresponded with Follen about the role of German learning and literature in America, and about his own travel experiences in Germany and personal literary tastes.[92] The review by George Ripley is one of the most comprehensive and positive evaluations and defenses of German thought and literature produced in America at that time. Not only did Ripley laud Follen for his work to make German culture available to American intellectuals, but he himself also attempted to make that culture seem attractive and meaningful to his readers.[93] Ripley lamented the fact that too little attention had been paid so far to things German in American intellectual life. That a professorship in German language and literature had finally been established at an American university showed that New Englanders were finally overcoming their suppositions that German thought was "all given to mysticism, rhapsody, wild and tasteless inventions in poetry, and dark and impenetrable reasonings in metaphysics."

Ripley recognized that many Americans had found German philosophy to be obscure; "but what great science, we would ask, is not obscure, before its nomenclature is understood, and its definitions studied?" He too denied the prevalent idea that German philosophy was irreligious and given to "materialism and skepticism." Ripley thought that Germans had not aided the spread of atheism, but rather had made the doctrines of Christianity believable in a new way. Indeed they had also opposed materialism and stood overwhelmingly on the side of idealism and faith. Diversity of opinion, as Follen had pointed out, was not necessarily to be taken as atheism, but should be understood as the right climate necessary for a search for truth in religion. Ripley ended his review with an expression of optimism concerning both the spread of German thought in New England and the role which Charles Follen was to play within that process:

> It would be superfluous for us to recommend the Discourse, of which we had been given this slight notice to the attention of our studious men. It has been extensively read, and has received the testimony of public favor to which it is richly entitled. We hope to see other fruits of the Professorship which the author holds, equally valuable with this Discourse.

## Follen's Views on German Theology, Philosophy, Literature, and Science

The arguments of Schleiermacher and De Wette,[94] as well as those of Kant, were made much more accessible to New Englanders by the lectures of Charles Follen, at Harvard and elsewhere. German idealism and in particular Kant's transcendental philosophy were by the 1830s to become a major influence on the American Transcendentalists, who wished to learn as much about these matters as possible. They could turn to Follen as a mediator: he had become very familiar with the ideas of Kant and Schleiermacher during his studies in Germany, and had forged a personal friendship with De Wette during his time in Switzerland.

Friedrich Schleiermacher stands as one of the most influential German theologians of the nineteenth century, and certainly had a great influence on the beliefs of Charles Follen. In Schleiermacher's anonymously published work *Über die Religion: Reden an die Gebildeten unter ihren Verächtern* (1799), the young minister working at Berlin's Charité hospital attempted to regain for Christianity the following that it had recently lost among the German educated classes. French philosophical materialism and a powerful faith in science had, according to Schleiermacher, displaced true religion. For him, religion had to do less with rigid dogmas, rationality, and action than with human feeling and intuition. From Schleiermacher's work, Follen could gain access to a form of religion that did not directly conflict with modern science and rationalism and did not restrict the inquisitiveness of the human spirit in any way; rather, religion was to be perceived as an inborn, intuitive, emotional aspect of man and a deeply romantic respect for life, creation, and eternity.

Wilhelm Leberecht De Wette was a close friend of Schleiermacher, and just as Schleiermacher had attempted to do in his *Über die Religion*, De Wette wished to reconcile rationalism and supernaturalism. For both theologians, religion was neither a purely rational discipline nor a mere series of historical events. Rather, it was a "living phenomenon" related to the personal emotions of a religion of sentiment *(Gefühlsreligion)*, with emphases on individual conscience and the Christian community.[95] De Wette published numerous works concerned with a historic-critical examination of the Bible, lectures on the history of religion, and a novel entitled *Theodor; or, The Sceptic's Conversion* (written between 1819 and 1822, and published in America in 1841). The novel portrays a young student of theology who is subject to religious experiences and doubts while studying with the philosopher Jacob Friedrich Fries at Jena. The novel was translated into English by James Freeman Clarke, who in his introduction pointed out the great similarities he discerned between the religious crises which Theodor had to face and the theological disputes of New England during the 1830s and 1840s.[96]

De Wette's works appeared in English translation just at the time when the general controversy over German theology in America, between 1820 and 1850, had reached its peak. The new theological interpretations imported from Germany seemed to many American theologians, such as Andrews Norton and Moses Stuart, to promote atheism and immorality. While he was certainly not openly pronounced an atheist as was Ludwig Feuerbach (who was to publish *Das Wesen des Christentums* in 1841), De Wette was controversial as a theologian who was attempting to explain the validity of the gospel accounts and explore the question of whether they were fact or fiction, with the use of concepts such as myth and "poetry of history." At the same time, however, De Wette was able to capture a rather large American intellectual readership. William Ellery Channing, George Ripley, and James Freeman Clarke all read his works. George Ripley published two translations of works by De Wette, put forth in his successful and influential series "Specimens of Foreign Standard Literature."[97] Theodore Parker became most preoccupied with this German theologian's theological liberalism and critical method. He translated De Wette's study of the Old Testament, and also directly applied what he read in De Wette, and his methods of scientific inquiry, to his own work. In 1844 Parker finally visited De Wette personally in Basel, and had lengthy discussions with him on theology and philosophy.[98]

To educated New Englanders of the time, who were searching actively for a way to reconcile reason and faith and had become unsure on the issues of revelation and miracles, De Wette offered a solution. He even demonstrated to them that they could maintain their faith entirely within the framework of an established church to which they might belong. De Wette could succeed in being a religious believer and at the same time remain a committed scholar who freely engaged in every form of biblical criticism. He represented to New Englanders a nearly perfect balance between rationalists and supernaturalists, and between religious liberalism and orthodoxy. As in politics, De Wette was in theology an exponent of a liberalism best expressed in terms of "balance, moderation, and reasonableness."

To explain the fame of De Wette in New England and the popularity of his writings, the historian Siegfried Puknat has cited the personal influence of Charles Follen and his travel companion, Charles Beck. Both were extremely well qualified for this role. Follen had been De Wette's colleague at Basel for several years, and had contributed to a scholarly journal edited by him. He had been exposed directly to his ideas, and had come to share most of De Wette's assumptions about theology. Charles Beck was the theologian's stepson. After Beck's mother, a widow, had married De Wette in 1809, the relation between stepfather and son (born 1798) had been excellent, and it was due to De Wette's influence that Beck had decided to study theology, along with classics. While Beck had learned about theological issues from his stepfather, the young student had called De Wette's attention to the political issues discussed by his fellow students at the time, including the case of the murderer Carl Sand, to whose mother De Wette had written.[99]

In the realm of philosophy, the thought of Kant steadily gained influence in American intellectual life in the 1830s, and it is certain that Charles Follen was part of this process. However, intellectual historians have disputed the actual degree of Follen's personal allegiance to Kant's ethics. In the early 1940s, René Wellek denied that Follen had thought highly of Kant, and Wellek also did not share later assertions that there was such a thing as a distinct "Kantian phase" in the American intellectual life in general, or specifically in the thought of Ralph Waldo Emerson during the 1830s.[100] According to Wellek, Follen criticized Kant in most regards, and did not find Kant a useful guide in his own life. Wellek argued that Follen's attitude to Kant was in fact "extremely unsympathetic," and that he could "scarcely be described as a propagandist for German idealist philosophy."[101]

In contrast, Henry Pochmann, the leading expert of his time on German cultural influence in America, writing fifteen years after Wellek, has shown how Charles Follen was strongly concerned with the ideas of Kant. Pochmann even claimed that Follen firmly believed Kant to have laid the basis for all modern intellectual life, and that Follen's own entire system of moral thought and action was derived from Kantian thought. It now remained for Follen to convey the essence of Kant, as he understood him, to Americans. Pochmann also argued, however, that Follen disagreed with Kant on the Categorical Imperative, and in several cases criticized the philosopher whom he otherwise very much recognized as "the master" of current intellectual life. Still, in America, Follen held fast to the idea of Fries, derived from Kant, that the individual had to decide for himself what his own personal "moral duty" was, and how he was to stay true to it and fulfill it.[102]

Recent work on the central significance given to the concept of freedom in the thought of Immanuel Kant has provided circumstantial evidence that Pochmann is right, and that Follen could in fact glean a great deal directly from that philosopher's writings for his own practical moral principles.[103] The British philosopher Henry E. Allison has dealt extensively with the important role Kant assigned to the concept of freedom in the following moral situations: the attainment of virtue and holiness, the fulfillment of duty, the curbing of radical evil, and the striving after moral self-perfection. Allison's study shows that the moral problems with which Follen concerned himself, and which he used to guide his own life, were available as blueprints in the writings of Kant.

Whether or not he subscribed directly and uncritically to Kant's Categorical Imperative, Follen's own intellectual position of radical subjectivism and absolute adherence to the individual conscience, which he had preached in Giessen and Jena, and which could not exist without confronting the thought of Kant, certainly did not change during his time in America.[104] In her biography of Follen, published in 1936, the German historian Julia Wüst denied that Charles Follen remained an Unconditional in America, subjectively interpreting his duty which he had to actively fulfill in the world. She argued, instead, that in the second half of his life he turned from a nationalist radical into a humanitarian reformer.[105] It is more likely, however, that Follen remained an Unconditional in the United States as much as he had been during his stay at the University of Jena. He continued to actively transmit the main tenets of this radical philosophical position, and the ideals of absolute moral duty and individual self-perfection—which were certainly derived from a popularized version of Kant's thought—to those around him.[106]

The best place to examine Follen's own philosophical stance is his "Lectures on Moral Philosophy," delivered in Boston during the winter of 1830–31.[107] The lectures included a definition of moral philosophy, an analysis of important issues in the history of philosophy and ethics, and a detailed exposition of Follen's own opinions on these matters.[108] Much of the subject matter which Follen had discussed shortly before with his students at the Harvard Divinity School was also incorporated.[109] Follen began by stating that he wished to help clarify what morality was and should be; the concept had lost its "state of simplicity" and would have to be redefined. Moral philosophy was a combination of morals, religion, and law, a "science of good life" and "the science of duty." Follen intended to examine what forms of government and of religion were truly moral and which were not.[110] He reaffirmed one of his most basic principles: that the true meaning of life lay in the "conquest of the self," and "the striving for divine perfection." The Gospels, he argued, should be acknowledged as a perfect code of duty and as a divine revelation of the moral nature of man. They would show the perfect "path to truth," and allow humans to free themselves from "the bondage of error."

In his first lecture, Follen began with a historical commentary on the ancient philosophers Plato, Aristotle, Zeno, Epicurus and on the modern thinkers Spinoza and Kant. From these historical models, Follen turned to delineate his own system of moral thought and declared: "It is the object of moral philosophy to break the spell of authority, and emancipate reason, that it may establish, by its own industry, a household of truth supported by faithful inquiry."[111] Accordingly, there were three areas he wished to discuss: the foundation of morals and religion in human nature (Follen here argued that morals and religion were not merely products of education and civilization but were in fact innate human qualities); the development of these principles by education (here he weighed household and public education against each other); and their establishment in society, chiefly by civil and religious institutions, church and state (here Follen discussed the relationship of the individual to church and state authorities in various areas, respecting, for example, capital punishment or taxation).[112] The only object of the civil government, Follen concluded, was to secure equal rights and justice for all.[113] As in his articles written in Switzerland, Follen once again began his examination of modern conditions by referring to the writings of Baruch Spinoza. He recalled that Spinoza had in many ways built a system of necessity and pantheism, which did not allow man any ability to act as a free agent and shape his own life. Follen now argued, however, that without free will, a moral system was in fact impossible. He thus reaffirmed his own belief in the absolute necessity of individual freedom as a basis for making a truly moral decision.[114]

But the key philosopher of modern time, he said, was Immanuel Kant. The final portion of the fourth lecture and much of the fifth lecture were devoted entirely to him, and the rest of the lectures showed how central Kant was for Follen. Some of the most important passages of the lectures dealt with Kant's concept of duty and the functioning of the individual's conscience and moral decision making.[115] The moral individual was led by individual conviction and the guidance of reason. He was bound by a self-defined and socially defined duty, and by social responsibility. Follen was also explicitly critical of some of Kant's teachings. He thought that the notion of the Categorical Imperative was Kant's "great mistake," and that it was too vague to be at all effective. Follen thus may not have improved the American opinion of Kant; American scholars tended to argue that this philosopher could easily be interpreted as atheistic and morally ineffective. And yet Follen's American friends, such as William Ellery Channing, now for the first time began to carefully scrutinize and even adopt Kant's views.[116] His American biographer George Washington Spindler has argued that Follen played a great role in bringing Kant's influence to the American intellectual elite, and that the *Lectures on Moral Philosophy* were "in all probability the first public discussion in this country [America] of German philosophical thought, especially that of Kant."[117]

After lecture five, Follen departed from his historical account of philosophical thought and turned to his own conceptions and convictions: individual conscience as the foundation of morality; man's capacity for moral free agency, which gave him the power and necessity of choosing his own course; and the primacies of virtue and of feeling. Striving for perfection, every individual was expected to assign himself his own duty. Moral philosophy as a whole, in fact, should be conceived of as "a system of human perfection." Self-assigned duties could not be the same for all; it was important, however, to speak not "the language of slaves" but, rather, that of free, self-responsible men.[118] Just as in the years before 1820, Follen was once again speaking as the political Unconditional. Another revealing moment occurred when, throughout lecture fourteen, Follen discussed the issue of the use of force in order to oblige individuals to fulfill their own duties to themselves. While "moral inducements" to deviant persons were preferable to violent means, Follen still did not rule out the latter. If moral suasion failed, violent means would have to be used as a last resort. This discussion is very reminiscent of Rousseau's conception of "forcing men to be free" in *The Social Contract*. It also might have been taken directly out of Follen's "Draft of the Constitution for a Future German Empire" of 1818–19. The problem of violence and rigid political coercion thus lingers without any great modifications throughout Follen's entire life, and it was clearly stated here that violence had its place in the political and moral world.

While men thus might be forced to be virtuous, Follen still warned at the same time that one "cannot make society into a jail." Man could in the end only be virtuous and true to himself (that is, socially responsible and free) out of his own motivation. The "natural rights" or "personal rights" of man, as Follen referred to them, always had to be protected. These were personal liberty; the protection of private property; personal security; an opportunity for useful labor; and social or political privileges, including above all the right to an education for children and students. Perhaps the most efficient way to bring man to morality was to foster his interest in religion, which was "the highest form of love, or the vital interest of man in perfection," an innate quality present in everyone at birth. The main theme in lecture fifteen, the last of the series, was religion. Follen believed that eventually "all men can meet on this ground of a common religious capacity and interest." A religious community composed of free individuals, who have gone through an earnest stage of skepticism and have arrived at personal faith, could best lead to the moral perfection of the individual and society.

An intense intellectual dispute ensued after Follen had delivered his lectures, when he received a letter from a man who had been in the audience.[119] The listener accused Follen of having presented "a sort of Fanny-Wrightism for the higher classes" and of having promulgated conceptions of "materialism and atheism." The upper classes were particularly in danger of becoming infected with atheism and infidelity, the listener claimed, and of eventually handing these beliefs down to the lower classes. The listener further expressed the fear that some preachers would lead their congregations to doubt that "the Bible is true as nothing else in true; that it is to be taken as the beginning and the foundation of all wisdom, as in itself perfectly beyond the question of reason." In the sermons and lectures which some scholars, including Follen, gave, there was the strong inherent evidence that "reason is perpetually trying to forget that she is a servant." The writer of the letter argued that infidelity springs from "the supposition that human reason is strong and sufficient." Follen, in reply, defended his own position by stating that he had in no way espoused the views of the freethinker Frances Wright, but had merely said that her doctrines, often described as materialism and atheism, were alternative views, not better ones. He insisted on his own belief in Christian principles, but also stressed again his idea that all people, whatever their beliefs might be, could make a contribution to Christian truth and had a fundamental right to do so.

In the field of literature, as we have seen, Charles Follen played a considerable role in changing the taste and reading behavior of many New Englanders as he began to lecture and publish throughout the 1830s. The poet whom Follen most often and most highly praised after 1830 was Friedrich Schiller. Follen's lectures entitled *On Schiller's Life and Dramas* (delivered in public during the years 1831–32), which include a short impressionistic biography of the poet, and his edition of Carlyle's *Life of Schiller* (1833) forcefully introduced this great poet and Weimar "freedom fighter" (as Follen saw him) to the American public. To Follen, Schiller was not only a superior poet in terms of his aesthetic abilities, but also treated the sort of political and social issues with which Follen could identify. Schiller was thus at the same time the perfect artist and the perfect morally engaged individual.[120] In his description of the poet's youth, Follen emphasized the excellent, if repressive, education Schiller received, his medical studies, and his early interest in religious topics and problems. In his first major success, the drama *The Robbers,* Schiller had aimed to show that even the most ardent love of justice and freedom, the most heroic resistance to every kind of oppression, was bound to lead to error and crime, if it "did not induce us first to dethrone the selfish passions, and establish the perfect law of liberty in our own souls."[121] Follen's consideration of his own life as parallel to, and involved with, that of Schiller became explicit when he remarked that the latter stayed near Dresden with the father of Theodor Körner, the poet who meant so much to Follen's generation. The fact that Schiller was appointed professor of history at the University of Jena in 1789 provided another point of contact with Follen's own life, learning, and experience. It is important to point out in this context that, while in Jena, Schiller became closely acquainted with the philosophy of Kant. At just the same time, Schiller's interest in history and politics increased; this pattern was much like Follen's own experience. Schiller had been one of the great favorites of the German student generation of 1813, and his poetic and dramatic works had inspired many students as they went to fight in the Wars of Liberation.

Schiller had also strongly influenced the Burschenschaft movement. Follen himself and the Giessen Blacks had been very excited by plays such as *Wilhelm Tell,* in which they recognized their own willingness to fight for the cause of freedom from any sort of oppression.[122] Schiller was also important to these students because of his positive attitude toward the reform of Christianity and its blending with nationalist ideals. In the introduction to the 1837 edition of *The Life of Schiller,* Follen briefly discussed Schiller's morality, seeing him as a "poet of truth" with a powerfully exercised "poetic mission." Upon moving to Weimar in 1787, Follen went on, Schiller eventually came into close contact with Goethe. Although he later became good friends with the greatest living German poet, Schiller from the first had his doubts about the possibility of a close relationship.[123]

The image of Goethe, Schiller's great contemporary, literary competitor, and friend, had been almost entirely negative in America until the 1830s. Orthodox Calvinists had always considered his writings atheistic and full of immorality, especially of a hedonistic and an erotic kind. The great German poet was thus seen as an unbeliever, who placed the role of art in life above that of God and faith. Goethe's attitudes toward human behavior and beliefs could not have appeared more foreign and disreputable to New England Calvinists.[124] Even in the 1830s, the intellectual descendants of these strict Calvinists, while themselves liberal Christians, still carried with them an initial moral distrust of Goethe's character and work, and this distrust was to continue far into the future. Frederick B. Wahr has examined the case of Emerson, who read Goethe with great interest, studied German in order to read his works in the original, and discussed his personality in his lectures on "Representative Men" (1845–46), but eventually came to the conclusion that his own views were opposite to those of Goethe. The distrust of Goethe which Emerson introduced into American intellectual life was that of a "moral idealist and ethical teacher," who was passing judgment on a "realist and artist."[125]

Follen added in an important way to Goethe's negative reputation, though for different, quite personal and political, reasons: he thought that Goethe had not shown enough interest in supporting the cause of German liberalism.[126] Where Schiller had taken sides, and had supported the progress of mankind toward political and social freedom, Goethe had tried to find freedom in altogether different ways. Instead of immortalizing man's struggle against oppression, he had engaged in an apotheosis of art and the senses. Charles Follen wrote of Goethe's main interests in his lectures "On Schiller's Life and Dramas":

> It was the natural effect of such constant and ever-increasing success upon a susceptible and accommodating disposition, to make Goethe essentially satisfied with things as they are, with the powers that be. . . . His course was not that of a reformer. He kept aloof from all the great questions that divided men in politics and religion. He devoted his talents and himself wholly to the study of nature and art, to intercourse with men of genius, and men of rank.[127]

According to Follen, Schiller's political engagement, social conscience, and public morality were far superior to Goethe's aestheticism and philosophical abstraction in every respect which truly counted in human existence.

Although both poets were concerned with freedom, Schiller was superior in that he adopted the views of Kant:

> In what, now, I would ask, consists the individual literary character of Schiller as a dramatic poet? Goethe, in speaking of the individual tendency of Schiller's poetic nature and his own, said, "Schiller preached the gospel of freedom; I would not allow the rights of nature to be encroached upon." The word freedom is to be taken here in the sense of Kant's philosophy, as synonymous with the moral nature of man. His enthusiasm for freedom was manifested in his resistance against all kinds of unnatural and unreasonable restraint; freedom from oppression, from fear, from prejudice, and from sin.[128]

Follen announced a conclusion which demonstrated his own most important values more than it in fact signified a qualified criticism of Goethe:

> Hence, among all his correct and beautiful portraits of human life and character, we find not one moral *beau idéal*. He has access, and does justice, to every motive, to all the longings of the heart after the highest, the ordinary, and the lowest gratifications, except that one mysterious desire after infinite perfection, which, from all its very nature, appears more in failure than in successful efforts, and thus produces the highest form of heroism, the character of the martyr.[129]

This judgment by Follen, perhaps without any true understanding of the very personal political issues involved, was followed in America. Even during the years from 1832 to 1845, when there was an active interest among Transcendentalists and other educated Americans in the work of Goethe,[130] and when the earlier disinterest in things German had vanished, Goethe was not easily accepted in the United States—and remained so until much later in the century.

Beyond his interest in German theology, philosophy, and literature, in America Follen always remained as informed as possible about the most recent developments in German intellectual life. In November of 1832, Follen delivered the funeral oration for the well-known German phrenologist Gaspar (or Johann Christoph Kaspar) Spurzheim (1776–1832). This oration was later printed as a pamphlet.[131] Phrenology had recently become very popular in America, and by the 1820s it had turned into what was then considered a full-fledged science.[132] Allegedly, a person could learn from a phrenological examination exactly who he was and how to improve himself within society. In 1832 Spurzheim visited the United States "on what amounted to a triumphant tour" and influenced many American scientists as well as less educated people. After Spurzheim suddenly died during his visit, Charles Follen drew a very positive portrait of him in his funeral oration.

Follen also began to make a contribution to another discipline, psychology, which was being introduced to the American scientific community.[133] "Mental philosophy," as psychology was largely called in America until the 1840s (and in Germany, *Seelenkunde*), was increasingly considered important by thinkers such as Theodore Parker. In 1836 Charles Follen began to draft a systematic treatment of psychological principles and concepts.[134] He argued that the study of psychology would aid man in his mission to "know thyself," and to explore in greater depth than ever before "the systematic knowledge of the soul." He thought that "the better we are acquainted with our own souls, their actual condition, disposition, and capacity, so much the fitter are we to apply our faculties to any given purpose, to control our passions, and cultivate our intellectual and moral nature." Psychology, like phrenology, thus enabled humans to "regulate our conduct, with a view to our own improvement and that of our fellow-men."

## Follen Leaves Harvard

The intense commitment to political activism which Follen stressed even in his lectures about Schiller and Goethe, as well as his propensity to challenge established authority, was much in evidence at Harvard University during his employment there. The decades of the 1820s and 1830s were years of unrest and change, of attempted curriculum reforms, and of severe quarreling between an unruly student body on the one hand, and the administration, which longed for order, on the other. In 1823 and during the years 1834–1838, the Harvard campus was affected by student rebellions which seriously obstructed the course of teaching.[135] Charles and Eliza Follen were accused of playing a sizable role in the latter episodes of student unrest.

A serious student rebellion took place at Harvard during the years from 1834 to 1838. Josiah Quincy, the conservative and formal president of the university, was not skilled at addressing student protest. He introduced a standardized grading scale for all students which called for the evaluation of almost every move they made while enrolled. Quincy's ranking system for the student body, which grew out of the grading scale, and his insistence on very strict discipline led to great protests. By 1834 Quincy had not been able to prevent the situation at the university from becoming very tense, and he was being attacked by faculty members as well as by students.[136] The students went on strike against Charles Beck, who was by now professor of Latin. Beck had come to Harvard in 1831, and lasted much longer than Follen. He was able to work together in an agreeable way with Josiah Quincy, and his reform proposals, which called for the introduction of a prototype of modern graduate studies, were well received (although they too eventually failed to be successful).[137] It is ironic that Beck, a student radical in Germany fifteen years before, now himself became the target of student hostilities. He had required his students to know greater parts of their Latin grammar book by heart. When their protest against this requirement was not considered by Beck, his windows were broken, his furniture destroyed, and the college bell was rung in the middle of the night. Finally, in May of 1834, all sophomores were dismissed and ordered to leave town until the campus had quieted down again.[138] Because Follen took the students' side, showing sympathy for their claims against Beck, the relationship of the two men can only have suffered considerably during the time they spent together at Harvard.

When Josiah Quincy decided to quell the student rebellion with severe disciplinary measures, including expulsions, the suspension of almost the entire senior class, and invoking the state courts, several faculty members openly opposed him. Apparently the leader of this dissident group was Charles Follen, who had called for "less outward government in college" and thought that "the young men should govern themselves." Eliza Susan Quincy, the wife of the president, writing years later, was of the opinion that Charles and Eliza Follen were the main instigators of the student rebellion. She thought that the Follens had maintained too close a contact with students, hosting them in their home, and that Charles Follen had attempted to diminish Josiah Quincy's support among the Harvard faculty. The president in any case had labeled Follen a "troublemaker" who had fallen from his favor by 1834, at the latest.[139] For several years after 1835, the German language was taught at Harvard by a lecturer, not a full professor. Samuel Eliot Morison speculated in 1936 on Charles Follen's and his wife's roles in the student riots, and also on Follen's dismissal as professor of German in 1835:

> Follen's friends let it be known that the reason for his being dropped
> was his ardent espousal of the anti-slavery cause and his ringing

"Address to the People of the United States" (1834) to get rid of the evil. It seems more likely that the real reason lay in the fact that Professor Follen opposed President Quincy's autocratic methods, and that Mrs. Follen, a rival queen to Mrs. Quincy, fermented the student rebellion "by her wit and talent."[140]

Throughout his employment at Harvard, Follen had tried to keep alive his dream of a "Germania in America," an independent free state of Germans, who would return to a free and politically reformed Germany one day.[141] The gymnastics movement which Follen helped to initiate in the United States in 1825, immediately after his arrival, was, along with literature and philosophy, an affirmation of German culture in American exile.[142] He was responsible for the building of the first athletics grounds at Harvard University, and for the introduction of classes on physical education. During the academic year of 1826–27, Follen was appointed superintendent of the newly established Harvard gymnasium and regularly supervised athletic exercises that proved to be very popular among the students. Follen's reports written for the Department of Modern Languages indicate the success of gymnastics at Harvard.[143] On September 27, 1827, for instance, Follen wrote in his report about the attendance of students and the duration of exercises:

> About the middle of this term the Gymnasium was well attended by a number of about 70 students, who went on the Delta every Wednesday and Friday, while I instructed the monitors every Monday. The regular exercises on the Delta continued for about one hour and a half; and those with the monitors, one hour.

By the end of 1827, however, Follen himself retired from the athletics program in order to devote more time to other activities. In a report of September 28, 1827, he stated, in English that was not as good as it had been in previous reports, that there had lately been a lack of attendance at his athletic exercises:

> The Gymnasium was well attended in the beginning of this term by about 70 students. But I found it impossible to keep them to the regular exercises; so that many preferred withdrawing from all exercise; and toward the end of the term only a few went out to exercise regularly on the Delta.[144]

When *Turnen* had gone out of style at the university, Follen continued his quest in another area and in October 1834 drew up a plan for the establishment of an independent institution of higher education in the United States, to be based on German learning and organizational principles.[145] It was conceived just before Follen lost his professorship at Harvard in 1835. He needed a steady income, and also felt that his many ideas for the reform of Harvard had been ignored; thus he thought of founding a private school which he referred to as a "seminary." This new institution was to be based completely on the principle of academic freedom *(Lernfreiheit)*, with as few external restrictions on the students as possible. Professors should be hired who represented various divergent schools of thought, so that students could make up their own minds about the answers and suggestions which were available to them. Discipline was to be loose and consist of guidelines only. The students would democratically establish their own rules and regulations, similar in general to the Burschenschaften in Germany, and specifically to the *Ehrenspiegel* code of the Giessen University students. Finally, the new institution conceived by Follen was not supposed to be dominated by any one religious group.[146] Follen's new school, however, came to exist only on paper, because the necessary financial means could not be raised. Although he tried to interest prominent friends such as George Ticknor, who himself was frustrated in his attempts to reform the Harvard curriculum, Follen's ideas had no practical success.

By the latter part of the 1830s, Follen came to focus exclusively on American theological and social problems, and to abandon his previous faith in a return to Germany. In a letter to his father and family at Giessen, written in 1826, Follen had already speculated that he was now "politically dead for Europe";[147] ten years later, he knew that this was almost certainly true. Several letters that Follen had received from Germany, dated from 1825 onward, show the consequences which Follen's radicalism had already had for the family in Hesse, especially for the career of his father. In a letter of March 11, 1827, Follen's father wrote that he had "asked for dismissal from his professional position, and separated himself entirely from Giessen." In fact, it seems that Follenius had lost his position as a judge at the Giessen law court on account of the revolutionary activities of his sons. He went on to say:

> I stand in relations which endanger my remaining small property, and your brothers and sisters, who are of age, have already renounced their

claim to inheritance. You will do the same, and send me the proper document.[148]

On July 28, 1829, Follenius spoke of the possibility of visiting his son in America, for "I consider it dangerous for you to come to us." In August of 1830 he complained to his son about the situation he found himself in, in Hesse. Evidently, Follen's father had experienced severe conflicts with the government and police authorities: "They consider me a poor orphan, a demagogue."[149]

Charles Follen realized that both the construction of a secluded German community in America and a speedy return to Europe were unlikely, and he became a genuine American, if hesitantly. A trip to Switzerland, which he hoped to take in 1839, turned out to be impossible, and Follen never saw Europe again. He kept himself well informed throughout the 1830s, however, and remained as opinionated as ever, as can be gathered from a letter he wrote to General Lafayette in Paris in 1832:

I gladly avail myself of this opportunity to call myself to your remembrance. Your introduction to some distinguished men in this country has opened to me the way to a sphere of usefulness and independence in this university where I am now appointed as professor of the German language and literature. . . . I am naturalized and married to an American lady, an ardent lover of liberty and a warm admirer of yours. I need not say, and could not find words to express the deep interest I feel in the great events of your country since the last glorious revolution. . . . By deserting Poland your present government has renounced the principle to which it owes its own existence; the cause of liberty has lost its standard, because the army left its defense to the brave but single-handed standard-bearer. I look with dismay on the cold indifference of my native land for whose liberty I have toiled and become an exile in its service. I look with distress yet with hope and trust upon the awakened spirit of France, that it will not submit to have its glorious effort of July 1830 recorded against her as a noble inconsistency. Pardon the idle words of one who in his separation from the great struggle between liberty and despotism has nothing but words and tears to offer at the altar of suffering humanity. If you should wish at any time information on the affairs of this country from a frank uncompromising republican who stands aloof from the existing parties, I shall be happy to give you such as I can obtain. I should be grateful to you for a few lines assuring me of your health, and continued friendship.[150]

In giving up his original speculations of creating an autonomous German state within the United States, Charles Follen was not unique. The efforts of his younger brother Paul, who arrived in Missouri with his Giessen friend Friedrich Münch and a number of Hessian settlers in 1834, were soon disappointed as well.[151] Paul Follen and Friedrich Münch had founded a Giessen Emigration Society in 1833, and described their aims in a pamphlet which they published.[152] A large group of Hessian settlers was to emigrate to the American West, and to claim and develop land there. While certain concessions would have to be made to the environment—such as learning the English language—the community was to remain together as much as possible, and to retain its German lifestyle and political ideals. Charles Follen wrote a letter filled with advice to his stepmother in Germany on July 1, 1833:

> As a lawyer he might find here probably a considerable income, if he were to perfectly master the English language, and should bring with him a competent knowledge of English law. Then he would require two years in order to turn the application of this to American affairs. . . . People of ability and upright intentions may succeed also in other business, but this depends on many circumstances which cannot be foreseen. . . . The Arkansas Territory is not suitable for German emigrants, as other western regions, partly because the climate is for the most part too warm, and especially, because in this Territory, as in the other Southern States, the slavery of the colored people is recognized by the laws. Ohio, Indiana, Illinois, and Michigan Territory offer greater advantages.[153]

After they arrived in America with their group of settlers, Paul Follen and Friedrich Münch tried for years to build up a thriving farming community in Warren County, Missouri, but owing to an unexpectedly harsh climate and problems among the German emigrants, their project never had the success which they had hoped for. Eventually the close-knit German group disintegrated, and the political ideals of the 1830s were largely lost.[154] Paul Follen died of tropical fever on his farm in 1844; Friedrich Münch eventually did go on to become a successful large-scale farmer and

Missouri politician. The latter was flexible enough to realize that success could not come within an autonomous German group or "free state," but only by adaptation to American economic and political standards.[155] In a similar way, from the 1820s onward, Charles Follen had been struggling with this problem himself.

# 5

# RELIGION AND FREEDOM

In July of 1828 Charles Follen was accepted as a candidate for the Unitarian ministry. He was finally ordained as a minister eight years later, in 1836, the year after his dismissal from Harvard. That this one-time radical revolutionary and advocate of social violence and planned terror would wish to preach to a Christian congregation, seems highly unlikely. The continuities in Follen's life which are evident in his transition from Germany to America, and from revolutionary to religious thought, however, were much stronger and more binding than one might think. In Germany, Follen had always maintained a decided interest in religious issues. The mystical religiosity of the Giessen Blacks (as shown in the "Great Song"), the nationalistic celebrations of the Burschenschaft at the Wartburg festival, and the open political involvement of theologians such as De Wette and Schleiermacher all did their part to link religious themes to political agendas. In his "Draft of the Constitution for a Future German Empire," Follen had seen religion as a force which could be used to create and build up national feeling among an educated elite and at the same time encourage libertarian and egalitarian opinions in the general population. It was essential for Follen to bring his German interest in religion to the United States; his personality would have been incomplete without it.

At a meeting of religious reformers in the United States, which he attended in the late 1820s, Follen described his German religious background and the tremendous change in the religious mood of Germany during the last fifteen years for his listeners. Coming from a family which initially did not place very much emphasis on socially conventional religious ideas and practice, during his youth Follen was nevertheless deeply impressed, he related, by the religious revival which was taking place all around him in Hesse:

I was born in Germany . . . during an era that was practically atheistic. The Catholic religion was established in the region where I lived; but the cultivated classes did not profess to believe it. My own first impression of Christianity was that it was a superstition of the vulgar, only less tasteful in its imaginary objects than those presented by the symbolic Mythology of Greece and Rome. I had no thought that any one believed it,—not even its priests and dispensers, if they were at all cultivated. There is no part of Germany so entirely irreligious now. The wars of Bonaparte produced indirectly a general religious movement among the Catholics of Germany, as well as among the Protestants.[1]

During the same discussion, Follen went on to describe how he was first forced to confront the issue of religion in a serious way during his time at school in Giessen:

I was a student, and once, on an examination occasion, I was shut up alone in a room . . . and my task was to write a theme explaining the well known fact that a man could die for the object of his thought and affection. This hour began a new era in my life. My first thought was utter despair. I had never reflected on the subject and had nothing to say. But there was a necessity upon me—I asked myself how I was to gain the power to originate thoughts on my theme, and I was brought to see that this intellectual power that was to be aroused within me, must have a fountain of supply homogeneous with it; . . . . This idea of living communion with my Creator gave me a flood of light, and, with unquestioning faith that power would be given me to comprehend my subject, I began to consider the several objects which history proved could induce a man to give up his life. . . . That there was something immortal in the human consciousness was proved by the fact that there was something mortal that could be separated from him and given away by it. The unconscious prayer of faith, which my intellect was making, thus brought a revelation of immortality as its immediate answer. . . . I remembered that the nucleus of the popular religion was a death. Having finished my theme, this last fact. . .drew me to inquire into the history of Christianity: and at length I found and read the New Testament.[2]

Through this experience, the idea that Jesus Christ had died to save humankind particularly caught Follen's attention. Jesus became for him, from the completion of this essay onward, the prime example of willingness to sacrifice one's worldly existence for higher purposes and ideals. Jesus was so convincing in Follen's eyes because he was able to do two things: to acquire a powerful and definite belief which he would never surrender, and about which he would never make a compromise; and to sacrifice his own life for that belief.

The reformer and Transcendentalist Elizabeth Peabody (1804–1890), a close friend of William Ellery Channing, recorded for posterity the above statements made by Follen, and believed that "Dr. Follen tended towards sacrificing individualities to laws, and individuals to humanity."[3] The important fact about Jesus in society, then, was that he was willing to sacrifice himself for his ideals and ultimately for the well-being and progress of all of humanity. The idea of self-sacrifice and even martyrdom became central to Follen's understanding of religion, and at the same time also greatly influenced his political activities. Follen praised the readiness of the individual to surrender his own life for the sake of a larger group, be it a nation or humanity at large. Moreover, what Jesus had done in the realm of religion, man had to do in the realm of political and social reform. The only way to bring about a transformation of human society and the happiness of all humans was through the self-sacrifice of individuals, for the sake of ideals which they had recognized as correct and worth pursuing. During his time with the Jena Unconditionals, and when he organized the Youth League during his exile in Switzerland, Follen had preached this same conception of the individual's role in political change. He brought it with him to the United States.

After 1815, during Follen's youth, there had arisen a wave of religious fervor that had spread throughout the German states. In a similar development, American religion had been strongly affected by a wave of awakenings and revivals shortly before Follen arrived. The mood of contemporary Protestantism in the United States had become evangelical and activist: Christians believed in their duty to save others and to win new converts. A great emphasis was placed on the necessity of personal conversion and on inner conviction, rather than religious ritual, as the true measure of faith. Charismatic figures such as Lyman Beecher (1775–1863) and Charles Grandison Finney (1792–1875) were able to convey their evangelical Christian message to thousands at camp meetings held during the 1820s and 1830s.[4] Charles Follen was inclined to oppose revivalism and the completely pietistic religion of the heart, as did most leading members of the Unitarian denomination.[5] The kinds of religious activity and belief that Follen now tended toward were those associated with religious liberty, reason and rational thought, and readiness to engage in political involvement. These principles, in Follen's view, were the ones provided by the new denomination known as Unitarian. It is clear that Follen was not interested in adhering to orthodox religion, or in being pressed into the framework of a fixed denomination. Nor was he a believer in evangelical Christian missionizing. Rather, he thought that religion should be socially relevant as well as an aid to reform. He also thought religion should liberate the human mind from prejudices and doctrinaire assumptions about society and morals. His wife wished to spread a similar message in her writings.[6]

The Unitarian Church, to which Follen turned three years after his arrival in America, was recognized by its supporters as liberal, tolerant, and interested in genuine social reform. But at a time of interior disputes among many religious denominations,[7] it was also a hotbed of intellectual ferment in New England, and in conflict with orthodox Calvinism. In the mid- to late 1820s, when Follen appeared upon the scene, Unitarians stood in the midst of a heated controversy on what a modern denomination ought to be and to believe.[8] Many Unitarians were highly active intellectuals who were engaged in redefining American religious creeds, social conventions, and intellectual traditions.[9] Unitarianism was the main spiritual root out of which New England Transcendentalism grew.[10] Both of these religious and intellectual movements, Unitarianism and Transcendentalism, derived much from the influence of German theological and philosophical thought. Charles Follen was thus a living representative of German philosophical idealism and theological liberalism, both much admired by leading figures in American theology such as William Ellery Channing and Henry Ware, Jr., as well as by the Transcendentalists Ralph Waldo Emerson, Theodore Parker, and George Ripley.

There were two main continuities between Follen's previous political and educational activities and his new career as a Unitarian preacher and minister. One was that he once again attempted to use the ministry to propagate his own belief in the idea of freedom. Unitarian religion was understood to contribute to the liberation of people not only from the narrow dogmas and doctrines which other denominations forced upon their believers, but also from any kind of social or political oppression which might manifest itself in the structure of American society. Yet Follen's career as minister shared the pattern of his previous life in that once again he was too radical, too unorthodox for those around him and was for this rejected by the mainstream of American liberal Christians. He occupied a position as lecturer at the Harvard Divinity School in 1830, but soon thereafter resigned. Although he had some success as a preacher, his tract entitled *Religion and the Church* (published in 1836) was a total failure on the book market.[11] After being ordained in 1836, he went to New York to serve a congregation, but was eventually dropped as minister because of the radical antislavery views included in his sermons. Follen was again publicly offering more "freedom" than his audience was willing to accept.

During the first half of the 1830s, Follen's life was enriched by newly established friendships, as with William Ellery Channing and the Harvard theologian Henry Ware, Jr. Follen also began to gather extensive experience as a preacher in several different places, including Boston, Lexington, and Newburyport, Massachusetts; New York City; and Washington, D.C. He published several well-argued tracts on religion, and delivered lecture series on religious topics. There also developed during this time, however, a growing sense of the fragility of the secure and prosperous position this one-time refugee had recently attained. Eliza Follen became very ill in the summer of 1832, and the Follens' new house had to be given up soon thereafter because she was told to travel to a healthier climate by her physician. Furthermore, as had previously happened during his time as a schoolteacher at Chur in Switzerland, the religious opinions which Follen voiced were increasingly irritating to the public attending his services and lectures.

## Ferment in American Religion

When he was hired as lecturer in German at Harvard in the fall of 1825, Charles Follen entered into a complicated and conflict-ridden religious scene involving the Congregational Church. New England Unitarianism, in the period from 1800 to 1840 (the years which are essential for Follen's involvement), represents an important problem in American religious history,[12] consisting of a reaction both to the strict tradition of orthodox Calvinism which had dominated the New England Congregational Church before 1800 and also to the rationalistic philosophy of eighteenth-century Scotland and France. The followers of Unitarianism rejected the doctrine of the Trinity, and believed instead that Jesus had been a great man, but quite distinct from God. God Himself was not awful or wrathful, but intent on helping humanity help itself.[13] To Unitarians, man himself had the potential to continuously improve himself and the world around him; he could aspire to become increasingly like God. But not only could the individual work on his own self-perfection, he could permanently transform his environment into a better place as well. Other key points on which orthodox Calvinists were challenged by Unitarians included the concepts of original sin and election (Unitarians believed that all humans were good at the beginning, not depraved, and that, as free agents, all were capable of noble deeds if society helped them into this role); the place of individual responsibility in the life of the believer (Unitarians stressed the active and benevolent role a believer had to play in society); and the traditional view of atonement for sins committed (atonement was not stressed by Unitarians, since they believed in the possibility of universal salvation).[14]

The leading figures of the new liberal religion, such as William Ellery Channing, did not want to coerce believers into the same sort of fixed categories and required beliefs as the established Congregational Church had done. Every Christian had to make his own personal decision regarding what, in detail, he believed. Individual conscience was the best guide in this process. Again, these were ideas with which Follen could very easily sympathize; during his career in Germany, he had, along with the philosopher Jakob Friedrich Fries, always emphasized the important role of *Überzeugung* (personal conviction) in individual moral decision making. Orthodox Congregationalists were both surprised and angered when faced with such firm opposition from Unitarians. They agreed with the biblical scholar Moses Stuart (1780–1852) of Andover Theological Seminary (which always remained orthodox), who had argued in 1819 that Unitarianism was "a half-way house to infidelity," and that the increasing laxity of theological doctrines would lead directly to a rapid and devastating loss of faith not only among scholars and the educated classes but also among the common people. The Unitarians, however, held on to their individualized beliefs and to the new-found religious freedom which they favored, and which their new denomination was to provide. When Follen arrived in Boston, the first cornerstones in the subsequent strong development of Unitarianism in the northeastern United States had already been laid. These were the election of the liberal scholar Henry Ware to the Hollis Professorship of Divinity at Harvard in 1805, thus breaking the orthodox hegemony there;[15] William Ellery Channing's definitive sermon, entitled "Unitarian Christianity," which he delivered at the First Unitarian Church in Baltimore in 1819 and which outlined the basics of Unitarian beliefs for years to come;[16] and the formation of the American Unitarian Association in 1825.[17]

The era from 1835 to 1865, a period when Unitarians were extremely successful in many areas of public life, may be called the "golden age" of American Unitarianism. Harvard University remained firmly dominated by Unitarian scholars, such as Andrews Norton, George Bancroft, and George Ticknor, along with Josiah Quincy, Henry Wadsworth Longfellow, and James Russell Lowell. Boston intellectual life was carried largely by Unitarian personalities, and Unitarians excelled in reform activities, some even becoming involved in the controversial antislavery movement.[18] The voice of the Unitarian elite in Boston which was to have the most influence, however, was the *Christian Examiner*. It appeared from 1824 to 1869, and carried countless articles on religious and philosophical as well as literary topics.[19] Leading scholars and ministers such as Ripley and Channing published articles on religious issues here. There were also a large number of pieces of high quality on German theology and general thought.

Almost immediately after his arrival in the city of Cambridge, Charles Follen inevitably came into contact with the Unitarian elite at Harvard.[20] Ever since it had been freely admitted during the presidencies of Samuel Webber (1806–1810) and John Thornton Kirkland (1810–1829), this group prevailed among the intellectual leaders at Harvard University as much as it had among the families of wealthy Boston merchants.[21] One of the characteristics of Boston and Harvard Unitarianism which was paradoxical, however, and which caused Charles Follen a great deal of difficulty, was its intellectually liberal but socially conservative position.[22] Although Unitarians could agree on increasing religious and theological freedom, they could not necessarily condone the changes in their society which some reformers were beginning to advocate. The Unitarian elite among Boston businesspeople, as well as among Harvard scholars, was skeptical, for instance, about the antislavery cause which was to grow in importance in Boston during the 1830s. Once he became involved in this movement, Follen was forced to weigh his own radical political views against the conservative and elitist attitudes of the social circles in which he was moving.

During the 1820s, his rapport with this group had still been positive. By 1827, for example, Follen had had considerable contact with Henry Ware, Jr., and had discussed both political and religious issues with him.[23] He had also been able to offer Ware detailed information on contemporary German theologians, their writings, and their teachings.[24] Follen's personal relationship with the Unitarian Church became more complicated when, eventually, after the success which Unitarianism had achieved in establishing itself as an independent denomination, it itself experienced a split between liberals and conservatives. While William Ellery Channing had helped create a distinct unity and agreement among Unitarians during the 1820s, the religious views voiced by former ministers such as Ralph Waldo Emerson became too liberal for Unitarian intellectuals such as Professor Andrews Norton at Harvard. When the newly formed Transcendentalist movement grew out of the Unitarian Church in the 1830s, it faced strong criticism and opposition from the conservative Unitarian wing.[25]

As much as they would later come into conflict with Unitarianism and its main beliefs, Ralph Waldo Emerson and most other Transcendentalists had their backgrounds in the Unitarian church, which Emerson described in the 1830s as "an icehouse" and "corpse-cold Unitarianism"; not a few of them had once been ministers themselves.[26] The training ground of most of those Transcendentalist intellectuals who had attended college was Harvard University and its divinity school.[27] Charles Follen is known to have been associated with the Transcendental Club, founded by Ralph Waldo Emerson and Frederic Henry Hedge. As is well known, this loose group of scholars began to meet regularly in June of 1836 at the homes of prominent intellectual Bostonians, and provided a forum in which the ideas of Transcendentalism were first discussed and formulated by its main proponents. While Follen was by no means a central figure here, it is nevertheless clear that he was frequently invited to come because of his acute knowledge of German idealism and its tenets.[28] His participation, however, necessarily had negative implications for his esteem among conservative Unitarians.

When Follen was active as a lecturer on ethics and eccesiastical history at the Harvard Divinity School from 1828 to 1830, Unitarianism had still been firmly entrenched and unchallenged there. After 1800, the orthodox wing of the Congregationalist Church had no longer been able to tolerate the prevalent religious opinion at Harvard University; and in 1808 it had founded Andover Theological Seminary in order to train men in the orthodox tradition.[29] The Harvard Divinity School had at this point been surrendered to the Unitarians. In the middle and late 1830s, however, under Follen's eyes, the intellectual makeup of religious opinion prevalent at the divinity school changed dramatically once more. The thought of Ralph Waldo Emerson and Theodore Parker now invaded the teachings promulgated there. An increasing number of both students and faculty accepted the new ideas. The openly heretical ideas of the Transcendentalist movement, as seen in Emerson's essay *Nature* of 1836 or his "Divinity School Address" of 1838, seemed more appropriate now to the intellectual pioneers than the liberal and reasonable interpretation of Christianity which Unitarianism had previously offered. Indeed, Unitarianism was now described by Theodore Parker as outmoded and regressive.[30]

These strong statements not only drew angry and scandalized replies from orthodox Congregationalists, but they also prompted many Unitarian leaders to decide that now Emerson and his friends had gone much too far. Thus what has become known as the "Transcendentalist Controversy" was born, and Andrews Norton, who had supported the Unitarian viewpoint during the earlier "Unitarian Controversy," now wrote an answer to Emerson entitled "The Latest Form of Infidelity." He delivered it as an address before the alumni of the Harvard Divinity School on July 19, 1839.[31] Norton insisted that the recent attacks on revealed religion made by Emerson had been out of place and false. "Certain facts," such as a belief in miracles or the conviction that Jesus was really divine and the Son of God, had to be the basis of everyone's creed or the entire religious system would break down.

Along with intellectual conceptions of religion, beliefs in its social application were also changing. Gary L. Collison has closely examined the minutes of the Harvard student Philanthropic Society, recorded between 1831 and 1851. Students at the divinity school at this time began to find a convincing way out of their previous religious dissatisfaction, lack of interest, and doubt by an increasingly strong commitment to social reform. The Philanthropic Society began, according to its own constitution, to concern itself with "Missionary, Bible, Tract, Prison Discipline, Temperance, and Peace Societies . . . Sunday Schools, Education generally, the Prevention of Crime, Poverty, &c." As the 1830s continued, however, the society became more and more involved with a dangerous and frowned-upon new crusade: the antislavery movement. Henry Ware, Jr., the former pastor of the Second Unitarian Church in Boston (where Ralph Waldo Emerson served as assistant pastor) who had become Professor of Pastoral Theology and Pulpit Eloquence at Harvard, following in the footsteps of his father, stimulated the students' interest in antislavery. The other key persons who turned the students' attention in this new direction, Collison finds, were the Rev. Samuel J. May (1797–1871), a Unitarian reformer who was pastor of the Unitarian church in Brooklyn, Connecticut; and Professor Charles Follen of Harvard.[32] Along with a group of reformers, Follen was thus beginning to apply new concepts of religion (eventually spelt out by Emerson and Parker) to concrete social and political purposes.

## Friendships

As was mentioned earlier, in September 1828 Follen had married Eliza Lee Cabot, who came from one of Boston's most prominent and wealthy families. Eliza Follen managed to maintain a delicate balance between the social norms of her upper-class family and her own radical beliefs. This discrepancy between elite social values and radical politics remained a basic theme throughout her life. Her marriage to Charles Follen certainly increased the tension. Elizabeth Bancroft Schlesinger has described Eliza Follen's friendship with the American novelist Catherine Sedgwick (1789–1867).[33] The latter was a prominent intellectual woman in her time who must have encouraged Eliza to write. Sedgwick did not, however, at any time allow reform or antislavery sentiments to enter into her unpolitical literary works, such as the historical romance *Redwood* (1824), the first book Charles Follen had read in English upon his arrival in America. While, except on a political level, she managed to remain friends with Eliza Follen, Sedgwick eventually lost her friendship with the English writer and reformer Harriet Martineau (1802–1876), who in turn became very close to the Follens.[34] The declining relationship of, and stark contrast between, Eliza Follen's friends Catherine Sedgwick and Harriet Martineau is a typical example of the way in which dedication to reform activities could transform the reformer's friendships, personal life, and social standing.[35]

The long-standing friendships which Eliza Follen had maintained before she met her husband were increasingly threatened by her own heightened political engagement. This new, stronger dedication to political and social issues was largely due to the influence of Charles Follen, who reinforced his wife's previously much milder interest in calling for social and political change in America. Eventually, personal relations were better for Eliza Follen with reformers such as William Lloyd Garrison and Harriet Martineau than with unpolitical literary friends such as Catherine Sedgwick or even with members of her own family in Boston. While Charles Follen gave Eliza new passionate interests and issues as objects of her energies and convictions, he also separated her more and more from friends who were not reform-minded or simply not as radical.

On her part, Eliza Follen was able to provide much more for Follen than mere domestic happiness: she had direct and intact connections to Boston's intellectual and religious elite. Her husband could utilize these contacts in order, first, to gain a certain measure of social acceptance, and, second, to put forth his own reform proposals and intellectual ideas to those who held positions of power in Boston. Eliza was able better than anyone else to introduce Follen into Boston society and to actively involve him in the intellectual and social issues of concern to the educated upper-class Bostonians of the day. It was Eliza who first brought her future husband Charles along to the meetings of Sunday school teachers held at the private home of William Ellery Channing. Whatever questions Follen may have had about how the American religious and social system worked, he was free to ask them in that setting. Nobody could give Follen a better sense of what Americans were concerned with, what they wished to discuss or change in their society, than Channing. Through his acquaintance with Channing, Follen had arrived at the center of the American theological and social reform impulse.

At the close of one of the meetings of the Sunday school teachers in early 1827, Eliza first suggested to Follen that he himself should attempt to become a Unitarian preacher. She sensed his deepening interest in religious issues, and his desire to tell others about it. Follen had always been a person driven by the idea that he had a mission to improve the lives and minds of people. Becoming a Unitarian preacher was one of the best ways to reach a large and devoted audience. Preaching appeared to Follen to be a powerful tool for the religious and social reformer; it was one of those elements of the Christian tradition which Ralph Waldo Emerson would still accept as highly valuable in his "Divinity School Address" of 1838. After initial doubts about his lack of qualification as a preacher to American congregations (language difficulties and lack of systematic theological training), Follen proceeded with the idea. He soon began private theological training during frequent visits with William Ellery Channing. Their conversations, which took place several times a week beginning in the winter of 1827–28, formed the backbone of Follen's turn toward an active participation in religious thought and action. The subjects discussed, drawn from the areas of religion, philosophy, and literature, included for instance the moral and religious education of children, immortality, the defects of Christianity as it presently existed, and gratitude.[36]

Follen began to keep a regular diary on theological issues, in which he recorded his own progress toward faith and the understanding of the nature and purpose of religion in its entirety. The diary was referred to by

Eliza Follen as having been "too personal to print." However, in her biography of Charles Follen she did provide excerpts in order to document Follen's preparation for becoming a preacher.[37] These extracts show how Follen was reinterpreting many of the intellectual speculations which he had always had in a religious way. He was discovering the uses of religion as a means of accomplishing social and political change as well as personal self-perfection. The diary excerpts also reveal the great variety of religious topics which Follen was now considering, and they indicate clearly how Follen was to interpret religion in the future. In the first entry, he recorded a conversation with Henry Ware, Jr., in which they discussed religious problems typical of Follen's interests: heretics and religious dissent. Considering the results of dissent, which he himself had previously experienced and would see much of in the near future, Follen spoke of "feuds in families, brothers not speaking to each other, civil wars."[38] Still, he believed that dissent was a necessary ingredient in finding the way toward true religion. In another part of the diary, Follen dealt with the question of Providence. He thought in general that the universe was "so constructed that the destination of each being is provided for"; however, Follen also firmly stated his belief in the free agency of man, saying that "our nature is made such as to be able, and called upon, to transmute all evil into good," and that it was possible for humans "to improve through our own exertions." He thus connected religious considerations with his own belief in self-perfection and the necessity of a commitment to reform.[39]

The religious diary also contains records of a multitude of discussions on other topics. These included what Follen called "the immortality of our moral nature," and the necessity of an active rather than entirely meditative Christian life. Here Follen recalled that he had once said to William Ellery Channing, that "moral satisfaction, without which there is no other real satisfaction, is not founded upon having once been virtuous, but upon our actually being so; and we rise in happiness as we rise in virtue."[40] Follen also writes of conversations about religious education for children, the supposedly dangerous and destructive teachings of recent German theologians, and the idea of gratitude. On the last point, Follen argued that we should be as grateful and understanding toward our enemies as toward our benefactors. Asked whom he would save in a life-threatening situation, if he could only save either his parent or a well-known benefactor of mankind, Follen opted for the latter, arguing that his duty to mankind was greater than that to his own family and friends.[41]

Finally, Follen noted many discussions he had taken part in which dealt with issues of literature, social reform, law, and philosophy. He also described the circle of persons in which he was now moving. Follen was invited to the private houses of many prominent Bostonians, and met there with George Ticknor, Henry Ware, Jr., Catherine Sedgwick, and Charles Folsom, among others. He also regularly met with a German friend named Gräter, with whom he discussed German literature and philosophy. Follen's closest friend, however, was William Ellery Channing. Born in 1780 in Newport, Rhode Island, Channing came from a prominent family. At Harvard College he received his theological training and first encountered what was known in New England as Deism and "Infidelity."[42] After graduation, Channing went to Richmond, Virginia, to work for the United States Marshal for that state. He began to reflect on the problems of the slavery system which he saw all around him. He also combined his political liberalism and sympathy for humanistic aspects of the French Revolution with a complete rejection of the violence committed in France and a strong sense of personal piety.[43] In June of 1803, Channing was ordained a Congregational minister and accepted a position at the Federal Street Church in Boston.

By 1805 Channing was advancing liberal religious views, and he was quickly more engaged in the great controversy which had begun within his church than he had ever wished to be. The "new theology," soon to be called "Unitarianism," which Channing now embraced, seemed to him better suited for the modern, socially and politically dynamic age in which he was living than did the Congregational tradition.[44] He took a stand on many theological, social, and political issues, developed a strong interest in education, and believed that religion and government were the proper way in which the mind of man could be freed and elevated.[45] He supported political freedom just as he did religious freedom and toleration; both concepts for him were interwoven with each other, and in many ways paralleled those of Charles Follen. Channing went beyond an opposition to "mental slavery," as he called it. Born in a northern state which had for many decades played a central role in the North American slave trade[46] and being informed about the harsh realities of slavery through several trips to the American South and the West Indies, after 1833 he could not avoid speaking out on this new controversy.[47] The great link between Channing and Follen concerning the problem of slavery will be discussed in Chapter 6.

The friendship with William Ellery Channing was the deepest and most influential which Follen was to have in America. In a letter to Follen,

Channing remarked: "There are few with whom I feel myself so strongly united, and the years are fast flying in which I can enjoy such friendships on earth. But we cannot dispose of ourselves here. We will cherish unity of spirit; and this will secure a meeting at last."[48] The relationship of the two men hinged on the major points on which their minds and spirits intersected. Both were firmly convinced of the important role which religion played in the moral and spiritual life of human beings. Religion would provide a spirituality, it would set guidelines for human social behavior, and convey a positive, hopeful view of man and his possibilities during life on earth. Both men furthermore believed that man was capable of self-perfection, and of bettering and reforming the world in which he lived. Channing once wrote that "there is such a thing as a serene, immovable conviction."[49] This term had been a crucial concept for Follen as well, ever since his earliest student days. Channing was also concerned with human self-knowledge and wrote an essay on "Self-Culture" in which he claimed that man must educate himself in order to be effective in the world and make life better for everyone else. The "old unity of piety and action," as Andrew Delbanco has phrased it,[50] would come alive when the individual was faced with a moral dilemma (such as was posed, for instance, by slavery). Piety and action would be combined and used for self-liberation, in the general pursuit of human freedom.

In July of 1827 Follen had already written a letter to Channing for advice on religious issues, and announced his visit to the minister's summer residence:

> There are several theological subjects concerning which I desire your opinion and advice. . . . Our next college vacation begins about the middle of this month, and continues to the end of August. I wish to employ this time principally in the study of the New Testament, and in writing down, in a series of lectures, my ideas on religion, moral and rational law. For this purpose, I need and request your kind assistance; and if you are not averse to having near you a greedy pupil, who threatens to encroach on your spare hours, I should take lodgings near yours, at Newport, about the beginning of next month.[51]

Channing answered on July 17, 1827:

> I thank you for your kind letter. It was, of course, gratifying to me. To know that I have contributed at all to the peace or progress of such a

mind as yours, is a great happiness. I wish you to feel, that you have paid your debt. My interviews with you have been highly interesting; and I owe to them views and impressions, which have quickened and enriched my mind. I shall be glad to see you and have you for a neighbour.[52]

Follen spent the late summer of 1827 in Newport, Rhode Island, filling in as a guest minister at a local church. This made it possible for him to be near William Ellery Channing even in the summer time, when he did not have teaching obligations at Harvard and could concentrate exclusively on his new interests in the field of theology. While Channing gave Follen advice on religious and social matters of importance in America, and trained Follen in Unitarian theology, Follen was able to respond by reporting on recent developments in German literature, philosophy, and theology. It was through Follen that Channing was able to get first-hand information about the work and writings of such important thinkers as Kant, Fries, Schiller, Schleiermacher, and De Wette. Channing became interested in German thought, and introduced those concepts which he considered useful into American religious discourse.

Elizabeth Peabody, a very close friend of Channing's who recorded many episodes of his personal life for posterity, wrote that at the first meeting of Follen and Channing, an "immortal friendship" ensued. Peabody's *Reminiscences of the Reverend William Ellery Channing*, published in 1880, may be the best source on the Channing-Follen relationship. The work, while highly subjective and selective, shows clearly that while Follen was Channing's pupil in theology during the fall of 1827, he certainly was a teacher to Channing in other areas as well.[53] Follen brought to Channing an appreciation of such diverse areas of German thought and social practice as child rearing, psychological theories of the human mind, and socialism. He introduced him to various aspects of German literature. Perhaps most important, Follen also opened Channing's eyes to the problem of slavery in the United States.[54] Channing for his part was most impressed not only with Follen's wide knowledge but also with his personality. He saw in him the most perfect "friend of freedom, of the Right," whom he had ever met, and immediately suggested after their first intellectual exchange: "Sir, we must know each other better!"[55]

In 1828, with Channing's help and advice, Follen was allowed to become a Unitarian minister, after he had been admitted as a candidate on July 28 of that year. After initial difficulties formulating his thoughts in the English language, Follen gradually became a more proficient preacher. This took time, however. A contemporary of Follen's remarked in a personal reminiscence written during the year 1853:

In the pulpit, a certain foreign accent and slowness of enunciation rendered his delivery less agreeable. But he had acquired great command of the language, and his pronunciation was surprisingly correct. In public discourse he was distinguished by a certain fervent simplicity, a kind of boyhood of mind, which he ever retained. He was also distinguished by a poetic reverence which is characteristic of the preachers of his native land, which showed itself still more in the tone of his voice than in his language. His enthusiasm, which was large, never seemed to find full vent in the pulpit. His treatment of a subject might sometimes be esteemed common-place. He rarely stirred the deepest sensibilities of his audience. His preaching was usually neither pungent nor commanding. But there was a persuasive gentleness and sincerity of tone, a fairness and a candour in argument, and a maturity of thought, which gained the respect and affectionate assent of the hearer.[56]

In July of 1828, Follen was also appointed lecturer on ethics and ecclesiastical history at Harvard Divinity School, and was assigned to offer lectures and other instruction to theological students and undergraduates. The salary was to be $700 a year. He would present an ethical problem to his students, on which each of them had to write an essay. Follen would then read and critique all the essays, and finally summarize himself what he considered to be the most important points on the subject under consideration. While avoiding dogmatism, he would present his own view, considering himself "still a learner with his pupils, only in, perhaps, an advanced class." The main themes of his teaching were "the nature and destiny of the human mind," and "the foundations of moral obligation."[57]

Follen thus was living on a very busy schedule from 1828 onward, teaching German at Harvard College three days a week, giving a talk on history there once a week, and lecturing on ethics at the divinity school once a week. At the same time, he also wrote sermons which he delivered in his capacity as a Unitarian preacher.[58] In September of 1830, however, Follen left his post at the Harvard Divinity School, because he was disappointed with his assignment as assistant instructor of ethics. In order to survive financially, he resolved instead to deliver his series of popular lectures on moral philosophy.[59] In the fall of 1830, he turned down a permanent position as pastor of a Unitarian congregation in Newburyport on the northern shore of Massachusetts, where he had spent the summer of 1830, preaching for six weeks.[60] As we have already seen, Follen instead chose to accept his newly established professorship of German literature at Harvard. While he now concentrated on conveying the essence of German literature to his students, Follen certainly did not cease to be concerned, in writing, with theological and philosophical speculation and, at the same time, with a steady improvement of his preaching.

## The Intersection of German Radicalism with American Religion

Follen soon sought to come to terms, in written form, with some of the new thoughts to which he had now been exposed. His European background was retained and blended with the new American influences. In order to digest American ideas, he found he could still use much of his European intellectual framework. Thus his American writings on philosophical and theological topics do not seem like a completely new endeavor; rather, they are in many ways a continuation of problems with which he had dealt in Germany and Switzerland. Having profited from the American religious and philsophical environment, he wished to combine it with his German intellectual background. Follen had always been interested in following philosophical debates and engaging in philosophical speculations, whether he was disagreeing with Jakob Friedrich Fries at Jena or cooperating with Wilhelm Leberecht De Wette at Basel. In America, his interest in philosophy took an increasingly religious turn. Follen began to look for ways in which he could link German philosophical idealism with those issues in American theology and philosophy which were under intensive discussion at the time.

In 1829 Follen completed an essay entitled "On the Future State of Man." It dealt with the possibility of human life after death, and was linked to the two articles of 1824 which he had published in the *Wissenschaftliche Zeitung* at the University of Basel. The new essay was published in three installments in the *Christian Examiner* of January, March, and July, 1830. The first part was called "On the Future State of Man," the second "The Immortality of the Affections," and the third "The Immortality of the Moral Powers."[61] At the outset, Follen asked what in fact would happen to the individual person after death. He argued that while the flesh would eventually die, certain features of man would not die. Man would never lose certain key "affections" such as the love for his fellow man, and he would also never lose the striving for morality which was necessary for survival.

Follen began the first part by providing a historical sketch of what various cultures in world history had thought of as an explanation for the question of life after death. In the second part, he stated his own opinion of what a modern answer might entail. In the third, he analyzed the "moral powers" of man that constituted his immortality. In all this, Follen wished to probe what would be the "kind, degree, and duration" of life after death. He was clear that "the future state will be an ultimate exhibition and complete vindication of divine justice." Man himself had the ability to sense with his own moral sense the "true nature of justice" which would apply to him. Follen argued at the start that what has always been "the deepest and most powerful of all the desires of man" was his "yearning after an endless continuation of his existence." He assumed that the body could not be maintained endlessly; thus the question arose of what could carry on living after the body had died. Follen argued that "the elements of man's immortality do not lie in the body, but in his mind." The human intellect, providing information and problem-solving abilities, survived and was passed on from one generation to another, and could thus be considered immortal.

In the second installment, Follen set out to show the importance and immortality of three principal human feelings: pain, pleasure, and desire. He argued: "Believing, as I do, that man in the life to come will still be essentially the same being, I conclude that the nature of his feelings will remain the same forever." A particularly important aspect associated with man's feelings was his innate ability to improve and perfect his own being. The "love of perfection" could eventually make man himself better, and also strengthen relations with others: "The growth, the permanence of our love to our fellow men, depends on their, and our own, growing excellence."

By the "moral powers," discussed in the third part, Follen meant man's conscience and his will. As opposed to animals, man had the ability of free choice. He could freely control his own life and could resist certain instincts which the animal had to follow. Most important was man's ability "to choose between selfish and disinterested desires." He could also listen to his conscience, a vital part of human existence which the animal lacked. Individual conscience must regulate human behavior in society, the state, and education. It was crucial for man to engage in actual "moral exertion," and to prove himself. This ability and sense of achievement would not be lost in a life to come. Conscience and the possibility of truly moral and just action, Follen argued, would always survive in man. By touching on the issues of immortality and human morality as well as the ethical self-determination and potential self-perfection of each individual Follen had not only explained theological positions that had recently surfaced in Germany. He had also directly intervened in the current theological discussion in America. Follen's message was directed against many of the central beliefs of orthodox Calvinism, and he provided valuable insights for New England Unitarians who wished to define their own position within the American religious context.

In March of 1832 Follen published a review which made European thought accessible to the American audience. In an effort to link religious with political principles, he critiqued a work by the French liberal thinker Benjamin Constant, whom he had met in Paris twelve years before, for the *American Quarterly Review.* Follen's own religious views in America may be clearly discerned in his review, which dealt specifically with Constant's work on religion.[62] He admired Constant's stress on religion as a free, libertarian, and individualistic concept which would thrive best if interpreted by each individual for himself. Follen always sought out and critically examined voices such as this one in order to clarify his own religious standpoint and to provide support for his social and political agenda. Turning away from a focus merely on politics, Constant had now written a book on religion. For some time Follen had been very interested in the political views of this publicist who was a major proponent of liberalism. He turned to Constant's religious opinions, as set forth in *De la Religion,* a work which Constant had recently published in Paris in 1825–1831. Follen was surprised that "a man who was known only as a politician, and a general scholar, should appear before the world as the author of a theological work." However, Follen was particularly interested in how political liberalism could be applied to religion, and how both religion and politics could interlock and aid each other.

It is in this review that Follen offered to the reader some of his strongest, most revealing statements about his own political beliefs. In the *American Quarterly Review* he raised echoes of his own European revolutionary past. Follen wrote:

When the French Revolution streched forth its spectral hand in the midst of the banquet hall of despotic Europe, her thousands of lords looked with trembling upon the bloody fingers, and not one of her political soothsayers had wisdom enough to read the mysterious hand-writing, or courage enough to make known the interpretation thereof. Indeed, the friends of freedom, not less than its enemies, saw with fear the first instinctive outbreakings of a spirit which seemed directed not only against the prevailing despotism, but against all social order, religion, civilization, and refinement. . . . True, this spirit of liberty has at times appeared as a destroying angel; but the angel has passed over the great interests and hopes of mankind, which have in the soul of man a safe habitation, secured by the protecting hand of God. . . . It is despotism in every shape, persecuting or patronizing, destroying or corrupting, at which the finger of Providence is pointed.[63]

Follen then drew the connection between these historical-political considerations and religion. He argued that this connection was in fact inescapable:

The intimate and indissoluable connection between liberty and religion, and the self-destroying tendency of those who have thought of loyalty to freedom inconsistent with loyalty to faith, have never been more deeply felt, and more eloquently set forth, than by B. Constant. . . . It is clear, then, that religion and liberty are not antagonist, but kindred principles.

Follen had thus found in Constant a legitimizing work in support of his own viewpoint. He had come upon terms to justify his own combining of religion with political liberalism. Constant brought credibility to Follen's own use of religion in order to reinforce political lessons he wished to convey to the American public, and thereby to change the political order of America. Follen's religion was that of spiritual emancipation and practical political liberation.

Even before he published these essays, Follen had begun to formulate his own religious agenda for American life: he made plans for the renewal of American religion through self-examination and criticism, and thus the creation of what he thought of as a true church and a true religion. He stressed the responsibility which all believers had for their social environment and for the universal rights of man. Finally, he tried to define just how the individual religious person must act in a given social situation. By 1825 Follen had already been considering what kind of religious reform program was needed in America. He had at that time written a letter to his Giessen friend Karl Christian Sartorius, who had by then emigrated to Mexico. In the letter, he stated:

Here, where complete freedom of conscience prevails, new sects are springing up daily, which indicates a vague religious aspiration. The chief defect, however, which all churches and sects have had since the earliest times is this: that they are all founded upon dogmas, upon a definite confession of faith. Everyone is reared in some creed, and so complies as a rule with that which his sponsors promised in his stead at his christening. This rests upon a complete misunderstanding of rational human nature, which impels man to a continuous perfecting of his character as also of his religious conviction. On the other hand all churches have hitherto presupposed that religion consists in the acceptance and adherence to a definite confession of faith. I say: Religion is piety. This consists in letting one's self be guided by God in all his actions, that is, in striving "to be perfect as his Father in Heaven is perfect," as Christ says. . . . In this manner it is possible to put an end forever to all schisms, while in the one general church each sect shall appear merely as the representative of a number of confessions, all of which are important for the information of the whole church.[64]

These ideas were very close to those which Schleiermacher had previously propagated in Germany, including what George Washington Spindler has called "the repudiation of unreasoning devotion to creeds," the separation of what was mere dogma from a true religion of feeling, and longing for a union of all sects in one church. Follen had brought these concepts from Europe.[65] Now he began to test them in the new American environment, attempting to adapt them to the issues of religious liberalism and rationality which were being debated in Boston when Follen arrived there. The theological principles which Follen had come to hold true were aired in several of his religious publications, but they were expressed in an especially clear way in the many sermons that he preached throughout the 1830s.[66] A total of thirty-four sermons are included in Volume II of the *Works*. All of them proceed from various passages of the Bible and explain the contemporary relevance of each biblical motive. Some of them were written for specific occasions (Christmas Day, Thanksgiving Day, to address the students at Harvard University).

Follen used his sermons primarily in order to lay his moral agenda before his listeners. In the eighth sermon, for instance, he stated: "When we say, that the pursuit of happiness, the greatest happiness of which he is capable, is the duty, the moral destiny of man, we are aware that this principle is liable to objections. . . . Happiness must not be confounded with pleasure."[67] Follen thus insisted on the close observance of moral duty by man, and as he had already done as a student in Germany, on an ascetic, simple way of life. In the eighteenth sermon he expanded on his conception of moral duty and on the role of the individual as an example to others around him:

> When we are commanded to love and to reverence, the direct object of such injunctions is the restraint of our selfish passions, over which the will has all requisite power, and which alone prevent those senti-ments, which are required of us as duties, from exercising their legiti-mate sway over our thoughts and our actions. There are various ways, in which men may be induced to receive and follow the voice of duty. With regard to duties of sentiment, more especially, there is, perhaps, no way so well fitted to bring them home to all hearts, as that of exhibiting them in living forms, by the example of men, whose char-acter was moulded by right sentiments.[68]

Follen's belief in the individual's freedom and power, and even obliga-tion, to shape the world according to God's will was stressed in another passage from the fifteenth sermon:

> But this admonition to seek happiness in action, in constant doing, is at variance with a very common opinion among men. They believe, that happiness is to be found in being at rest, and that rest consists in doing nothing. This notion I conceive to be an error; an error, too, which is the cause of much evil, and, still more, a great impediment to good. . . . The life of the inner man, the essence of the mind, consists in action. It is the nature of the human mind not to be satisfied with what it has done, or is doing, but to be constantly aiming at higher pursuits.[69]

Follen again expressed similar ideas about the power of individuals to shape their own lives in his sermon delivered to the students of Harvard University:

> But you must never forget that the grand and beautiful prospects in science and in life cannot be attained by a smooth and level road, but

by a steep and rugged ascent. . . . I say, do not stop at the dead letter of your profession. . . . Strive, then, to master the dead letter, and boldly follow the life-giving Spirit that leads into all truth. Strive to enter into the reason of all things; search the foundations of your own mind. Do not linger on the surface, but strike deep, until you have reached that blessed spring, whose living waters the winter frost and the summer heat of life cannot freeze or dry up, even the wellspring of wisdom from the deep waters of the heart.[70]

In his sermons Follen thus preached adherence to a self-imposed moral duty, but was also calling his listeners to action and emphasizing human freedom. These points had also been made in the "Lectures on Moral Philosophy" of 1830–31. In the sermons, he was again postulating that humans could work individually and in groups to shape and recast the world in which they lived according to divine will. Man could strive toward perfection, in his relationship with God, in morality, and in politics; that way, he could, in fact, begin to become more and more divine himself. Follen's religious sermons (part of a spiritual realm) were thus linked to an upright moral stance (ethical realm), and finally to an active form of political behavior (practical realm). Follen had succeeded in explaining the connection of spirituality, moral duty, and political action to his listeners. He had defined a relationship between religious faith and social action that was to be highly valuable in his American environment.

## Religion and Social Reform

As we have seen, Follen did not limit his interests to abstract, theoretical themes in religion and philosophy. Like many reformers of his time, he was interested in a variety of different areas of American life, and particularly in the specific application of his religious ideas to plans for social reform. In the fall of 1834 Follen was invited to deliver an address introducing the Franklin Lectures at the Masonic Temple in Boston.[71] Follen spoke to an assembly of Boston workingmen and discussed concerns he deemed of direct importance to them, including their individual and social rights. He argued that labor should be the true value which guided society. The new machines invented by Americans and now used in production allowed humans to work more efficiently and to expend more energy on culture and self-development. Machines had helped Americans progress out of a state of "chaos and barbarism," and advance from "savagery" to "civilization." Follen presented a strong argument that material progress was necessary, positive, and unavoidable, as well as compatible with human happiness.

There existed, however, certain obstacles to progress; these would have to be overcome by all Americans. Follen decried complacency and self-righteousness; at the same time he warned against underrating the achievements of American manufacturing. He also denounced what he called an unhealthy "mercenary spirit" that could spread among workers as well as employers. Other features of contemporary society which Follen considered "impediments" to the progress of manufacturing and the arts were the unnecessary attention paid to fashion in one's clothing, and especially the decline of religious piety. Follen here linked the concept of economic progress with religious themes, and subsequently turned to a lengthy discussion of religion as it was relevant for his audience. He said that there was indeed a record of errors and falsities in every human endeavor or discipline. There was, however, such a thing as a "true religion" to which humans could aspire. Follen made sure everyone understood that he did "not speak of creeds and forms of religion, but of the principle,—that fundamental principle of human nature which leads some men to believe in the Bible, others in the Koran, and others in the Veds [i.e., the ancient Hindu sacred texts known as the Vedas]."[72]

All religious creeds, according to Follen, sprang from the same "tendency of human nature to something infinite, something unattainable by an ordinary exercise of our faculties in this life, something that demands the highest exertion and an endless and ever-changing sphere of existence and action." Religion in fact was not stationary but progressive, and was an expression of the ability of man to strive for his own infinite improvement. The history of Christianity had shown that a religious creed must be developed through the ages by its followers; it could not stand still without change for long.[73] After relating the great influence and inspiration which religion had through the centuries brought to the arts, architecture, and music, Follen declared that religion was directly useful to the modern working man and his daily world. In fact, Follen believed, "if American industry aspires after perfection, it must drink deep of the living waters of religion."[74] Piety was the "essential, life-giving principle of every science." It had "a foundation which free inquiry did not undermine." For Follen, a religious attitude, no matter of what denomination, was thus not only the fulfillment of a basic, inborn human need, but it was also necessary for the achievement of self-improvement and the progress of society and the world.

After Follen had delivered this address, he received a critical letter attacking the statements that he had made, especially his concept of the progressive, ever-changing character of religion and the spirit of free inquiry which he thought of as central in human progress toward truth. Follen wrote a lengthy reply, defending himself and insisting on the necessity of "free inquiry" in order to reach any personal religious conviction that was valid. He told his correspondent to "free himself of his prejudices both for and against religion," and to, in his own conscience, separate religious belief from "superstition and bigotry." According to Follen, the listener should place greater trust in the powers of his own mind to progress toward religious truth and piety.[75]

Charles Follen continued to theorize about religious issues in other publications. In 1836 he completed an essay, "Religion and the Church," that shows the development of his religious views around the time of his ordination as a Unitarian minister.[76] This essay was radical in that Follen was once again speaking on behalf of freedom, and in favor of a critical attitude toward accepted doctrines in religion and society. His appeal could not be to a large group of readers, as he was contradicting and denying what the great majority of them held to be true. It appears that Follen's arguments were once again far too extraordinary to be heard by the intellectual mainstream of his environment. Follen had planned to write a whole series of essays on this topic; however, this more elaborate project was not completed because the first published contribution failed to be a success at the booksellers.

The ideas presented in the essay that Follen did publish (consisting itself of three parts) were very much influenced by the climate of religious liberalism fostered by recent theologians in Germany and Unitarians and Transcendentalists in America. Follen carefully avoided proclaiming the superiority of any particular religion, creed, or denomination over its various competitors. Rather, he argued in a way reminiscent of Lessing's play *Nathan the Wise* (1779): all religions, even those of the most primitive idolatry, were valid in their own right and were an expression of something that was common to all humans, a longing for worship of and contact with a force which created the world and kept it in motion.

The essay provides an intimate look into Follen's own religious views. Follen spoke about his personal religious development since the earliest days of his youth. He had spent his childhood in a belief system characterized by religious "wonder" and "curiosity," and then had become increasingly skeptical and dissatisfied with the simplistic explanations of established denominations as he grew older. Eventually, however, what he had been most attracted to was the self-sacrifice of Jesus for mankind. He had come to believe that the individual's sacrifice for humanity was the highest form of religious expression. Follen made clear that "Religion and the Church" was related in many ways to the articles on philosophy and law he had published in Basel during 1824. In America, Follen claimed, he was still dealing with many of the same questions which had occupied his mind more than twelve years before. In this essay he was thus not turning to a completely new subject matter. Rather, he was continuing his own spiritual development and was establishing connections to his previous thought patterns.

Follen's essay spoke to no creed or religious denomination in particular; all were equally addressed, whether Christian, Jew, Muslim, or any other religion. At the same time, none of these creeds was essentially superior to any other. Rather, Follen argued, religion was a "common tendency" of human nature, for everyone had an innate desire to speculate about the origins of the world and to strive for personal perfection. This made religious freedom all the more important, along with an enlightened view of the equal validity of all religions. Religion was described by Follen as "the tendency of the human mind to the infinite," as a "progressive principle" which would help man strive for perfection. He continued:

> The endless progress of man is the highest object of all finite improvement; and everything that tends to benefit, to refine, and to elevate the character and condition of the individual and society, must be considered as a means of religion.[77]

Follen was thus assuming that man was constantly developing in a positive way, that he would learn from his own experiences and ultimately be able to come to terms with most problems that presented themselves in life. In order for man to become more perfect, however, he necessarily had to engage in skepticism; only by testing his own concept of religion could he advance his own being to a higher state of existence. Even modern science was described by Follen as an aid in the individual's search for true religion: a creed which would not stand the test of science was not worth following.

Follen went on to postulate that "the universe . . . is a harmonious whole." He was convinced that there existed in the universe a "truth and harmony" in all things, if man could only become sophisticated enough to discover where this order lay. Both faith and theology, if examined in a skeptical and thorough way, would help man to eventually discover truth and order, to "solve the mysteries of divine wisdom." Religion should not isolate itself from the arts and sciences; on the contrary, it should use them in order to help man in his striving for perfection. Theology itself was a science based on the "observation of facts," and on "extensive and impartial inquiry." Its sole object was the search for truth. Man had to utilize all the tools available to him, all disciplines of knowledge, in order to understand the world better through religion. Science, however, would never be able to replace religion completely on man's path to perfection. The order of the universe was not merely mechanistic. God did not simply set the world in motion and then leave it to fend for itself; rather, God was present in a form which man could eventually discover only through religious activity. Even after the creation of the world through God, there remained "freedom and the possibility for change." "Free actions of men," and not only some form of general providence (as Calvinists would believe), accounted for many of the human events that took place in the world. But these free actions must be guided by a belief in God and by the moral standards and "knowledge of duty" which a religious creed provided.

On October 30, 1836, Follen was ordained as a Unitarian minister at William Ellery Channing's Federal Street Church in Boston. At least four prominent Unitarian ministers participated in the ordination ceremony. The Transcendentalist George Ripley, who had reviewed Follen's "Inaugural Discourse," was one who took part. Channing himself delivered the concluding prayer. But the preparations did not go completely smoothly; Eliza Follen remembered:

> One of the clergymen, whom he asked to assist at his ordination, before he consented, made, as he himself told me, a most vehement attack on Dr. Follen, for his devotion to the cause of Abolition. It was in the street. Dr. Follen heard him patiently to the end of his sharp rebuke, and then simply said, "Will you not, in spite of my offences, be willing to assist at my ordination?" He consented; and no man has ever been more eloquent than he in praising the virtues, which he had himself so severely and sternly tested.[78]

Soon after his ordination, Follen was ready to accept an appointment as a temporary minister with a congregation in New York City. He needed employment and a regular income, and was willing to move to New York immediately.[79] The First Unitarian Church in New York had been founded by New England Unitarians and a group of wealthy New York citizens and first incorporated on November 15, 1819. In 1821, William Ware (1797–1852), another son of the Harvard professor Henry Ware, Sr., was appointed the church's first permanent minister. By then the congregation had become quite large and included merchants, manufacturers, attorneys, lawyers, a broker, and a historian. One of the most prominent families was that of Eliza Follen's friend Catherine Sedgwick.[80]

In early October of 1836, the controversial William Ware resigned from his ministry. Having been referred to by some orthodox church members as "an instrument of the devil," Ware preferred to leave voluntarily after fifteen years of service and subsequently set out on a journey to Europe. For two weeks after his departure, Charles Follen was invited to preach as a replacement. Although the congregation was not entirely satisfied with Follen's performance, the trustees asked him to stay on as interim minister until May 1, 1837. But matters went well for Follen and his New York congregation only until his Thanksgiving Day sermon. He had been warned by those who had supported his application not to let political radicalism of any sort slip into his sermons. By Thanksgiving, however, Follen could no longer restrain himself, and lashed out against the slavery system in the American South. With a few sentences about slavery, Follen alienated many of the most powerful members of the congregation, who "rose and went out of the church, looking very angry."[81]

In other sermons which he preached in New York, moreover, Follen emphasized his favorite topic, freedom, to such a degree that he was criticized by members of the church both for his repetition and for his opinions, which were, they thought, needlessly radical. Follen was soon unequivocally told that his socially radical ideas had no place in the church services. The Transcendentalist Theodore Parker, a kindred spirit, described this conflict and Follen's struggle for religious faith in general, in a tribute to Follen in *The Dial* after the latter's death.[82]

Although Follen had expected a considerable degree of conflict between himself and the church trustees who had a stake in the continuation of the slavery system because their trade depended upon its productivity, he was still disappointed when a majority of them voted to let his term expire in March of 1837. He left New York and spent the month of April 1837 substituting as minister at a Unitarian church in Washington, D.C.[83] On May 1 Follen was allowed to return to the First Church in New York until another permanent pastor could be found. He began to preach regularly again, delivered a series of public "Lectures on Infidelity," and he and his wife had great success with a series of open-house socials for the members of the congregation. Follen spent his summer vacation in Stockbridge, Massachusetts, with his wife and son. In September they returned to New York. Follen began to feel that he had won over the congregation, and that, if he was careful politically, he could secure a steady job as minister there.[84]

But he soon encountered further difficulties. Apparently without his prior knowledge, his name was listed as part of the committee arranging a rally to be held in memory of the murder of the abolitionist Elijah Lovejoy in Alton, Illinois, in November 1837. Lovejoy had defended his printing press against a crowd of men who wanted to smash it; he became the victim when the level of violence was escalated by his attackers. This unwanted publicity, and the fact that Follen did actually attend the rally, caused a stir within his congregation. The sermon which he delivered a few days later, based on the text "I have come not to destroy, but to fulfill" and urging a sympathetic view of reformers, did not help the situation. Although many of the wealthy New Yorkers who had belonged to the congregation in 1836 were by now no longer worshiping at the First Unitarian Church, there still took place an intense discussion among the trustees whether to let Follen stay or to dismiss him. The only offer the trustees felt they could make was to keep him as minister temporarily until they could find some-one more to their own liking. Follen was very depressed by this decision, and decided to resign rather than stay on for an undetermined length of time. Donald Walter Kring speculates that factors other than his abolitionist views may have made the New York church decide against Follen, such as his stubbornness and his personal tendency to divide the congregation frequently along political lines.[85] In his last sermon in New York, preached after his decision to resign, Follen made a strong statement which put a final torch to his association with the First Unitarian Church and its mem-bers. He argued that if Jesus were to come back to earth at that moment, he would be crucified all over again by the very Christians who held him to be the center of their religion. After more than 1,800 years of Christianity, those who believed in Christ still had not understood even the most crucial part of his message.[86]

## American Counterattack against German Religious Views

In his "Lectures on Infidelity," read to the public in the spring of 1837 in his New York church, Follen had spoken to a large audience about the meaning and implications of skepticism and "infidelity" for the Christian tradition and its central beliefs. About the kind of person commonly referred to as an "infidel," he proclaimed:

I would rather call him an unbeliever than an infidel (I mean the consciencious sceptic), whose life is governed by the precepts of religion, though his mind is not satisfied with the evidence. To charge such a man with willful unbelief is as unjustifiable as to accuse a man of dishonesty, who, in casting up an account, has committed a mistake by which he himself is the loser.[87]

Nobody could call himself a true Christian who had not thought critically about his own religion and who had not at some point called his beliefs into question. All Christians were to skeptically consider what they believed, and thereby overcome their scruples. The spirit of free inquiry was one of the most important elements of true Christianity. By examining the works of writers such as the French Encyclopedists, the philosophers Thomas Hobbes and David Hume, the radical journalist Tom Paine, and the Scottish-American reformer Frances (Fanny) Wright, Follen concluded "that fair and free inquiry would lead to faith."[88] The "Lectures on Infidelity" were an open statement in favor of the rational religion for which the Unitarians were supposed to stand. Follen went on to say:

Many think that calling into question the truths of the doctrines of the New Testament is a kind of irreverence; but to me it seems, on the contrary, that the true foundation of our abiding belief in its truth is, that its fundamental doctrines may at all times be put to the test of fair reasoning, that its principles are not a mere matter of fact and history, but of free investigation and conviction. The Bible gives us only means of arriving at truth, not truth itself. I believe in the Bible because the Bible believes in me. I find the law and the prophets in my own soul.[89]

There was an opinion, widely prevalent among conservative American theologians, that Follen took great pains to contest here and elsewhere. This was the idea that much of the unrest und uncertainty which had recently come to trouble American religious life had been imported specifically from Germany. American ministers and theologians were increasingly putting their finger on German theology and declaring it an evil influence on American beliefs. The great influence of German theological thought in New England in the 1830s and the subsequent widespread American fears of German "atheism" were recalled by the Rev. Joseph Henry Allen in his Channing Hall Lecture of 1889 on "The Contact of American Unitarianism and German Thought."[90] Allen showed how thinkers such as Schleiermacher, De Wette, and David Friedrich Strauss had suddenly swept into New England and had forever changed religious thought and attitudes there. Americans such as James Freeman Clarke, Theodore Parker, George Ripley, Henry Ware, Jr., Edward Everett, and Ralph Waldo Emerson at once absorbed the new German philosophical and theological ideas and based many of their own works on them.

The religious historian C. H. Faust has described the deep fears and insecurities about the foundations of American religious life that developed after 1815.[91] Orthodox Congregationalists had always predicted the worst when the Unitarian movement gained strength in America around this time. They argued that the sort of doctrines Channing proclaimed in his Baltimore sermon of 1819 would lead inevitably to a dramatic decline of religious faith in America. It was the "German heretics" who received the blame. German philosophy was the ultimate root of all evil; it had induced men like Emerson and Parker to disseminate their provocative and intolerable views.[92]

The culmination of attacks on German theology and thought, to which Follen felt he had to reply in 1837, came from the Unitarian side in 1839 with Andrews Norton's "Discourse on the Latest Form of Infidelity."[93] Norton insisted that there had to remain certain "religious truths," certain facts which men could hold on to when they were religious believers. The great flux and incertainty which had come to New England religion had to be stopped. The first step, Norton said, was to disassociate oneself from "the influence of the depraving literature and noxious speculations which flows in among us from Europe." European authors were very popular, but their writings were "often disfigured by gross immoralities," and they "obstructed all correct knowledge" of religion. Germany was seen by Norton as the main country guilty of furthering infidelity. Not only vulgar elements were promoting it there, but in fact the very pillars of the culture:

> There is now no bitter warfare against Christianity, because such men as then waged it would now consider our religion as but a name, a pretense, the obsolete religion of the state, the superstition of the vulgar. But infidelity has but assumed another form, and in Europe, and especially in Germany, has made its way among a very large

portion of nominally Christian theologians. Among them are now to be found those whose writings are most hostile to all that characterizes our faith.[94]

Norton felt that, among these German cultural leaders, a great variety of false and dangerous doctrines were in circulation: "In Germany the theology of which I speak has allied itself with atheism, with pantheism, and with the other irreligious speculations, that have appeared in those metaphysical systems from which the God of Christianity is excluded." Addressing the question of miracles, and their treatment in German theological works, he then declared: "On this ground, however, the miracles of Christ were not indeed expressly denied, but were represented by some of the founders of the modern school of German infidelity, as only prodigies, adapted to rouse the attention of a rude people."

Follen was clearly dealing with a very sensitive subject in his "Lectures on Infidelity" and in his defense of German theology elsewhere in his sermons and writings. His views were prejudged as controversial even before they were uttered: he was German-educated himself, and was dealing with a dangerous and sensitive American issue. His continuously strong defense of religious liberalism and of the principle of free inquiry for the attainment of religious truth would serve to win him more enemies than friends.

In the winter of 1838–39, Follen continued on the same controversial course when he delivered a series of lectures on the history of pantheism in Boston. In these talks Follen set out to examine for his listeners the new theological challenges to Christianity arising in his time. In the "Divinity School Address" of 1838, Emerson had drifted away from orthodox Christianity and even from the Christian religion as it existed in the widest sense. Other liberal theologians were moving in the same direction; they emphasized the value of the human individual and the sacred rights he or she was always endowed with, but did not insist on holding fast to traditional Christian teachings. Many of the current pantheistic writers had been inspired by Spinoza; Follen had already began to study the thought of this philosopher in Switzerland.[95] Although Follen did not unconditionally embrace pantheistic ideas, he still considered them worth critical examination. In his notes for the lectures he stated:

The subject of investigation is, the relation between God and the world; whether there be a God of nature, or nature itself be God. These are questions which call indeed for the utmost exertion of the spirit that is endowed with the singular power, and impelled by the un-quenchable desire, to search all things, even the deep things of God.[96]

An excellent record of Follen's lectures exists in the notebook of John Moore, a Harvard student of the time.[97] According to Moore's record, Follen started his course of lectures with an attempt to draw a clear distinction between the beliefs of pantheism and atheism. He argued that "the doctrines of Pantheism originated undoubtedly in a devout religious spirit," and that "on the other hand the stern and bigoted opposition to Pantheism, wh. has marked its whole history, had its origin, probably, in a no less religious spirit." Follen recognized that "in the minds of many, Pantheism is inconsistent with man's free agency—destroys his responsi-bility—is at war with the idea of God as a father, as a separate, personal existence." Still, Follen argued that "Christianity has nothing to fear from the reflections of the meditative and the pious." Pantheism could contrib-ute, moreover, to "liberalizing the minds of many who are now wedded to fixed opinions." When studying pantheism closely, Christians would realize that the differences between the two belief systems "are more in names than in ideas." Follen began his survey of pantheistic ideas with an examination of Hinduism. He mentioned "the most ancient Hindoo writ-ings" such as the *Vedas* and the "Laws of Mayhnu."

Follen next considered what he called the "Unitarian system—the reduc-ing all things to one." A world view of this kind had arisen in ancient Egypt, in Asian civilizations, and, most notably, in classical Greece. Follen traced three main paths of Greek belief systems: pantheism (Thales); dual-ism and trinity (Anaxagoras, with the division of matter and mind, and Plato, with the division of mind, matter, and divine idea); and the theory that the world consisted of particles of matter, or atoms (put forward by Democritus). Follen argued, according to Moore, that in Greece "the system of Pantheism appears in 2 schools, Ionian and Eliatic." The Ionians were "Materialist Pantheists," while the Eliatic school consisted of "Ideal Pan-theists." The latter school eventually "degenerated into Skepticism." Follen went on to discuss the Kabala, Gnosticism, and the system of Zoroaster, "who reduced all things to 2 principles, light and darkness."

He continued his survey with a discussion of the thought of Plotinus, whose principle was that of "intuition, i.e. the immediate contemplation of the Deity within us." According to Plotinus, Follen said, "our knowledge of God is the self-knowledge of God, as reflected in human reason." The great problem with Plotinus was that his system could not account for sin, since he could not clearly decide whether man was in fact a free agent or not. The next important figure was the sixteenth-century Italian philosopher and pantheist Giordano Bruno (1548–1600), who was burned at the stake during the Inquisition. His main principle had been "to reason all is one, and one is all." There was matter, of which we could only see colors and forms; it was to be called "a phenomenon." But there were also "spiritual phenomena," such as hope or fear. All things, however, contained the two attributes of form-giving and form-receiving, "Receptivity and Efficiency, the attributes of the infinite one." According to Follen, Bruno had thus thought that "the creation of the world is a self-creation of the infinite substance into various forms."

In his next lecture, he went on to what he called "the most complete system of Pantheism," in the philosophy of Spinoza. After a brief section on the weak points of Spinoza's system, Follen finally turned to the modern German philosophers who had dealt with pantheism. His discussion of Fichte, even more than his renewed excitement about Spinoza, reiterates in a pantheistic context Follen's most basic conviction:

> He [Fichte] says I cannot but believe that I see objects before me, but these are but different forms of my own mind. "I know that I am"— this is the absolute I—this is Fichte's God. Knowledge is the subjective form of existence. Existence is objective. The basis of all reality, of all knowledge, is the personal freedom of man.

Follen briefly went on to talk about the contributions of Schelling, who had moved from pantheism to theism, and Hegel, who had argued that "the universe is the mind of God."

In his fifth lecture, Follen tried to establish his own definition of pantheism. He was highly critical of what he found:

> Pantheism is every system and every doctrine, which refers all things and events to one principle in such a manner as to exclude permanent individual existence, and free agency. All systems of Pantheism have this in common, that they deny all permanent individual existence and free-agency. They say, all is derived from one, and one from all—there is no permanency.

Follen concluded that "Pantheistic charity," practiced by the adherents of what he called "Sentimental Pantheism," "is founded upon the denial of the difference between right and wrong," and merely acquiesced to the belief that "it takes all sorts of people (good and evil) to make a world." This sort of Pantheistic system thus ignored the fact that "life is not mere acquiescence—it is work—it is individual responsibility." In a section on "Objections to Pantheism," Follen listed several more negative factors. He stressed again that there was a tendency to "annihilate the distinction between right and wrong" and "between virtue and vice"; there was the danger of "equivocation, or an undefined use of language"; some were unhappy with the role assigned to reason, which was seen as infinite, while understanding was considered finite; and a persistent vagueness in imagining the deity was caused by the pantheist objection to anthropomorphism. But, Follen concluded:

> We must not forget the great merits of Pantheism. Many of the most excellent minds and hearts have been pantheists. Pantheism has opposed Polytheism. In future, as in past times, we shall find two kinds of minds working in a one-sided way. One will have everything defined—the other everything vague. Still these last will do good, so long as they do not come forward as infallible prophets. And both classes by having mutual respect and charity will serve to advance truth.

The audience had thus been given an extended series of talks on the historical development of pantheism; but Follen had also used the lectures to once again advance certain themes fundamental to his own religious and philosophical agenda. Renewed emphasis had been placed on the idea that the most varied forms of religious discourse could make a contribution to the human search for truth and meaning. Hindu and Greek philosophical assumptions in conflict with or even in direct contradiction to the tenets of nineteenth-century American Christianity could legitimately be used in order to advance man's understanding of God and his own role in the world. Current religious doctrines should not be employed to limit or select the range and scope of philosophical discourse.

Follen had also managed to involve his listeners in a renewed discussion of the concept of human freedom. While recognizing the positive aspects of pantheism and specifically of Spinoza's philosophical system, he clearly rejected the idea that all men were ruled by necessity only and had no moral free agency whatsoever. It was crucial for Follen to assert that there was a clearly definable difference between what he wanted to see as "Good" and "Evil." Humans had to be free to make their own moral decisions and to contribute actively and consciously, in freedom, to the spread of "Good" and the increase of freedom throughout the world. A meaningful life for him was unthinkable without a belief that men could work toward a continuous increase of freedom for themselves and the entire world.

Follen delivered his "Lectures on Pantheism" twice. Originally, he spoke to a group of listeners in Boston. At the request of Henry Ware, Jr., Follen then repeated the lectures for the students at the Harvard Divinity School. Unfortunately for him, his audiences were very small, many thought the material overly dry, and the financial gain was so meager that it might have been better for him to stay at home.[98]

In the summer of 1838 Follen put the theoretical issues about which he had been preparing and delivering lectures to practical use when he joined those who came to the defense of the free-thinker Abner Kneeland (1774–1844), accused of blasphemy and atheism and awaiting trial in Boston.[99] Kneeland had published several articles extremely critical of established Christian doctrines in his newspaper, *The Investigator*. A particularly strong statement had appeared in the December 20, 1833, issue:

Universalists believe in a God which I do not; but [I] believe that their God, with all his moral attributes, (aside from nature itself,) is nothing more than a chimera of their own imagination.[100]

Kneeland's articles clearly constituted a violation of the Act of July 3, 1782 ("An Act against Blasphemy"), still in effect in Massachusetts. His first trial had taken place in Boston in January of 1834.[101] On March 8, 1836, after three previous trials had not settled the case, Kneeland had been found guilty and sentenced to several months in prison. Kneeland had again appealed this decision, this time to the Supreme Court of Massachusetts. In the spring of 1838 Kneeland's appeal was considered for a fourth time.[102]

That same spring several prominent Bostonians, including Charles Follen and, among others, William Ellery Channing, Ralph Waldo Emerson, William Lloyd Garrison, and Ellis Gray Loring, prepared a petition in Kneeland's favor, addressed to the governor of Massachusetts, and asking for Kneeland's "unconditional pardon for the offence of which he has been adjudged guilty."[103] The petition was eventually signed by as many as 168 Boston citizens. In their defense of Kneeland, Follen and his co-authors argued that it was the right of everyone to freely inquire into religious doctrines and their meaning, and to state his or her own opinions in public.[104] Follen, Channing, and Loring thought that "religion needs no support from penal law." In fact, the two needed to be separate in a modern political system. To imprison Kneeland for blasphemy was a decision "at variance with the spirit of our institutions and our age." Follen and his friends argued that "freedom of speech and the press is the chief instrument of the progress of truth and of social improvements, and is never to be restrained by legislation." The authors also warned that by harsh punishment, the courts would make Kneeland into a martyr for those who shared his "licentious opinions" and "hurtful doctrines." They argued that in countries where the law had curbed deviant religious opinions in an especially severe way, more such opinions had "by a natural reaction" secretly sprung up. This argument thus did not necessarily support Kneeland's statements at all; rather, Follen and his friends believed only that his opinions should not be opposed using such ineffective and outdated punitive methods.

By siding with Kneeland, Follen was here showing his own belief in a specific kind of freedom: the freedom to believe, profess, and discuss whatever an individual pleased. Follen was also, however, seeking to discredit those who were interested in keeping religion theological and spiritual rather than practical and worldly. Religion should not be used as a tool of social and moral control. Instead, it was for Follen more valuable as an agent which would release man's energies devoted to social improvement and change. Kneeland was in the end jailed for sixty days, and chose to migrate to the American West after his release from prison. Although the petition proved unsuccessful, it showed that Follen had earned a position of influence and respect among leading Bostonians when it came to religious matters and public discussion about them.

During that same summer of 1838, when Follen had to resign from his post as Unitarian minister in New York, he planned to found his own church in that city and to direct the congregation in accordance with his own rules and precepts. Eliza Follen wrote about these plans:

He wished to see a church established upon what he considered the true Christian principle, where the preacher did not address men as proprietors of pews, but as the possessors of immortal souls; he wished to minister to a church, the doors of which should be open to all whose creed was universal love and toleration.[105]

His new church would engage in what Eliza Follen later referred to as "a more truly social worship," which would entail active participation of the congregation in each service; hold religious conferences which would encourage more intercourse between minister and church members; do away with the high pulpit and the traditional construction of the church building, so as to further contact and equality among all those who wished to speak up; make women truly equal with men, as did the Society of Friends; let all participate in the music in equal parts; provide a learned minister who was also a strong leader; have members pay all fees by voluntary subscription; and welcome all people who wished to participate.

This elaborate plan, filled with enthusiasm but not entirely practicable, failed by the fall of the same year. Follen also thought of starting such a church in Boston if it proved impossible to do so in New York. Sufficient financial support, however, was lacking. Eliza Follen wrote of her husband's feelings when faced with another failure:

> Here, as in all other purposes, he felt his poverty; his daily bread was to be earned. He had, it is true, opportunities of preaching; yet he could only earn enough barely to support himself and family. This distressed him. . . . His poverty made him powerless, and the time passed without a single effort being made for this great, and, as he thought it, most desirable object. Of his numerous disappointments, Dr. Follen perhaps felt none more keenly than this.[106]

In the spring of 1839, however, Follen's situation improved. He was hired as minister by a group of Unitarians who had formed a society in East Lexington, Massachusetts. Follen had already preached here as early as 1835, and had been succeeded as preacher by Ralph Waldo Emerson. In May of 1839, when the society had managed to secure funds to become a regular congregation, Follen moved to Lexington and began to organize the new parish. The congregation planned to build its own church, which Follen designed himself. Construction began in July of 1839, and it was agreed that Follen was to dedicate the completed building in person on January 15, 1840.[107]

## Transition to Antislavery

By the mid-1830s, Follen was seeking to unite in himself the callings of religious man and social reformer. In this context, Eliza Follen discussed portions of a sermon which Follen had preached on the text "I have come not to destroy, but to fulfill."[108] While talking about Christianity and reform, he had also speculated on his own role:

In describing the true Christian reformer, Dr. Follen unconsciously portrayed himself. Progress and improvement were, indeed, the law of his nature; but all that actually existed, especially when hallowed by time and sentiment, was sacred to him, unless there was a higher motive for destroying, than for retaining it.

Follen asked in his sermon whether Jesus had been a conservative or a radical reformer in his time, or perhaps both. He sought to understand how the modern reformer was to interpret Jesus' activities, and how was he to engage in reform as a believing Christian. Follen went on:

> The great object of change and reform is not change and reform, but to find the most perfect, and therefore most permanent, form in law and religion, in science and art, in public and domestic life. On the other hand, we see the prejudiced conservative defending the present state of things because it does exist, or because he believes that nothing would come to pass without the permission of Providence, and that, therefore, whatever is is right. He who reasons thus, forgets that this view of Providence would protect and justify the liar, the robber, the murderer, and every kind of error or crime, as well as truth, virtue, and piety.[109]

Again Follen stressed the ever-changing character of religion, which, as all other areas of human experience, had to be adapted to the times. It had to be used in order to contribute to the cause of progress and finding a more perfect way of life for mankind. Reform in a Christian vein should fulfill the same object: it must not be interested solely in bringing about change for the sake of change. Rather, it must adapt human institutions to the needs of the age, and work only to better the lives of men and women.

Follen decried religion which promoted a withdrawal from worldly affairs. Rather, reformers had to sacrifice their own personal interests "even in their fidelity to an unpopular cause," and true believers should actively engage in the liberation of man from social oppression. In 1927 the intellectual historian Vernon Parrington commented on this same issue:

> To those who enjoy the little ironies of history, the easy subjugation of respectable Boston by that very Jacobinical heresy against which Boston was so bitter is too amusing to be overlooked. Changing its name and arraying itself in garments cut after the best Yankee fashion, the

gospel of Jean Jacques [Rousseau] presently walked the streets of Boston and spoke from its most respectable pulpits, under the guise of Unitarianism.[110]

Like quite a few other Unitarians, William Ellery Channing included, Follen eventually devoted most of his energy to the cause of antislavery. He recognized that his sermons in New York and elsewhere could be used in order to try and change the minds of those in the congregation about key social problems, and thus to combine religious faith with a commitment to social justice.[111] Not unlike the German nationalist student movement had tried to do from 1815 on, Follen thus attempted to legitimize and strengthen his own social ideas by referring to the Bible and to religious motifs.

# 6

# SLAVERY AND LIBERATION

Although Charles Follen's political behavior in public had been fairly uncontroversial in the United States up to the early 1830s, he subsequently came upon the issue of antislavery, which would from then on serve to satisfy his urge for freedom fighting. As always, his sense of moral duty and of absolute commitment to a cause which he believed to be just and true came before anything else. Follen became concerned with the freedom and the rights of those who were enslaved in America, just as he had taken sides with the peasants of Hesse a dozen years before. The consequences of his actions, as earlier, now appeared secondary to him. Beginning in the summer of 1833 Follen became passionately involved in antislavery agitation, and built up a new circle of acquaintances and friends who were all connected to this cause. He eventually became vice president of the Massachusetts Antislavery Society and a founding member of the Cambridge Antislavery Society. In order to fomulate and disseminate his views, Follen delivered several important speeches, published an abolitionist piece in the *Christian Examiner,* and produced antislavery essays. His wife Eliza joined him in the cause, and remained active in it after Follen's death in 1840.

Follen established and maintained significant and close contacts with the most energetic and well-known abolitionist, William Lloyd Garrison, visiting him in his office for the first time in the summer of 1833, and with William Ellery Channing, whom he encouraged to take a firmer stand in the antislavery campaign. Essentially, Garrison and Channing presented for Follen two alternative attitudes toward antislavery and toward American reform in general. Garrison was uncompromising in his attitudes, harsh in his language, and, despite his emphasis on nonviolence, extremely belligerent in his personal style. Channing was much more moderate, diplomatic, and, many thought, dignified. Follen was left with the choice of whose path to follow, that of the radical and aggressive Garrison, or that of his best American friend, the moderate and tactful, but less fiery, Channing. Follen attempted to find a balance between the two views in his approach to reform, and to retain a close personal relationship with both personalities. Once again, however, Follen also went too far for many of those who were willing to listen to him in Boston. His energy and intensity of commitment were stronger than his ability to convince those around him that his goals were reasonable and meant to improve rather than disturb his surroundings. Neither the Brahmin business people nor many of the academics, even those who held similar religious views and were not uninterested in reform issues, could accept, let alone share, his opinions.

The personal consequences of Follen's leading role in antislavery activities were great. Follen lost his professorship of German at Harvard. The Unitarian congregation to which he preached in New York City rejected his radical abolitionist views and asked him to leave after only one year of service. Nor did Follen's activities bear immediate fruit. As in Germany, he was about twenty years ahead of his time in demanding actions and reforms for which much of the American political elite, as well as the public in general, was not ready.[1] Because of his renewed radicalism, the second half of the 1830s was a time in Follen's life when anxieties about his professional and financial future were increasingly creeping into his everyday life. In the winter of 1835–36 and in the following spring, he found himself without a job or regular income.[2] He had remained politically active, but had failed to make his political statements conform to the expectations of his environment. Again Follen had a choice: either to compromise his personal agenda, and at least partly mute his political agitation, or to be socially and financially marginalized. Follen's response was characteristic of his entire career; he showed little regard for his own personal advantage, or even for the well-being and prosperity of his wife and child, when there was a moral crusade to engage in.

## Antislavery Leaders, Institutions, and Publications

Before the American Revolution, slaves had been held in Massachusetts as well as in the Southern colonies. The abolition of slavery had eventually been written into the Massachusetts state constitution in 1780.[3] In the early 1830s, a small but extremely devoted and strong movement formed in the city of Boston which aimed at abolishing slavery in the entire United States. The handful of abolitionists who started the movement were influenced by evangelical religion as well as by the many secular reform efforts of their time. They used Boston as their main base, and then swiftly expanded to other cities and areas of America. William Lloyd Garrison became the central figure of Boston abolitionism and the editor of the most influential antislavery newspaper, *The Liberator*. He had been born in 1805 and from early on had shown a "profound religious tendency" and unusual "strength of moral conviction."[4] In the summer of 1833 Charles Follen had out of curiosity made his first visit to Garrison's tiny printing office at Merchants' Hall in Boston, in order to find out more about the antislavery cause and the people who were contributing to it. Follen was at once deeply impressed by Garrison's firm convictions, his fervent activism, and humble personal style.[5] The connection between the two men became very close as time went on; Garrison considered Follen an important and powerful addition to the antislavery movement, and repeatedly praised his courage and engagement.[6] In 1840, he remembered:

> The time has been, when not a single friendly voice encouraged me; and not a single friendly hand was stretched forth. I stood alone. At that time, who sought me out in my utter obscurity, and cheered my heart with the words of his lips? It was Charles Follen. He found me at the outset of my labors, in the obscure chambers of Merchants' Hall. He aided, counselled, and strengthened, and cheered me. He labored to enlighten those who dwelt amongst, and made them sensible to the cause of enslaved humanity.[7]

There were many points of contact between Follen and Garrison that immediately bound the two men together. Garrison conceived of antislavery as a moral crusade against sin, and even as a religion; he equated abolition with salvation, and held a determined belief in Christian perfectionism.[8] But he was also harsh, stubborn, and fanatical and, as John Thomas has written, showed "the longings of an authoritarian mind concerned with getting and using power over others."[9] This combination of, on the one hand, purposeful and idealistic devotion to what had been subjectively recognized as good, and on the other hand, an inflexible and aggressive personal style, was as characteristic of Follen as it was of Garrison.

In the winter of 1831–32 the first American society aimed exclusively at the abolition of slavery was founded in Boston under the leadership of Garrison. Regular members included Ellis Gray Loring and David Lee Child, both lawyers; Isaac Knapp, publisher of the *Liberator;* Samuel J. May, the Unitarian minister; and several others. Women, including Maria Weston Chapman, Lydia Maria Child, and Eliza Follen, also soon played a prominent role in Boston antislavery, and eventually founded an anti-slavery society of their own.[10] After the goals of fighting the system of slavery in the American South and of helping slaves gain their freedom had been determined, the means of achieving these goals had to be defined. Some members advocated a "gradualist" approach toward the abolition of slavery; Garrison believed that slavery would have to be abolished immediately.[11]

Several other courses of action were open to the antislavery reformers. One was the possibility of moral suasion, which aimed at convincing slaveholders that slavery was both unchristian and undemocratic and should be abolished on moral grounds. There existed, furthermore, the possibility of legal action, such as legislation by Congress, or individual lawsuits. Other options were the possibilities of colonization, which meant transporting blacks back to Africa; and of the free soil movement, which aimed at containing slavery within certain specific geographical areas only. Finally, another possibility, if an extreme one, was to call directly for the abolition of the United States Constitution, which accepted the institution of slavery, and bring about the dissolution of the entire American Union.[12]

Charles Follen himself had been aware of the problem of slavery in the American South as early as 1831. A key experience in Follen's life which first called his attention to the abolitionist cause, as his wife reports in her biography, was an encounter with an elderly black man in the fall of that year. The episode which Eliza Follen describes has the character of a conventional "conversion story," as often found in religious publications. Follen and Eliza had recently moved to their new house in Cambridge, very close to Harvard College. One Sunday morning, Follen was returning from preaching and, riding in his horse-drawn carriage, he picked up an old black man standing on the road in the rain. This man first alerted Follen to the problems of slavery and to the existence of an antislavery crusade by telling him about an incendiary antislavery pamphlet recently written by the radical black abolitionist David Walker (1785–1830), which had appeared in Boston in the fall of 1829.[13] After his pamphlet was issued and had been sent to members of Congress and to prominent citizens in the South at Walker's expense, Walker had died very suddenly under mysterious circumstances, and many thought that he had been poisoned by his opponents.[14]

The pamphlet written by Walker was full of anger, and contained an appeal for some form of radical, even violent action to be undertaken by blacks in America in order to truly change their intolerable situation. Walker proceeded from the premise that "we [blacks in the United States] are the most degraded, wretched, and abject set of beings that ever lived since the world began." He decried what he called "the inhuman system of slavery," and announced that his pamphlet was written in "a spirit of inquiry and investigation respecting our miseries and wretchedness in this Republican land of liberty." He concluded that "the white Americans, having reduced us to the wretched state of slavery, treat us in that condition more cruel . . . than any heathen nation did."[15] Walker warned that if white Americans did not "repent" and free all slaves, the consequences for them would be grave. Blacks would first have to "go forth and enlighten their brethren." The next step would be violent struggle against white oppression.

Charles Follen was deeply impressed by the claims and accusations made in the pamphlet, and outraged by the fate its author had suffered. For him, "Walker's Appeal" brought to mind the rhetoric he himself had written in "The Great Song" while putting up resistance to the Hessian government in Germany. Walker was describing the kind of problems and outlining violent responses to them which Follen could very well understand. Again there was an entire people, a large group of human beings, who had to free themselves of the oppression they were forced to live under. Once again violent revolt seemed to be the only effective and appropriate solution to a complex social problem.

The idea of using violence was not without its effect on the antislavery movement and on its supporters in general. One of the most controversial questions for these Northerners was whether to actively encourage the use of violent uprisings in the South in order to end the social injustice there, as Walker had suggested. Charles Follen, from early on, speculated that the South's refusal to end the slavery system would ultimately lead to violent confrontation within Southern society and perhaps the American nation as a whole.[16] Increasingly, the Northern abolitionists were suspected everywhere of fostering dissent and violent conflict in America.

However, there was profound skepticism on the part of Garrison and his supporters on the question of whether slave uprisings and rebellions planned in the North would actually help the antislavery cause or harm it.[17] From the beginning, Garrison publicly disassociated himself from violent methods, and so did the majority of his most loyal followers. And neither Follen nor Garrison, at least in public statements, advocated the use of violence in order to bring about the end of slavery in the American South. However, there was still a sizable difference in what they thought would be most effective. Follen was in favor of pursuing a political solution to the problem of slavery over Garrison's desire to concentrate on intensive moral suasion.[18] Garrison eventually came to see the entire structure of the American government, as well as the wording of the United States Constitution, as sinful, and advocated a complete moral renewal. Follen, in contrast, wanted to work within the framework of the existing legal and political institutions and never publicly advocated an overthrow of the American government. In general, the relationship of Follen and Garrison was not free of conflict: Garrison's rhetoric seeemed to Follen overstated and thus not entirely useful.

Instead of mere moral pressure, verbal hostility to the government, or outright violent measures, Follen gradually came to favor a legal battle against recalcitrant public officials, in both the North and the South, who were unwilling to put what he considered the main principles of the Declaration of Independence into practice and thus guarantee equality for Americans of all races. He felt that the laws of the United States, as well as fundamental documents of American political life such as the Declaration of Independence and the Constitution, should form the principal weapons of the antislavery movement. The legal foundations of a free society had already been created in America; that battle had been won earlier than in Europe. These legal tools now had to, however, be reinterpreted, and then used and applied in the correct way.[19] It remained uncertain what measures Follen would advocate if his tactic of legal action failed.

The first surviving mention of slavery and abolitionism by Follen appears in a series of letters which form part of a correspondence with the British diplomat Sir John Bowring (1792–1872).[20] Bowring was the editor of the well-known radical periodical *Westminster Review,* and a fervent supporter of the British antislavery movement. In his letters, written in late 1832 and in 1833, Follen vehemently attacked the way slavery was accepted as a lesser evil by most American politicians who wished to avoid national divisions:

> Indeed, the experience of every day shows us, that a republic secures blessings to mankind only so far as it actually exists; I mean, so far as

it really acknowledges the equal rights of every individual. There are many in this country, who value the union of the States above every thing, higher even than the individual rights, the protection of which is the only lawful ground of its existence. This overrating of the union proceeds in some form from an honest superstition . . . which makes them shrink from calculating the value of the union.[21]

Although many Americans refused to acknowledge this, slavery stood in direct opposition to the professed central political principles of the United States:

Many are now recovering from the delusion, which was induced in a great measure by the magic spell of specious names, such as "the American system," "the patriotic principle," etc. Still, it is astonishing, as well as lamentable, to observe how few, among the advocates of those simple demonstrations of political economy, hold them on a general ground, as principles of philanthropic justice and practical Christianity, applied to the international intercourse of men.[22]

Finally, Follen complained to Bowring that "there is in the North of this country a decided and even persecuting opposition to the honest anti-slavery efforts of a few martyr spirits."[23] Bowring, in a letter to Follen of August 1834, in turn referred to slavery as "the opprobrium of the United States." He called upon Follen to "labor night and day, at sun-rising and sun-setting, at home and abroad" to abolish slavery and "get rid of the infirmities" of the United States. Follen fervently agreed, having already discussed his decision to join the Antislavery Society with Eliza by 1833.[24] His belief in freedom and its realization in America had been shaken by his increased exposure to what he saw as the illegal and unconstitutional character, as well as the clear immorality, of slavery.

Apart from the diatribe by the black abolitionist David Walker, another publication that immediately stimulated Follen's interest in antislavery was Lydia Maria Child's *Appeal in Favor of That Class of Americans Called Africans*, which he first read shortly after it appeared in Boston during the summer of 1833. This was one of the earliest and most complete and thorough abolitionist treatments of what slavery was, why it was considered evil, and what could be done to work toward its destruction. Follen garnered from this work the statistical and historical information he needed and also found there an outline of current abolitionist tactics.[25]

By 1833 Follen had thus become acquainted with the main ideas and problems of the antislavery crusade through personal encounters and by reading current pamphlets and books. Now he began to seek out specific institutions that would allow him to make an active contribution to the cause. By the mid-1830s, a whole spectrum of antislavery groups were available to Follen as institutional frameworks in which he could learn more about the plight of blacks and could voice his own ideas on the subject. The New England Antislavery Society (renamed Massachusetts Antislavery Society in 1835) was operating within his easy reach. The New England Society became the main institution through which William Lloyd Garrison and his followers were able to propagate antislavery opinions and goals.[26]

This new group soon successfully challenged the American Colonization Society, which had dominated New England thought about slavery and its problems during the preceding decade with its strong opposition to the integration of blacks as citizens. The Colonization Society wanted all blacks to be transported back to Africa, supplied with land and the basic necessities of life there, and left to their own devices. Garrison and his supporters, in contrast, called not only for an immediate and complete end to slavery but also for the full integration of blacks into American life. The New England Society and its "Garrisonian" attitudes, however, eventually proved too harsh in tone and too extreme in its goals for many more moderate antislavery activists. Another group, the American Antislavery Society, founded in Philadephia in December of 1833 by representatives from nine different states, soon became a strong national antislavery organization, able to capture the attention of many who were willing to engage in antislavery activities. Although the constitution and the "Declaration of Sentiments" of this society were written by Garrison, many abolitionists joined who were initially not as radical as the Garrisonians, and who would later disagree with their tactics.[27] Charles Follen became a member of the Executive Committee of the American Antislavery Society.

By February of 1834 the New England Antislavery Society was effective as a statewide organization only, and became a chapter of the national American Antislavery Society. With its head offices in Boston, it presided over many smaller regional chapters.[28] The influence and active participation of Charles Follen in the activities of the New England and the Massachusetts Antislavery societies can be seen from the annual reports which they published. At the first meeting, on January 9, 1833, Follen offered these resolutions to the members of the society:

- That this Society has for its sole object the abolition of slavery in the United States, without any reference to local interests, political parties, or religious sects.
- That it is the object of this Society so to direct public sentiment as to induce the slaveholders to liberate their slaves of their own accord, and to persuade the slaves to abstain from violent means, awaiting patiently the result of the peacable measures employed by their friends for the restoration of their rights.[29]

For the first New England Antislavery Convention, organized by members of the New England Antislavery Society and meeting in Boston from May 27 through May 29, 1834, Charles Follen served as chairman of the "Committee of Arrangements" that was formed in order to draft a public statement on antislavery. When the committee had finished its work, Follen spoke to the participants in an "Address to the People of the United States."[30] This speech was later printed and mailed to members of the United States Congress and to prominent citizens of the American South. The "Address"[31] was Follen's first major abolitionist contribution delivered before a sizable audience. In his speech, Follen did not set out to slander or indiscriminately attack slaveholders and their supporters. Rather, he systematically discussed all the major issues which made up the controversy on slavery at that time, political, moral, and economic. This sort of treatment would lead all Americans to "confess and repair our wrongs" and "to act in obedience to the law of liberty which we have proclaimed."

If the whole of American political behavior was to be meaningful and true to its own principles, Follen declared, slavery would have to be abolished immediately and completely. "Every Fourth of July," he argued, "is to us a day of exultation for what we have done, and a day of humiliation for what we have left undone." Follen saw the enslaved black person first and foremost as an American citizen who was being denied the most basic rights, all of which were freely granted to others. He furthermore argued that "freedom has a salutary, and slavery a hurtful, influence on the mind and disposition both of the master and the slave." Those who held slaves were thus in effect not only brutalizing other human beings and citizens but also betraying their own political principles.

Against all doubts raised by other voices on the slavery issue, Follen pleaded for immediate abolition of slavery. It, and the fulfillment of the rights of "personal independence and self-ownership," would not create political instability. There were no historical examples of this happening,

Follen claimed. In fact, a case like that of Haiti showed clearly that immediate abolition had had positive effects on the strengthening of fundamental humanistic legal principles, on the "advantages of the free-labor system," and on the moral state of both former masters and slaves. Haiti had
gained its national independence from France in 1804 under the leadership
of General Jean Jacques Dessalines, and had subsequently become the
earliest example of an autonomous black-ruled state. However, the political
stability of Haiti that Charles Follen praised did not in fact correctly
characterize the situation on the island. After independence, there had
occurred a massacre of whites, the assassination of General Dessalines, and
subsequently a number of violent uprisings and changes in regime. While
the example of Haiti was thus not very well chosen, Follen still believed
that immediate abolition in the United States would make the slave owners
feel better morally and bring them back into harmony with liberal political
principles and human rights. Converting slave labor into free wage labor
would also pay off in terms of economic profits. A free black worker would
work harder and would live a more economically satisfying, energetic life.
Instead of preventing the thorough education of slaves, as they presently
did, slave owners should further the education of black citizens in order
to transform them into productive and active members of the nation.

Follen also challenged the legal justification of slavery. He understood
that there were property laws in the United States which enabled persons
to keep slaves. However, he questioned whether the principles of the
Declaration of Independence did not overrule any of the laws later made.
The case against slavery simply required a reinterpretation, and perhaps
not even a change, of the American Constitution. Congress alone could
finally determine whether slavery was to be a legal form of enterprise in
the United States. If this body could be influenced to reinterpret the laws
of the United States and be reminded of the original precepts of the
Declaration of Independence, slavery could be abolished swiftly, without
economic instability or great social disturbances. Already in 1834, Follen
argued that the maintenance of slavery itself would in the end lead to
political instability in America. He said that "its existence is the chief cause
of our political dissentions," and that those who directly or indirectly
strove to secure the existence of slavery in the United States were increasing
"the danger of a servile and civil war . . . [which was] gaining every year,
every day." If a way to abolish slavery and rectify prolonged social injustice
could not be found very soon, open violence would be unavoidable in the
future. Follen then ended his speech in a dramatic way, challenging Ameri-

can political decision makers to be true to their promise of freedom and democracy, and expressing his disgust at European political traditions that were reactionary in spirit and practice:

> The world has heard the tocsin of truth, and is awaking. Man is felt to be man, whether European prejudice frown upon him on account of his station, or American prejudice because of his color. Europe, which had rekindled the extinguished lamp of liberty at the altar of our revolution, still nourishes the holy fire. . . . The despotism which our forefathers could not bear in their native country, is expiring, and the sword of justice in her reformed hands, has applied its exterminating edge to slavery. Shall the United States, the free United States, which could not bear the bonds of a King, cradle the bondage which a King is abolishing? Shall we, in the vigor and buoyancy of our manhood, be less energetic in righteousness than a kingdom in its age?

The reaction to Follen's "Address" and to the idea of mailing it to others was vigorous in many respects, and certainly not all positive. Eliza Follen reported that he received one copy back through the mail covered with derogatory remarks, "upon the subject of foreigners throwing firebrands, and other stereotyped remarks of the same sort." He was also personally attacked in a vehement way in the Boston press.[32] But even as Follen brushed these comments aside, many of those sympathetic to the cause of abolition were clearly afraid of what might befall the antislavery activists in the near future. In July of 1834, William Ellery Channing wrote of his personal alarm to Charles Follen:

> I have been much shocked by the late riots in New York. That mobs should break out there, however painful, is not surprising; for we know that materials for such explosions exist in all large cities. But in this case there was a toleration of the mob by the respectable part of the community, showing a willingness that free discussion should be brought down by force, and that slavery should be perpetuated indefinitely. This is a sad omen, a melancholy indication of the decay of the spirit of freedom and humanity.[33]

By 1834–35, the character of antislavery was changing. During the period of the next two years, often referred to as the "mob years," the abolitionists encountered a steadily growing measure of violent opposition to their ideas and activities. Northern antislavery agitators were confronted with threats against all public manifestations of their work, and against their very lives. Mobs that gathered in Boston and other Northern cities actively sought to disrupt and stop abolitionists' public meetings and demonstrations.[34] These "mobs" often included wealthy and influential Boston citizens, merchants and businessmen, who feared that the antislavery agitators would destroy Boston's commercial ties with the American South. During these difficult years of 1835 and 1836, Follen was active on the board of managers of the Massachusetts Antislavery Society. William Lloyd Garrison was physically attacked during 1835, and Samuel May was assaulted by mobs five times. Follen was shocked by the physical violence and the blows struck at abolitionists from various sides, but never showed any sign of abandoning the cause.[35] May remembered Follen's role at that time as having been very positive:

> It was during the most stormy period,—the time that tried men's souls. I have given some account of it in previous articles, and have made some allusions to Dr. Follen's fidelity and fearlessness. . . . He aided us by his counsels, animated us by his resolute spirit, and strengthened us by the heart-refreshing tones of his voice. In the crisis it was, at our annual meeting in January, 1836, that he made his bravest speech. There was not a word, not a tone, not a look of compromise in it.[36]

At the fourth annual meeting of the Massachusetts Antislavery Society, held in Boston in January 1836, Follen, in his capacity as vice president, delivered a resounding speech on the dangers and immoral behavior of the antislavery mobs threatening the work of the abolitionists. On the behavior of the mobs, and their acceptance by American civil society, he commented:

> Anti-abolition mobs, and the impunity of their authors, have been justified by our newspapers, ay, by men of high standing in society, by a mode of reasoning, according to which we ought to condemn and send to prison, not the thief and the cheat, but the man of property who has been robbed or defrauded.

In a radical and provocative passage, Follen then dealt with what he believed to be the reason for the recent mob activities:

There is, indeed, no denying that if there were no abolitionists daring to express their sentiments, there would be no such mobs. . . . The abolitionists are the authors of these mobs, they tempt and provoke the people to violence, as truly as the man of property tempts and provokes the thief, and is, therefore, the true author of the theft, and ought to be sent to prison. . . . Such are the arguments by which the enemies of freedom, the prophets, the perpetrators, and the advocates of mobs, amongst us, have outlawed law, and outreasoned reason.[37]

On the local level, Follen was active as a founding member of the Cambridge Antislavery Society, established in 1834.[38] It was meant to be a subsidiary of the Massachusetts Society, and was supported by a number of local citizens. The first president of this new association was Henry Ware, Jr., an abolitionist at heart who remained involved as long as he could, until antiabolitionist pressure exerted by Harvard University, his employer, became too great. Ware resigned, but always remained a sympathizer.[39] Charles Follen, in contrast, ignored warnings from Harvard, and remained an active participant. According to its constitution, this small society aimed at the "emancipation of all who are in bondage," and at the abolition of slavery, which was "inconsistent with our free institutions, subversive of the purposes for which man was made, and utterly at variance with the plainest dictates of reason and Christianity."[40] Follen fully agreed with these views, and supported them as actively in this small society as he did on a larger scale. However, Follen realized that he was here participating in a society that deviated from the abolitionist mainstream. Initially, one of the main objectives of this small society had in fact been to make more moderate the radical tone and aggressive style of antislavery as they were exemplified by William Lloyd Garrison. Although a group had gathered that felt a certain discomfort with the Garrisonian position, the latter prevailed very soon, and the Cambridge Society died in its infancy a year later.[41] For the time being at least, the Garrisonian attitude dominated the New England abolitionist movement.

## Estrangements and Fellowships

As a reform movement attracting many educated and highly skilled men and women of strong conscience, some of whom belonged to the upper classes of Boston and New York, the American antislavery movement was from the beginning intimately connected with the Unitarians. Many Unitarian ministers were among the most fervent antislavery agitators in Boston.[42] Unitarian laypeople were, in a similar way, instrumental in the antislavery crusade. Poets such as John Greenleaf Whittier (1807–1892) and James Russell Lowell (1819–1891), for instance, used their literary and social influence in order to attack what they saw as the greatest social and moral injustice in the America of their time. Prominent female writers such as Lydia Maria Child and Eliza Follen attempted to discredit slavery in their numerous books, pamphlets, and poems, and appealed to the moral sense of adult and young readers everywhere in the United States.[43] Predictably, however, the relationship of Unitarianism with abolitionism was never free of conflict. A strong tendency toward social conservatism was deeply ingrained in the new Unitarian denomination. Douglas Stange has argued that "no members of America's elite were more disturbed by the abolitionist agitation in the ante-bellum United States than were the Unitarian conservatives."[44] Stange has also shown the wealthy and educated Unitarians' "adoration of order and authority" and fear of a "true social democracy" in America. American government and American laws were seen as already having achieved a very high degree of perfection; the effects could only be negative if one tried to alter or even replace them.

Charles Follen did not subscribe to the social conservatism of the Unitarian majority. Instead, he continued to use his position as a Unitarian lay preacher and later as an ordained minister in order to reach the moral nerve of the people to whom he preached. He very soon recognized the potential power of the pulpit in the antislavery crusade. The congregations to which Follen preached represented an audience which he might persuade of his conviction that the problem of slavery was deeply related to Christian principles of morality and sinfulness. Follen thus believed that apart from reforming American laws and influencing politics, he could help end slavery by engaging in moral suasion. In a letter of May 9, 1837, William Ellery Channing clearly expressed his thoughts to Follen on the relation of religion and antislavery, making sure he understood the priorities involved:

> I feel strongly, that, by preaching Christianity in its length and breadth, by bringing out its true spirit clearly, powerfully, in the language of deep conviction, we are advancing the Antislavery cause most effectually. . . . I am less anxious that Antislavery should be preached, than that the spirit of Christianity should be set forth with clearness and energy. The great service which Antislavery is to do is to reveal this spirit with a new life and power.[45]

Follen's sermons, however, particularly the Thanksgiving Day sermon of 1836 which had caused consternation in his congregation and had eventually contributed to his dismissal, were intended specifically to further the antislavery cause.[46] The suggestions of Channing influenced Follen; but he very soon went far beyond them, and in fact took a much more radical stand. He preached antislavery more directly than Channing would ever have found appropriate. Follen's antislavery tirades and his overbearing stress on the importance of freedom for the individual human being led to considerable conflict with his parishioners at the First Unitarian Church in New York, as we have seen, and in his appearances elsewhere.[47]

Although in danger of losing his post in New York, Follen characteristically refused to give up the intellectual and moral position which would eventually lead to his resignation under fire. In a letter to Channing, Follen firmly stated in the spring of 1837: "I have never been so strongly impressed with the intrinsic anti-slavery tendency of Unitarianism, as taking its stand on the absolute worth and eternal destiny of human nature."[48] Follen then refused during the following year, under any circumstances, to change his own religious outlook or adapt his tactics to the tastes of those around him.

The intense friendship between Channing and Follen was apparent not only in the realm of religious thought but also in the relation of both men to antislavery. The most important document that shows the easy rapport and close cooperation of these friends in the antislavery movement is the *Memoir of William Ellery Channing* published by Channing's nephew William Henry Channing in 1848. Many letters of Channing to Follen on antislavery problems and other themes are assembled here.[49] They show that Channing was firmly convinced that Follen was making a great contribution to social reform in the United States, and that this tendency toward helping others live a better life had always been present in Follen. On reading Follen's "Great Song," Channing remarked:

> Those who have felt in their youth the enthusiasm of freedom, whose spirits have been stirred within them by the sight of oppression, will easily interpret the language of this song, written at the age of seventeen. They will see in its tone of violent indignation nothing cruel or unfeeling, but the natural utterance of intense, all-sacrificing devotion to the rights, dignity, and happiness of mankind.[50]

The role of Channing in the antislavery movement has been characterized by scholars as having been indecisive and as showing a lack of intensity.[51] At first, Channing was not at all eager to join the antislavery crusade as it presently existed. He found the harsh rhetoric that the abolitionists used distasteful, and instead favored an approach which pursued a dialogue between all those involved, including the Southern slaveholders. On July 7, 1834, he wrote to Follen on the question of whether he would join an antislavery society:

> There is no need of what is called unanimity in this or any other cause. Men are perpetually sacrificing their intellectual and moral independence to this idol. So great a subject as slavery cannot be viewed by all from one position, nor with entire agreement as to the modes of treating it. . . . I feel no freedom, as some sects say, to join any of your bodies, but the cause is very dear to my heart.[52]

With time, however, Channing gradually left his initial passivity and caution behind.[53] One incident in the mid-1830s, reported with great pleasure as a moral "conversion story" by radical abolitionists, was particularly important in changing Channing's attitude. This was the severe criticism voiced spontaneously one day by his protegé Samuel May, which caused Channing to recognize that a more intensive commitment from him was needed by the movement. During a discussion of the topic with Channing, May finally became furious and exclaimed:

> Dr. Channing, I am tired of these complaints. The cause of suffering humanity, the cause of the oppressed, crushed colored countrymen, has called as loudly upon others as upon us, who are known as the Abolitionists. It was just as incumbent upon others, as upon us, to espouse it. We are not to blame that wiser and better men did not espouse it long ago. The cry of millions, suffering the most cruel bondage in our land, had been heard for half a century and disregarded.

When he was so energetically attacked by May, Channing did not withdraw or become angry. Rather, he reflected in silence for a moment, and "then in a very subdued manner, and in the kindliest tones of voice," told May: "Brother May, I acknowledge the justice of your reproof. I have been silent too long."[54]

Channing became devoted to the antislavery cause, but he never became a radical abolitionist favoring the sort of personal manner or rhetoric which Garrison demanded of his followers. Channing still warned about the possible failings involved in abolitionism in a letter to Follen written as late as October 26, 1837:

> There is one subject on which I should like to write, but can promise nothing, and that is the character of Abolitionism. I should like to point out what I think its defects and dangers, and to do something towards helping people to comprehend it. Perhaps the Abolitionists themselves are not aware how little they are understood, both in the North and the South. They are supposed to be partly heated by ideas of rights and liberty, partly fevered by exaggerated ideas of the slaves's sufferings, partly stirred up by the passion for notoriety. That they have an affection for the colored man as a man and a brother, and wish to remove what crushes his humanity, is not suspected.[55]

Channing also wrote a long letter to the *Liberator* on December 14, 1837, criticizing its "modes of operation," its support for the "resort to force by Mr. Lovejoy," and its "disposition to violent forms of speech." William Lloyd Garrison soon responded that Channing's letter was "defective in principle, false in its charity, and inconsistent in its reasoning."[56] Life with the most radical of abolitionists was thus not easy for Channing. Predictably, a commitment to antislavery also had grave social consequences for Channing among the educated and wealthy citizens of Boston. Toward the end of his life, he was made to feel the indignation of those around him on account of his active participation in the antislavery crusade: many of his former peers as minister were no longer on speaking terms with him, and his own position at the Federal Street Church in Boston ended in discord. By tolerating, and even partly siding with, the radical antislavery views such as those of his closest friend, Charles Follen, Channing was obliged to make a choice as to who his friends were. He cut himself off, in the end, from the religiously devoted, but socially conservative Unitarian elite.[57]

Apart from sermons, Channing expressed his antislavery opinions in written tracts. The extensive work *Slavery*, published in 1835, and the many pamphlets which Channing eventually published in support of antislavery, were widely read. They influenced Charles Follen's thought, and Follen, as one of the main persons who pushed Channing toward an active engagement in the antislavery crusade, in turn influenced them in a decisive way. Because Channing's position in Boston Unitarianism was so prominent, and the slavery issue was causing such divisions within the denomination, it was expected that he would eventually set out his positions on slavery in writing. His statements were attacked by conservative Unitarians for their support of antislavery sentiment, welcomed by antislavery moderates for their moral earnestness, and torn apart by antislavery radicals such as Garrison for their comparative lack of fervor, their willingness to understand both positions, and the promise to mediate between them.[58]

In *Slavery*, Channing examined the "evils of slavery" by affirming the "God-given human rights" which should apply to slaves as well as to free persons, and by searching the Scriptures for proofs that a Christian should by all means stand on the side of emancipation. While Channing was lauded by many, after the publication of *Slavery*, for his clear stand on the necessity of emancipation and an end to the "evil system" of slavery, he was still criticized by most ardent abolitionists for the moderation which prevailed in his essay. For Garrison, of course, the style and tone of Channing's attack on slavery were not radical enough.[59] On December 16, 1835, Channing wrote to Follen about the probable reception of his book:

> That you find so much to censure in the book gives me no pain. I have to thank my friends for letting me off so easily. That you found so much to approve gives me sincere pleasure. I certainly did the best which I could under the circumstances; but whilst I am most grateful to God for the unexpected reception it has met with and the good it has done, I am as little satisfied with the execution of my task as any one can be.[60]

A tract by Channing which was more radical than *Slavery* was his "Letter to James G. Birney," published for general distribution in 1837.[61] Between 1839 and 1842, Channing published other pamphlets in support of the emancipation of the American slaves, such as *Remarks on the Slavery Question, In a Letter to Jonathan Phillips* (Boston, 1839); *Emancipation* (Boston, 1840); and *The Duty of the Free States, or Remarks Suggested by the Case of the Creole* (Boston, 1842). The last dealt with the question of violence, an issue which was always present in abolitionist circles, if often beneath the surface. Channing reviewed the case of the slave ship "Creole," sailing from Virginia to New Orleans, which had been taken over by blacks in a general mutiny. The slaves had sailed the brig into the port of Nassau in the Bahamas and had demanded their own freedom. Channing wished to demonstrate the morally justifiable act of the black slaves, and the cruelty of American demands for their immediate return. He thus directly contradicted the pacifist stance publicly propagated by William Lloyd Garrison; it is likely, however, that Follen strongly agreed with him in justifying violent self-defense as a valid last resort.

The relationship between Channing and William Lloyd Garrison was much more problematic. Even though Channing was willing, during the later 1830s, to take a firmer stand against slavery, he never fully gained the respect of Garrison until the 1840s. Rather, he generally remained, as his biographer John White Chadwick has commented, "between two fires," attacked by slaveholders and radical abolitionists alike.[62] By contrast, his friendship with Charles Follen always remained intact, and in fact grew stronger. More than most other abolitionists, Follen recognized that Channing had an important contribution to make to antislavery. Only when Garrison read the memoir of Channing, soon after it was published in 1848 by his nephew, could he say that he saw him now "in a better light," and proclaim Channing "a sincere man, and true to his own convictions of duty."[63] At the same time, he still thought that Channing was "not a reformer," and his "impressions of Dr. Channing were, that he was somewhat cold in temperament, timid in spirit, and oracular in feeling." Channing had for him been "a man whose hearty, personal cooperation [he] had longed to secure, and who had met with silence the only advances that could in delicacy be made for an interview that might remove mutual misunderstanding."[64] Continuing the same statement, Garrison went on to complain bitterly:

> Much to my regret, I had no personal acquaintance with this remarkable man, though I longed for at least a single interview. But the *Liberator* was not to his taste, and my manner of conducting the antislavery enterprise seemed to him harsh, repulsive, and positively injurious. As he never expressed a wish to converse with me, I did not feel free to intrude myself upon his notice. For twelve years, he saw me struggling against all that was evil in the land—in a cause worthy of universal acclaim—with fidelity and an unfaltering spirit—but during all that time he never conveyed to me, directly or indirectly, a word of cheer, or a whisper of encouragement.[65]

It is surprising that Charles Follen managed to retain the friendship and support of both men throughout the 1830s, considering their very different outlooks on reform. For once in his life, Follen was able to balance two contrary opinions, and to hold on to two connections that were vital to his own political and moral development. Eliza Follen characterized her husband's relationship with Garrison around 1836 in this way:

> He did not agree with Mr. Garrison upon some questions unconnected with the anti-slavery cause; his taste and feelings were offended by the language he occasionally used; he was deeply pained by his harsh attacks on individuals [Channing was undoubtedly meant here]; but he never allowed his perception of what he thought Mr. Garrison's faults, to overshadow his conviction of his great virtues. He reverenced his fearless devotion to principle; his uncompromising declaration and vindication of what he considered truth, against the weakness or mistakes of his friends, as well as against the open and determined opposition of his enemies.[66]

In addition to Channing and also Garrison, one of the closest friends of Charles and Eliza Follen in this phase of their lives was the English writer and reformer Harriet Martineau (1802–1876), who visited the United States several times in the 1830s and met the Follens early in 1835. Most of the letters from this period which were published by Eliza Follen in her husband's *Works* are to or from Harriet Martineau. They show that with this English woman, Charles Follen could fruitfully exchange ideas and formulate his own plans.[67] On her voyages to the United States between the years 1834 and 1836, Martineau critically viewed the institutions and the people of America, taking special interest in the possibilities of reform movements and the achievement of social improvement.[68] In the introduction to a modern edition of her *Society in America*, Seymour Martin Lipset has shown how the English reformer saw America as a "land of promise" and a "new society," important to observe for those working to achieve progress in European social arrangements and political systems. Martineau came to America for the first time in 1834, to examine to what extent the "American Creed" of human equality and an obligation to human justice, as it was described in the Declaration of Independence, in day-to-day life.[69] After a trip to the American South, Martineau became particularly interested in the slavery question. Eventually she could no longer conceal her own sentiments, which were strongly in support of the antislavery movement. Stephen Bloore has described how she was careful at first not to speak out publicly about antislavery, so as not to offend her hosts and not to fall into disfavor in American public opinion and with the press. Eventually, however, Martineau felt obliged to publicly and unambiguously side with the antislavery movement, thus risking social ostracism from the majority of the conservative New England elite. Among those who worked hardest to enlist Martineau's support and great intellectual influence for antislavery was Charles Follen.[70]

In her *Autobiography*, published in 1877, Martineau reported on the invitation she received in 1835 from Charles Follen to attend an antislavery meeting for the first time in her life. On a visit to Henry Ware, Jr., in Cambridge, she met the Follens. They immediately inquired whether she would have time to come to the next meeting of the Boston Female Antislavery Society, to which Eliza Follen belonged. When Martineau, after an initial hesitation, agreed to come, "the Follens had not been gone many minutes before the invitation arrived." Charles and Eliza Follen had thus played the decisive role in introducing her directly to members of the antislavery movement in Boston.[71] Later in her autobiography Martineau expressed her positive view of Charles Follen and his achievements, tying together his German past with his socially involved American present:

Dr Follen, the patriot hero of Germany, the student, the poet, the philosopher, the victim of the Holy Alliance, the Christian teacher, the American abolitionist, and the victim of American despotism. . . . He was one of those rare great spirits that find no alternative at the call of a great cause but obedience. He was the only European exile of that vintage who declined to prosper as an American by flattering the nation's sin,—so rare is the virtue that can pour out of its life-blood twice. While suffering proscription from the land of his birth, he identified himself with Garrison among the earliest, and suffered, with the rest, a fresh proscription from the land of his love and his adoption.[72]

One of the first letters she received from Charles Follen shows clearly how the latter wished to influence her. It is written in a style highly typical of Follen; the vocabulary is reminiscent of the religious mysticism of the "Great Song." Definitions of Follen's key concepts of "principles" and "martyrdom" are included:

Those principles in which we live and move and have our being, though as old as the creation of man, are still a new doctrine, the elements of a new covenant, even in civilized, republican, Christian America. They are as the bread and wine of the altar, to which all are

invited, but of which few partake, because they dread to sign in their
own hearts the pledge of truth which may have to be redeemed by
martyrdom. . . . But if the world separate itself from us, it leads us to
find a world in ourselves and in each other; not to form a new
aristocracy of a somewhat higher stamp, but to unite our strength to
break down every wall of our partition that interferes with man and
our fellow-man. Our meeting with you, dear Harriet, was a blessed
recognition, rather than a new acquaintance; our friendship had a
pre-existence in kindred principles.[73]

Lipset has written that "abolitionists were [Martineau's] heroes in
American society," as can be seen in her sympathetic 1839 article entitled
"The Martyr Age of the United States." She made it clear how much harder
the abolitionists' stand was in America than in Britain, where slavery no
longer existed. Furthermore, Lipset has claimed that in Britain, there were
not the same pressure groups whose livelihood depended on the economic
well-being of the American South and thus on an intact slavery system. It
is clear in any case that the American abolitionists constituted a small
minority which braved the social opprobrium of "polite society in the
North" and fought a bitter struggle against the great odds of bigotry, social
and economic pressure, and threats of violence.[74]

The intimacy between the Follens and Martineau established a link
between two of the most controversial reform campaigns of the time: those
for the emancipation of women and of American slaves. In "The Martyr
Age," Martineau took special note of the important role that women played
in the antislavery movement. She told the background story of the recently
established Boston Female Antislavery Society, which was "composed of
women of every rank, and every religious sect, as well as of all complex-
ions." Martineau was happy to observe that, in the society, "all sectarian
jealousy is lost in a great cause."[75] Under the leadership of Maria Weston
Chapman, the women established their own office in downtown Boston.
They kept meeting even though they were increasingly subject both to the
criticism of male abolitionists and to the dangers posed by proslavery
mobs. Eventually, Martineau observed, the slavery and the women questions became entangled as one issue, and could only be solved together.
There could be no abolition of slavery without full legal equality for
women as well. By their willingness to fight for the rights of black Americans, women showed that they too were entitled to the sort of treatment
which they demanded for blacks. To support this argument, Martineau

quoted from a speech delivered by Charles Follen before the Massachusetts Antislavery Society in 1836, in which he strongly urged all abolitionists to recognize without hesitation the equal rights of women not only within the antislavery movement, but also in society at large:

> I maintain that, with regard to the Anti-Slavery cause, men and women have the same duties and the same rights. . . . It is indeed a proof of uncommon moral courage, or of an overpowering sense of religious duty and sympathy with the oppressed, that a woman is induced to embrace the unpopular, unfashionable, obnoxious principles of the abolitionists. . . . It is on this account that I look upon the formation of the Ladies' Anti-Slavery Societies as an event of the highest interest. . . .[76]

The importance of the women's issue for antislavery in the later 1830s has been increasingly recognized in recent scholarship. The consistent position of perfect equality of the sexes supported by Garrison and Follen alike was not shared by all abolitionists; rather, the question whether to admit women to all antislavery meetings and make them regular members of all abolitionist societies divided the reformers. Antifeminist abolitionists, as Aileen Kraditor has called them, attempted to block the proposals for equality put forth by Garrison and Follen.[77] Eliza Follen herself belonged to an ever-increasing group of socially active women who were important to the abolitionist movement because of the support they lent to it and also because of the challenge they presented to those male abolitionists who had to become accustomed to accepting women reformers as their equals. With many of her pamphlets, tracts, and poems, such as "The Liberty Cap" (1846) or "To Mothers in the Free States" (1855), Eliza Follen also contributed significantly to the antislavery movement by influencing the mood of her readership, which consisted of adults and particularly children.[78] She was never able to influence American public opinion as much as Harriet Beecher Stowe did several years later with *Uncle Tom's Cabin* (first published serially in 1851–52), but she attempted with considerable success to work in the same direction. Her goal was to appeal to the moral conscience of her audience, and to show that slavery was above all morally wrong and sinful.

Eliza Follen's personal acquaintance with William Lloyd Garrison continued until her death in 1860. Its closeness is apparent in several letters which she wrote to him. In 1850, for example, she paid a visit to her son

Charles Christopher, who was then studying at the University of London. To Garrison she wrote:

> Now that I am established here in London for the winter I am very anxious to be sure of having the *Liberator.* I left directions for it to be sent during my absence to Mrs. Pomeroy of Cambridge, but now I wish it to be sent here to me, as it is also sent or was last year to Dr Hutton I suppose that it can be sent to me in the same way. I set my heart so much upon getting it, as I think it will aid me in my purpose of agitating a little in London. . . . Mrs Chapman says that she shall send me the *Standard* but I depend most upon the *Liberator*—I have this moment received a letter from H. Martineau saying that she had sent 20 pounds to Mr E. G. Loring to be divided equally between the *Standard* and the *Liberator.* . . .[79]

Remaining loyal to her own reform mentality at all times, Eliza Follen found a new circle of like-minded friends among British reformers during her stay in England. Jane Carlyle, the wife of the British writer Thomas Carlyle, mentioned her in a letter of 1851:

> What a douce and intelligent looking woman that Mrs Follen is! I quite took to her before I knew her name. Luckily, because I should not have taken to her after having at one time of my life been perfectly bored with her praises from several quarters, but chiefly from one, an Italian painter Gambardella who used to declare that she and I were the only two women in the world.[80]

## Nationality and Abolition

Charles and Eliza Follen contributed greatly to the antislavery movement through organizational work, essays, and speeches. In 1836 Follen gave two public talks which were later printed. Throughout these publications, there remained a continued stress on the concepts of freedom and liberty as the most important abstract values in Follen's life, and on their negative opposites, slavery and oppression. Follen spoke before the Massachusetts Antislavery Society at its annual meeting in Boston on January 20, 1836.[81] He said that the antislavery crusade was first and foremost one of philanthropy, or the "love of man." Its followers must recognize that slaves were indeed humans, as they themselves were, and naturally endowed with the same rights and duties. All members of antislavery societies were called to strive for the freedom of their fellow Americans who were black. Follen called upon the abolitionists to help fulfill the principles of the Declaration of Independence and its provisions for universal legal equality and individual human rights. This document was currently a "dead letter," and had to be "raised from the dead." Slavery and its abolition was thus described by Follen as an American political issue, but also as a question relevant for all mankind.

Although he knew it would keep away many potential white antislavery supporters, Follen was in support of admitting black abolitionists to the Massachusetts Antislavery Society meetings. The most important fact which Follen wished to teach everyone, from the Southern slaveholder to the Northern antislavery sympathizer, was "that the colored man is a man." If the antislavery crusade was to be credible, blacks would have to be permitted to attend its meetings in the North and actively contribute to the shaping of their own future. Follen also observed in the same vein that, in the antislavery campaign, "foreigners and citizens have the same duties and the same rights." Here he was speaking at least partly in self-defense, having recently been attacked several times as a "foreign meddler" in American affairs who did not have the right to demand changes in American legal and social life. Follen made it clear that foreigners had their role in striving for freedom and equal rights as they did in every country where these assets were absent. Nor was American slavery the only issue Follen raised in his speech. His scope was much broader:

> Our cause is the cause of man; therefore our watchword from the beginning has been, "Our country is the world,—our countrymen are mankind." We reverence patriotism as a virtue, so far as it is philanthropy applied to our country, while we look down upon it as a vice, so far as it would sacrifice the rights of man,—the moral to the selfish interests of our nation.[82]

Follen went on to denounce organized and extensive violence as a means of political change, whether it was applied by the mobs who engaged in the tarring and feathering of abolitionists or by the antislavery activists themselves. At the same time, Follen strongly pleaded for the individual's right to defend his own freedom and human dignity. Depriving any human being of his natural rights in an artificial way was for Follen an act of violence in itself which had to be countered. The abolitionist reformers must work against this violence, and ensure, at the same time, that they "defend the rights, and respect the feelings of all men." A further issue which Follen addressed in this speech was the question of women's rights. Women must be allowed to take an active part in antislavery meetings, and the contribution which they could make must be gladly accepted. He echoed the view of Harriet Martineau that it was impossible to press for the rights of American blacks, if these rights were not also guaranteed to American women. Follen deplored the fact that "men have at all times been inclined to allow women particular privileges, while withholding from them essential rights."

At the end of his speech Follen rallied his listeners to take up their cause with enthusiasm and to use every possible method short of violence in order to help abolish slavery. "Family connections, commercial relations, political and religious interests" bound the Northern abolitionists to their fellow Americans in the South. Thereby, the Southerners could be influenced in a tireless campaign "to restore the slave to his natural rights." Follen exclaimed that "we contend with a national prejudice; we aim at a national reform." He felt that the abolitionist crusade must use all possible channels of communication, and must be as broad and sweeping as possible. In his view, Americans had the ability to actively mold and to morally perfect their own national community, and the future course of mankind:

> We are told, we must not agitate this subject;—let it alone, and it will remedy itself. This is not the course of Providence. Such reformations are never accomplished without human means. God will not indulge us in our indolence, and do the work without our instrumentality.

The essay "The Cause of Freedom in Our Country" placed Follen's argument more directly in the American national context. It was published in the *Quarterly Antislavery Magazine* in October of 1836. Here Follen set out, in a similar way to his January speech, to examine critically how far the principles of freedom and liberty had been realized in the United States. Again he constrasted liberty with oppression:

> The internal history of every nation, every republic in particular, consists of the workings, the successful or unsuccessful conflicts, of the principles of Liberty and of Oppression. . . . I mean by Liberty, the possession of all the inalienable equal rights which belong to each human being as a necessary moral attribute of human nature—the

right of each individual to use all his facilities of mind and body in any way not inconsistent with the equal freedom of his fellow men. . . . And I mean by Oppression, any infringement, and undeserved or unneccessary abridgement, of those natural rights.[83]

Follen had thus set up a dichotomy by which to test the national environment in which he lived. To his displeasure, he found that in the case of the United States, "the worm of Oppression is gnawing every fibre of the frame." The "causes and means of personal advancement," such as "the acquisition of property; the comforts, and refinements of life; personal bravery, talent, learning, and skill; honor and office" were, according to Follen, being used in an unjust way, and their "perversion into instruments of Oppression" was unacceptable to both a legal thinker and a Christian. In theory, America possessed all the attributes, including great natural resources and wealth and a republican form of government, to make every one of its citizens prefectly happy. The fathers of democracy and republican government in America had succeeded in all they wanted to achieve. Follen argued that "the great experiment that was to determine the fitness of man for self-government, has been successful, wholly successful so far as it has actually been tried." However, all the natural endowments that they could utilize, and the political ones they had themselves created, were not being used in a moral or even an efficient manner. Instead, slaveholders were marring the image of all America as the land of freedom and justice. Follen insisted that "slavery is not a local evil, that strikes only the spot in which it settles, with barrenness; it is a stagnant pool that infects the whole neighborhood, and aggravates every minor disorder in the body politic."

If Americans, in obvious contradiction to their own Constitution, accepted slavery as an integral part of their political system, then other vices would soon be allowed as well. The whole country would eventually fall back in its development from the ideal of liberty into the stage of feudalism, inequality, political privileges, and prejudice against color. Furthermore, there was great danger that racial oppression would also harm other population groups in America: Follen specifically mentioned the American Indians, whom he saw as victims of white hypocrisy and greed. Native Americans had clearly and repeatedly shown themselves "susceptible of civilization and true religion"; all "the Christian, the Republican white man" had given them, however, had been "broken treaties, gun-powder and rum." Follen argued that "closely allied with the love of distinction, and still more extensive in our country, is the eager pursuit of wealth."

Greed and profiteering were phenomena which led directly to the acceptance of slavery, and sustained it as a social system. Excessive regard for money making thus led not only to social injustice but also to the undermining of ideals set forth in the Declaration of Independence and the Constitution. Follen called upon the "friends of freedom" to unite in order to fight "the enemy" which relied on the racial and financial exploitation of fellow Americans. The principle that "all men were born free and equal" had to be defended as an indispensable American right. The dignity of human nature, and the equal rights of every citizen of the United States, obliged Follen and his friends, he said, to fight for liberty and against oppression. Slavery was indeed a problem of the highest national import; if it were not abolished as soon as possible, then the entire moral foundation of American political life would break down.

By 1835 Follen had become completely open in his antislavery activities, and along with his closest circle of associates, eventually tried to force political concessions from the Massachusetts government. He employed all the legal skills and the forceful argumentative style which had been his trademarks in Europe. This next stage of his involvement in the antislavery struggle was reminiscent of the way he had petitioned the government in Hesse at the beginning of his radical career. In December of 1835, the Massachusetts Antislavery Society had been denounced by the governors of several Southern states because it had sent through the mails a great amount of abolitionist literature to the South. Governor Everett of Massachusetts and the state attorney general were pressured by their Southern counterparts to put an end to these mailings. In addition, northern abolitionists had mailed so many petitions to the House of Representatives in Washington that the members voted to no longer consider them individually, but instead to treat them collectively as one petition. Under pressure from Washington as well, the Massachusetts government decided that the local abolitionists were "guilty of an offense against the laws of their country, and were liable to prosecution."[84] What was being proposed was the so-called Gag Bill, which would make it illegal to discuss many of the issues central to the antislavery movement in pamphlets and magazines, and to send these to Washington politicians or slaveholders in the South by mail.[85] The abolitionists decided to protest against the proposed bill, and demanded a public hearing. A Massachusetts House committee of five representatives, led by the Honorable George Lunt, subsequently met twice at the State House in Boston with a committee sent by the Antislavery Society. The antislavery committee, for both hearings, was made up of

Charles Follen, Samuel May, William Lloyd Garrison, Ellis Gray Loring, and William Goodell.

Harriet Martineau described the scene at the first hearing on March 4, 1836. Charles Follen, "looking German all over, and a deeper earnestness than usual overspreading his serene and meditative countenance,"[86] delivered a fiery speech, accusing the Massachusetts legislature of political failure in not officially denouncing slavery as a moral and political evil. Freedom of speech for all citizens, he argued, was essential to the preservation of the spirit of the U.S. government and to the Constitution. To threaten "liberty of speech" and "to muzzle the press" would seriously injure the American political system. Follen argued that the sort of censorship which the abolitionists were experiencing was more typical of the mobs which had recently gathered in Faneuil Hall than of a state government. Perhaps it would be enough if "the mob let loose again their bloodhounds upon us." George Lunt interrupted at this point and said: "Stop, Sir. You may not pursue this sort of remark. It is insulting to this committee, and to the Legislature, which they represent." Follen countered that he did not think he had said anything illegal or indecent. Lunt answered: "The committee consider the remarks you have made very improper, and cannot permit you to proceed." Follen was thus forced by the chairman to stop talking and to sit down.[87] When Samuel May protested, Lunt simply said:

> Whatever you Sir . . . may think of the remarks of Dr. Follen, it is for the committee to decide whether they were proper or improper. . . . It is a subject of special favor that you are admitted to this interview at all—and now you must be subject to our direction.

Although a quarrel over whether the abolitionists even had a right to call for a hearing now ensued, William Lloyd Garrison did manage to lead the participants back to the actual topic under discussion, and used the speaking time he was given to deliver a scathing attack on slavery.

A second meeting was held on March 8. Charles Follen once again spoke at length, and this time the legislative committee could find no grounds to interrupt him or keep him from speaking out altogether. Instead, he put forth an intense and convincing statement against legislative censure and the misrepresentation of the abolitionists as undisciplined ruffians. Freedom of speech had to be guaranteed to all Americans, and "Judge Lynch," as used by the mobs trying to persecute abolitionists in Boston, should be banned from the civilized resolution of political issues.[88] Follen formulated his defense of free speech in general, and his own right to participate in public discussion specifically, in this way:

> I have been eleven years a resident, and six years a citizen, of this republic. The principles on which the anti-slavery societies are founded, are the same which brought me to this country, and without the enjoyment of which I could not wish to remain in it. The principles of freedom, and especially the right of free discussion, are secured to the citizens in the Constitution and laws of the country.[89]

He also used his right to speak openly as a platform in order to promote the cause of antislavery. His awareness of the dangers involved in the conflict between antislavery and proslavery supporters is prominent. His overly methodical and even stubborn style is evident as well:

> It is now admitted, that the voice of the civilized world, out of this country, is with the Abolitionists. The civilized nations of Europe have already done, or are fast doing, what must be done in this country at some time or other. Emancipation must come. Mr. Jefferson prophesied truly, when he said, many years ago, that an end to slavery must come. Whether it will come in peace, by argument and persuasion, or in blood, as it did in St. Domingo, rests upon ourselves to determine. The Abolitionists' feeling, in the spirit of the prophecy of Jefferson, that emancipation must come, seek to bring it about in peace, by rousing the country to a sense of the dangers growing out of this institution, and increasing so long as it remains among us.

After Follen spoke the abolitionist William Goodell, who also addressed the hearing on these issues, became agitated and exclaimed:

> Censured for what? It is not the Abolitionists you will censure, but you will censure the first principles of freedom. . . . No, I will not fear.—Blessed be God, though the mountains be removed, and though the depths be broken up, yet I will not fear. I fear not for myself, but I fear for the liberties of my country.

Lunt countered: "Stop, Sir, the committee will hear no more of this. You will not be permitted to proceed in this manner." Goodell was now cut off. Eliza Follen reported:

Dr. Follen thus had at last the satisfaction of being allowed to express his own views without further opposition to himself personally; but he had the pain, directly afterwards, of hearing his collegue stopped in his address, and then ordered to sit down. Mr. May, also, was silenced by the chairman. When rudely spoken to himself, he had been calm; but this insulting tone to others, he told me, severely tried his temper. I saw the glow of indignation in his face.[90]

Eventually the abolitionists reached a complete deadlock with the committee chairman, and they recognized that nothing they could say would change his mind or force him to make concessions. The hearing had, however, been public, and many who were in attendance had begun to sympathize with the antislavery arguments which had been presented. The main reason for this sympathy was the openly hostile treatment of the abolitionists at the hands of the committee.[91] The reaction to Follen's remarks in the Boston press, however, was much less favorable. Again he was attacked *ad hominem,* and his arguments were twisted and ridiculed.[92] The Gag Bill itself was not rescinded until 1844.

The entire entourage of abolitionists, with spouses and supporters, had been present at both hearings of 1836. However, the most dramatic manifestation of support occurred when William Ellery Channing suddenly and unexpectedly entered into the room. Harriet Martineau described his arrival at the State House:

> During the suspense the door opened, and Dr. Channing entered—one of the last people that could on that wintry afternoon have been expected. He stood for a few moments, muffled in cloak and shawl-handkerchief, and then walked the whole length of the room, and was immediately seen shaking hands with Garrison (he afterwards explained that he was not at the moment certain that it was Mr. Garrison, but that he was not the less happy to have shaken hands with him). A murmur ran through the gallery, and a smile went round the chamber. Mrs Chapman whispered to her neighbor, "Righteousness and Peace have kissed each other."[93]

In November of 1838, Charles Follen published another abolitionist article in *The Christian Examiner,* entitled "Antislavery Principles and Proceedings." It provides a valuable summary of and insight into the complex and productive activities of the American antislavery movement, and a synopsis of various positions and debates which had recently taken place within it. The relationship of the American Antislavery Society to its smaller local member organizations was debated; as was the question of the actual coordinated goals of these numerous societies; the means by which they intended to accomplish it; the probable effects of recent political measures aimed at the abolitionists and especially of the Gag Rule imposed by Congress; and finally the connections between American antislavery societies and similar foreign societies. Follen went to great lengths to show that the abolitionists did not want to incite the slaves to rebellion, and did not want to prepare for the use of violence themselves. Their sphere was exclusively that of "moral action" and the tactic of persuasion. This struggle would be fought with pamphlets and newspapers, not with guns or swords.

The drawing up of the Declaration of Independence, according to Follen, recognized the illegal and criminal character of holding some in slavery while others were allowed to oppress them. Slavery clearly went against the maxim of "all men are created equal." Thus the duty of all politicians and legislators, if they indeed interpreted the Declaration of Independence and the Constitution correctly, was to press for the unlimited and immediate emancipation of all slaves. The experiences with slave emancipation in the British West Indies were presented as very positive, and as not providing any cause for concern. The black citizens had found their place in these societies by themselves, and the transition from slavery to freedom and justice had been tranquil and easily manageable. Follen even argued that "experience has also shown, that with the exception of some cases in which relief should, and would be given, the abolition of slavery is a great economical gain for the slaveholder."[94]

In an 1839 article entitled "Peace and War," Follen went beyond these suggestions and again dealt with violence, an issue which was vital both to the antislavery crusade and to Follen's entire political life in general.[95] By this time Follen was no longer a German radical revolutionary, but an American reformer who sympathized with the work of the American Peace Society and the cause of pacifism. Still, the question of the use of force was occupying his mind as much as it had twenty years before. Evidently the unconditionally pacifist ideas which Follen had espoused in his article "Antislavery Principles and Proceedings," written to please his abolitionist friends, were not satisfying to him personally as a final answer. In December of 1837, William Ellery Channing had written to Follen on the relation of antislavery and violence:

As to my letter to the Abolitionists, I rested on the incongruity of a work of philanthropy and bloodshed. I did not take the ground of expediency, but intended to lay down a principle. I felt, that, after having had so much to do with the Abolitionists, I owed it to the truth and myself to show where I agreed and where I disagreed with them.[96]

Channing clearly came down on the side of peace as a precondition to reform, and wished to avoid violence at any cost. Not only Channing, but an increasing number of American reformers in general, were supportive of pacifism, and were becoming increasingly convinced that the use of force should be banned completely from political life throughout the world.

The American Peace Society and the New England Non-Resistance Society were advocating complete abstinence from the use of force, even if they recommended significantly different paths toward the same goal. William Lloyd Garrison and several of his abolitionist friends left the American Peace Society in 1838 in order to form the more radical New England Non-Resistance Society. The "Declaration of Sentiments" of this group, written by Garrison that same year, outlines its members' readiness to fight against slavery and social injustice of any kind with words, but never with violent means.[97]

Charles Follen was familiar with Channing's, as well as with Garrison's, nonviolent stance. He also welcomed the controversy developing between the peace societies, including the dispute over the radical antigovernment ideas put forth by Garrison, because it was forcing citizens to actively reflect on the nature and meaning of their government and of reform. It was this debate among pacifists that prompted Follen to write the article "Peace and War" in 1839. He searched the Bible, especially the episodes in the life of Jesus as recorded in the Gospels, for evidence on how a Christian was to relate to the question of armed struggle. Much in Christian teaching, he found, spoke against any use of force directed by one human against another. The life and acts of Jesus, Follen argued, signified the eventual prevalence of pacifist behavior over brute force. The Old Testament had in fact already provided the commandment "Thou shalt not kill." Jesus then extended the relevance of this principle by abstaining in general from any violence, even when faced with persecution and certain death. Peter had once attempted, immediately after Jesus' arrest, to defend his teacher; but Jesus had disapproved of his use of violence. Yet Jesus had thrown the moneylenders out of the Temple in a violent way, and Follen came to the general conclusion that Jesus' teachings did not completely exclude securing the basic rights of man with the use of force. Certain instances of the use of violence were in fact not contrary to the Gospels and the principle of love. In the end, Jesus had never established absolute nonresistance as an unalterable rule.

Having examined biblical authority in this way, Follen himself rejected complete and unconditional abstinence from political violence. While the goal of all governments and all individual citizens had to remain to use violence only as an absolute last resort, and to work steadily toward the abolition of aggressive behavior, the rights of states and citizens still should be defended with force if all other methods had failed. Within a state, an individual possessed the intrinsic right to defend his or her own life and basic rights and principal interests with legitimate force. In addition, the state itself had the right to defend its internal security and interests. The right to self-defense could not be stripped away from anyone. Follen stated that among citizens of the same state, "liberty is the only sure foundation of true peace," and that it thus had to be defended at all costs, even with the use of violence. In the international realm, as well, there could indeed be "just wars," which had to be fought against "tyrants" who wished to deny the self-government of people within a nation, or of a whole nation itself. In the face of injustice and oppression, according to Follen, war became not only a right but even a duty of the victimized party. Military successes could thus be seen as moral if they conformed to the principles of the fulfillment of duty and resulted from an exalted effort of will and a spirit of self-sacrifice. Just wars, in turn, had the following aims: they should have only the reestablishment of justice as their object; they should be started only after all peaceable attempts to solve the conflict had failed; and they should inflict no injuries except those absolutely necessary.

In the long run, however, Follen argued, the best solution to international conflict was to entirely change the internal political structures of as many nations as possible. The ideas of an international Congress of Nations and of a World Court were highly favored by Follen, as by most peace societies. Follen was confident that the world's nations, and its individual governments, would eventually be able to limit violence very strictly, and perhaps even outlaw it completely as a means of solving conflicts. But he doubted whether this positive change could take place quickly. The more liberal the individual government was, and the more personal rights it granted its citizens, the more likely it was that it would be able to work for world peace. Authoritarian and backward governments would have a much harder time outlawing war and violence. Major problems would in fact arise for a Congress of Nations or a World Court if they were composed of nations which were too heterogeneous in their form of government. The attainment of world peace could thus be made most feasible by "republicanizing the world." If this could be accomplished, most reasons for war, Follen believed, could be effectively eliminated. To this end, Americans should work for an abolition of the authoritarian governments that remained in Europe. Americans had to learn how to bear arms, in order to preserve their own liberty, and also to extend their republican system of government to other areas of the world.

In this article Follen revealed many of the political ideas he had developed while residing in the United States. He supported peace societies and their reform agenda, and considered the U.S. Constitution, rightly interpreted, as the fulfillment of his own political ideals. However, he had retained some of the patterns of belief learned in Germany more than twenty years before. Even at the end of the 1830s, Follen did not exclude the use of violence from his conception of political life. He still asserted the right, even the duty, of the victim of oppression to rise up, take up arms, and destroy the tyrant, whether it was another individual, an unjust and ineffective government, or a foreign power. What he had added to these convictions was America's particular belief in rights and duties in the attainment of political justice. Follen did not attempt to apply the argument in "Peace and War" explicitly to the American antislavery movement. However, it can easily be extrapolated that his own view, as moderate as it may have been in public debate and in the image created of him by his own wife, may indeed have been quite close to that of the black abolitionist David Walker. The latter had warned white Americans that if they did not abolish the slave system and give blacks equal rights, then blacks would exercise their right to liberate themselves in a violent way. Charles Follen undoubtedly would have been on their side. The lurking issue of violence, which remained on Follen's mind both during his time as a European revolutionary and when he became an American abolitionist, would burst forth in the American Civil War twenty years later.[98]

## Exile Again

By the late 1830s, Charles Follen was thus an experienced, important, and committed abolitionist. But his success in establishing himself as a figure to whom abolitionists looked up, and whom slaveholders detested and feared, had serious side effects. From 1835 until 1838, paralleling his rise to abolitionist respect and even fame, Follen experienced a string of professional disasters, including the loss of his Harvard professorship in German literature, his dismissal as a minister in New York City, and subsequent grave financial problems. One of the main questions in connection with Follen's recurring professional problems is whether Follen in fact lost his Harvard professorship mainly because of his devotion to the antislavery cause, as Eliza Follen claimed. She argued in her *Life of Charles Follen:*

> Dr. Follen received repeated warnings, that his interests in the College would be materially injured by his devotion to this hated cause. He was told, that anti-slavery would never be tolerated in Harvard University; but he did not on that account think it right, neither did he feel disposed, to desert a cause, which he thought of more importance than all others, and in comparison with which, the interests of any individual were a petty concern. "The question," he said, "is, whether this is my duty; what will be the consequences, is a secondary matter."[99]

Samuel Eliot Morison has written that it was mainly Follen's involvement with student rebellions, and his personal dislike of Harvard's president Josiah Quincy, that ended his career as the first professor of German.[100] Douglas Stange has argued that the university dropped Follen for financial reasons.[101] However, Follen had evidently been warned by the university administration not to speak up too loudly in support of the antislavery cause; antislavery therefore must have played some role in his dismissal. Josiah Quincy certainly is remembered as an opponent of the radical abolitionism with which Follen was associated. In his *History of Harvard University,* published in 1840, Josiah Quincy passed over Follen in a very swift and unemotional way, and when considering him merely remarked:

> Charles Follen . . . was appointed Professor, and continued acceptably to fulfill the duties of his office until 1835, when it ceased by the terms of its original foundation. During his short connection with the university, his services were characterized by learning, labor, and fidelity.[102]

The outcome remains, in any event, that his advocacy of radical social reform made it impossible for Charles Follen to live a normal middle-class life appropriate to his educational background and social position. Unlike in Europe, in the United States he was not persecuted by the police, and his writings were not censored. He was socially shunned and financially marginalized, however, because of his commitment to antislavery. When he had lost both his professorship and his post as a minister, the financial situation of his small family became increasingly problematic. Follen was not only marginalized in a financial way. Although he had by then lived in the United States for many years, and held American citizenship as well, he was described in the antiabolitionist press as a "foreign meddler" who had no business criticizing American institutions or political arrangements but should rather keep quiet.[103]

When Follen was not losing promising, well-paid positions, he was losing minor ones. In the spring of 1835, Follen had been forced to take on pupils from a rich family in order to earn extra money, and the Follens moved to Watertown, Massachusetts. His new responsibilities involved the education of the sons of a Bostonian named James Perkins for a salary of two thousand dollars per year. Follen at first enjoyed his new job and set up a rigorous plan of education for the boys. With his adequate salary, Follen was able to afford a comfortable house for Eliza and himself and their young son. In the fall of the same year, however, Follen again had to leave his new employment. Eliza said that there were distinct reasons, "which there would be a manifest impropriety in making public."[104] Evidently Follen had again come into conflict with members of the Boston upper class, on whom he depended financially, but whom he also wished to lecture on political and social issues.

After his employment as Unitarian minister in New York had ended in May of 1838, the Follens moved back to Massachusetts, this time to the town of Milton. That summer, Follen's plan to found a free church in New York failed. By the end of 1838, he was severely dejected by the series of failures which he had experienced, and thereupon Follen thought of something which had not come up for years: the idea of a permanent return to Germany, or at least of an extended trip to Europe. Eliza Follen commented in her biography:

> He had long been thinking of a visit to his own country, and this seemed to him to be a favorable moment. He hoped, that, when he returned, his prospects for the future might become brighter, and, if nothing more satisfactory should offer, he could open a school. . . . He often occupied himself in laying out the plan of our journey through France to his brother's residence in Zurich, and in arranging the way we should pass our time in Switzerland.[105]

Depressed about his many professional failures, and unsure how he was going to survive financially, in January of 1839 Follen wrote to his brother August in Switzerland to convey his current downcast state of mind. He had, while in church, had a vision of an end to his earthly existence, and of being taken up into heaven by God:

Again, I looked up, and, in the place of the martial, gigantic eagle, I beheld with delight the gentle form of a dove. Now the chant of the children resounded from below; the dove spread out her wings and rose to the ceiling. Now the roof of the house flew open like a double gate, and revealed the dome of heaven; and the dove, borne upward by the swelling chorus from below, ascended higher and higher. With my whole soul bent upon her upward flight, I strove to catch the last visible movement of those celestial wings, when the gentle touch of a human hand on my shoulder, waked me from my reverie. The aged minister, whose services I had come to lighten on this day by my labor of love, stood by my side, and bade me welcome to his pulpit.[106]

In 1839, at the height of his antislavery activities, and increasingly a social outcast, Follen was mentally turning back to his youth. In January he wrote of his plan to visit Europe in a letter to his former Harvard student Frederick Huidekoper:

It is very probable though not perfectly certain that we shall sail from New York about the middle of May for Havre. Then we intend to make a stay of about a fortnight in Paris, and go on to Switzerland. We shall pass some time at Zurich where I have a brother residing, and some time at Bern, with my sister. . . . In Germany and even in Italy so far as the influence of Austria extends I should not be safe from political persecution.[107]

A few months later, however, Follen found a new purpose when he was offered his position as minister to the congregation in East Lexington. He accepted that position and canceled his European travel plans, writing to Frederick Huidekoper again in April of 1839:

I have delayed answering your last letter which I received about a week ago, in order to inform you of the result of an inquiry I made at New York. I am sorry to have to say to you that we are not going to Europe this year. We shall spend this summer at Lexington, about 8

miles from Boston. As soon as we received your letter Mrs Follen wrote
to New York to ascertain in what time, and in what vessel Mr Robert
Sedgwick, and his wife Catherine Sedgwick are going; and in order
to make them acquainted with you, in case you should determine to
sail with them. . . . Glück auf die Reise![108]

A letter written by Follen in October of 1839 mentioned the Hesse radical
Friedrich Ludwig Weidig, about whom he had most likely not thought or
written for a long time:

I received today from New York a letter from a German whose name
is Frederic Emminghaus who has probably by this time sailed for
Europe, requesting me to translate into English the Biography of Dr
F. L. Weidig which has lately been published in Germany. Dr Weidig
was an early and intimate friend of mine who suffered most cruelly
and died for the same cause for which I came into exile to this country.
I am able to bear testimony to the upright and elevated character of
that persecuted man, and probably to add some facts to the German
work. I understand there are some of Weidig's Sermons and Poems in
the little volume that contains his Biography; and I am desirous to
comply, if my engagements in any way permit, with this request.[109]

On November 5 of the same year, Follen began a series of lectures on
the history of Switzerland in Boston. The lectures, as did his letter about
Weidig, showed his longing to return to Europe, and at the same time
his failure to succeed in America: the audience for the lectures was very
small, and composed mainly of his and his wife's personal acquaintances.
According to Eliza Follen, "no one saw him struggling to repress his
feelings of disappointment; they saw that he did repress, did conquer
them entirely."[110] At that moment, it seemed uncertain whether Charles
Follen would once again manage to overcome his social isolation and
financial crisis.

## Follen's Death and Reactions to It

In January of 1840, Follen was earning extra income by delivering a series
of lectures to audiences at the Merchants' Library Union in New York City.
Shortly before he had succeeded in settling matters with his new congregation in East Lexington. The congregation was small, but determined to

construct a new meetinghouse, and begin to serve the community. Follen's stipend as minister was not very generous, but he was pleased to have it.[111] Follen had agreed to return from New York to East Lexington on January 13, 1840, in order to meet with the church members and dedicate the new church building. Follen left his wife, who had become ill during the trip, and his son, in New York City and set off for Boston on board the steamboat "Lexington." He had sought to postpone his trip back to Boston, but the leaders of his new congregation insisted that he must come at once if he was still interested in the job as minister. So Follen set out. At 7 P.M., four hours after its departure, the ship caught fire and sank in a storm off Long Island Sound. Nearly all of the seventy-six passengers, including Charles Follen, and the entire crew of thirty-five, were killed in the accident. The news of this disaster did not reach East Lexington until the next morning.[112] John S. Dwight, an acquaintance of Follen's, wrote to Mrs. Eli Robbins at the East Lexington Unitarian Community immediately after the accident had occurred: "I have just seen Mr Hillard who has had a letter from a friend in New York, dated since the accident, stating that Dr Follen *was* on board, and that Mrs Follen and Charles certainly were *not*."[113]

In her *Life of Charles Follen*, Eliza Follen placed much of the blame for her husband's death on the congregation which had hired Follen in Lexington. Why, she repeatedly asked herself, had they insisted that Follen had to return at once in order to assume his duties, even though his wife was ill and unable to travel? In a letter of February 1840, D. Weston, an acquaintance of Eliza Follen, wrote to his sister Anne Warren Weston: "The story about Mrs Follen down here is that she is now in an insane asylum."[114] Although this statement may have been based more on rumor than on fact, there is no doubt that Eliza Follen was much afflicted by her loss. She vented her anger and despair at those whom she held at least indirectly responsible for her husband's early and tragic death. "The people at Lexington," she wrote, "thought only of themselves, of their own wishes, and what they supposed would be their own interests. Who can ever compute the effects of a single selfish act?"[115] She at once gave up her connections with the new community that her husband had hoped to serve. Samuel Cabot, her brother, wrote to the head of the Unitarian community at East Lexington in July of 1840:

Although as a matter of course I presume you have caused . . . the . . . House occupied by the late Dr Follen as terminated by his death, yet my sister Mrs Follen has thought you may be prevented from letting it by the idea that she might wish to retain it . . . (I) am therefore to inform you that she shall have no wish to do so.[116]

Eliza decided soon thereafter that the only way to come to terms with her husband's death was by describing his life story and record of achievements for her son, her friends, and posterity:

> I feel an unutterable shrinking from thus removing the veil of privacy from all that is most dear and holy to my own existence; but by no other means could the beautiful image of his life and character be given. No one knew him as I did. Therefore, with an unhesitating faith and a cheerful courage, I commit this inadequate record of my husband's life to the public, remembering, that the weak feeling which makes this act a sort of self-crucifixation, will pass away, and that, while the hand that drew it will be forgotten, this faithful picture of human excellence will live for ever in the minds of many.[117]

She set to work immediately in the latter months of 1840, and edited the *Works* of her husband in five volumes. The first volume, her six-hundred-page biography, was completed on November 17, 1841.

One of the people most shaken by Follen's death was William Ellery Channing, who in 1840 published a "Discourse Occasioned by the Death of the Rev. Dr. Follen," dealing with the necessity of suffering and ill fate in God's scheme for humanity. Follen's sudden and unnecessary death shook the foundations of Christian faith for Channing and many of his other friends such as Samuel May. Channing wrote that Follen had lived for the cause of bettering the world for humanity. His sudden death was not to be seen only as a terrible loss, but also as a part of God's plan. Follen's early death did not diminish his achievements in Channing's eyes. In fact, Follen's stature was increased, and he was elevated to become a symbol of devotion to humanity and a martyr for the rights of all those for whom he had fought. Later, on February 1, 1841, Channing wrote in a letter:

> The loss of Dr. Follen is, indeed, one of the greatest bereavements of my life. In his case, I had found that spiritual ties may be as strong as those of nature. He was one of the few men who won my heart and confidence at first. I saw almost intuitively that he was a true man,— that he had an unconquerable force of soul joined with the sweetest

affections,—that he was not the slave of opinions or circumstances, but that he obeyed freely a divine law in his own soul. He has done me good.[118]

Channing was extremely upset when several close friends, who wished to arrange a memorial service for Follen, were denied a church room in which to hold it. Channing applied for the use of every Unitarian and several of the Orthodox Congregational churches in Boston, and every one in turn refused. Follen's steady and outspoken opposition to slavery had produced such a hardened spirit of reaction among the conservative elements of Boston that it had become an act of considerable courage merely to remember him in a public ceremony. Even Channing's Federal Street Church, which he had served for decades, after a meeting of its trustees declined the use of its facilities. It was not until April 17, 1840, that the Massachusetts Antislavery Society was able to secure the Marlborough Chapel in Boston in order to hold the funeral service.[119]

Follen's death also prompted a number of other memoirs. The "Discourse on the Life and Character of the Rev. Dr. Follen" by Samuel May formed the centerpiece of the memorial service held for Follen in the Marlborough Chapel. In a lengthy, detailed review of Follen's life and achievements, May described how Follen had always been a freedom fighter, even before he came to the United States. "But he soon saw, after his arrival here, that his labors and sacrifices in the cause of liberty were not ended." Most impressive about him was that "he spoke so boldly for freedom."[120] There was also an obituary article for Follen in the *Christian Examiner* of September 1842. The author of this article was Channing's nephew William Henry, and the title was "Life and Writings of Dr. Follen." It was a review of and first reaction to Eliza's *Works*, which had recently appeared that same year. Channing found that Eliza Follen was not disqualified from telling the public about her husband's life and achievements merely because she had been so close to him emotionally. He argued that "love alone has insight," and that Eliza was more apt to have discovered the real Charles Follen than anyone else. Interestingly, William H. Channing concentrated heavily on Follen's German period of activity. The image of Follen constructed here was a complete apotheosis. Charles Follen had made an important contribution to the radical reform movement supported by persons such as William H. Channing, and now his German past was made to appear virtuous and socially engaged in every way possible as well. As a boy, Follen had already attempted to strive for "Christ-like perfection"; he had "commenced the life of reform with himself." Follen's tendency toward fanaticism, and his possible involvement in the Kotzebue murder (which Channing conceded), here served to brighten his image as a devoted, radical reformer even more. Channing claimed that Follen was "perfect" when in the United States, with his religiosity, his moral conviction, and his defense of human rights. Through the filter of Eliza Follen's narrative, the author had gone to great lengths to show where Follen's intensive commitment to reform in America came from, and to what great lengths he was willing to go. Channing also used the story of Follen's life to give new inspiration and psychological aid to all American reformers; his essay had the character of a call to arms.

The description of Charles Follen by Theodore Parker, published in the *Dial* in January of 1843, was also largely based on Eliza Follen's biography of her husband. It also contained very personal comments by a personal acquaintance who sought to provide an image of Follen which was both just and lifelike. The article complemented that of William Henry Channing in that its basic evaluation of Follen's character was very similar, and because, unlike William Henry Channing, Parker dealt mostly with Follen's career in America. He felt that Follen was a man most distinguished not primarily by his intellectual, but by his moral powers. He "belonged to the class . . . of men of moral action." Follen's "whole life was a warfare against sin," distinguished by "his pious love of freedom" and "his abhorrence of all that had the savor of oppression about it." Parker also dwelt at length on the tragic failures which occurred so frequently in Follen's life, such as his loss of several positions and the seeming impossibility of converting people to his moral and social standpoint. Parker did not feel, however, that Follen had been hindered by all the setbacks he had to endure; rather, he affirmed about Follen that "defeat gave him courage, not dismay."

The leading historian of Unitarians and their relationship to antislavery, Douglas Stange, was certainly correct in his remark that Follen upon his death became for the Garrisonian abolitionist a sort of martyr, a true believer in their cause who had suffered for his convictions and had now been taken away by a premature death.[121] And yet Follen's abolitionism was perhaps not as radical as Garrison and his followers liked to portray it. Follen, after all, was in favor of a political solution to the problem of slavery. He was not on the radical wing of the Garrisonian movement, and was apparently quite opposed to the harsh tones which Garrison used in his tactic of intensive moral suasion.[122] Stange's categorization of Follen as a "Garrisonian" within the broader reaches of American antislavery, however, is based on the image created by Eliza Follen and a few very dedicated friends. Precisely what Follen's private ideas were about a resolution of the slavery controversy in the United States will be forever uncertain unless Follen's complete private papers are one day discovered. The article "Peace and War," written as late as 1839, shows that even at the very end of his life, Follen had not abandoned the possibility of violent solutions to political stalemates. After the failure of a primarily legal way of proceeding against the system of slavery, what Follen's reaction to the Civil War would have been is impossible to know.

# CONCLUSION

In 1854 Elizabeth Palmer Peabody, an educated Bostonian and close friend of William Ellery Channing's, evaluated Charles Follen as he had appeared to her:

> When considering the subject of gratitude to men, I remember Dr. Follen took ground against cultivating the sentiment of gratitude to any great extent. He said the despotisms of Europe were cemented, to a great degree, by grateful sentiments, which induced fidelity to princes who conferred favors, to the destruction of a sensibility to the liberty of humanity in general. . . . I have said he would sacrifice individuals to humanity; but this was guarded by a clear sense of justice. All the sacrifices he believed in were self-sacrifices. . . . Earnestness was perhaps his most distinctive trait. . . . His method of treating a subject was to begin with the fundamental fact or principle, and build it up with honest fidelity; working long about the foundations and neglecting nothing; so that, in our "fast" country, he was liable to be left in the rear by competitors who were altogether inferior to him. His mind was comprehensive of principle, but he did not carry his brain in his hand so much as in his heart. . . . I think his mind was not at all creative—it certainly was not imaginative.[1]

Follen had devoted his entire life to the ideals of individual freedom and human liberation. In addition, he had defined for himself a clear framework of moral convictions, viewing it as his duty to adhere to it. But toward the end of his life, during the year 1837, Follen himself had begun to reflect on his own standards, his goals, and his methods for achieving them, in a deeper way than ever before. Increasingly, he began to ask why, in the first forty years of his life, he had not been able to change the world around him more, according to his own will. Why had he failed to transfer his own self-perfection onto humanity at large? Was his failure to do so a result of intellectual deficiencies on his part?

Describing her husband's state of mind during that year, Eliza Follen commented:

> Dr. Follen occasionally, at these times, but not often, alluded to the fact, that his whole life, as it regarded worldly success, had been a series of failures. . . . "Had I been willing," he has said, "to lower my standard of right, the world would have been with me, and I might have obtained its favor."[2]

Perhaps this passage provides a better explanation for the basic problem of Charles Follen's life than that of intellectual backwardness: it stresses his personal rigidity and uncompromising nature when he felt called upon to correct a wrong, and at the same time his inability to justify his behavior to the world around him.

In March of 1837 Follen had been ousted by his New York congregation, although he ultimately chose to resign. He was very downcast about this and said to his wife, as she remembered: "Through my whole life I have labored for the highest objects, and have been actuated by the most elevated purposes, and in all things I have apparently failed. I cannot help feeling this deeply." Eliza Follen answered: "This is not failure . . . this is what we both expected; others prefer bonds, you prefer freedom, and we must be willing to pay the penalty annexed to the choice."[3]

Although Eliza Follen aimed at a sanctification of her husband as a courageous fighter for causes which he knew were just, as a hero unswerving in his own convictions, it is obvious from these scenes that her husband was in fact shaken by a deep crisis of faith. At forty, he had come to doubt something fundamental to his own existence: his own ability to actively change the world around him and to shape his own life and the lives of others. In so many areas of his activity, Follen's ideas had not been accepted by those whom he was trying to persuade. His own lack of flexibility and his placing the fulfillment of personal conviction above the demands of the society in which he lived had prevented him from being an effective proponent of reform, over and over again. Follen had been forced to recognize that history did not always move by cause and effect, and that the achievement of moral and political progress did not occur in a process which was rationally controllable. Dreams of justice and freedom could not always be realized in a rigid and systematic way; at the end of the century, Henry Adams and others moved far beyond Follen's nineteenth-century faith in progress when they described the world as increasingly complex, irrational, and uncontrollable.

At the same time, one may very well conclude that Follen's tragedy was one of being chronologically out of place, and that he was simply too far ahead of his time to be heard. He was a Jacobin and Republican in Germany long before the historical hour of these people could possibly have come. He advocated antislavery in the United States twenty years before this movement actually had its strongest impact on American society. He fought for a new sort of personal and civic freedom and individual human rights in a world still far removed from such thought, Germany, and one not yet pursuing this course thoroughly enough, the United States. Follen was one of those rare personalities willing to give up a normal civil life and to devote himself completely to the political and social causes which he pursued. In many ways, Follen's actions were not representative of what other reformers of his time wanted to achieve; rather, he tested the limits of acceptable behavior in all those societies in which he lived. His visions were those of the future, not of the present. Charles Follen was a person with strong convictions and high ideals, a fighter for increased freedom and human perfection, as he understood them. But he was also almost by definition an outsider, one who was not accepted and not listened to by the mainstream, an individual overwhelmed by the inertia of society around him and by the inapplicability of his own dreams to social and political reality.[4]

Even his wife's description of his life promised to be controversial as soon as it appeared. On December 21, 1841, William Ellery Channing wrote to Eliza Follen, expressing these fears:

Few things are so uncertain as the immediate reception of a book. Its merit is no pledge of public favor. Books which amuse, or which pander to the prejudices, passions, party spirit, sectarian spirit, and selfish interests of the day, succeed best. When we publish, we must prepare ourselves for neglect, indifference, and even unkind remarks. I am sure there are prepared spirits for your work. I hope not a few, but I expect no sensation from it. You offer to your fellow beings a portrait of the mind, heart, labors, conflicts, thoughts, aspirations, of a good and great spirit. Leave it to do its work, to act on all souls, and dismiss all anxiety. I hope for the best. I shall not be troubled by whatever takes place.[5]

For Eliza Follen, however, the characterization of her husband remained radiantly positive at all times. On March 28, 1848, she wrote to her friend Mary Carpenter describing her experiences while writing:

Dear Friend! For so I must call you—how precious, how very precious is your letter! Nothing in life is so dear to me saving my child as the spiritual communion and I may say spiritual love which has spring [*sic*] up I may say from the ashes of my deep sorrow. He alone who has the heart can sound the deep agony, or know the holy joy I experienced while writing the simple story of my dear husband's life—I wanted the whole world to know that a man even here could be like Christ, but as to immolate myself as to speak of all those hallowed days we passed together—oh how did my hand sometimes refuse to move—how often did I almost sink into utter despair—but these moments were very few and a power not my own soon came to strenghten me—and an intense joy visited me, which I could not account for and cannot describe.[6]

When Charles Follen died, his wife was fifty-three and had a ten-year-old son, Charles Christopher. She moved to West Roxbury, Massachusetts, and began to write short books, pamphlets, and poetry in order to supplement her slim financial reserves. Her publications were mainly antislavery works and books for children.[7] Both *Anti-slavery Hymns and Songs* and *A Letter to Mothers in the Free States* were published in 1855. These works were written in a moralizing tone, to convince as many as possible of her readers of the immoral and destructive character of slavery.[8] The death of her husband did not end Eliza Follen's interest in antislavery; in fact her commitment to it intensified in the 1840s. And yet she never fully recovered from the loss of her husband. Toward the end of her life, in 1857, she wrote to a friend about her own psychological situation:

Rough winter weather is a terrible battle for life when one is no longer young and every victory we win over it is at the expense of some faculty of these poor bodies of ours, not as it seems to me of the animating spirit that governs and directs, that grows in many respects brighter and braver. Is not the consciousness of the entire separation of our true selves from our instruments of action and means of manifestation perhaps the strongest argument in favor of the separate existence of the spirit. . . . Mrs Maria Child whom I met at the Fair, asked me one day, if I was willing to hear a message which my husband sends me from the land of the spirits—you may imagine my emotions—as soon as I was calm—I said yes I would hear it. . . . At last the medium described my husband, but did not give his name—she said this spirit was higher than are the others and more perfect—the personal description was perfect. The medium was asked what he said—"He says" she replied "that he loved this person while in this world and loved her more now." "Tell her," the spirit then said "that souls exist in the land of spirits"—"Why do you tell her this?" "Because she has lately been a great deal with a dear one belonging to me and I wish her to carry her this message from me."[9]

In February 1860, when Eliza Follen died, Lydia Maria Child sent the following lines to Charles Christopher Follen:

I know too well how unavailing are any words that can be spoken, while the heart lies crushed under a heavy load of sorrow. Time, and time alone, can heal such wounds; and we never again can be precisely what we were. Your good mother's life was a constant preparation for the angelic world, the influences of which shone through her countenance, and rendered her very looks a benediction to all who saw her. She looked like one of the eight beatitudes; and as you stopped to consider which of that holy family she most resembled, you found she looked like all of them. Garrison said truly, that her face needed no change to become that of an angel; and certainly the same was true of her large, loving sympathizing soul. But why do I say this to you? You know it already, far better than I can express it. You know that she was a blessing here, and that she has gone to the blest above. But my heart yearns towards you, and her dear, afflicted sister; and the necessity is upon me to say how dearly I loved her, and how much I deplore her loss. I remember very distinctly the last look she ever gave me. It was at the Anniversary Meetings in May. We had been sitting together for hours, having a very cosy and animated time. I left her there, and went out through the crowd, to take the cars home. She drew me back, detained me a little, and said, with one of her most loving smiles, "Do come to see me soon. You are a comfortable creature to be with." Oh! how little I thought that was my last look on her beaming countenance, and those the last words I should ever hear from that loving voice. The last note she wrote to me, inviting me to come to Brookline on the 24th, was so cheerful and so strong, so full of life, and hope, and love, that it never occurred to me that the writer was no longer young. Always she presented herself to my mind clad in immortal youth. But when I went all joyfully to meet her, with a thousand things that I wanted to say, already anticipating her smiles, and witticisms, and outbursts of eloquent indignation, as I recounted to her my various experiences, I was arrested by your mournful message; and then I remembered, with sad forebodings, that she was old. Dear Charles, how I sympathize with the loneliness of your bereaved heart! You have two guardian angels now. That calm, wise, great-hearted father; that tender, sympathizing, generous mother. But even that consciousness will not fill the aching void. For many months, you will have unutterable longing, at times, for "the touch of a vanished hand, and the sound of a voice that is still.". . .You are the true son of a lineage spiritually noble; and those who have formed your character must necessarily be near you, because you are walking in the same paths, by which they went to the Heavenly Kingdom.[10]

Charles Christopher Follen, who had graduated from Harvard in 1849,[11] and studied in London during the early 1850s, became a landscape architect. Prior to the Civil War, he was a partner in the architectural firm of Follen and Curtis. After 1867, he was active with the firm of Lee and Follen.[12] He had gone on to take an active part in the antislavery movement, as his parents had done. Charles Christopher supported the Union side in the American Civil War, and in 1864 rented an abandoned plantation in Murfreesboro, Tennessee. He grew cotton there for some time, but was taken prisoner by Confederate troops in mid-December and treated quite badly for several weeks. After being abandoned by his guards on December 23, 1864, Charles Jr. was finally rescued by friends. He compiled a report as well as a lengthy narrative on his experiences while in captivity.[13] Charles Christopher Follen too passed away unusually young on November 6, 1872, at the age of 42. He thus died even younger than his father had. The cause of death was a brain disease. He never married, and left no children.[14] Shortly after his death, Maria Weston Chapman wrote a statement in commemoration addressed to all his friends and acquaintances:

> Private sorrow must ever give place to public calamity: but there are griefs stronger than misfortune; and one such grief is the death of Charles Follen. He died in Boston, his birthplace, the week before the recent disaster. He was the only son of distinguished parents: Dr. Charles Follen, the devoted friend of freedom in both hemispheres, and Eliza Lee Cabot, daughter of Samuel Cabot. Both fervently engaged in the moral battle for the abolition of slavery in America. Their son Charles was born in 1830 and his whole life was passed in the ranks of that cause. When, by efforts like those of his parents and his own, that moral conflict had moved[?] the Northern people to assume the actual one, he joined a Massachusetts battalion and underwent hardships in his country's service. . . . He was a graduate of Harvard, greatly beloved by his fellow-students and honored by all who have ever known him for his perfect integrity and high sense of justice and entire disinterestedness. . . . For his death appeared so untimely, knowing that his life was dedicated to the principles of freedom. He was a member of the Executive Committee of the Massachusetts Antislavery Society and a devoted friend of William Lloyd Garrison and his associates, who lament with no common sorrow this last bearer of a bright name.[15]

The younger Charles Follen carried on the commitment to the establishment of freedom in American society which his parents had instilled in him. By contrast, however, the German world of his father, and his father's true past in Europe, remained dark and unknown to him throughout his lifetime. Although his father's life had represented a personal, philosophical, and political unity, the full extent of that unity would never be exposed.

# NOTES

## Introduction

1. On the German idea of *Bildung* in the nineteenth century, see Walter Horace Bruford, *The German Tradition of Self-Cultivation: "Bildung" from Humboldt to Thomas Mann* (Cambridge: Cambridge University Press, 1975).

2. Eliza Lee Cabot Follen, ed., *The Works of Charles Follen, with a Memoir of His Life*, 5 vols. (Boston: Hilliard and Gray, 1841). Hereafter cited as *Works*. The first volume is a six-hundred-page biography of Charles Follen written by his wife.

3. Two examples may be cited here. The rector of the University of Giessen, Franz Josef Arens, had student rooms searched for incriminating evidence when he suspected illegal Burschenschaft activities at Giessen. The Mainz Central Investigation Commission, which was appointed by the German Confederation in 1819 to investigate the extent of political radicalism in Germany, based its allegations against individuals largely on the personal papers which it was in many cases able to seize.

4. Invaluable work was done in the early twentieth century by the Kommission für burschenschaftliche Geschichtsforschung, headed by Herman Haupt, Karl Schneider, Georg Heer, and Paul Wentzcke. They initiated the *Quellen und Darstellungen zur Geschichte der Burschenschaft* (Heidelberg: C. Winter, 1910–1940), continued after 1945 as *Darstellungen und Quellen zur Geschichte der Deutschen Einheitsbewegung* (Heidelberg: C. Winter, 1957–present). Haupt, the university archivist at Giessen, published many works dealing directly with Follen, especially "Karl Follen und die Giessener Schwarzen," in *Mitteilungen des Oberhessischen Geschichtsvereins*, NF 15 (1907): 1–156. Wentzcke and Heer contributed to the *Quellen und Darstellungen* series with their two-volume *Geschichte der Deutschen Burschenschaft* (Heidelberg: C. Winter, 1919, 1927). Important work was also done on this phenomenon in the former German Democratic Republic, especially by Günter Steiger in *Aufbruch: Urburschenschaft und Wartburgfest* (Leipzig: Urania, 1967) and Willi Schröder in *Burschenturner im Kampf um Einheit und Freiheit* (Berlin: Sportverlag, 1967). Today the Archiv

der Deutschen Burschenschaft (where the *Darstellungen und Quellen* are published) is in a side wing of the Bundesarchiv branch in Frankfurt am Main.

5. Major work on Hessian radicalism in the 1810s and 1820s, as well as its relationship to the rise of modern German nationalism, has been contributed by Erich Zimmermann, archivist at Darmstadt, in *Für Freiheit und Recht: Der Kampf der Darmstädter Demokraten im Vormärz (1815–1848)* (Darmstadt: Hessische Historische Kommission, 1987); Siegfried Büttner, *Die Anfänge des Parlamentarismus in Hessen-Darmstadt und das du Thilsche System* (Darmstadt: Historischer Verein für Hessen, 1969); Adolf Müller, *Die Entstehung der Hessischen Verfassung von 1820* (Darmstadt: Hessischer Staatsverlag, 1931); and most recently Karin Luys, *Die Anfänge der Deutschen Nationalbewegung von 1815 bis 1819* (Münster: Nodus, 1992). The 1830s have been dealt with by Thomas Michael Mayer, Büchner specialist at Marburg University, in his "Büchner und Weidig," in *Georg Büchner: Text und Kritik Sonderband,* ed. Heinz Ludwig Arnold (Munich: Edition Text und Kritik, 1979).

6. Literature in this area began in the nineteenth century with works such as Gustav Phillip Körner, *Das Deutsche Element in den Vereinigten Staaten von Nordamerika 1818–1848* (Cincinnati: A. E. Wilde, 1880). Important examples published more recently are Henry Pochmann, *German Culture in America* (Madison: University of Wisconsin Press, 1957), and Stanley Vogel, *German Literary Influences on the American Transcendentalists* (New Haven: Yale University Press, 1955). Both works pay a great deal of attention to Follen and his role as a transmitter of German culture.

7. See, above all, the works by Conrad Wright, *The Liberal Christians* (Boston: Beacon Press, 1970); David Robinson, *The Unitarians and the Universalists* (Westport, Conn.: Greenwood Press, 1985); George H. Williams, ed., *The Harvard Divinity School: Its Place in Harvard University and in American Culture* (Boston: Beacon Press, 1954); William Hutchison, *The Transcendentalist Ministers* (New Haven: Yale University Press, 1959); and Daniel Walker Howe, *The Unitarian Conscience: Harvard Moral Philosophy, 1805–1861* (Cambridge, Mass.: Harvard University Press, 1970).

8. Anne Rose, *Transcendentalism as a Social Movement* (New Haven: Yale University Press, 1981). See also the anthology by Perry Miller, ed., *The Transcendentalists* (Cambridge, Mass.: Harvard University Press, 1950).

9. Douglas Stange, "The Making of an Abolitionist Martyr: Harvard Professor Charles Theodore Christian Follen," *Harvard Library Bulletin,* 24 (1976): 17–24; and Stange, *Patterns of Antislavery among American Unitarians* (Rutherford, N.J.: Fairleigh Dickinson University Press, 1977).

10. A few examples: Heinrich von Treitschke considered Follen an unstable, disoriented, and ruthless character in his *Deutsche Geschichte im Neunzehnten Jahrhundert* (Leipzig: S. Hirzel, 1879–1889), vol. II, pp. 437–443. Follen had done more to prevent than to further the German unity under Prussian auspices which Treitschke so strongly supported. Furthermore, he was to be considered "the gravedigger of the *Burschenschaft.*" The Marxist historians of the German Democratic Republic who became interested in Burschenschaft history in the 1960s, Günter Steiger and Willi Schröder, saw Follen essentially as a historical

actor who advocated the use of violence where and when it was most inappropriate and thus contributed nothing to the rise of socialism or democracy in Germany.

11. See Richard Pregizer, *Die Politischen Ideen des Karl Follen: Ein Beitrag zur Geschichte des Radikalismus in Deutschland* (Tübingen: J. C. B. Mohr, 1912); and the politically tendentious Julia Wüst, "Karl Follen," *Mitteilungen des Oberhessischen Geschichtsvereins*, NF 33 (1936): 1–139.

12. On Haupt, see note 4. Spindler's biography is entitled *Charles Follen: A Biographical Study* (Chicago: University of Chicago Press, 1917).

## 1. Unity and Freedom

1. See Otto Dann, ed., *Nationalismus und sozialer Wandel* (Hamburg: Hoffmann and Campe, 1978), p. 116. An excellent survey has recently been put forth by Michael Hughes, *Nationalism and Society: Germany, 1800–1945* (London and New York: E. Arnold, 1988); see especially pp. 1–100.

2. Dann, *Nationalismus*, p. 113. See also Hans Gerth, *Bürgerliche Intelligenz um 1800* (Göttingen: Vandenhoeck and Ruprecht, 1976), pp. 29–79. Karin Luys, *Die Anfänge der Deutschen Nationalbewegung von 1815 bis 1819* (Münster: Nodus, 1992), pp. 14–15, echoes the assertion that modern German nationalism began as an elite phenomenon after 1800 and its social base gradually widened after the 1830s.

3. The important role of the "political professor" at this time has been shown convincingly in Willi Real, "Geschichtliche Voraussetzungen und Erste Phasen des Politischen Professorentums," *Darstellungen und Quellen zur Geschichte der Deutschen Einheitsbewegung*, 9 (1974): 7–95. The *Darstellungen und Quellen* will be cited as *DuQ*; the earlier series, *Quellen und Darstellungen* (see Introduction, note 4), as *QuD*.

4. On "unity" and "freedom," see the article by Werner Conze, entitled "Freiheit," in *Geschichtliche Grundbegriffe*, ed. Otto Brunner et al. (Stuttgart: E. Klett, 1972–present). See also Ernst Rudolf Huber, *Deutsche Verfassungsgeschichte seit 1789* (Stuttgart: W. Kohlhammer, 1960), vol. I, pp. 4–5. Finally, see the two volumes by Jürgen Schlumbohm: *Freiheitsbegriff und Emanzipationsprozess: Zur Geschichte eines politischen Wortes* (Göttingen: Vandenhoeck and Ruprecht, 1973); and *Freiheit: Die Anfänge der bürgerlichen Emanzipationsbewegung in Deutschland* (Düsseldorf: Schwann, 1975).

5. Eliza Lee Cabot Follen, ed., *The Works of Charles Follen, with a Memoir of His Life* (Boston: Hilliard and Gray, 1841), vol. I, pp. 1–2. This biography is the most important source we have for facts about Karl Follen's life. It is hampered by the extreme devotion of a loving wife to her husband. Eliza Follen could not see her husband in a negative or even an objective light. Her knowledge of Follen's German past was limited, and her overview of his activities as a young man is by no means complete.

6. See the article entitled "Follenius," in *Neue Deutsche Biographie* (Berlin: Duncker and Humblodt, 1953–present). See also *Deutsches Geschlechterbuch* (Görlitz: C. A. Starke, 1920), vol. 32, p. 190.

7. Biographical details on the Follen family circumstances in about 1800 can be gleaned from Karl Vogt, *Aus meinem Leben* (Stuttgart: E. Nägele, 1896), pp. 10–13. Vogt, a Swiss medical doctor, was the son of Karl Follen's sister Luise. At the time of Karl Follen's birth, his family was still known as "Follenius." August, Karl, and Paul Follen later dropped the latinized form.

8. *Works*, vol. I, p. 5.

9. Ibid., vol. I, pp. 6–7.

10. Ibid., vol. I, pp. 7–13.

11. On Follen's religiosity as a child, see Herman Haupt, "Karl Follen und die Giessener Schwarzen," *Mitteilungen des Oberhessischen Geschichtsvereins*, NF 15 (1907): 20–21. For a careful description of German protestant childrens' education in the late eighteenth century, focusing on the example of Ernst Moritz Arndt, see Günther Ott, *Ernst Moritz Arndt: Religion, Christentum, und Kirche in der Entwicklung eines deutschen Publizisten und Patrioten* (Düsseldorf: Presseverlag der Evangelischen Kirche im Rheinland, 1966), pp. 23–56.

12. For more details on Follen's religiosity as a child in Germany, and, connected to this, as an adult in the United States, see Chapter 5.

13. Karl Follen to his friend Zurbuch at Darmstadt, dated 1811. Staatsbibliothek Preussischer Kulturbesitz, Berlin: Sammlung Darmstädter, 2 L 1814. The translations of German primary documents, and of the early writings of Karl Follen, are all mine, unless otherwise stated.

14. Quoted in Richard Pregizer, *Die politischen Ideen des Karl Follen. Ein Beitrag zur Geschichte des Radikalismus in Deutschland* (Tübingen: J. C. B. Mohr, 1912), p. 12.

15. Johann Andreas Demian, *Beschreibung oder Statistik und Topographie des Grossherzogtums Hessen* (Mainz, 1824–25), vol. II, p. 367.

16. Karl Glöckner, ed., *Giessen, 1248–1948* (Giessen: Brühlsche Universitäts-Druckerei, 1948), pp. 19–20.

17. J. R. Dieterich, "Die Politik Landgraf Ludwigs X. von Hessen-Darmstadt von 1790–1806," *Annalen für Hessische Geschichte*, NF 7 (1910): 421.

18. For a detailed study of German-French relations in the Rhineland during this period, see T. C. W. Blanning, *The French Revolution in Germany: Occupation and Resistance in the Rhineland, 1792–1802* (Oxford: Clarendon Press, 1983). Blanning sets out to "explain why and how the great majority of the Rhinelanders rejected and resisted both French practice and French principles."

19. Elisabeth Fehrenbach, "Verfassungs- und sozialpolitische Reformprojekte in Deutschland unter dem Einfluss des napoleonischen Frankreich," in *Deutschland zwischen Revolution und Restauration*, ed. Helmut Berding and Hans-Peter Ullmann (Düsseldorf: Droste, 1981), pp. 65–90.

20. Heinrich Leo, *Meine Jugendzeit* (Gotha: F.A. Perthes, 1880).

21. The career of Friedrich Ludwig Weidig will be discussed in Chapter 2.

22. See the provocative work by Wolf Kittler, *Die Geburt des Partisanen aus dem Geist der Poesie: Heinrich von Kleist und die Strategie der Befreiungskriege* (Freiburg: Rombach, 1987). While analyzing the powerful effect of war on Heinrich von Kleist's thought and writings, Kittler provides a clear image

of the generally militant mood among German nationalists in 1813–1815. The contributions of Kleist to this mood will be discussed in more detail in Chapter 2.

23. Glöckner, *Giessen, 1248–1948*, p. 46.

24. For details on this situation, see Heinrich Ulmann, "Hessen-Darmstadt am Scheideweg im Herbst 1813," *Annalen für Hessische Geschichte*, NF 9 (1913): 292.

25. *Works*, vol. I, p. 18.

26. Friedrich Meinecke, *Das Zeitalter der Deutschen Erhebung* (Bielefeld and Leipzig: Velhagen and Klasing, 1913).

27. For details, see Georg Thudichum, *Tagebuch niedergeschrieben auf dem Zug der hessischen freiwilligen Jäger nach Lyon im Jahr 1814*, ed. Karl Esselborn (Darmstadt: H. L. Schlapp, 1923), p. 5.

28. See Karl Bader, "Zur Geschichte des Grossherzoglich Hessischen Freiwilligen Jägercorps, 1813–1814," *Annalen für Hessische Geschichte*, NF 2 (1899): 507–515.

29. Ibid., p. 517; Thudichum, *Tagebuch*, p. 11.

30. Friedrich Gottlieb Welcker in a letter to Karoline von Humboldt, dated April 14, 1814. *Karoline von Humboldt und Friedrich Gottlieb Welcker: Briefwechsel 1807–1826*, ed. Erna Sander-Rindtorff (Bonn: Ludwig Röhrscheid, 1936), pp. 163–164.

31. In his article entitled "Freiheit" contributed to *Historische Grundbegriffe*, Werner Conze has emphasized the difference between the terms "Wars of Liberation" *(Befreiungskriege)* and "Wars of Freedom" *(Freiheitskriege)*. The patriots soon began "to speak of the so-called Wars of Liberation, because they 'liberated' nobody except the German princes." What was demanded by the veterans returning home were real internal reforms of German political life and constitutional arrangements, rather than simply a successful completion of the campaign against France and a quick return to old arrangements.

32. On the background of these eighteenth-century fraternities, see the opening of Haupt, "Karl Follen und die Giessener Schwarzen."

33. This document is reproduced in Joachim Leopold Haupt, *Landsmannschaften und Burschenschaft* (Leipzig: F. A. Brockhaus, 1820), pp. 206–224.

34. For many examples, see the articles published on this period in the *QuD* or in the official periodical *Burschenschaftliche Blätter*, published 1885–present.

35. Quoted in Haupt, "Karl Follen und die Giessener Schwarzen," p. 3.

36. See Rolland Ray Lutz, "The German Revolutionary Student Movement, 1819–1833," *Central European History*, 4 (1971): 215–241. Gary D. Stark, "The Ideology of the German Burschenschaft Generation," *European Studies Review*, 8 (1978): 33–38. Maria Wawrykowa, "Die studentische Bewegung in Deutschland im ersten Jahrzehnt nach dem Wiener Kongress," *Bourgeoisie und bürgerliche Umwälzung in Deutschland, 1789–1871*, ed. Helmut Bleiber (Berlin: Akademie-Verlag, 1977), pp. 49–63.

37. For an overview of the founding and further history of the Jena *Burschenschaft*, see Günter Steiger, *Aufbruch. Urburschenschaft, und Wartburgfest* (Leipzig:

Urania, 1967), pp. 33–79. See also the historical sketch by Herman Haupt, "Die Jenaische Burschenschaft von ihrer Gründung bis zum Wartburgfeste," *QuD,* 1 (1910): 18–113.

38. See Herman Haupt, "Die Verfassungsurkunde der Jenaischen Burschenschaft vom 12. Juni 1815," in *QuD,* 1 (1910): 114–161.

39. Ibid., pp. 141–153.

40. On Karl von Grolman, see Wolfgang Paul, *Die Grolmans: Eine preussische Adelsfamilie 1777–1856* (Esslingen and Munich: R. Bechtle, 1989), pp. 327–329. He will be discussed in detail in Chapter 2.

41. There is information available on Karl Follen's studies in Giessen in various places. See Herman Haupt, "Zum Gedächtnis Karl Follens," *Deutsch-Amerikanische Geschichtsblätter,* 14 (1914): 7–55. See also the records on Karl Follen in the Universitätsarchiv Jena: in several letters to the Jena University senate written when he was applying for employment as a lecturer there, Follen outlines his studies and the topics he had taught in Giessen. Follen writes: "At the end of the next-to-last semester, after I passed a double exam and a public disputation, I received a doctorate in both laws [civil and canon law], as you can see from the diploma I am including. My dissertation . . . which could not yet be printed since I was ill, will appear soon, along with several articles in the next issue of the legal periodical edited by von Grolman and Löhr [both Giessen professors of law]. In the same semester in which I received my degree, I taught an 'Examinatorium and Disputatorium' on the Pandects, in conjunction with legal history. In my last semester I taught common civil law, as well as Roman inheritance law."

42. Peter Moraw, *Kleine Geschichte der Universität Giessen, 1607–1982* (Giessen: Ferbersche Universitätsbuchhandlung, 1982), p. 116. Much information about student radicalism at Giessen may be gleaned from the meticulous work of the Mainz Central Investigation Commission (Zentraluntersuchungskommission). The main source here is vol. XVI of the records it compiled beginning in 1819, entitled "Über die Verbindingen und Umtriebe in Giessen." Wiesbaden, Hessisches Hauptstaatsarchiv (HHStA), Abt. 210, Nr. 12540. This record contains three hundred paragraphs describing the principal individuals involved in the Giessen student scene, all their activities, as far as these could be determined, and an evaluation of all written materials which the commission had managed to acquire. The main facts about Giessen University's radical students are also contained in condensed form in the printed *Hauptbericht der Mainzer Zentraluntersuchungskommission* (1827), Wiesbaden, HHStA, Abt. 210, Nr. 7483.

43. Alexander Pagenstecher, *Aus Gärender Zeit: Lebenserinnerungen, 1816–1850* (Leipzig: Voigtländer, 1913), pp. 38–42.

44. Haupt, "Karl Follen und die Giessener Schwarzen," p. 10. See also Hans-Georg Werner, "Die politische Lyrik der Giessener 'Schwarzen,'" *Wissenschaftliche Zeitschrift der Universität Halle,* 15 (1966): 53–73.

45. They wore a black gown over a white shirt, and a large black cap with a silver cross on it. The German Reading Society and the Blacks are also discussed in Luys, *Anfänge der Deutschen Nationalbewegung,* pp. 131–174. How-

ever, as she states on p. 137, the biography of Karl Follen is "only of marginal interest" for Luys.

46. See "Leben und Wirken des Giessener Schwarzen Karl Christian Sartorius," in *Beiträge zur Geschichte der Giessener Urburschenschaft*, ed. Herman Haupt and Hans Schneider (Darmstadt: F. Bender, 1931), p. 19.

47. Pagenstecher, *Aus Gärender Zeit*, pp. 54–55.

48. Ibid., p. 55.

49. For the German text, see Follen's *Works*, vol. I, pp. 609–610.

50. For the German text, see the collection of poetry entitled "Die Giessener Schwarzen," ed. Friedrich Harzmann, *QuD*, 12 (1930): 77–98.

51. August Adolf Follen collected the poems and songs of the Blacks and published them in his anthology *Freye Stimmen frischer Jugend* (Jena: Kröker, 1819). On these poems, see also Werner, "Die politische Lyrik," pp. 58–66.

52. See Haupt, "Karl Follen und die Giessener Schwarzen," pp. 15–16.

53. This episode is recounted in ibid., pp. 26–33.

54. See Herman Haupt, "Zur Geschichte des Giessener Ehrenspiegels," *QuD*, 2 (1911): 202–214.

55. A list of the 1817 *Ehrenspiegel* adherents is to be found at the university archives in Giessen, Allg. L 8, Nr. 1298. There is also a published list in *Burschenschafterlisten*, ed. Paul Wentzcke (Görlitz: Starke, 1942), vol. 2, pp. 48–51. Wentzcke also lists the members of the Giessen German reading society, and of Germania. See pp. 43–44, 45–47.

56. Friedrich Ludwig Jahn, *Die Deutsche Turnkunst* (Berlin, 1816). For extensive biographical information on Jahn, see Heinrich Pröhle, *Friedrich Ludwig Jahn's Leben* (Berlin: F. Duncker, 1872).

57. See August Follen, *Freye Stimmen frischer Jugend*.

58. One close connection of gymnastics and nationalist agitation, see especially Dieter Düding, *Organisierter Gesellschaftlicher Nationalismus in Deutschland* (Munich: R. Oldenbourg, 1984). Düding remarks about the Giessen Blacks: "Their activities within the gymnastics movement were thus dictated by the thought of strengthening a socially quite broad nationalistic 'partial movement,' and of gradually pushing it into a revolutionary and radically democratic direction" (p. 128).

59. Friedrich Ludwig Jahn, *Deutsches Volksthum* (Lübeck: Niemann and Comp., 1810).

60. Ernst Moritz Arndt, *Entwurf einer Teutschen Gesellschaft* (1814). On the development of Arndt's nationalism, see Hans Kohn, "Arndt and the Character of German Nationalism," *American Historical Review*, 54 (1949): 787–803.

61. Karl Follen, *Beiträge zur Geschichte der teutschen Samtschulen seit dem Freiheitskriege 1813* (1818). The text is included in *Der Giessener Ehrenspiegel*, ed. Carl Walbrach (Frankfurt am Main: Verlag der Deutschen Burschenschaft, 1927), pp. 1–53.

62. Ernst Moritz Arndt, *Geist der Zeit* (Berlin: Realschulbuchhandlung, 1806–1818).

63. Alfred G. Pundt, *Arndt and the Character of German Nationalism* (New York: Columbia University Press, 1936), p. 153.

64. Ibid., p. 160.

65. For a list of the festival participants, see Günter Steiger, "Die Teilnehmer des Wartburgfests von 1817: Eine kritische Ausgabe der sog. 'Präsenzliste,'" *DuQ*, 4 (1963): 65–133.

66. Lutz Winckler, *Martin Luther als Bürger und Patriot: Das Reformationsjubiläum von 1817 und der politische Protestantismus des Wartburgfestes* (Lübeck: Matthiesen, 1969), p. 7.

67. See Ibid., especially pp. 44–77.

68. The speech by Heinrich Riemann is available in printed form in *Das Wartburgfest am 18. Oktober 1817*, ed. Hugo Kühn (Weimar: A. Duncker, 1913), pp. 58–63.

69. Ibid., pp. 64–67.

70. Ibid., pp. 72–74.

71. Saul Ascher, *Die Germanomanie: Skizze zu einem Zeitgemälde* (Berlin: Achenwall, 1815). For background information, see Walter Grab, "Saul Ascher: Ein Jüdisch-Deutscher Spätaufklärer zwischen Revolution und Restauration," *Jahrbuch des Instituts für Deutsche Geschichte der Universität Tel Aviv*, 6 (1977): 131–179; see especially pp. 166–170.

72. On the drafting of the "Principles and Resolutions," see Hans Ehrentreich, "Heinrich Luden und sein Einfluss auf die Burschenschaft," *DuQ*, 4 (1913): 82–88. The complete text, with a short introduction, is printed in the same article, on pp. 109–129.

73. The "Principles and Resolutions" are reproduced in full in ibid., pp. 113–129.

74. Ibid., pp. 121–123.

75. In English translation, "Contributions to the History of the German Universities since the Wars of Liberation in 1813."

76. The *Beiträge* and the *Ehrenspiegel* texts are both included in Walbrach, *Ehrenspiegel*. The editor, a Burschenschaft historian who published this modern edition of Follen's two essays in 1927, criticized Follen's pamphlet severely in a short introduction. According to Walbrach, Follen had, above all, the problem of unrealistic goals and a "lack of understanding of what was achievable" in his time.

77. Walbrach, *Ehrenspiegel*, pp. 5, 9.

78. Ibid., pp. 19–29.

79. See the excellent study of Willy Real, "Geschichtliche Voraussetzungen und erste Phasen des Politischen Professorentums," *DuQ*, 9 (1974): 7–95. Real traces the development of political professors from eighteenth-century figures such as Johann Gottfried Herder and Friedrich Schiller to the mid-nineteenth-century men Karl von Rotteck and Karl Theodor Welcker. Among many others, he discusses Johann Gottlieb Fichte, Friedrich Schleiermacher, and Ernst Moritz Arndt. Real's treatment ends with the "Göttingen Seven" of 1837. A section of his article is also devoted to Karl Follen.

80. William M. Calder ed., *Friedrich Gottlieb Welcker: Werk und Wirkung* (Stuttgart: F. Steiner Verlag, 1986), p. 46. This work is a collection of recent essays on Welcker's life and scholarship.

81. Reinhard Kekulé, *Das Leben Friedrich Gottlieb Welcker's* (Leipzig: B. G. Teubner, 1880), p. 164. Kekulé's book contains many autobiographical notes and letters by Welcker himself.

82. Friedrich Gottlieb Welcker, *Einleitung zu Vorträgen über die deutsche Geschichte,* ed. Robert Fritzsche (Giessen: J. Ricker, 1898), pp. 1–14.

83. Ibid., pp. 19–33.

84. Ibid., p. 33.

85. Karl Betz, *Friedrich Gottlieb Welcker. Ein Leben für Wissenschaft und Vaterland* (Grünberg: Thraum, 1986), p. 74.

86. See especially Karl-Heinz Bloching, "J. F. Fries' Philosophie als Theorie der Subjektivität" (Ph.D. diss., University of Münster, 1969). Bloching has shown convincingly how Fries arrived at his "subjective philosophy," making the individual's own conscience the ultimate guide for discerning what was moral and what was not.

87. See Huber, *Deutsche Verfassungsgeschichte,* vol. I, pp. 712–13. On Fries, see also Ernst Henke, *Jakob Friedrich Fries* (Leipzig: F. A. Brockhaus, 1867). The latter is still the most comprehensive biography.

88. Huber, *Deutsche Verfassungsgeschichte,* vol. I, p. 715.

89. Heinrich Luden, *Einige Worte über das Studium der Vaterländischen Geschichte: Vier öffentliche Vorlesungen* (Jena: Akademische Buchhandlung, 1810), p. 8.

90. Ehrentreich, "Luden," p. 51.

91. Ehrentreich, "Luden," pp. 51–58. Luden, *Einige Worte,* pp. 16–35.

92. Luden, *Einige Worte,* p. 15.

93. Ehrentreich, "Luden," pp. 67–69; 89.

94. See ibid., pp. 70–84.

95. Ibid., p. 92.

96. See Huber, *Deutsche Verfassungsgeschichte,* vol. I, p. 723.

97. The constitution is printed in Joachim Leopold Haupt, *Landsmannschaften und Burschenschaft,* pp. 257–264. The two main principles quoted here appear on p. 257.

98. See ibid., pp. 259–264.

## 2. Freedom and Violence

1. The German financial term is *Schuldentilgungsanstalt.*

2. This letter to Follen, signed by the mayors of several small Hesse villages, is dated August 30, 1818. It is included in Eliza Lee Cabot Follen, ed., *The Works of Charles Follen, with a Memoir of His Life* (Boston: Hilliard and Gray, 1841), vol. I, pp. 62–63.

3. Follen wrote this petition in September of 1818. See *Works,* vol. I, p. 64.

4. Detailed information on the Giessen group at this time is in the Mainz Central Investigation Commission (MZUK) report XVI: "Über die Verbindungen und Umtriebe in Giessen." HHStA Wiesbaden, Abt. 210, Nr. 12540.

5. On the Darmstadt revolutionary group, see Erich Zimmermann, *Für Freiheit und Recht: Der Kampf der Darmstädter Demokraten im Vormärz (1815–1848)*

(Darmstadt: Hessische Historische Kommission, 1987), especially pp. 17–80. See also Ilse Spangenberg, *Hessen-Darmstadt und der Deutsche Bund, 1815–1848* (Darmstadt: Historischer Verein für Hessen, 1969), pp. 40–57; Herman Haupt, "Karl Follen und die Giessener Schwarzen," *Mitteilungen des Oberhessischen Geschichtsvereins,* NF 15 (1907): 109–118; Karl Wegert, "The Genesis of Youthful Radicalism: Hesse-Nassau, 1806–1819," *Central European History,* 10 (1977): 183–205.

6. On Heinrich Karl Hofmann (sometimes spelled Hoffmann), see Herman Haupt, "Heinrich Karl Hofman, ein süddeutscher Vorkämpfer des deutschen Einheitsgedankens," *QuD,* 3 (1912): 327–404; Friedrich Meinecke, *Die Deutschen Gesellschaften und der Hoffmannsche Bund* (Stuttgart: J.C. Cotta, 1891); Friedrich Meinecke, "Zur Geschichte des Hoffmannschen Bundes," *QuD,* 1 (1910): 4–17.

7. *Hauptbericht der Mainzer Zentraluntersuchungskommission,* HHstA Wiesbaden, Abt. 210, Nr. 7483, p. 39.

8. Ibid., p. 42.

9. That these constitutions were indeed to be liberal and democratic in the modern sense, and not merely representational according to estates, was a claim the Blacks were making. The *Bundesakte* did not at all closely define what was meant by *Landständische Verfassungen* in its thirteenth article; the correct interpretation of the article henceforth became a matter of heated contention between the Hesse-Darmstadt government authorities and the constitutional movement. A significant number of legal experts began to contribute in written form to the rising controversy over this question; see Karin Luys, *Die Anfänge der Deutschen Nationalbewegung von 1815 bis 1819* (Münster: Nodus, 1992), p. 184.

10. See Zimmermann, *Für Freiheit und Recht,* pp. 23–25.

11. Adolf Müller, *Die Entstehung der Hessischen Verfassung von 1820* (Darmstadt: Hessischer Staatsverlag, 1931), pp. 13–14. See also Hans Andres, *Die Einführung des konstitutionellen Systems im Grossherzogtum Hessen* (Berlin: E. Ebering, 1908), pp. 118–149; and Spangenberg, *Hessen-Darmstadt und der Deutsche Bund,* pp. 40–57.

12. *Hauptbericht,* p. 44.

13. Ibid., p. 45.

14. Ibid., p. 46.

15. Müller, *Hessische Verfassung,* pp. 9–13.

16. Ibid., p. 29, n. 74. See also Wegert, "Youthful Radicalism," pp. 194–205.

17. Wegert, "Youthful Radicalism," p. 187.

18. Müller, *Hessische Verfassung,* pp. 35, 51. See also Siegfried Büttner, *Die Anfänge des Parlamentarismus in Hessen-Darmstadt und das du Thilsche System* (Darmstadt: Historischer Verein für Hessen, 1969), pp. 6–23.

19. Müller, *Hessische Verfassung,* pp. 35–50.

20. Ibid., p. 39. On von Grolman and his career, see Karl Esselborn, *Hessische Lebensläufe* (Darmstadt: Hessische Historische Kommission, 1979), pp. 128–138.

21. Büttner, *Anfänge des Parlamentarismus,* p. 13.

22. See Heinrich Ulmann, ed., *Denkwürdigkeiten aus dem Dienstleben des Hessen-Darmstädtischen Staatsministers Freiherr Du Thil* (Osnabrück: Biblio, 1967).

23. Ibid., pp. 275–282.

24. Georg Rühl, *Warum müssen wir Landstände haben, und wozu nutzen sie?* (Frankfurt am Main: Eichenberg, 1819).

25. *Hauptbericht,* p. 75. This principle became known as Follen's *Grundsatz.* It is described in detail in MZUK report XVI: "Über die Verbindungen und Umtriebe in Giessen." See especially paragraph 143 of this report, which is entitled "Der Grundsatz: Der Zweck heiligt die Mittel. Sommer 1818." This report is available at the HHStA Wiesbaden, Abt. 210, Nr. 12540.

26. The entire document, referred to in German as "Grundzüge für eine künftige teutsche Reichsverfassung," is printed in Carl Ernst Jarcke, *Carl Ludwig Sand und sein, an dem kaiserlich-russischen Staatsrath von Kotzebue verübter Mord* (Berlin, 1831), pp. 88–111, and also in Hartwig Brandt, ed., *Restauration und Frühliberalismus 1814–1840* (Darmstadt: Wissenschaftliche Buchgesellschaft, 1979), pp. 121–131. It is discussed in *Hauptbericht,* p. 65. Herman Haupt, in "Karl Follen und die Giessener Schwarzen," gives the "Grundzüge" very little attention and calls the document "an unusually childish and immature concoction" of ideas. It is certainly worth more attention, however.

27. Brandt, *Restauration und Frühliberalismus,* p. 17.

28. For a useful overview of the Jacobin tradition in Central Europe, and in Germany specifically, see Helmut Reinalter, *Der Jakobinismus in Mitteleuropa: Eine Einführung* (Stuttgart: Kohlhammer, 1981). Reinalter presents various current definitions of Jacobinism. Most of these point in the direction of a commitment to social equality, popular sovereignty, mobilization of the lower classes, and readiness to employ violent means. Karl Follen adds the concept of national unity.

29. Ernst Rudolf Huber, *Deutsche Verfassungsgeschichte seit 1789* (Stuttgart: W. Kohlhammer, 1960), vol. I, p. 725.

30. On Christoph Follenius's favorable attitude toward Jews, see Karl Vogt, *Aus meinem Leben* (Stuttgart: E. Nägele, 1896), p. 11.

31. See Oskar Franz Scheuer, *Burschenschaft und Judenfrage: Der Rassenantisemitismus in der Deutschen Studentenschaft* (Berlin: Verlag Berlin-Wien, 1927), pp. 6–7.

32. On the Jews at German universities in the early nineteenth century, see Monika Richarz, *Der Eintritt der Juden in die Bürgerlichen Berufe* (Tübingen: J. C. B. Mohr, 1974). Compare also the surprisingly brief treatment of anti-Semitism in Luys, *Anfänge der Deutschen Nationalbewegung,* pp. 231–232.

33. See Eleonore O. Sterling, "Anti-Jewish Riots in Germany in 1819," *Historia Judaica,* 12 (1950): 116.

34. See Walter Grab, "Saul Ascher: Ein Jüdisch-Deutscher Spätaufklärer zwischen Revolution und Restauration," *Jahrbuch des Instituts für Deutsche Geschichte der Universität Tel Aviv,* 6 (1977): 131–179.

35. This comment was part of the speech made at the Wartburg festival by the student Hans Ferdinand Massmann; it is discussed in Chapter 1. The portion quoted here is printed in Scheuer, *Burschenschaft,* p. 15.

36. See Grab, "Saul Ascher," p. 170. In Volume 8 of Heinrich Luden's *Nemesis,*

a writer using the pseudonym "Christlieb" speculates in detail on various schemes to either expell all Jews from Germany or to eliminate them by "shooting to death," "clubbing to death," or "drowning."

37. See Scheuer, *Burschenschaft*, p. 26.

38. Sterling, "Anti-Jewish Riots," pp. 120–131. See also Müller, *Hessische Verfassung*, pp. 52–53. Müller comes to the conclusion that the Blacks were indeed anti-Semitic in their intellectual stance and in their actions.

39. Müller, *Hessische Verfassung*, pp. 53–54.

40. On Weidig's life and ideas, see Karl Mihm, "Alexander Friedrich Ludwig Weidig," *Archiv für Hessische Geschichte und Altertumskunde*, NF 15 (1928): 348–384; 574–608. See also Harald Braun, *Das politische und turnerische Wirken von Friedrich Ludwig Weidig* (St. Augustin: H. Richarz, 1983). Erich Zimmermann also gives much attention to Weidig in *Für Freiheit und Recht*. Finally, see Thomas Michael Mayer, "Büchner und Weidig" in *'Georg Büchner': Text und Kritik Sonderband*, ed. Heinz Ludwig Arnold (Munich: Verlag Text und Kritik, 1979).

41. Braun, *Weidig*, pp. 34–35.

42. On the contacts between Follen and Weidig, see Haupt, "Karl Follen und die Giessener Schwarzen," pp. 130, 137. See also Braun, *Weidig*, pp. 36–39.

43. Braun, *Weidig*, p. 38.

44. Although Weidig had been first investigated in as early as 1818, sufficient proof could never be compiled by the Hesse government in order to prosecute him for a specific political crime. The case against him was therefore temporarily halted in April of 1820, and his personal connections to Karl Follen and other Hesse radicals were not further examined for the time being. See ibid., pp. 46–51.

45. Hans Mayer, *Georg Büchner und seine Zeit* (Frankfurt on Main: Suhrkamp, 1972), p. 148.

46. Karl-Ludwig Ay, "Das Frag- und Antwortbüchlein des Darmstädtischen Offiziers Friedrich Wilhelm Schulz," *Zeitschrift für Bayerische Landesgeschichte*, 35 (1972): 728. For extensive information on the cooperation of Weidig and Büchner, see Thomas Michael Mayer, "Büchner und Weidig," pp. 16–287. See also Zimmermann, *Für Freiheit und Recht*, pp. 141–143.

47. Braun, *Weidig*, p. 80.

48. See Friedrich Noellner, *Actenmässige Darlegung des wegen Hochverraths eingeleiteten gerichtlichen Verfahrens gegen Pfarrer Dr. Friedrich Ludwig Weidig* (Darmstadt: C. W. Leske, 1844); and Friedrich Noellner, *Die Kritik der gerichtlichen Verfahrens gegen Pfarrer Weidig* (Braunschweig: Vieweg und Sohn, 1845); and Carl Welcker, *Die geheimen Inquisitionsprozesse gegen Weidig und Jordan* (Karlsruhe: Braunsche Hofbuchhandlung, 1843).

49. In many historical works, he is referred to only as Wilhelm Schulz, in others as Wilhelm Schulz-Bodmer.

50. On Schulz, see Walter Grab, *Der Mann der Marx Ideen gab* (Düsseldorf: Droste, 1979), and *Dr. Wilhelm Schulz aus Darmstadt* (Frankfurt on Main: Büchergilde Gutenberg, 1987). See also Karl Esselborn, "Eines hessischen Demagogen

Werdegang, Verurteilung und Flucht," *Aus Babenhausens Vergangenheit*, 4 (1932): 1–31.

51. An English translation would be: "Book of Questions and Answers about many Issues which are particularly important for the German Fatherland. For the German Burgher and Farmer." On this pamphlet, see Ay, "Das Frag- und Antwortbüchlein," pp. 728–770. The pamphlet was recognized as a major concern by the MZUK. It is covered in a special report available at the HHStA Wiesbaden.

52. Ay, "Frag- und Antwortbüchlein," p. 728.

53. See Wilhelm Schulz, *Briefwechsel eines Staatsgefangenen mit seiner Befreierin* (Mannheim: Bassermann, 1846). See also Ay, "Frag- und Antwortbüchlein," p. 758.

54. Letter of Georg Büchner to his family, dated Strasbourg, April 5, 1833. Quoted in Georg Büchner, *Werke und Briefe* (Munich: Deutscher Taschenbuch Verlag, 1980), p. 248.

55. The German titles are "Das grosse Lied" and "Teutsche Jugend an die teutsche Menge." Handwritten contemporary copies of the "Great Song" are in the Hessische Landesbibliothek Kassel and at the Archiv der Deutschen Burschenschaft in Frankfurt am Main. An English translation by Eliza Cabot Follen is published in *Works*, vol. I, Appendix I, pp. 593–600.

56. Quoted in George Washington Spindler, *Karl Follen: A Biographical Study* (Chicago: University of Chicago Press, 1917), p. 41.

57. Helena Szépe, "Zur Problematik von Karl Follens 'Grossem Lied,'" *Monatshefte für deutschen Unterricht*, 63 (1971): 335–340.

58. There is considerable material in the Universitätsarchiv Giessen on the crackdown led a year later by Rector Franz Josef Arens on student political activities. See Allg. L 14, Nr. 1315: "Anstellung des Ausserordentlichen landesherrlichen Bevollmächtigten auf der Landesuniversität." This special agent of the state for the University of Giessen was to be Franz Josef Arens. He now held special powers to search student rooms, interrogate students, and dissolve any meetings or clubs which seemed suspicious to him. See Allg. L 14, Nr. 1314: "Der Bundestagsbeschluss vom 20. September 1819. Die Ausstellung der Zeugnisse wegen Teilnahme an Verbindungen der Studierenden." All students were henceforth required to apply for a certificate clearing them of the charge of political agitation before being allowed to take their exams and enter a profession. See also Allg. L 8, Nr. 1299: "Die Bundesbeschlüsse in Ansehung der teutschen Universitäten." This file explained the provisions of the new "University Law" formulated by the Carlsbad Decrees and pased by the Bundestag in Frankfurt in September of 1819.

59. "Untersuchung gegen Dr. Carl Follenius," Universitätsarchiv Giessen, Jur. K 8. This file reveals the way in which university authorities in Giessen were trying to make up their minds about the role of Karl Follen in student radicalism. While there was heavy debate whether to provide Follen with a certificate clearing him of all charges that he had participated in illegal student radicalism, the senate of the university finally did write the document out for

him. None of the professors dealing with Follen's case, including Franz Josef Arens, were at this point sufficiently aware of the major role he had played in Giessen student life. Follen's tactic of keeping his political moves as secret as possible had worked with regard to the university authorities at Giessen.

60. Universitätsarchiv Jena. Akte Karl Follen.

61. See Goethe's "Aktenmässige Nachricht über die seit dem 10. Junius 1792 auf der Akademie zu Jena vorgefallenen Unruhen." It is published in Johann Wolfgang Goethe, *Sämtliche Werke* (Munich: C. Hanser, 1985–present), vol. 4.2, pp. 824–830. A discussion of Jena University, emphasizing the model character of the institution for the whole of Germany, the excellence of the faculty, as well as the "rowdy" character of the student body before and after 1800, is available in Theodore Ziolkowski, *German Romanticism and Its Institutions* (Princeton: Princeton University Press, 1990), pp. 218–308.

62. Erich Maschke, *Universität Jena* (Cologne and Graz: Böhlau, 1969), pp. 49–92.

63. Max Steinmetz, ed., *Geschichte der Universität Jena* (Jena: G. Fischer, 1958), vol. I, p. 240.

64. Heinrich Luden, *Rückblicke in mein Leben* (Jena: F. Luden, 1847), pp. 167–176.

65. *Hauptbericht*, p. 85.

66. Haupt, "Karl Follen und die Giessener Schwarzen," p. 127. Wesselhöft's lengthy evaluation of Karl Follen's role in Jena is contained in his pamphlet *Teutsche Jugend in weiland Burschenschaften und Turngemeinden* (Magdeburg: W. Heinrichshofen, 1828), pp. 65–100. On p. 67, he refers to Follen as a "German devil." See below for more detailed discussion.

67. On Follen in Jena, see the MZUK report XXIV: "Über die politischen Umtriebe und Vereine auf der Universität Jena," HHStA Wiesbaden, Abt. 210, Nr. 12546. See also *Hauptbericht*, p. 88–91. The following secondary literature also deals with this subject in detail: Günter Steiger, *Aufbruch. Urburschenschaft, und Wartburgfest* (Leipzig: Urania, 1967), pp. 173–175; and Herman Haupt, "Karl Follen und die Giessener Schwarzen," *Mitteilungen des Oberhessischen Geschichtsvereins*, NF 15 (1907): 126–129.

68. See Haupt, "Karl Follen und die Giessener Schwarzen," p. 130; and *Works*, vol. I, pp. 68.

69. Johannes Wit, genannt von Dörring, *Fragmente aus meinem Leben und meiner Zeit* (Leipzig: H.E. Gräfe, 1827–1830), vol. III, part 1, p. 208.

70. On Wit von Dörring, see Josephine Blesch, *Studien über Johannes Wit, genannt von Dörring* (Berlin and Leipzig: W. Rothschild, 1917), especially pp. 1–13. See also the useful introduction in Rainer Thierbach, ed., *Wit von Dörring—Revolutionär, Zuchthäusler, Spion* (Heidenheim: Heidenheimer Verlagsanstalt, 1973), pp. 8–18.

71. Wit, *Fragmente*, vol. 3, part 1, pp. 207–208.

72. Gerhard Schulz, *Die Deutsche Literatur zwischen Französischer Revolution und Restauration* (Munich: C. H. Beck, 1989), p. 71.

73. See Gordon Craig, "German Intellectuals and Politics, 1789–1815: The Case of Heinrich von Kleist," *Central European History*, 2 (1969): 3–21. The play

is also described in detail in Gerhard Schulz, *Die Deutsche Literatur*, pp. 54–58, 654–658. For the political implications, see Wolf Kittler, *Die Geburt des Partisanen aus dem Geist der Poesie: Heinrich von Kleist und die Strategie der Befreiungskriege* (Freiburg: Rombach, 1987), pp. 228–255. Kittler spells out very clearly Kleist's political position: he believed in using partisan military tactics in order to destroy Germany's enemies, particularly the French armies.

74. Gerhard Schulz, *Die Deutsche Literatur*, pp. 56–60. In his notorious poem "Germania an ihre Kinder," written just after the *Hermannsschlacht* and first published in 1813, Kleist suggested in an explicit way how to deal with French perpetrators and answer aggression head on:

A lustful hunt, as if gunners
Are tracking down wolves!
Knock him dead! The last judgment
Will not ask you for the reasons!

75. The play *Die Hermannsschlacht* was glorified during the National Socialist period in Germany, and thereafter strictly rejected by literary critics in the second half of the twentieth century. Only in 1982 was the drama rediscovered in a successful production on the German stage. For details, see Kittler, *Die Geburt des Partisanen*, p. 15.

76. For many excerpts from Sand's diary and letters, see *Carl Ludwig Sand, dargestellt durch seine Tagebücher und Briefe von einigen seiner Freunde* (Altenburg: C. Hahn, 1821). The most recent critical treatment of the Sand case is Günther Heydemann, *Carl Sand: Die Tat als Attentat* (Hof: Oberfränkische Verlagsanstalt, 1985).

77. On Sand, see the work of Carl Ernst Jarcke, a noted conservative criminalist in Berlin who undertook a systematic legal investigation in 1831. More recent are the studies of Wilhelm Hausenstein, "Karl Ludwig Sand," *Süddeutsche Monatshefte*, 3 (1906): 178–201; Karl Alexander von Müller, *Carl Ludwig Sand* (Munich: Beck, 1925); and Heydemann, *Carl Sand*. The following archival sources are also available: the MZUK report XXX on "Carl Sand" at the HHStA Wiesbaden, Abt. 210, Nr. 12550; and the records of the Hofgericht Mannheim on the Sand case, to be found in the Badisches General-Landesarchiv (BGLA) Karlsruhe, Abt. 233, Nr. 4181, and Nr. 4182. The latter record, Nr. 4182, was written on the evening of the murder; it contains the very first impressions of the Mannheim police when they arrived on the murder scene, and details on Sand's health after his suicide attempt.

78. See *Carl Ludwig Sand, dargestellt durch seine Tagebücher und Briefe.*

79. Heydemann, *Carl Sand*, p. 82.

80. This document is included in ibid., Appendix, pp. 119–122.

81. See the *Hauptbericht*, and the Hofgericht Mannheim records at the BGLA Karlsruhe, Abt. 233, Nr. 4181 and Nr. 4182. Furthermore, Jarcke, Treitschke, Haupt, Pregizer, and Wüst have all dealt with this question.

82. See Hausenstein, "C. L. Sand," pp. 178–201; J. Hermann, "Zur Kritik der Nachrichten über die Attentate von 1819," *Forschungen zur Deutschen Geschichte*, 23 (1883): 571–592; Hans Schneider, "Das Attentat des Apothekers Karl Löning auf den Präsidenten Ibell (1819)," *QuD*, 5 (1920): 153–170.

83. *Hauptbericht*, p. 103.

84. Ibid., p. 103. On this same question, see also the records of the Hofgericht Mannheim, at the BGLA Karlsruhe, Abt. 233, Nr. 4181 and Nr. 4182.

85. Friedrich Münch, *Erinnerungen aus Deutschlands trübster Zeit* (St. Louis and Neustadt a.d. Haardt: Witter, 1873). The most significant parts of Münch's memoirs, relating to the connection of Follen and Sand, were published earlier in an article entitled "Follen, Sand, und Löning: Neues Licht in altes Dunkel," *Die Gartenlaube* (1872): 722–725.

86. See Wit von Dörring, *Fragmente*, vol. III, part 1, pp. 190–214.

87. Wit von Dörring, *Fragmente*, vol. III, part 1, pp. 206–209.

88. Heinrich Leo, *Meine Jugendzeit* (Gotha: F. A. Perthes, 1880), pp. 188–189.

89. This letter from De Wette to Sand's mother, dated March 31, 1819, is printed in the article by Wilhelm Hausenstein, "Dokumente zur Geschichte des Studenten Karl Ludwig Sand," *Forschungen zur Geschichte Bayerns*, 15 (1907): 160–183, 244–270. An excerpt, containing the most important passages, is printed in Heydemann, *Carl Sand*, pp. 132–133.

90. Hans Schneider, "Das Attentat des Apothekers Löning auf den Präsidenten Ibell (1819)," *QuD*, 5 (1920): 154–155.

91. Schneider, "Löning," pp. 159–161. The case is also dealt with extensively, using archival documents, in W. Sauer, *Das Herzogtum Nassau in den Jahren 1813–1820* (Wiesbaden: W. Kreidels, 1893).

92. See the suspicions voiced in the MZUK report "Über des Apothekers Löning Theilnahme an demagogischen Umtrieben und dessen Mordversuch," HHStA Wiesbaden, Abt. 210, Nr. 12551.

93. These thoughts are clearly expressed in Münch, "Follen, Sand, und Löning," p. 724.

94. Schneider, "Löning," p. 166.

95. Written in Elberfeld in July 1819. Quoted in Gottfried Fittbogen, "Briefe aus dem Lager der Unbedingten," *Euphorion*, 27 (1926): 380.

96. Wit von Dörring, *Fragmente*, vol. 3, part 1, p. 210.

97. *Hauptbericht*, p. 113.

98. See for instance Leo, *Meine Jugendzeit*, p. 186. Leo divides the Unconditionals into two groups: those who were willing to "engage in common crimes" (bear false witness, steal), and those who were willing to murder their enemies. Karl Follen clearly belonged in the latter, very small category.

99. See *Works*, vol. I, pp. 72–73.

100. Ibid., vol. I, p. 72.

101. See Leo, *Meine Jugendzeit*, pp. 179–181.

102. For the text, see Wit von Dörring, *Fragmente*, vol. III, part 1, pp. 194–200.

103. See Heinrich von Treitschke, *Deutsche Geschichte im Neunzehnten Jahrhundert* (Leipzig: S. Hirzel, 1879–1889), vol. II, pp. 437–443. For a critique of Treitschke's stance toward Follen and the *Burschenschaft* and *Turner*, see Starr Willard Cutting, "Heinrich von Treitschke's Treatment of Turner and Burschenschafter," *Philological Quarterly*, 1 (1922): 31–48.

104. See Erwin Schuppe, *Der Burschenschafter Wolfgang Menzel: Eine Quelle zum*

*Verständnis des Nationalsozialismus* (Frankfurt am Main: G. Schulte-Blumke, 1952), pp. 23–24.

105. Wesselhöft, *Teutsche Jugend*, pp. 67–86.

106. Julia Wüst, "Karl Follen," *Mitteilungen des OberhessischenGeschichtsvereins*, NF 33 (1936): 64–65.

107. Ibid., p. 132.

108. Steiger, *Aufbruch*, pp. 161–164.

109. See Huber, *Deutsche Verfassungsgeschichte*, vol. I, pp. 731–732.

110. See Ernst Münch, *Erinnerungen, Lebensbilder, und Studien* (Karlsruhe: Müllersche Hofbuchhandlung, 1836), vol. I, p. 460. Also quoted in Schuppe, *Menzel*, p. 24.

111. Münch, *Erinnerungen*, vol. I, pp. 459–460.

112. See the discussion in Richard Pregizer, *Die Politischen Ideen des Karl Follen: Ein Beitrag zur Geschichte des Radikalismus in Deutschland* (Tübingen: J. C. B. Mohr, 1912), pp. 59–77.

## 3. Stages of Exile

1. See Universitätsarchiv Giessen, Jur. K 8: "Untersuchung gegen Dr. Carl Follenius."

2. For background on this, see especially Eberhard Büssem, *Die Karlsbader Beschlüsse von 1819* (Hildesheim: Gerstenberg, 1974), pp. 129–155.

3. See Günter Steiger, "Das 'Phantom der Wartburgverschwörung' 1817," *Wissenschaftliche Zeitschrift der Universität Jena*, 15 (1966): 191.

4. According to Günter Steiger, Karl Albert von Kamptz did not believe that the politicized student movement, as it existed in 1819, could inflict serious damage on the Prussian state through individual terrorist acts or small-scale violent action. He was, however, concerned about the change in "spirit" which had taken place among German youth in the universities. Although the students seemed incapable of causing a revolution, they could progressively influence others in subversive ways. It was the new emphasis on an "inner conviction," preached by Jacob Friedrich Fries, and more dangerously by Karl Follen, that Kamptz intended to curb.

5. Steiger, "Wartburgverschwörung," p. 194.

6. On the Prussian police, its personnel structure, methods, and aims, see Hans Branig, *Fürst Wittgenstein: Ein preussischer Staatsmann der Restaurationszeit* (Cologne and Vienna: Böhlau, 1981). Many records of the Prussian "Immediat-Untersuchungskommission" in Berlin-Köpenick relevant to this study are collected in Friedrich Schnapp, ed., *E. T. A. Hoffmann: Juristische Arbeiten* (Munich: Winkler, 1973). The original records of this commission are in the Deutsches Zentralarchiv Merseburg.

7. Quoted in Günter Schönbrunn, ed., *Geschichte in Quellen. Band 5: Das bürgerliche Zeitalter, 1815–1914* (Munich: Bayerischer Schulbuchverlag, 1980), pp. 83–84.

8. Ibid., p. 84.

274

9. The text of the most important new laws is printed in Ernst Rudolf Huber, ed., *Dokumente zur Deutschen Verfassungsgeschichte* (Stuttgart: W. Kohlhammer, 1961), vol. I, pp. 90–102. The standard work on the Carlsbad Decrees is Büssem, *Karlsbader Beschlüsse.*

10. The original documents of the Mainz Commission have been destroyed. However, several copies, made in the 1820s, are still available. These may be found at the Hessisches Hauptstaatsarchiv in Wiesbaden and at the Bayerisches Staatsarchiv in Munich. A full listing of the more than eighty individual reports compiled by the commission is in A. Petzold, "Die Zentraluntersuchungskommission in Mainz," *QuD,* 5 (1920): 217–222, n. 125.

11. The latter has been used extensively for this work.

12. *Bundestagsprotokolle,* 1827, 10. Sitzung, Section 78. The basic investigation results are listed here. There are also statements by the individual state representatives; for Hesse, this is made by the Hofgericht in Darmstadt. Again there is a complete listing of the more than eighty individual reports compiled.

13. On the Mainz commission, see A. Petzold, "Die Zentral-Untersuchungskommission in Mainz," *QuD,* 5 (1920): 171–258. See also Eberhard Weber, *Die Mainzer Zentraluntersuchungskommission* (Karlsruhe: C. F. Müller, 1970), passim.

14. Eliza Lee Cabot Follen, ed., *The Works of Charles Follen, with a Memoir of His Life* (Boston: Hilliard and Gray, 1841), vol. I, p. 73.

15. On the investigations of Sand and Follen at Mannheim, see the records of the Hofgericht Mannheim, at the BGLA Karlsruhe, and the MZUK report on "Carl Sand," HHStA Wiesbaden, Abt. 210, Nr. 12550.

16. See Ernst Rudolf Huber, *Deutsche Verfassungsgeschichte seit 1789* (Stuttgart: W. Kohlhammer, 1960), vol. I, p. 748.

17. "Untersuchung gegen Dr. Carl Follenius," Universitätsarchiv Giessen, Jur. K 8.

18. The university authorities had, for example, been able to compile an extensive list of the students who were believed to belong to the Giessen Burschenschaft and subscribe to Follen's *Ehrenspiegel* code. This list is in the Universitätsarchiv Giessen, Allg L 14, Nr. 1315. In Allg L 8, Nr. 1299, there is also information on Franz Josef Arens's objectives, and his reports on what he had been able to find out about secret student societies in Giessen.

19. On the petition movement, which called for the introduction of a liberal constitution in Hesse-Darmstadt and was organized by the Darmstadt Blacks, supported by Giessen students, see Chapter 2.

20. August Follen to Ludwig von Mühlenfels, May 12, 1819. Printed in Gottfried Fittbogen, "Briefe aus dem Lager der Unbedingten," *Euphorion,* 27 (1926): 376–377.

21. "Untersuchung gegen Dr. Carl Follenius," Universitätsarchiv Giessen, Jur. K 8. In the university archives at Giessen, as noted above, there are also records of Franz Josef Arens's appointment and duties as special state investigator. Arens attempted to investigate the Burschenschaft group which had existed at Giessen, kept a close watch on current student politics, and issued the necessary evaluations students needed in order to certify their political reliability and fitness to take exams or seek government employment.

22. It was customary for executioners to ask the forgiveness of those whom they were about to kill. Still, the extensive legends which sprang up among German radicals about the death of Carl Sand emphasize that all the people in the audience, the executioner, and everyone except the reactionary government officials were on Sand's side.

23. See Günter Steiger, *Aufbruch: Urburschenschaft und Wartburgfest* (Leipzig: Urania, 1967), p. 210. Chips from the wooden block used during Sand's execution can still be seen today in the office of the Archiv der Deutschen Burschenschaft in Frankfurt am Main.

24. Follen did not leave Germany a moment too soon. By 1820 the Prussian authorities were increasingly interested in trying him for possible involvement in political radicalism. In the former East German DZA Merseburg, Rep. 77 XXI, Spez. F Nr. 2, Bd. 1, there was a letter from Duke Carl August of Saxony-Weimar, dated March 14, 1820, explaining the case of Follen to the Berlin investigation committee, and stating that Follen had been at Jena in 1819, but had left several months earlier. There was also an official report on Follen's stay in Jena at the DZA Merseburg.

25. *Works*, vol. I, p. 101.

26. Hans Fraenkel, "Politische Gedanken und Strömungen in der Burschenschaft um 1821–1824," *QuD*, 3 (1912): 252. On Follen and Wit in Paris during May and June of 1820, see also the *Hauptbericht*, pp. 125–131.

27. *Hauptbericht*, p. 126.

28. On the relationship of Follen and Cousin, see ibid., pp. 129–130. The Mainz officials were here using two main sources: the statements Cousin made in Berlin after he was arrested on a trip to Germany in the early 1820s, and the statements of Wit von Dörring after his arrest about the same time.

29. On the Benzel-Sternau family, see the *Neue Deutsche Biographie* (Berlin: Duncker and Humboldt, 1953–present), vol. II, pp. 59–60.

30. *Works*, vol. I, p. 107.

31. See the discussion in Ernst Brand, "Die Auswirkungen der deutschen Demagogenverfolgungen in der Schweiz," *Basler Zeitschrift für Geschichte und Altertumskunde*, 45–47 (1946–1948): 148–149.

32. See *Works*, vol. I, pp. 105–111.

33. Ibid., vol. I, p. 110.

34. Brand, "Auswirkungen der Demagogenverfolgungen," p. 150.

35. Proof of how much the "Preussische Immediat-Untersuchungskommission" was finding out may be seen in Schnapp, *E. T. A. Hoffmann*.

36. Andreas Staehelin, *Geschichte der Universität Basel, 1818–1835* (Basel: Helbing and Lichtenhahn, 1959), pp. 49–50.

37. See Ernst Staehelin, *Dewettiana: Forschungen und Texte zu W. M. L. De Wettes Leben und Werk* (Basel: Helbing and Lichtenhahn, 1956). Contained in this work are the most important dates concerning De Wette's life and a list of his publications. There is also a collection of his letters, many of them to Jakob Friedrich Fries. De Wette's letter to Carl Sand's mother is printed on pp. 85–87. The theologian claimed: "The error [which your son made] is excused and in some ways pushed aside by the strength and honesty of his conviction."

276

38. That there was, even after 1819, still contact betwen Fries and prominent liberals, and also between Fries and Karl Follen, can be seen in Fries's correspondence. He wrote to Karl Follen and heard from him several times after the latter had left Jena and gone to Switzerland. See Fries' personal papers, at the Universitätsbibliothek in Jena. An edition of Fries's letters is being prepared by Professor Gerd König at Bochum.

39. Staehelin, *Geschichte der Universität Basel*, pp. 74–76.

40. See Wilhelm Oechsli, *Geschichte der Schweiz im neunzehnten Jahrhundert* (Leipzig: S. Hirzel, 1903–1913), vol. II, pp. 632–633.

41. For details on Follen's planned Swiss work, and for the titles of Follen's lectures, see Felix Staehelin, "Demagogische Umtriebe zweier Enkel Salomon Gessners," *Jahrbuch für Schweizerische Geschichte*, 39 (1914): 20–21.

42. Karl Follen, "Über die Bestimmung des Menschen," *Wissenschaftliche Zeitschrift herausgegeben von Lehrern der Baseler Hochschule* (Basel, 1824): 56.

43. Ibid., p. 75.

44. Ibid., p. 103.

45. Ibid., pp. 111–113.

46. Karl Follen, "Über die Rechtslehre des Spinoza," *Wissenschaftliche Zeitschrift herausgegeben von Lehrern der Baseler Hochschule* (Basel, 1824): 4.

47. Ibid., p. 53.

48. A complete discussion of the location of Follen's conception of natural law within the German tradition is not possible here. It is significant, however, that during the 1820s and 1830s, Germans were turning away from western European and American natural law and toward a conception of law centered on the historical development of the nation state, as developed in the thought of Hegel. See Hajo Holborn, "Der Deutsche Idealismus in Sozialgeschichtlicher Beleuchtung," *Historische Zeitschrift*, 174 (1952): 359–384.

49. Staehelin, "Demagogische Umtriebe," pp. 21–25.

50. See Hans Fraenkel, "Politische Gedanken und Strömungen in der Burschenschaft um 1821–24," *QuD*, 3 (1912): 270–271.

51. See Silbernagl, "Die geheimen Verbindungen der Deutschen in der ersten Hälfte des neunzehnten Jahrhunderts," *Historisches Jahrbuch der Görres-Gesellschaft*, 14 (1893): 786–795.

52. See Oechsli, *Geschichte der Schweiz*, vol. II, pp. 695–696.

53. Staehelin, "Demagogische Umtriebe," pp. 6–7.

54. Ibid., pp. 9–12.

55. These guidelines established by Karl Follen are published in ibid., pp. 14–15.

56. See Silbernagl, "Die geheimen politischen Verbindungen," pp. 788–789.

57. See ibid., pp. 788–789.

58. See ibid., pp. 790–791. On Wesselhöft's prominent role within the league and his incresing lack of faith in its potential for success from early 1822 onward, see also Carl Follenberg (= Ferdinand Neigebaur), "Acten-Stücke über die unter dem Namen des Männer-Bundes und des Jünglings-Bundes bekannten demagogischen Umtriebe," in Leopold Friedrich Ilse, *Geschichte der geheimen Verbindungen der neuesten Zeit* (Leipzig: J. A. Barth, 1833), part 7,

pp. 1–15. Wesselhöft increasingly felt in 1822 that "at the moment I could not think of the means by which the victory of truth and reason in German politics could be hastened along. The people are only willing to work for justice if they can make a material gain for themselves in the process."

59. See Herman Haupt, "Zum Gedächtnis Karl Follens," *Deutsch-Amerikanische Geschichtsblätter*, 22/3 (1922–23): 31.

60. At the Congress of Troppau in October of 1820, Metternich's agents even claimed that Karl Follen had already attempted to found a secret political group with various other German exiles while still teaching at Chur. See Brand, "Auswirkungen der Demagogenverfolgung," pp. 143–144.

61. *Hauptbericht*, pp. 125–130.

62. See Fraenkel, "Politische Gedanken," p. 257.

63. On Wittgenstein and his cooperation with Kamptz, see Hans Branig, *Fürst Wittgenstein* (Cologne and Vienna: Böhlau, 1981), especially pp. 101–111. In the Prussian police ministry, Wittgenstein was police minister, and Kamptz was "Wirklicher Geheimer OberReg. Rat und Direktor." Wittgenstein had direct connections to the Prussian court, and thus often had an easy time convincing the king of what he wished to do in police matters. Details about the Berlin "Immediate Commission," its methods and goals, are also provided in the introduction to Schnapp, *E. T. A. Hoffmann: Juristische Arbeiten*, pp. 5–13, and passim.

64. See Schnapp, *E. T. A. Hoffmann: Juristische Arbeiten*. This is a very careful edition of Hoffmann's legal works, and it includes transcriptions of all reports Hofmann compiled on the Burschenschaft members Carl Bader, Carl Ulrich, the gymnastics enthusiast Franz Lieber (soon to emigrate to America and become the first political scientist there), August Follen, and Friedrich Ludwig Jahn.

65. See Eckart Klessmann, *E. T. A. Hoffmann oder die Tiefe zwischen Stern und Erde: Eine Biographie* (Stuttgart: Deutsche Verlagsanstalt, 1980), pp. 447–450.

66. The legal proceedings against August Follen are very well documented. Many related documents were formerly at the DZA Merseburg, Rep. 77 Spec. Lit F Nr. 2 Bd 1 through Bd 5. These include lengthy official protocols of his court case, letters written to friends describing his trial, his personal poetry book, and newspaper articles relating to his imprisonment. See also Gottfried Fittbogen, "Der Prozess gegen Adolf Ludwig Follen," *Deutsche Revue*, 47 (1922): 34–43. The most recent treatment of August Follen's life is in Edmund Spevack, "August Adolf Ludwig Follen (1794–1855): Political Radicalism and Literary Romanticism in Germany and Switzerland," *Germanic Review*, 71 (1996): 3–22.

67. Fraenkel, "Politische Gedanken," pp. 289–293.

68. Quoted in ibid., p. 298.

69. The crisis in the Youth League is decribed in detail in the memoirs of a student who joined toward the end of its existence: see Arnold Ruge, *Aus früher Zeit: Lebenserinnerungen* (Berlin: F. Duncker, 1862–1867), vol. 2, pp. 366–367.

70. Paul Wentzcke and Georg Heer, *Geschichte der Deutschen Burschenschaft* (Heidelberg: C. Winter, 1919 and 1927), vol. 2, p. 120.

71. Staehelin, "Demagogische Umtriebe," pp. 37–39.

72. See Fraenkel, "Politische Gedanken," p. 300.

73. See Paul Wentzcke and Georg Heer, *Geschichte der Deutschen Burschenschaft*, vol. 2, pp. 180–181.

74. Four of Wit von Dörring's articles are reprinted in Harald Braun, *Das politische und turnerische Wirken von Friedrich Ludwig Weidig* (Sankt Augustin: H. Richarz, 1983), pp. 182–212. The translation of the Latin motto is: "If medicine will not cure [the German political situation], iron will cure it; if iron will not cure it, fire will destroy it." The last word is misprinted in Braun; it should read "tunabit."

75. Letter of Karl Follen to Ferdinand Wit, dated October 20, 1820. It is included in *Hauptbericht*, pp. 296–297.

76. Staehelin, "Demagogische Umtriebe," p. 42.

77. See Oechsli, *Geschichte der Schweiz*, vol. II, pp. 697–699.

78. See Ruge, *Aus früher Zeit*, vol. 2, pp. 176–177, 366–367.

79. Friedrich List to August Follen, June 1824. Reproduced in Friedrich List, *Tagebücher und Briefe, 1812–1846,* ed. Edgar Salin (Berlin: R. Hobbing, 1933), vol. 8, p. 297.

80. Friedrich List to August Follen, July 2, 1824. See ibid., vol. 8, pp. 292–293.

81. Printed in Herman Haupt, ed., "Follen-Briefe," *Deutsch-Amerikanische Geschichtsblätter*, 14 (1914): 15.

82. This phase of Karl Follen's life is well documented. In the former DZA Merseburg there were many documents relating to Follen's persecution by Berlin, including physical descriptions of what Follen looked like; police reports on where he might possibly be at any given time; records of the testimony of Wit von Dörring against him; and the reports of the Prussian police agent, who was searching for Follen in Switzerland, back to Berlin.

83. See Oechsli, *Geschichte der Schweiz*, vol. II, pp. 634–641.

84. See Staehelin, "Demagogische Umtriebe," p. 46.

85. Haupt, "Follen-Briefe," p. 13.

86. On August Follen's illness, which was so severe that it lasted for eighteen months, see Hans-Günther Bressler, "Der Spätromantiker A.A.L. Follen in Psychiatrischer Schau," *Schweizerische Medizinische Wochenschrift*, 79 (1949):868.

87. Brand, "Auswirkungen der Demagogenverfolgungen," p. 165.

88. Printed in Haupt, "Follen-Briefe," pp. 20–21.

89. Quoted in Brand, "Auswirkungen der Demagogenverfolgungen," p. 175.

90. See Oechsli, *Geschichte der Schweiz*, vol. II, pp. 676–677.

91. Quoted in Haupt, "Zum Gedächtnis Karl Follens," p. 27.

92. The German title is "Denkschrift über die Gründung einer Deutsch-Amerikanischen Universität." The entire document, discovered and edited by Herman Haupt, is printed in *Deutsch-Amerikanische Geschichtsblätter*, 22/23 (1922–23): 56–76.

93. On Follen's "Memorandum," see the Mainz commission's *Hauptbericht*, p. 119. The commission members were worried about Follen's supposed purpose of "bringing together the Germans of North America into one state, to be represented in Congress, which could become an example for the home country, and could in many ways contribute to its liberation." A critical discussion

of the "Memorandum" appears in Stefan von Senger und Etterlin, *Neu-Deutschland in Nordamerika* (Baden-Baden: Nomos, 1991), pp. 81–88.

94. See Karl Follen, "Die Gründung einer Deutsch-Amerikanischen Universität," pp. 72–73.

95. See Paul Follen and Friedrich Münch, *Aufforderung und Erklärung in Betreff einer Auswanderung im Grossen aus Teutschland in die nordamerikanischen Freistaaten* (Giessen, 1833). This pamphlet explains the entire scheme developed by Paul Follen, including travel, finances, social organization, and goals for the German group in the New World.

96. On Karl Follen's flight, see Brand, "Die Auswirkungen der deutschen Demagogenverfolgungen," pp. 186–192. Once Follen had fled Switzerland, the Prussian authorities immediately found out. At the DZA Merseburg, there was a police report specifically evaluating the idea that Follen might have escaped to America, and considering what steps might perhaps still be taken against him in the future.

97. The journal is partly reproduced in *Works*, vol. I, pp. 127–133.

98. Karl Follen to his parents and siblings, dated Philadelphia, January 13, 1825. Printed in Karl Buchner, "Dr. Karl Follen," *Der Freihafen*, 4 (1841): 71–76.

## 4. German Culture and American Reform

1. In the American half of his life, Follen remained just as secretive as in Europe. As noted in the Introduction, the complete letters and papers of Charles Follen have never been discovered. George Washington Spindler searched for them in 1917, and Erich Geldbach did so in the 1980s. The papers have not turned up in an archive thus far. A letter of April 27, 1915, in the folder on Follen at the Harvard University Archives (HUG 300) points to the fact that letters and journals of Charles Follen were left to a relative of Eliza Follen, John H. Cabot of Brookline. About 1900, Professor Kuno Francke of Harvard asked Cabot if he had any letters or journals belonging to the Follens. Cabot sent him what he had, and received from him a letter acknowledging their receipt. Perhaps Francke filed them in the library of Harvard College. The letter is from a descendant of Eliza Follen's, Marian C. Rimann (Mrs. James J. Rimann [?]), and addressed to a Mrs. Lane. Unfortunately, among the Kuno Francke Papers (Harvard University Archives), there is no indication that Francke was in fact in the possession of Follen materials. There are, however, a number of Follen papers and letters, concerning his career in America, at the Boston Public Library, in the Harvard University Archives, and at the Massachusetts Historical Society. Small collections on Follen can be found in various other libraries such as Cornell University Library and the Pierpont Morgan Library.

2. For recent evaluations of Follen's American career in secondary literature, see Heinrich Schneider, "Karl Follen, a Re-appraisal and Some New Biographical Materials," *Society for the History of the Germans in Maryland: 30th Report* (Baltimore, 1959), pp. 73–86; Wolfgang Martin Freitag, "Mit der Sonne nach Westen hin: Karl Follen," in Kurt Schleucher, ed., *Deutsche Unter Anderen Völkern* (Darmstadt: Turris, 1975), vol. 4, pp. 92–136; Douglas Stange, "The

Making of an Abolitionist Martyr: Harvard Professor Charles Theodore Christian Follen," *Harvard Library Bulletin*, 24 (January 1976): 17–24; and Walter Donald Kring, *Liberals among the Orthodox: Unitarian Beginnings in New York City, 1819–1839* (Boston: Beacon Press, 1974), chaps. 13–15.

3. This account by the Rev. George Simmons of Albany, New York, is included in William Buell Sprague, *Annals of the American Pulpit* (New York: R. Carter and Bros., 1857–1869; reprint New York, 1969), vol. 8, p. 544.

4. This document is fully discussed in Chapter 3.

5. See Edward Pessen, *Jacksonian America: Society, Personality, and Politics* (Urbana and Chicago: University of Illinois Press, 1985), pp. 53–148, 197–232, 324–327. Pessen presents a more current and critical view of the period, its problems and characteristics, than do two earlier works, Arthur Schlesinger, Jr., *The Age of Jackson* (Boston: Little, Brown and Co., 1945), and John William Ward, *Andrew Jackson: Symbol for an Age* (New York: Oxford University Press, 1955).

6. On the American nationalism of the period, see Laurence J. Friedman, *Inventors of the Promised Land* (New York: Knopf, 1975); Hans Kohn, *American Nationalism: An Interpretative Essay* (New York: Macmillan, 1957); Paul C. Nagel, *This Sacred Trust: American Nationality 1798–1898* (New York: Oxford University Press, 1971).

7. On the development of an automomous American literature in the 1830s to 1850s, see Larzer Ziff, *Literary Democracy: The Declaration of Cultural Independence in America* (New York: Viking Press, 1981).

8. See Russel Blaine Nye, *Society and Culture in America 1830–1860* (New York: Harper and Row, 1974), pp. 1–31. Nye argues that the "frame of American belief" in the period described was dominated by four ideas: nationalism, mission, romanticism, and progress.

9. Nye, *Society and Culture*, pp. 3–31.

10. Bernhard zu Sachsen-Weimar-Eisenach, *Reise durch Nord-Amerika in den Jahren 1825 und 1826*, ed. Heinrich Luden (Weimar: W. Hoffmann, 1828).

11. Francis Lieber, *The Stranger in America* (Philadelphia: Carey, Lea, and Blanchard, 1834). See also the standard work by Frank Freidel, *Francis Lieber: Nineteenth-Century Liberal* (Baton Rouge: Louisiana State University Press, 1947).

12. Letter dated May 12, 1827. Quoted in Thomas Sergeant Perry, ed., *The Life and Letters of Francis Lieber* (Boston: J. R. Osgood and Co., 1882), pp. 69–70.

13. Ludwig De Wette, *Reise in die Vereinigten Staaten und Canada im Jahr 1837* (Leipzig: Weidmann, 1838). This work by De Wette, a physician from Basel, is an insightful, objective, and reliable source.

14. Ibid., pp. 12–13, 345–348.

15. Ibid., pp. 44, 353–354.

16. Quoted in Follen, *Works*, vol. I, p. 128.

17. These letters are published in Karl Buchner, ed., "Dr. Karl Follen: Mit Benutzung von noch ungedruckten Briefen desselben aus Amerika in die Heimath," *Der Freihafen*, 4 (Altona, 1841): 59–78 and 113–146. More letters are published in Herman Haupt, ed., "Follenbriefe," *Deutsch-Amerikanische*

*Geschichtsblätter*, 14 (1914): 7–83. Several are also included by Eliza Follen in *Works*, vol. I, pp. 139–148.

18. Letter from Charles Follen to his parents and siblings, dated January 13, 1825. It is printed in *Works*, vol. I, pp. 144–148. The letter is also included in Buchner, "Dr. Karl Follen," pp. 71–76; and in Haupt, "Follenbriefe," pp. 22–27. The quotation here is from Buchner, p. 74.

19. Same letter as cited in note 18. This quotation is from *Works*, vol. I, p. 146. The German text may be found in Buchner, "Dr. Karl Follen," p. 73.

20. See especially Clifford S. Griffin, "Religious Benevolence as Social Control," and John L. Thomas, "Romantic Reform in America," in David Brion Davis, ed., *Antebellum Reform* (New York: Harper and Row, 1967), pp. 81–96 and 153–176.

21. Nye, *Society and Culture*, pp. 34–35.

22. Davis, *Antebellum Reform*, pp. 1, 6. On the problems of interpreting the attitudes and activities of antebellum reformers today, see Ronald G. Walters, *American Reformers* (New York: Hill and Wang, 1978), Introduction. Compare also Lawrence J. Friedman, *Gregarious Saints: Self and Community in American Abolitionism, 1800–1870* (Cambridge and New York: Cambridge University Press, 1982).

23. Letter from Charles Follen to his parents and sisters, dated December 19, 1826. It is included in *Works*, vol. I, pp. 164–169.

24. Peter Stephen DuPonceau to John Davis, dated June 12, 1825. American Philosophical Society Library, Philadelphia. Misc. ms. Collection.

25. Quoted in *Works*, vol. I, pp. 140–143.

26. See ibid., vol. I, pp. 144–148. This letter is dated January 13, 1825.

27. On the history of the Round Hill School, established by Joseph Cogswell and George Bancroft, see Erich Geldbach, "Die Verpflanzung des deutschen Turnens nach Amerika: Beck, Follen, Lieber," *Stadion*, 1 (1975): 331–376.

28. See *Works*, vol. I, p. 163.

29. For an overview of the history of Harvard College at the time, see Samuel Eliot Morison, *Three Centuries of Harvard* (Cambridge, Mass.: Harvard University Press, 1936), and the "official history" by Harvard president Josiah Quincy, *History of Harvard University* (Cambridge, Mass.: J. Owen, 1840). The reforms in the university and the expansion of the entire institution under President Kirkland have most recently been discussed in Bernard Bailyn, "Why Kirkland Failed," in Bernard Bailyn, Donald Fleming, et al., *Glimpses of the Harvard Past* (Cambridge, Mass.: Harvard University Press, 1986), pp. 19–44. For many valuable insights into Harvard history during the 1820s and 1830s, see also Robert A. McCaughey, *Josiah Quincy, 1772–1864: The Last Federalist* (Cambridge, Mass.: Harvard University Press, 1974).

30. Morison, *Three Centuries of Harvard*, chaps. 9–11, pp. 195–272.

31. See McCaughey, *Josiah Quincy*, pp. 139–143.

32. George Huntston Williams, *The Harvard Divinity School: Its Place in Harvard University and in American Culture* (Boston: Beacon Press, 1954), pp. 21–77; Van Wyck Brooks, *The Flowering of New England, 1815–1865* (New York: E. P. Dutton and Co., 1936), esp. chap. 2. See also Henry Pochmann, *German Culture*

*in America, 1600–1800* (Madison, Wisc.: University of Wisconsin Press, 1957), pp. 81–82.

33. Records of Follen's involvement with Harvard University, his teaching positions and performance, his salary and lecture topics, are in the Harvard University Archives. See the Bertha Illsley Tolman Catalogue of University Records 1636–1870 for details.

34. Thomas Wentworth Higginson, *Cheerful Yesterdays* (Boston: Houghton Mifflin, 1898), and Andrew P. Peabody, *Harvard Reminiscences* (Boston: Ticknor, 1888; reprint New York, 1972). Peabody paints a very positive image of Follen, and also discusses Charles Beck. He includes his experience with Follen as a teacher, a literary critic, and an outspoken opponent of slavery, and as a friendly and concerned host to students at his house in Cambridge.

35. These notes have never been discussed in the secondary literature and are available in the Harvard University Archives. The General Catalogue at the Harvard University Archives lists "George Moore, A.B. 1834, Notes of Dr. Follen's lectures on German literature, 1834. Texts for sermons, and skeletons. Notes to Dr. Follen's lectures on Pantheism, 1839," and "Henry Burroughs, A.B. 1834. Notes to Professor Follen on German literature, 1834" (HUC 8833.324 and HUC 8833.376). The notes of George Moore are also dealt with in Chapter 5.

36. These reports and papers are in the Harvard University Archives, file no. UA III 28.26.

37. George Washington Spindler, *Karl Follen: A Biographical Study* (Chicago: University of Chicago Press), p. 104. See also Louis Viereck, *Zwei Jahrhunderte Deutschen Unterrichts in den Vereinigten Staaten* (Braunschweig: F. Vieweg und Sohn, 1903), pp. 27–29.

38. See Charles Follen, *Deutsches Lesebuch für Anfänger* (Boston: Hilliard and Metcalf, 1826), pp. x–xii.

39. On the German Society at Harvard and its members, compare Spindler, *Karl Follen,* p. 110; and Pochmann, *German Culture* in America, p. 563, n. 454. See also Leonard L. Mackall, "Briefwechsel zwischen Goethe und Amerikanern," *Goethe-Jahrbuch,* 25 (1904): 3–37. Mackall believes that the discussions on German literature and culture reported in *Works,* vol. I, pp. 209–210, 221, are records of Follen's statements while meeting with the German Society. He lists the members of Follen's society as having been: "S. A. Eliot, G. Ticknor, S. H. Perkins, Wm. T. Andrews, F. C. Gray, J. Pickering, N. I. Bowditch, E. Wigglesworth, F. Lieber, Mr. Miesegaes, T. Searly, J. M. Robbins." See Mackall, p. 23.

40. Reginald Phelps, "The Idea of the Modern University—Göttingen and America," the *Germanic Review,* 29 (October 1954): 175–190. Thomas Wentworth Higginson, "Göttingen and Harvard Eighty Years Ago," *Harvard Graduates' Magazine,* 6 (1897–98): 6–18. See also the extensive discussion in Stanley Vogel, *German Literary Influences on the American Transcendentalists* (New Haven: Yale University Press, 1955), pp. 22–49. Finally, an important work in this context is Carl Diehl, *Americans and German Scholarship, 1770–1870* (New Haven: Yale University Press, 1978). Chapter 3 is entitled: "Innocents Abroad: American Students in German Universities, 1815–1870."

41. For short intellectual portraits of these men, see Emma Gertrude Jaeck,

*Mme. de Stael and the Spread of German Literature* (New York: Oxford University Press, 1915), pp. 251–270.

42. Many useful documents on the German experiences of Ticknor, Cogswell, and Bancroft are included in Richard Hofstadter and Wilson Smith, eds., *American Higher Education: A Documentary History* (Chicago: University of Chicago Press, 1961), vol. I, pp. 251–265. The Americans returning from Germany soon became involved in reforming the universities in their home country, in many cases according to the German model. For articles such as "Ticknor and the Harvard Reforms of the 1820s" and "Francis Lieber on the Purposes and Practices of Universities," see Hofstadter and Smith, pp. 269–300. See David Tyack, *George Ticknor and the Boston Brahmins* (Cambridge, Mass.: Harvard University Press, 1978), for biographical details and social background. See also George Ticknor, *Life, Letters, and Journals* (Boston and New York: J. R. Osgood, 1876), and Van Wyck Brooks's chapters 4 and 5 in *The Flowering of New England.*

43. Vogel, *German Literary Influences,* pp. 50–60. Morison, *Three Centuries of Harvard,* pp. 234–238. On Francis Lieber, see Freidel, *Francis Lieber,* and August Kirsch, "Franz Lieber: Turner, Freiheitskämpfer und Emigrant" (Ph.D. diss., University of Cologne, 1953). Lieber first came to the United States as a gymnastics instructor, but later turned to more important work as an encyclopaedist and as the first professor of political science at Columbia University. On Carl Beck's American career, see William Newell, *Christian Citizen: A Discourse Occasioned by the Death of Charles Beck—Delivered March 25, 1866, before the First Parish Church in Cambridge* (Cambridge, Mass., 1866).

44. Charles Follen to Francis Lieber, dated February 21 and February 22, 1927. Huntington Library, San Marino, California. LI 1461 and LI 1462.

45. On Lieber's entire career, see Freidel, *Francis Lieber.* For specific information on the background of his new job in Boston, see Geldbach, "Die Verpflanzung des deutschen Turnens," pp. 359–376.

46. For details, see Geldbach, "Die Verpflanzung des deutschen Turnens," pp. 331–376.

47. Phelps, "Idea of the Modern University," pp. 175–190.

48. See ibid., p. 183.

49. There is information on the Massachusetts of the time in Arthur B. Darling, *Political Changes in Massachusetts, 1824–1848* (New Haven: Yale University Press, 1925). See especially chaps. 1 and 2.

50. Ann Rose, *Transcendentalism as a Social Movement* (New Haven: Yale University Press, 1985), passim. See also Justin Winsor, *The Memorial History of Boston* (Boston: J. R. Osgood, 1881), 4 vols.; it contains detailed articles on philosophy (vol. 4, pp. 295–330), Unitarianism (vol. 3, pp. 267–282), and antislavery (vol. 3, pp. 369–400) in Boston. A short overview is given by Roland N. Stromberg, "Boston in the 1820s and 1830s," *History Today,* 11 (1961): 591–598. Finally, see Martin Green, *The Problem of Boston* (New York: Norton, 1968).

51. Ronald Story, *The Forging of an Aristocracy: Harvard and the Boston Upper Class, 1800–1870* (Middletown, Conn.: Wesleyan University Press, 1980).

52. Friedman, *Gregarious Saints,* pp. 43–45.

53. See Green, *Problem of Boston,* pp. 75–76.

54. See Spindler, *Karl Follen*, p. 107. See also the chapter entitled "Carl Follen's View" in Camillo von Klenze, *Charles Timothy Brooks, Translator from the German, and the Genteel Tradition* (Boston: Modern Language Association, 1937), pp. 15–19.

55. On the Follen-Channing relationship, see *Works*, vol. I, and also Pochmann, *German Culture in America*, pp. 115; 172–246. Pochmann also points out the ties Charles and Eliza Follen had to many other members of the Boston intellectual elite, including Harvard professor Henry Ware, Jr.; Unitarian clergyman and historian John Goreham Palfrey; conservative Unitarian clergyman Andrew Preston Peabody; and James Marsh, theologian and president of the University of Vermont. In general, the Follens were associated with prominent Unitarians inside and outside the Harvard "College Circle," but also with theological students.

56. On Follen and his knowledge of Kant, see Pochmann, *German Culture in America*, p. 119. See also René Wellek, "The Minor Transcendentalists and German Philosophy," *New England Quarterly*, 15 (1942): 652–680.

57. See *Works*, vol. I, pp. 171–172. Pages 182–246 contain extracts from a diary which Follen was keeping at the time; all his intellectual discussions at William Ellery Channing's are recorded.

58. The most complete statements of German influence of these kinds in America can be found first of all in Henry Pochmann, *German Culture in America*, and second in Vogel, *German Literary Influences*. The phrase "German craze" appears in Pochman, p. 114. See also Orie William Long, *Literary Pioneers: Early American Explorers of European Culture* (Cambridge, Mass.: Harvard University Press, 1935), and von Klenze, *Charles Timothy Brooks*. A provocative and divergent account is also Harold S. Jantz, "German Thought and Literature in New England, 1620–1820," *Journal of English and Germanic Philology*, 41 (1942): 1–45. Jantz proves that German influence in New England, if not very prominent, went much further back than the early nineteenth century.

59. On Mme. de Staël's role, see Vogel, *German Literary Influences*, pp. 63–64. In *Madame de Stael*, Jaeck has shown the influence of Mme. de Stael in both England and America. She has also individually discussed many of the most important intellectuals in both countries who furthered the attractiveness of German culture to the scholarly and general public.

60. George Ripley reviewed Follen's "Inaugural Discourse" for the *Christian Examiner* in January 1832, pp. 373–380. This review is partly reprinted in Perry Miller, ed., *The Transcendentalists: An Anthology* (Cambridge, Mass.: Harvard University Press, 1950), pp. 59–63. Ripley's most important contribution was the *Specimens of Foreign Standard Literature*, which he edited from 1838 on. He thus made the works of many German and French authors, including Goethe, Schiller, Eckermann, Menzel, and De Wette, and their most important works available to the American reading public. An important treatment of Ripley's role is Arthur R. Schultz and Henry A. Pochmann, "George Ripley: Unitarian, Transcendentalist, or Infidel?" *American Literature*, 14 (1942–43): 1–19. Ripley is shown here to have been a difficult, ever-changing man who had great problems finding a workable relationship to German culture, specu-

lative philosophy, and religion. The most well-known biography is Octavius Brooks Frothingham, *George Ripley* (1882; reprint New York: AMS Press, 1970). See also Charles Robert Crowe, *George Ripley: Transcendentalist and Utopian Socialist* (Athens, Ga.: University of Georgia Press, 1967), and Henry L. Golemba, *George Ripley* (Boston: Twayne, 1977).

61. Margaret Fuller published a study of Theodor Körner in the *Western Messenger* in 1838. Follen had previously praised Körner very highly. She also translated Eckermann's *Conversations with Goethe in the Last Years of His Life* (Boston: Hilliard, Gray, 1839). See also Joel Myerson, *Critical Essays on Margaret Fuller* (Boston: G. K. Hall, 1980).

62. See Theodore Parker, "The Life and Character of Dr. Follen," *The Dial,* January 1843. In this article Parker was very positive toward Follen, lauding the latter's great and consistent commitment to moral action. The article by Parker was primarily a review of Charles Follen's *Works,* published in 1841; it does also show, however, a close familiarity on Parker's part with Follen's life and ideas. There is a short sketch of Parker's general interest in German literature and philosophy in Jaeck, *Mme. de Stael,* pp. 318–323.

63. Several letters from Emerson to Charles Follen, and letters mentioning Follen are published in *The Letters of Ralph Waldo Emerson,* ed. Ralph Leslie Rusk (New York: Columbia University Press, 1939). Some letters from Follen to Emerson are in the Houghton Library at Harvard University. For references, see Heinrich Schneider, "Karl Follen: A Re-appraisal," p. 86. See also Ralph Leslie Rusk, *The Life of Ralph Waldo Emerson* (New York: C. Scribner's Sons, 1949); Joel Porte, *Representative Man: R. W. Emerson and His Time* (New York: Oxford University Press, 1979); and Robert E. Burkholder and Joel Myerson, eds., *Critical Essays on R. W. Emerson* (Boston: G. K. Hall, 1983).

64. For precise details, see René Wellek, "Emerson and German Philosophy," *New England Quarterly,* 16 (1943): 41–62.

65. The exact relationship of Emerson and Follen is hard to reconstruct. It is very probable, however, that Emerson had noticed Follen by 1831, and was scrutinizing his public statements made in lectures and publications. See Pochmann, *German Culture in America,* p. 567, n. 499. Emerson mentions Follen in a letter to Carlyle in 1835, saying that "a respectable German here, Dr. Follen, has given lectures to a good class upon Schiller." See Vogel, *German Literary Influences,* p. 66.

66. For a recent assessment of Hedge's life and influence, see Bryan F. LeBeau, *Frederic Henry Hedge: Nineteenth Century American Transcendentalist* (Allison Park, Penn.: Pickwick Publications, 1985).

67. Frederic Henry Hedge, "Coleridge's Literary Character," *Christian Examiner,* 14 (1833): 108–129; and "Life of Schiller," *Christian Examiner,* 16 (1834): 365–392.

68. Frederic Henry Hedge, *Prose Writers of Germany* (Philadelphia: Grey and Hart, 1848).

69. See Frank Luther Mott, "The *Christian Disciple* and the *Christian Examiner,*" *New England Quarterly,* 1 (1928): 197–207. Follen contributed several articles to the *Christian Examiner,* including "The Future State of Man," pub-

lished between January and July 1830, and "Antislavery Principles and Proceedings," published in November of 1838. "Professor Follen's Inaugural Discourse," delivered when Follen assumed his chair as professor of German at Harvard in 1830, was reviewed in the *Christian Examiner* in January 1832. In September of 1842, William Henry Channing published his lengthy commemorative article "Life and Writings of Dr. Follen" in the same periodical. For research on the *Christian Examiner*, there is one essential work: William Cushing, "Index to the Christian Examiner" (Boston: J. S. Cushing, 1879), reprinted in Kenneth Walter Cameron, ed., *Research Keys to the American Renaissance* (Hartfort, Conn.: Transcendental Books, 1967).

70. George Willis Cooke, *An Historical and Biographical Introduction to Accompany "The Dial"* (New York: Russell and Russell, 1961), is most helpful. *The Dial* itself is available in a recent reprint edition. See also Joel Myerson, *The New England Transcendentalists and "The Dial"* (Rutherford, N.J.: Fairleigh Dickinson University Press, 1980).

71. For full discussion of this article, see Chapter 6.

72. For details on Eliza Cabot Follen's family background, see Lloyd Vernon Briggs, *History and Geneology of the Cabot Family* (Boston: C. E. Goodspeed and Co., 1927), vol. I, pp. 197–231. On the role of Eliza Follen as reformer: Elizabeth Bancroft Schlesinger, "Two Early Harvard Wives: Eliza Farrar and Eliza Follen," *New England Quarterly*, 38 (1965): 147–167.

73. The commercial successes of Eliza Follen's branch of the Cabot family, particulary of her father and brothers, are evident when one reads the Samuel Cabot Papers, and the J. H. Cabot Papers at the Massachusetts Historical Society. Many of these letters are related to foreign trade, such as the China trade, and some were written overseas. For further details, see Briggs, *History and Genealogy of the Cabot Family*, vol. I, pp. 197–230.

74. *Dictionary of American Biography* (New York and London: Charles Scribner's Sons, 1931), vol. VI. See also Briggs, *History and Geneology of the Cabot Family*, vol. II, pp. 595–596.

75. Eliza Follen is described in Schlesinger, "Two Early Harvard Wives," pp. 147–167.

76. See *Works*, vol. I, pp. 163–164.

77. See ibid., vol. I, p. 256.

78. See Charles Christopher Follen, Manuscript Autobiography in Class Notes of 1849, Harvard University Archives.

79. See *Works*, vol. I, pp. 275–277. The others involved in the funding of Follen's chair were Samuel Cabot's father-in-law, Col. Perkins, and a friend of the family named Jonathan Phillips.

80. Charles Follen to Charles Folsom, dated 20 July, 1830. Folsom ms. Collection. Boston Public Library.

81. Charles Follen to Charles Folsom, dated 9 August 1830. Folsom ms. Collection. Boston Public Library.

82. Today, just to the north of Waterhouse Street in Cambridge, lies Follen Street, named after Charles Follen.

83. See *Works*, vol. I, pp. 303–304.

84. Ibid., vol. I, pp. 256–259.

85. A.H.L. Heeren, *History of the States of Antiquity* (Northampton, Mass.: S. Butler, 1828); and *History of the Political System of Europe and Its Colonies, from the Discovery of America to the Independence of the American Continent* (Northampton, Mass.: S. Butler, 1829). Follen's review appeared in the *American Quarterly Review*, 5 (1829). The full text is reprinted in *Works*, vol. V, pp. 99–124.

86. For extensive information on the historical development of German instruction in the United States, and on the contribution specifically made by Charles Follen, turn to Viereck, *Zwei Jahrhunderte Deutschen Unterrichts*.

87. Samuel Cabot Papers, Massachusetts Historical Society, Boston.

88. Charles Follen, "Inaugural Discourse Delivered before the University in Cambridge, Massachusetts, September 3, 1831." Published in *Works*, vol. V, pp. 125–152.

89. Ibid., vol. V, p. 132.

90. See ibid., vol. V, pp. 135–142.

91. Ibid., vol. V, p. 148.

92. For the letter of John Quincy Adams to Follen, and the latter's reply, see ibid., vol. I, pp. 305–312.

93. An abridged version of the review, with a short introduction to it, may be found in Miller, *The Transcendentalists*, pp. 59–63.

94. Siegfried B. Puknat, "De Wette in New England," *Proceedings of the American Philosophical Society*, 102 (1958): 376–95. Puknat's article is very valuable: it shows which aspects of De Wette's work were especially well received in New England, and what role Follen and the theologian's stepson, Charles Beck, played in introducing them there. Puknat has also published a helpful article on "Channing and German Thought," *Proceedings of the American Philosophical Society*, 101 (1957): 195–203. Here Follen is shown as a major influence on William Ellery Channing's intellectual acceptance of German theology.

95. Puknat, "De Wette," p. 381.

96. Ibid., pp. 388–389.

97. See ibid., pp. 380–395; as well as pp. 384–385, for a list of the many great foreign works which Ripley edited. He translated many of them himself.

98. On the relationship of Parker and De Wette, see ibid., pp. 386–388. Parker described his encounter with De Wette in an 1844 letter to his friend and mentor Convers Francis. It is quoted in ibid., on pp. 387–388.

99. Ibid., pp. 377–395.

100. See his essay "Emerson and German Philosophy," *New England Quarterly*, 16 (1943): 44–48.

101. See René Wellek, "Minor Transcendentalists and German Philosophy," *New England Quarterly*, 15 (1942): 659.

102. See Pochmann, *German Culture in America*, pp. 116–120.

103. See Henry E. Allison, *Kant's Theory of Freedom* (Cambridge: Cambridge University Press, 1990).

104. See Spindler, *Karl Follen*, p. 124.

105. See Julia Wüst, "Karl Follen," *Mitteilungen des Oberhessischen Geschichtsvereins*, NF 33 (1936): 121.

106. On Follen's definition of morality, see Pochmann, *German Culture in America*, p. 566, n. 477.

107. Follen wrote a letter to the trustees of the Boston Athenaeum in order to arrange for his lectures, dated November 6, 1830. Boston Athenaeum.

108. The lectures, which were published as vol. III of the *Works*, are discussed in Pochmann, *German Culture in America*, pp. 116–117; and p. 566, n. 476–477.

109. See Spindler, *Karl Follen*, p. 123.

110. See *Works*, vol. III, pp. 1–17.

111. Ibid., vol. III, p. 15.

112. See ibid., vol. III, pp. 15–19.

113. See the discussion in Spindler, *Karl Follen*, p. 124.

114. See *Works*, vol. III, p. 78.

115. On conscience, duty, and virtue, see especially lectures 7 and 8, in ibid., vol. III, pp. 136–171.

116. See Pochmann, *German Culture in America*, p. 119; and pp. 564–565, n. 469.

117. Spindler, *Karl Follen*, p. 125.

118. See *Works*, vol. III, pp. 172, 207–215, 235.

119. For details on this controversy, see ibid., vol. I, pp. 290–299.

120. Follen's *Lectures on Schiller* form vol. IV of the *Works*. Follen summarized and discussed nine dramas, and provided a short "Life of Schiller" and note on the dramatic sketches. His favorite was *Wilhelm Tell*; he never finished the English commentary section on it, and lectured largely without notes on this play.

121. *Works*, vol. IV, p. 18.

122. See Albert Ludwig, *Schiller und die Deutsche Nachwelt* (Berlin: Weidmann, 1909), pp. 47–52, 117–120.

123. *Works*, vol. IV, p. 34.

124. For a glimpse of the American attitude toward Goethe at this time, turn to the pieces by Frederic Henry Hedge or Margaret Fuller on Schiller and Goethe reprinted in Miller, *The Transcendentalists*, pp. 78–82 and 369–372.

125. Frederick B. Wahr, *Emerson and Goethe* (Ann Arbor: G. Wahr, 1915), pp. 74, 181–182.

126. This view of Charles Follen's relationship to Goethe's works, was first stated in Wahr, *Emerson and Goethe*, p. 44. It was reiterated in Johannes Urzidil, *Das Glück der Gegenwart: Goethes Amerikabild* (Zürich and Stuttgart: Artemis, 1958), pp. 29–30. Urzidil writes: "Goethe, so verkündete Follen. . .stehe den Freiheitsbestrebungen seiner Epoche verständnislos gegenüber. Goethe, so rief er von Lehrstuhl und Kanzel, sei seinem Wesen nach ein Heide und führe eine moralisch anfechtbare Lebensweise. Einzig Schiller-und dies mögen die frei-heitsbewussten Amerikaner bedenken-einzig Schiller sei der wahre Dichter der Deutschen und der echte Protagonist der Freiheit." On the other hand, Heinrich Schneider, in "Karl Follen: A Re-Appraisal," feels that Urdizil's picture is overdrawn, and that Follen has been unfairly held responsible for the American opinion that Goethe was "immoral" and a "heathen." See Schneider, p. 76.

127. *Works*, vol. IV, p. 384. Also quoted in Wahr, *Emerson and Goethe*, p. 44.

128. *Works*, vol. IV, p. 388.

129. Ibid., vol. IV, pp. 385–386.

130. Wahr, *Emerson and Goethe*, p. 39.

131. For the complete text of this oration, see also *Works*, vol. V, pp. 153–188.

132. On the impact of phrenology on American medicine and scientific thought, see Nye, *Society and Culture*, pp. 334–336.

133. On the impact of psychology in America, see ibid., pp. 331–334.

134. Unfortunately, he was only able to finish the introduction and part of the first book. For the complete text of Follen's fragment, see *Works*, vol. III, pp. 323–363.

135. Samuel Eliot Morison has provided us with two main discussions of the riots. See "The Great Rebellion at Harvard," *Proceedings of the Massachusetts Historical Society*, 27 (1927–1930): 54–112. This article focuses on the 1823 riots. His *Three Centuries of Harvard* deals with both 1823 and 1834–1836. See pp. 230–232, 252–253.

136. McCaughey, *Josiah Quincy*, pp. 148–149.

137. Ibid., pp. 173–174.

138. Morison, *Three Centuries of Harvard*, pp. 251–252.

139. McCaughey, *Josiah Quincy*, p. 157.

140. Morison, *Three Centuries of Harvard*, p. 254.

141. The term "Germania in America" is used by Richard O'Connor, *The German-Americans: An Informal History* (Boston: Little, Brown, 1968), pp. 67–97. See also John A. Hawgood, *The Tragedy of German-America* (New York and London: G.P. Putnam's Sons, 1940). Colin Ross, *Unser Amerika: Der Deutsche Anteil and den Vereinigten Staaten* (Leipzig: F. A. Brockhaus, 1936) provides helpful information, but its interpretations are no longer useful today.

142. See Geldbach, "Die Verpflanzung des deutschen Turnens," pp. 336–338.

143. Harvard University Archives, file no. UA III 28.26.

144. Department of Modern Languages, Charles Follen Reports and Papers, 1826–1828. Harvard University Archives, file no. UA III 28.26. Follen's involvement with gymnastics at Harvard, which remained strong until he turned toward the pursuit of new interests in theology and eventually antislavery, is described in detail in Spindler, *Karl Follen*, pp. 126–137; and in Geldbach, "Die Verpflanzung des deutschen Turnens," pp. 340–352.

145. See the "Plan for a Boston Seminary," in *Works*, vol. I, pp. 623–626. There is also a discussion in Spindler, *Karl Follen*, pp. 137–139.

146. See Spindler, *Karl Follen*, p. 138.

147. The letter is printed in Herman Haupt, "Follenbriefe," pp. 42–47.

148. Quoted in *Works*, vol. I, p. 323.

149. Both letters quoted in ibid., vol. I, p. 324.

150. Charles Follen to General Lafayette, dated April 2, 1832. Cornell University Library.

151. See Gustav Phillip Körner, *Das Deutsche Element in den Vereinigten Staaten von Nordamerika, 1818–1848* (Cincinnati: A. E. Wilde, 1880; reprint New York, Frankfurt, and Berne: Peter Lang, 1986), pp. 301–307.

152. Paul Follen and Friedrich Münch, *Aufforderung und Erklärung in Betreff*

*einer Auswanderung im Grossen aus Teutschland in die nordamerikanischen Freistaaten* (Giessen, 1833).

153. See *Works,* vol. I, pp. 318–320.

154. See Mack Walker, *Germany and the Emigration* (Cambridge, Mass.: Harvard University Press, 1964), pp. 66–69; and Stefan von Senger und Etterlin, *Neu-Deutschland in Nordamerika* (Baden-Baden: Nomos, 1991), pp. 178–185. Walker emphasizes that "the Giessen Society was a product of politically colored emigration." He shows how the Hessian group failed to retain its cohesion in the new American environment, owing to organizational and financial problems.

155. Friedrich Münch, *Erinnerungen aus Deutschlands trübster Zeit* (St. Louis and Neustadt an der Haardt: Witter, 1873). See "Das Leben von Paul Follenius," pp. 57–71, and "Das Leben von Friedrich Münch," pp. 72–91.

## 5. Religion and Freedom

1. Quoted in William Buell Sprague, *Annals of the American Pulpit* (New York: R. Carter and Bros., 1857–1869), vol. VIII, p. 545.

2. Quoted in ibid., vol. VIII, pp. 545–546.

3. Quoted in ibid., vol. VIII, p. 547.

4. See Russel Blaine Nye, *Society and Culture in America, 1830–1860* (New York: Harper and Row, 1974), pp. 285–292.

5. Sidney Ahlstrom, *A Religious History of the American People* (New Haven: Yale University Press, 1972), p. 391.

6. See especially Eliza Cabot Follen, *The Skeptic* (Cambridge, Mass.: J. Munroe and Co., 1835).

7. Nye, *Society and Culture,* p. 305. Nye's argument is that, after 1800, "divisions, disputes, and secesssions within secessions continued to complicate the contemporary religious picture."

8. The Unitarian Controversy is best covered in Earl Morse Wilbur, *A History of Unitarianism in Transsylvania, England, and America* (Cambridge, Mass.: Harvard University Press, 1952), pp. 401–434. See also George Willis Cooke, *Unitarianism in America* (Boston: American Unitarian Association, 1902), pp. 92–123. A concise introduction is in Conrad Wright, ed., *A Stream of Light: A Sesquicentennial History of American Unitarianism* (Boston: Unitarian Universalist Association, 1975), chap. 1, pp. 3–32.

9. For an overview of the history of Unitarianism in New England, see David Robinson, *The Unitarians and the Universalists* (Westport, Conn.: Greenwood Press, 1985). Robinson calls the years 1820–1860 "the classic period" of Unitarianism. See pp. 39–46.

10. On the connections between Unitarianism and Transcendentalism in New England, see William R. Hutchison, "Boston Unitarianism—the Context of Transcendentalist Reform," in *The Transcendentalist Ministers* (New Haven: Yale University Press, 1959), pp. 1–21. Hutchison also shows the influence of German thinkers such as Kant on the American religious and philosophical leadership. See pp. 22–28. For a recent statement that the roots of New England

Transcendentalism may to a great extent be found in Unitarianism, see Ann Rose, *Transcendentalism as a Social Movement* (New Haven: Yale University Press, 1981), pp. 1–44. The problems of the Unitarian-Transcendentalist relationship are also shown in C. H. Faust, "The Background of the Unitarian Opposition to Transcendentalism," *Modern Philology*, 35 (1937–38): 297–324. The questions of whether Transcendentalism was a native American or an imported German-French-Indian intellectual current, and how its relationship to American religion developed, are discussed in Perry Miller, "From Edwards to Emerson," *New England Quarterly*, 13 (1940): 589–617.

11. This tract is printed in Eliza Lee Cabot Follen, ed., *The Works of Charles Follen, with a Memoir of His Life* (Boston: Hilliard, Gray, 1841), vol. V, pp. 254–313.

12. For a valuable introduction to sources relating to the Unitarians in New England, see David B. Parke, ed., *The Epic of Unitarianism: Original Writings from the History of Liberal Religion* (Boston: Starr King Press, 1957). A detailed explanation of Unitarian beliefs and practices is available in Joseph Henry Allen, *Our Liberal Movement in Theology* (Boston: Roberts Bros., 1882). Cooke, *Unitarianism in America,* also provides a detailed view of Unitarian involvements and achievements. See also Ahlstrom, "The Emergence of American Unitarianism," in *A Religious History*, pp. 388–402.

13. See Ahlstrom, *A Religious History*, pp. 391–393, for a detailed discussion of the most important Unitarian beliefs.

14. See Wright, *A Stream of Light*, p. 6.

15. For a detailed description and documents relating to the Ware election, see Conrad Wright, "The Election of Henry Ware," *Harvard Library Bulletin*, 17 (July 1969): 245–278.

16. The sermon may be found in *The Works of William Ellery Channing* (Boston: American Unitarian Association, 1890), pp. 367–384. It is also available in David Robinson, ed., *William Ellery Channing. Selected Writings* (New York: Paulist Press, 1985), pp. 70–102.

17. The best brief guide to Unitarian history in the United States may be found in Wright, *A Stream of Light.*

18. See ibid., pp. 30–43. An extensive and systematic listing of Unitarian achievements in education, philanthropies, reform, American literature, and many other fields is given in Cooke, *Unitarianism in America.* Cooke demonstrates the dominance of Unitarians in New England intellectual life from 1820 to 1860.

19. See Frank Luther Mott, "The *Christian Disciple* and the *Christian Examiner*," *New England Quarterly*, 1 (1928): 197–207.

20. For an overview of the intellectual climate at Harvard concerning philosophy, see Edgeley Woodman Todd, "Philosophical Ideas at Harvard College, 1817–1837," *New England Quarterly*, 16 (1943): 63–90. Todd emphasizes the influence of Scottish philosophy as having been the most important. For the best discussion of Unitarian influence at Harvard, however, see George H. Williams, ed., *The Harvard Divinity School: Its Place in Harvard University and in American Culture* (Boston: Beacon Press, 1954), pp. 21–95. There is also the

detailed work by Daniel Walker Howe, *The Unitarian Conscience: Harvard Moral Philosophy, 1805–1861* (Cambridge, Mass.: Harvard University Press, 1970), passim. The conditions at Harvard are also described by Van Wyck Brooks in *The Flowering of New England, 1815–1865* (New York: E. P. Dutton and Co., 1936), pp. 21–45, 89–110.

21. A major portion of Williams, *The Harvard Divinity School,* is devoted to this issue. See also Gary L. Collison, "'A True Toleration': Harvard Divinity School Students and Unitarianism, 1830–1859," in Conrad Edick Wright, ed., *American Unitarianism, 1805–1865* (Boston: Massachusetts Historical Society, 1989), pp. 209–237.

22. See Cooke, *Unitarianism in America*, p. 122: "Although the liberal ministers and churches led the way in securing religious freedom, yet they were socially and intellectually conservative. Radical changes they would not accept, and they moved away from the old beliefs with great caution." Daniel Walker Howe has spoken of the Unitarian elite in Boston as "religious liberals and social conservatives," "elitists in a land dedicated to equality," and "reformers who feared change." See *The Unitarian Conscience*, p. 12.

23. Henry Ware, Jr., taught at Harvard as Professor of Pulpit Eloquence and the Pastoral Care from 1830 to 1842.

24. Follen's greatly increased interest in religion after 1825, fostered strongly by his new acquaintance with Eliza Cabot, is documented in the journal that he kept at the time. While Eliza Follen thought that much of the journal was "too personal to be printed," selections are printed in *Works*, vol. I, pp. 182–246. In this journal, Follen recorded several conversations he had had with Henry Ware, Jr., and William Ellery Channing.

25. On the Transcendentalist controversy which ensued, see Wright, *A Stream of Light*, pp. 43–61; and Robinson, *The Unitarians and the Universalists*, pp. 75–86.

26. On the relationship of the key personalities of both Boston Unitarianism and Transcendentalism, and thus on the similarities and divisions of both movements, see Lentheniel H. Downs, "Emerson and Dr. Channing: Two Men from Boston," *New England Quarterly*, 20 (1947): 516–534. Downs chronicles how Channing at first influenced Emerson greatly with his sermons, until the later developed his own philosophical ideas and finally shocked Channing with utterances such as the "Divinity School Address" of 1838. Emerson's bitter attacks on the Unitarian denomination as it had established itself are treated in Perry Miller, "From Edwards to Emerson," *New England Quarterly*, 13 (1940): 589–617, and especially pp. 611–612.

27. On the evolution of Transcendentalism in New England, see Alexander Kern, "The Rise of Transcendentalism," in Harry Hayden Clark, ed., *Transition in American Literary History* (Durham: Duke University Press, 1953), pp. 247–314. On the relation of Unitarianism and Transcendentalism, see also Wright, *A Stream of Light*, pp. 43–61.

28. See Joel Myerson, "A History of the Transcendental Club," in Philip F. Gura and Joel Myerson, eds., *Critical Essays on American Transcendentalism* (Boston: G. K. Hall, 1982), pp. 596–608. See also H. C. Goddard, "Unitarianism

and Transcendentalism," in Brian M. Barbour, ed., *American Transcendentalism: An Anthology of Criticism* (Notre Dame: University of Notre Dame Press, 1973), pp. 159–178. Follen is expressly mentioned as having been a member of the original club in George Willis Cooke, *An Historical and Biographical Introduction to Accompany "The Dial"* (New York: Russell and Russell, 1961), p. 53. Cooke has an entire chapter on the formation and meetings of the Transcendental Club. See pp. 40–55.

29. See Parke, *The Epic*, p. 80.

30. Theodore Parker, "Discourse on the Transient and Permanent in Christianity (1841)." For the text, see Parke, *The Epic*, pp. 111–114.

31. See Wright, *A Stream of Light*, pp. 48–51.

32. Collison, "A True Toleration," pp. 216–221.

33. See Elizabeth Bancroft Schlesinger, "Two Early Harvard Wives: Eliza Farrar and Eliza Follen," *New England Quarterly*, 38 (1965): 157–159.

34. On Sedgwick's life and literary career, see Mary Michael Welsh, *Catherine Maria Sedgwick: Her Position in the Literature and Thought of Her Time up to 1860* (Washington, D.C.: Catholic University of America, 1937). A biographical sketch is provided on pp. 7–20.

35. See the documents assembled in Bertha-Monica Stearns, "Miss Sedgwick Observes Harriet Martineau," *New England Quarterly*, 7 (1934): 533–541.

36. See *Works*, vol. I, pp. 191, 194, 205–207, 213–220.

37. See ibid., vol. I, pp. 182–246.

38. Ibid., vol. I, p. 183.

39. Ibid., vol. I, p. 187.

40. Ibid., vol. I, p. 188.

41. Ibid., vol. I, pp. 195, 213–214.

42. Arthur W. Brown, *Always Young for Liberty: William Ellery Channing* (Syracuse: Syracuse University Press, 1956), pp. 1–31; Andrew Delbanco, *William Ellery Channing: An Essay on the Liberal Spirit in America* (Cambridge, Mass.: Harvard University Press, 1981), pp. 19–26. On Channing, see also Arthur W. Brown, *William Ellery Channing* (New York: Twayne, 1961); and Madelaine Hooke Rice, *Federal Street Pastor: The Life of William Ellery Channing* (New York: Bookman Associates, 1961).

43. Delbanco, *Channing*, pp. 25, 29. Channing spoke out against what he considered the "Jacobin menace" in France, and prided himself on his own Federalist stance in the United States.

44. On Channing's religious development away from orthodox Calvinsim, see Brown, *Always Young for Liberty*, p. 111. On his ideas about the what Andrew Delbanco has called the "discrediting of the American past," and about the anxiety felt by Channing regarding the rapidity of social change in America, see Delbanco, *Channing*, pp. 55–82.

45. Brown, *Always Young for Liberty*, pp. 184, 186.

46. Newport, Rhode Island, was a very active port in the slave carrying business even before the American Revolution. By 1808, when the slave trade was officially outlawed (but still illegally practiced), Newport merchants had

transported more than 100,000 Africans to the American South, Cuba, and Barbados.

47. One view of Channing's involvement with the antislavery movement after 1833 is presented in Brown, *Always Young for Liberty*, chap. 16. See also Jack Mendelsohn, *Channing: The Reluctant Radical* (Boston: Little, Brown, 1971), pp. 223–283. Finally, "Slavery and the Problem of Evil," are discussed in Delbanco, *Channing*, pp. 116–153. There will be a full discussion of Channing's attitude toward slavery below in Chapter 6.

48. William Henry Channing, *Memoir of William Ellery Channing* (Boston: William Crosby and H. P. Nichols, 1848), vol. III, p. 315.

49. Quoted in Mendelsohn, *Channing*, p. 11.

50. See Delbanco, *Channing*, p. 135.

51. Follen to Channing, July 1, 1827, quoted in *Works*, vol. I, p. 177.

52. See ibid., vol. I, p. 178.

53. See Elizabeth Palmer Peabody, *Reminiscences of the Reverend William Ellery Channing* (Boston: Roberts Bros., 1880), esp. pp. 189–369. A discussion of Peabody's points on Channing's relationship with Follen may be found in Siegfried B. Puknat, "Channing and German Thought," *Proceedings of the American Philosophical Society*, 101, no. 2 (April 19, 1957): 195–203.

54. See Peabody, *Reminiscences*, pp. 257–267, 339–341, 358–361.

55. Ibid., p. 217.

56. These memories of Follen, provided by the Reverend George Simmons of Albany, New York, and written in 1853, are quoted in Sprague, *Annals of the American Pulpit*, vol. VIII, p. 544.

57. See *Works*, vol. I, pp. 251–254. For a description of Follen's teaching methods, see p. 260.

58. On Follen's work schedule and daily routine during the years 1828–1830, see ibid., vol. I, pp. 260–264.

59. See ibid., vol. I, pp. 287–290.

60. Ibid., vol. I, pp. 271–276.

61. The essays are also reprinted in *Works*, vol. V, pp. 3–98. In a footnote to his series of articles in the *Christian Examiner*, Follen noted that "the principles contained in this article I first advanced in a treatise 'On the Destiny of Man,' published 1823, in the first two numbers of the Literary Journal of the University of Basle." See *Christian Examiner*, July 1830, p. 293n.

62. Charles Follen, "Benjamin Constant's Work on Religion," *American Quarterly Review*, 11 (March 1832): 103–120. Cf. Orestes Brownson in *The Christian Examiner*, 17 (1834): 66–77.

63. See Follen, "Benjamin Constant's Work on Religion," pp. 103–104.

64. This letter printed in George Washington Spindler, *Karl Follen: A Biographical Study* (Chicago: University of Chicago Press, 1917), pp. 159–160. It is also reproduced in Herman Haupt, "Follen-Briefe," *Deutsch-Amerikanische Geschichtsblätter*, 14 (1914): 32–36.

65. Spindler, *Karl Follen*, p. 160.

66. They form vol. II of the *Works*.

67. *Works,* vol. II, p. 95.

68. Ibid., vol. II, p. 221.

69. Ibid., vol. II, pp. 176–177.

70. Ibid., vol. II, pp. 324–325.

71. For the text, see ibid., vol. V, pp. 228–253.

72. For Follen's section on the essence of what he called "true religion," see ibid., vol. V, pp. 246–248.

73. Ibid., vol. V, p. 247.

74. Ibid., vol. V, p. 253.

75. Ibid., vol. I, pp. 351–355.

76. Only two chapters of what was supposed to become a much larger work were initially published. A third chapter, left by Follen in manuscript form, was published by Eliza Follen in ibid., vol. V, pp. 293–313.

77. See ibid., vol. V, p. 297.

78. Follen's antislavery activities will be discussed in Chapter 6. For details on his ordination, see ibid., vol. I, pp. 420–421. See also Sprague, *Annals of the Unitarian Pulpit,* vol. VIII, p. 543.

79. This period of Follen's life has been very well described by the church historian Walter Donald Kring in his history of All Souls Unitarian Church in New York City. See *Liberals among the Orthodox: Unitarian Beginnings in New York City, 1819–1839* (Boston: Beacon Press, 1974), chaps. 13–15, pp. 204–245. A short overview of the development of All Souls in New York is also available in an anonymous pamphlet entitled *The Unitarian Church of All Souls: First Congregational Church Founded 1819* (New York, n.d.).

80. Kring, *Liberals,* pp. 45, 69–71, 262–263.

81. Ibid., *Works,* vol. I, pp. 424–425.

82. Theodore Parker, "Life and Writings of Dr. Follen," *The Dial* (January 1843): 343–362. On Follen's conflicts in New York, see esp. pp. 352–353.

83. *Works,* vol. I, p. 440; Kring, *Liberals,* p. 218.

84. *Works,* vol. I, p. 445; Kring, *Liberals,* pp. 222–224.

85. See Kring, *Liberals,* pp. 227–231.

86. See ibid., p. 234.

87. See *Works,* vol. I, p. 446.

88. For details, see ibid., vol. I, pp. 446–449.

89. Quoted in ibid., vol. I, pp. 448–449.

90. Included in *Unitarianism: Its Origin and History—A Course of Sixteen Lectures Delivered in Channing Hall, Boston, 1888–1889* (Boston: American Unitarian Association, 1890).

91. C. H. Faust, "The Background to the Unitarian Opposition to Transcendentalism," *Modern Philology,* 35 (1937–38): 297–324.

92. Ibid., pp. 304, 316.

93. Andrews Norton, *A Discourse on the Latest Form of Infidelity: Delivered at the Request of the Association of the Alumni of the Cambridge Theological School, on the 19th of July, 1839* (Cambridge, Mass.: John Owen, 1839).

94. Ibid., p. 9. The following quotes appear on pp. 10 and 22.

95. Details on these lectures may be found in *Works,* vol. I, pp. 501–505.

96. Quoted in ibid., vol. I, p. 503.

97. Moore's notebook, which also contains good quality notes to Follen's lectures on the history of German literature at Harvard (pp. 1–11), is in the Harvard University Archives, file no. HUC 8833.324. The notes to the "Lectures on Pantheism" appear on pp. 59–80.

98. *Works,* vol. I, p. 504.

99. For the text of Follen's petition, see *Works,* vol. I, pp. 635–637. Details regarding the Kneeland case, Kneeland's four trials, and his personal career may be found in Henry Steele Commager, "The Blasphemy of Abner Kneeland," *New England Quarterly,* 8 (1935): 29–41.

100. Quoted in *Works,* vol. I, p. 636. See also Henry Steele Commager, *The Era of Reform, 1830–1860* (Princeton, N.J.: Von Nostrand, 1960), p. 159.

101. Commager, "Blasphemy," p. 32.

102. Ibid., p. 37.

103. This petition by Charles Follen et al. may be found in *Works,* vol. I, Appendix VIII, pp. 635–637. It is also printed in Commager, *The Era of Reform,* pp. 159–161. In William Henry Channing, *Memoir of William Ellery Channing,* there is likewise a reproduction of the text (vol. III, pp. 103–105), as well as a discussion of Channing's and Follen's role in the forming of the petition (vol. III, pp. 101–108).

104. H. A. Rattermann, "Karl Follen," *Americana Germanica,* 4 (1902): 257–258.

105. *Works,* vol. I, p. 496.

106. See ibid., vol. I, pp. 498–500.

107. See Charles Hudson, *History of the Town of Lexington* (Boston and New York, 1913), vol. I, pp. 343–347. See also Douglas Percy Brayton, *The History of the Follen Church* (East Lexington, Mass., 1939), pp. 5–11.

108. For Eliza Follen's discussion of her husband's sermon, see *Works,* vol. I, pp. 467–470. This New Testament motto can also be found written beneath a small portrait of Follen which is in the possession of the Boston Public Library. In many ways, it sums up Follen's entire career, and his conception of moral and social duty.

109. *Works,* vol. I, pp. 469–470.

110. Vernon L. Parrington, *The Romantic Revolution in America, 1800–1860* (New York: Harcourt, Brace, 1927), pp. 313–320. See also *Works,* vol. I, pp. 466–470. On the role which both Unitarianism and Transcendentalism played for social reform, see Rose, *Transcendentalism as a Social Movement.* Finally, see Conrad Wright's essay "The Minister as Reformer," in *The Liberal Christians: Essays on American Unitarian History* (Boston: Beacon Press, 1970), pp. 62–80.

111. On the problem of antebellum reform and its propagation by religious groups, see Clifford S. Griffin, "Religious Benevolence as Social Control," in David Brion Davis, ed., *Antebellum Reform* (New York: Harper and Row, 1967), pp. 81–96, and the reply by Lois W. Banner, "Religious Benevolence as Social Control: A Critique of an Interpretation," in John M. Mulder and John F. Wilson, eds., *Religion in American History* (Englewood Cliffs, N.J.: Prentice Hall, 1978),

pp. 218–235. See also John F. Thomas, "Romantic Reform in America," in Davis, *Antebellum Reform*, pp. 153–176.

## 6. Slavery and Liberation

1. The most recent treatment of Follen's antislavery activities may be found in Douglas C. Stange, "The Making of an Abolitionist Martyr: Harvard Professor Charles Theodore Christian Follen (1796–1840)," *Harvard Library Bulletin*, 24 (1976): 17–24.

2. See Eliza Lee Cabot Follen, ed., *The Works of Charles Follen, with a Memoir of His Life* (Boston: Hilliard, Gray, 1841), vol. I, pp. 360, 404.

3. Louis Filler, *The Crusade against Slavery, 1830–1860* (New York: Harper, 1960), p. 10.

4. Justin Winsor, *The Memorial History of Boston* (Boston, J. R. Osgood, 1881), vol. 3, p. 371. On Garrison, see Aileen S. Kraditor, *Means and Ends in American Abolitionism* (New York: Pantheon Books, 1969); Russel B. Nye, *William Lloyd Garrison and the Humanitarian Reformers* (Boston and Toronto: Little, Brown, 1955); John L. Thomas, *The Liberator: William Lloyd Garrison—A Biography* (Boston and Toronto: Little, Brown, 1963).

5. *Works*, vol. I, p. 304. On Follen's first meeting with Garrison, see Samuel Joseph May, *Some Recollections of Our Antislavery Conflict* (Boston: Fields, Osgood and Co., 1869), p. 253. See also Douglas Stange, *Patterns of Antislavery among American Unitarians* (Rutherford, N.J.: Fairleigh Dickinson University Press, 1977), p. 53.

6. See Wendell P. Garrison and Francis J. Garrison, *William Lloyd Garrison, 1805–1879: The Story of His Life, Told by His Children* (New York: Century Co., 1885–89), vol. I, pp. 441, 463–466.

7. *Massachusetts Anti-Slavery Society: Eighth Annual Report* (Boston: Massachusetts Anti-Slavery Society, 1840; reprint, Westport, Conn.: Negro Universities Press, 1970), p. viii.

8. Thomas, *The Liberator*, pp. 5, 227–228.

9. See ibid., p. 457.

10. See Stange, *Patterns of Antislavery*, pp. 53–54, and also Winsor, *History of Boston*, vol. 3, p. 375. For the constitution and proceedings of the Society, see *New England Anti-Slavery Society: First Report* (Boston: New England Anti-Slavery Society, 1833), *Second Report* (1834), and *Third Report* (1835) (Reprint, Westport, Conn.: Negro Universities Press, 1970). The series is continued from 1836 under the new name, Massachusetts Antislavery Society.

11. The early controversy among abolitionists whether to strive for either gradual or immediate emancipation is presented in Kraditor, *Means and Ends*, pp. 26–32.

12. See Russel B. Nye, *Society and Culture in America, 1830–1860* (New York: Harper and Row, 1974), pp. 65–66.

13. David Walker, *Appeal to the Colored Citizens of the World, in Particular and Very Expressly to Those of the United States* (Boston: D. Walker, 1829). The third

edition was published in Boston in 1830. See May, *Some Recollections*, pp. 133–134, for further details on Walker's *Appeal*.

14. *Works*, vol. I, p. 304.

15. All these quotations are from Walker, *Appeal*, pp. 3–9.

16. See Stange, *Patterns of Antislavery*, p. 57. This opinion was formally expressed in Follen's 1834 "Address to the People of the United States on the Subject of Slavery," to be discussed below. For the relevant passages, see *Works*, vol. V, pp. 213, 217.

17. See John Demos, "The Antislavery Movement and the Problem of Violent Means," *New England Quarterly*, 37 (1964): 501–526.

18. For a definition of the differences in approach, see Stange, *Patterns of Antislavery*, pp. 70–71. See also *Works*, vol. I, pp. 379–380.

19. See Staughton Lynd, "The Abolitionist Critique of the United States Constitution," in Martin Duberman, ed., *The Antislavery Vanguard: New Essays on the Abolitionists* (Princeton: Princeton University Press, 1965), pp. 209–239. According to Lynd, many abolitionists in fact saw the ideals of the American Revolution betrayed when the Constitution was adopted as a compromise in its present form.

20. *Works*, vol. I, pp. 330–338.

21. Letter dated December 31, 1832. Reproduced in ibid., vol. I, pp. 332–334.

22. This letter is dated October 10, 1833. It is reproduced in ibid., vol. I, p. 336.

23. Letter dated October 10, 1833. Printed in ibid., vol. I, pp. 335–338.

24. Ibid., vol. I, p. 338.

25. Lydia Maria Child, *An Appeal in Favor of That Class of Americans Called Africans* (Boston: Allen and Ticknor, 1833; reprint, New York: Arno Press, 1968). On Follen's reaction to this work, see also *Works*, vol. I, p. 340, and Stange, "Abolitionist Martyr," p. 19.

26. See Roman J. Zorn, "The New England Antislavery Society," *Journal of Negro History*, 42 (1957): 157–176; Stange, *Patterns of Antislavery*, pp. 53–54.

27. May, *Some Recollections*, pp. 79–91; Zorn, "New England Antislavery Society," pp. 175–176.

28. Zorn, "New England Antislavery Society," p. 176; Elaine Brooks, "The Massachusetts Antislavery Society," *Journal of Negro History*, 30 (1945): 311–330.

29. *New England Anti-Slavery Society: First Report*, p. 8.

30. For a description of Follen's participation, see May, *Some Recollections*, p. 255. May devoted a whole section of his book to eulogizing Follen; see ibid., pp. 248–259.

31. It is reprinted in *Works*, vol. V, pp. 189–227.

32. See ibid., vol. I, pp. 342–343.

33. Quoted in William Henry Channing, *Memoir of William Ellery Channing* (Boston: William Crosby and H. P. Nichols, 1848), vol. III, p. 159.

34. See Harriet Martineau, "The Martyr Age of the United States," *London and Westminster Review*, 32 (1839): 1–59. On the mob year, see pp. 13–21.

35. *Works*, vol. I, pp. 378–379.

36. May, *Some Recollections*, p. 255. For Follen's speech mentioned here, see *Works*, vol. I, Appendix VI, pp. 627–633.

37. *Massachusetts Anti-Slavery Society: Fourth Annual Report*, pp. 49–50. The New England Society had been renamed Massachusetts Antislavery Society in February of 1835. Follen also delivered another speech at the same convention, later printed as the "Speech before the Massachusetts Antislavery Society" and included in *Works*, vol. I, Appendix VI, pp. 627–633.

38. For details on this small abolitionist society, see *Works*, vol. I, p. 343.

39. John Ware, *Memoir of the Life of Henry Ware, Jr.* (Boston: J. Munroe and Co., 1846), vol. II, pp. 146–155.

40. See Stange, "Abolitionist Martyr," p. 19. George Willis Cooke, *Unitarianism in America* (Boston: American Unitarian Association, 1902), p. 359.

41. See Stange, *Patterns of Antislavery*, p. 31.

42. See Cooke, *Unitarianism in America*, pp. 353–367. May, *Some Recollections*, as well as Stange, *Patterns of Antislavery*, offer full discussions of this topic.

43. See Cooke, *Unitarianism in America*, pp. 366–367. For an account of how Follen directly influenced John Greenleaf Whittier, see May, *Some Recollections*, p. 265. Whittier published many antislavery poems, and also wrote one specifically in Follen's honor. See the poem entitled "Follen," in John Greenleaf Whittier, *Anti-Slavery Poems: Songs of Labor and Reform* (Boston: Houghton Mifflin, 1898), pp. 24–28.

44. Douglas Stange, "Abolitionism as Treason: The Unitarian Elite Defends Law, Order, and the Union," *Harvard Library Bulletin*, 28 (April 1980): 152–170. This passage appears on page 152.

45. Quoted in William Henry Channing, *Memoir of William Ellery Channing*, vol. III, p. 191.

46. Follen's Thanksgiving Day sermon plainly expressed his antislavery views. See *Works*, vol. II, pp. 187–200 (Sermon 16).

47. See *Works*, vol. I, pp. 463–464. Walter Donald Kring, *Liberals among the Orthodox: Unitarian Beginnings in New York City, 1819–1839* (Boston: Beacon Press, 1974), p. 216.

48. *Works*, vol. I, p. 444.

49. See William Henry Channing, *Memoir of William Ellery Channing*, vol. III, especially chap. 4, pp. 134–241, entitled "The Antislavery Movement."

50. Quoted in ibid., vol. III, p. 243.

51. See Stange, *Patterns of Antislavery*, pp. 75–90, 94–99. On Channing's role in the antislavery movement, see also Arthur W. Brown, *Always Young for Liberty: A Biography of William Ellery Channing* (Syracuse, N.Y.: Syracuse University Press, 1956), esp. pp. 222–241 on "The Slavery Question."

52. See William Henry Channing, *Memoir of William Ellery Channing*, vol. III, p. 159.

53. Cooke, *Unitarianism in America*, pp. 358, 365.

54. On this incident, see May, *Some Recollections*, pp. 173–175. The quotation here is from this source. The scene is also reported in William Henry Channing, *Memoir of William Ellery Channing*, vol. III, pp. 156–158.

55. Quoted in William Henry Channing, *Memoir of William Ellery Channing*, vol. III, p. 217.

56. This long letter, as well as Garrison's response, are reproduced in ibid., vol. III, p. 218–229.

57. Reported in ibid., vol. III, pp. 231–233. See also Jack Mendelsohn, *Channing: The Reluctant Radical* (Boston: Little, Brown, 1971), pp. 267–269.

58. See the detailed discussion in Mendelsohn, *Channing: The Reluctant Radical*, pp. 223–283.

59. For Garrison's angry reaction, see the report in John White Chadwick, *William Ellery Channing: Minister of Religion* (Boston: Houghton Mifflin, 1908), p. 276. Garrison denounced *Slavery* as "utterly destitute of any redeeming, reforming power," and as "calumnious, contradictory, and unsound."

60. Quoted in William Henry Channing, *Memoir of William Ellery Channing*, vol. III, p. 174.

61. William Ellery Channing, *Letter of William Ellery Channing to James G. Birney* (Boston: J. Munroe, 1837).

62. See Chadwick, *Channing*, pp. 259–295.

63. Wendell P. Garrison and Francis J. Garrison, *William Lloyd Garrison*, vol. III, pp. 239–240.

64. Ibid., vol. III, pp. 238–239.

65. Quoted in ibid., vol. III, pp. 241–242.

66. *Works*, vol. I, pp. 379–380.

67. On the beginning of the friendship between Harriet Martineau and the Follens, see ibid., vol. I, pp. 373–374. In the last third of this volume, Eliza Follen included many letters written by Harriet Martineau.

68. See Martineau, "Martyr Age," pp. 1–59. Harriet Martineau, *Retrospect of Western Travel* (London: Saunders and Otley, 1838), 2 vols; Harriet Martineau, *Harriet Martineau's Autobiography*, ed. Maria Weston Chapman (Boston: Houghton Mifflin, 1877), 2 vols.

69. Seymour Martin Lipset, "Introduction" to Harriet Martineau, *Society in America* (abridged edition, New York: Transaction Books, 1962), pp. 5–41.

70. See Stephen Bloore, "Miss Martineau Speaks Out," *New England Quarterly*, 9 (1936): 403–416.

71. See Martineau, *Autobiography*, vol. I, pp. 347–348.

72. Ibid., vol. II, pp. 279–280.

73. This letter from Charles Follen to Harriet Martineau, dated November 30, 1835, is quoted in ibid., vol. II, pp. 280–281.

74. See Lipset, "Introduction," pp. 33–34.

75. Martineau, "Martyr Age," p. 18.

76. Charles Follen at public antislavery meeting in 1836. For the complete text, see *Works*, vol. I, Appendix VI, pp. 630–631. The speech is also partially quoted in Martineau, "Martyr Age," pp. 38–39.

77. See Kraditor, *Means and Ends*, pp. 39–77; and Ronald G. Walters, *The Antislavery Appeal: American Abolitionism after 1830* (Baltimore: Johns Hopkins University Press, 1976), pp. 101–109.

78. How important antislavery propaganda specifically directed at women

and also at children was in contributing to the moral suasion of American society at large, has been shown in Walters, *Antislavery Appeal*, pp. 96–98.

79. Eliza Cabot Follen to William Lloyd Garrison, dated 1850. Eliza Follen letters, Boston Public Library.

80. Jane Carlyle to Mrs. Wilkinson, dated April 23(?), 1851. Follen Papers, Massachusetts Historical Society.

81. The text is printed in *Works*, vol. I, Appendix VI, pp. 627–633.

82. Ibid., vol. I, p. 629.

83. This and the following passages are all taken from Charles Follen, "The Cause of Freedom in Our Country," *Quarterly Antislavery Magazine* (October 1836): 61–73.

84. *Works*, vol. I, p. 388.

85. The text of the Gag Bill, and a discussion of its background, are to be found in Harriet Martineau, "Martyr Age," pp. 30–33. For more information, see also Kraditor, *Means and Ends*, p. 6.

86. Martineau, "Martyr Age," p. 30.

87. This scene is recounted in *Works*, vol. I, pp. 391–392.

88. The scene is recorded in ibid., vol. I, pp. 392–403; and in George Washington Spindler, *Karl Follen: A Biographical Study* (Chicago: University of Chicago Press, 1917), pp. 210–212.

89. This and the following quotation are recorded in *Works*, vol. I, pp. 392–394.

90. Ibid., vol. I, p. 401.

91. *An Account of the Interviews Which Took Place on the Fourth and Eighth of March, between a Committee of the Massachusetts Anti-Slavery Society, and the Committee of the Legislature* (Boston: Massachusetts Anti-Slavery Society, 1836).

92. See *Works*, vol. I, p. 402.

93. Martineau, "Martyr Age," pp. 30–31.

94. Charles Follen, "Antislavery Principles and Proceedings," *Christian Examiner*, 25 (November 1838): 238.

95. The text is included in *Works*, vol. V, pp. 314–373. The article first appeared (in a shortened version) in the *United States Magazine and Democratic Review*, 5 (1839).

96. Quoted in William Henry Channing, *Memoir of William Ellery Channing*, vol. III, p. 229.

97. The text of Garrison's "Declaration of Sentiments" is included in Staughton Lynd, ed., *Nonviolence in America: A Documentary History* (Indianapolis and New York: Bobbs-Merrill, 1966), pp. 25–31.

98. See Walters, *Antislavery Appeal*, pp. 28–29. Walters writes that "although abolitionist nonviolence rested upon a firmly Christian base, Protestantism contained countercurrents that helped reformers, as they lost faith in pacifism, to explain and even anticipate violence. . . . Despair and predictions of godly retribution gathered strength from political developments after 1845."

99. *Works*, vol. I, p. 343. Follen's letter of resignation, and the vote of the Harvard Corporation to accept this statement are on pp. 357–360 in the same volume. Evidently the decision had been very hard on Follen, and a period of

depression and sadness followed the loss of the professorship in the spring of 1835.

100. Stange, "Abolitionist Martyr," pp. 19–20; Samuel Eliot Morison, *Three Centuries of Harvard* (Cambridge, Mass.: Harvard University Press, 1936), p. 254.

101. Stange, "Abolitionist Martyr," pp. 19–20.

102. Josiah Quincy, *The History of Harvard University* (Cambridge, Mass.: J. Owen, 1840), vol. II, p. 49.

103. See Spindler, *Karl Follen*, p. 203.

104. *Works*, vol. I, p. 377.

105. See ibid., vol. I, p. 508.

106. See ibid., vol. I, pp. 510–515, for the text of the letter that Charles Follen wrote to his brother August Follen in Switzerland.

107. Charles Follen to Frederick Huidekoper, dated January 7, 1839. Harvard University Archives. File no. HUG 1402.5.

108. Charles Follen to Frederick Huidekoper, dated April 2, 1839. Harvard University Archives. File no. HUG 1402.5.

109. Charles Follen to "My dear Sir," dated October 13, 1839. Miscellaneous Papers–Charles Follen, Rare Books and Manuscript Division, the New York Public Library, Astor, Lenox, and Tilden Foundations.

110. See ibid., vol. I, pp. 546–548.

111. The church is now called "Follen Unitarian Church," and still stands in East Lexington, Massachusetts. For historical information, see Douglas Percy Brayton, *The History of the Follen Church* (East Lexington, Mass., 1939).

112. See Brayton, *Follen Church*, pp. 8–10.

113. John S. Dwight to Mrs Eli Robbins, dated "Friday morning," 1840. Follen Papers, Massachusetts Historical Society, Boston.

114. D. Weston to Anne Waren Weston, dated February 1840. Boston Public Library. MS A.9.2.13.21.

115. *Works*, vol. I, pp. 573–574.

116. Samuel Cabot to Stephen Robbins, dated July 10, 1840. Follen Papers, Massachusetts Historical Society, Boston.

117. *Works*, vol. I, pp. 581–582.

118. Quoted in William Henry Channing, *Memoir of William Ellery Channing*, vol. III, p. 316.

119. Mendelsohn, *Channing: The Reluctant Radical*, pp. 268–269; May, *Some Recollections*, pp. 257–259; Stange, "Abolitionist Martyr," p. 22.

120. Samuel Joseph May, *A Discourse on the Life and Character of the Rev. Dr. Follen* (Boston: H.L. Devereux, 1840). This publication includes the "order of services" at the memorial service for Follen. Included were a prayer by Henry Ware, Jr., a hymn by John Pierpont, the discourse by Samuel J. May, a hymn by Maria W. Chapman, and a benediction by J. V. Himes.

121. See Stange, "Abolitionist Martyr," pp. 17–24. See also Fawn M. Brodie, "Who Defends the Abolitionist?" in Duberman, *Antislavery Vanguard*, p. 65. When discussing the self-description of several leading abolitionists as "martyrs," Brodie includes a critique of Hazel C. Wolf, *On Freedom's Altar: The Martyr*

*Complex in the Abolitionist Movement* (Madison, Wisc.: University of Wisconsin Press, 1952). Wolf writes, for instance, that the abolitionist Theodore Weld stated about himself that he "gloried in the persecution he suffered," and "lovingly wore the martyr's crown of thorns." This image was also projected upon Charles Follen by those who survived him.

122. See Stange, "Abolitionist Martyr," p. 23.

## Conclusion

1. Included in William Buell Sprague, *Annals of the American Pulpit* (New York: R. Carter and Bros., 1857–1869), vol. VIII, p. 547.

2. Eliza Lee Cabot Follen, ed., *The Works of Charles Follen, with a Memoir of His Life* (Boston: Hilliard, Gray, 1841), vol. I, p. 541.

3. Ibid., vol. I, p. 440.

4. While the mainstream of Boston society certainly rejected Follen and his views, for certain reform circles he became a true martyr or even cult figure, and several Boston families began to name their children after him. There were Charles Follen Garrison and Charles Follen Folsom; Charles Follen McKim, the architect of the Boston Public Library; Professor Charles Follen Atkinson, to whom Follen's son left all he owned; and the twentieth-century author Charles Follen Adams.

5. Quoted in William Henry Channing, *Memoir of William Ellery Channing* (Boston: William Crosby and H. P. Nichols, 1848), vol. III, p. 372.

6. Eliza Cabot Follen to Mary Carpenter, dated West Roxbury, Mass., March 28, 1848. J. H. Cabot Papers, Massachusetts Historical Society, Boston.

7. Elizabeth Bancroft Schlesinger, "Two Early Harvard Wives: Eliza Farrar and Eliza Follen," *New England Quarterly*, 38 (1965): 165.

8. See Eliza Follen, *To Mothers in the Free States. Anti-Slavery Tracts, No. 8* (New York: American Antislavery Society, 1855).

9. Eliza Follen to "Dear Friend," dated Brookline, January 24, 1857. J. H. Cabot Papers, Massachusetts Historical Society, Boston.

10. Lydia Maria Child to Charles Follen Jr., dated February 5, 1860. Follen Papers, Massachusetts Historical Society, Boston.

11. See his short, hand-written autobiography. It is in the records of the Class of 1849, in the Harvard University Archives. Follen describes his childhood up until he entered Harvard College as a student.

12. See the *Boston City Directories* for the 1850s, 1860s, and 1870s. Available on microfiche at the New England Historic-Genealogical Society in Boston.

13. Both documents are handwritten. The report is eleven pages, and the narrative fifty-seven pages long. They are available in the J. H. Cabot Papers at the Massachusetts Historical Society, Boston. An edited version is available in Edmund Spevack, "Charles Christopher Follen's Civil War Report and Narrative," *Tennessee Historical Quarterly* (Summer 1997), forthcoming.

14. See the death notice in the *Massachusetts Vital Records*, available on microfiche at the New England Historic-Genealogical Society in Boston. In his will, Charles Christopher Follen left all his belongings, including his books and

personal papers, to a close friend, who had been named for his father, Professor Charles Follen Atkinson of Cambridge, Massachusetts. The will of Eliza Follen (1860) may be found in the Suffolk County Probate Court, Dedham, Massachusetts. The wills of Charles Follen, Jr. (1870), and Charles Follen Atkinson (1914) may be found in the Supreme Judicial Court Archives, Boston.

15. Draft for a document on the death of Charles Follen, Jr. Maria Weston Chapman's handwriting. Boston Public Library. MS A.4.6A.1.p54.

# INDEX